THOMAS PAINE

RIGHTS OF MAN:

BEING AN

ANSWER to Mr. BURKE's ATTACK

ON THE

FRENCH REVOLUTION.

BY

THOMAS PAINE,

SECRETARY FOR FOREIGN AFFAIRS TO CONGRESS IN THE
AMERICAN WAR, AND
AUTHOR OF THE WORK INTITLED *COMMON SENSE*.

LONDON:
PRINTED FOR J. JOHNSON, St. PAUL's CHURCH-YARD.
MDCCXCI.

Rights of Man. First edition flyleaf

COMMON SENSE:

ADDRESSED TO THE

INHABITANTS

OF

AMERICA.

On the following interesting

SUBJECTS.

I. Of the Origin and Defign of Government in general, with concife Remarks on the English Conftitution.

II. Of Monarchy and Hereditary Succeffion.

III. Thoughts on the prefent State of American Affairs.

IV. Of the prefent Ability of America, with fome mifcellaneous Reflections.

Written by an ENGLISHMAN.

By Thomas Paine

Man knows no Mafter fave creating HEAVEN;
Or thofe whom choice and common good ordain.
THOMSON.

PHILADELPHIA, Printed
And Sold by R. BELL, in Third-Street, 1776.

Common Sense. First edition flyleaf

THOMAS PAINE

HIS LIFE, WORK AND TIMES

by AUDREY WILLIAMSON

London GEORGE ALLEN & UNWIN LTD
Ruskin House   Museum Street

ISBN 0 04 923061 1

Printed in Great Britain
in 11 on 12 pt Baskerville type
by T. & A. Constable Ltd
Edinburgh

In memory of my father
HERBERT EDGAR WILLIAMSON
(1886–1972)
Socialist and trade unionist

PREFACE AND ACKNOWLEDGMENTS

Paine's works 'form the most important part of his life', wrote his friend and biographer Thomas Rickman, and another friend, the American poet Joel Barlow, expressed much the same opinion in 1809, the year of Paine's death: his 'own writings are his best life'. He was reticent on personal matters and some details are still questionable. I have tried to present a fair psychological picture and sift truth from legend, while giving all the salient material where the evidence is conflicting. Although he had an exciting and eventful life, and took part in some of the major historical events of his time, Paine was primarily a writer, a humanitarian, and a political philosopher and reformer. His character emerges from his work, and the true task of a biographer, to my mind, is to study both. For it was through his work that Paine made an imprint on his time, and remains of living interest in our own.

There has probably never been a time in history when his writings have seemed more pertinent and 'contemporary'. We live in times of renewed upheaval, with the young in particular, throughout several continents, either questioning long-established systems of government and ways of life, or actively propagating revolution. With the innovation of space travel, the world has come to a scientific acceptance of the probability of other planets, in other galaxies, inhabited by intelligent life, a theory advanced by Paine in *The Age of Reason* almost one hundred and eighty years ago. His principle of a welfare state has for a quarter of a century been an accepted feature of the British social system; the United Nations is at least an attempt to provide the channel for a peaceable solution of international difficulties that Paine envisaged as a substitute for war; and the emergence of Black Power has shown how right was his prophecy that the treatment of the American slaves, and failure to liberate them, would bring in the future disasters to the white state and hatred for their abusers among Africans.

The nuclear bomb and other barbarities have carried the devastation of war into regions of savagery and suffering which would have appalled the Quaker-born Paine, antipathetic to war on principle. But in this area only has he failed to influence the world for the better. Science, his love and ally, has defeated him. But even though often overlooked or forgotten, his yeast still works within the bread of human society, and interest in him has of late steadily revived.

A great deal of this contemporary relevance has emerged during the 1960s, since the biography of Paine, *Man of Reason*, by Alfred Owen Aldridge, in 1959. To Professor Aldridge's research into the *minutiae* of American and French papers relative to Paine historians owe a debt; but some of it did not appreciably add to one's knowledge of Paine, the man or the political thinker, and does not need detailed repetition. The English side of Paine's life, and in particular the six years at Lewes, have not been thoroughly researched since Moncure D. Conway's biography of 1892, and the Lewes period has now yielded entirely new and important material.

Conway, like Aldridge and almost all Paine's biographers, was an American, and the American emphasis in so much written on Paine has meant a certain underestimate of English social and political backgrounds and their formative effect on his character and outlook. The significance of his French Revolution contacts has also been somewhat overlooked. This book seeks to balance this by placing Paine in his social, political and scientific context in a way which it is hoped will make clear to general readers, not only historians, his importance as a figure in our democratic history. To do this it has been necessary to give some picture of his times and the characters who surrounded him, both in England and in France; for no man lives and works in isolation.

Paine was the victim of virulent and successful political propaganda which scholars have long realized invalidates the two earliest biographies: by 'Francis Oldys' (a pseudonym for a government official, George Chalmers), in 1791, the year of publication of *Rights of Man*, and by James Cheetham in 1809, the year of Paine's death. Both these biographies were the origin of a 'black legend' about Paine which persists in modern times. It was perpetuated even to some extent in Paul Foster's play, *Tom Paine*, for the La Mama Experimental Theatre Club, performed in New York and at the Edinburgh International Festival in 1967, which gave a brilliantly impressionistic picture of Paine's ideas through actual quotations, yet still preserved the Cheetham myth of a drunken profligate.

In 1819 Paine's most loyal and intimate English friend, the author and classical scholar Thomas (known as Clio) Rickman, published a life which expressed deep indignation at the legend and attempted to put Paine's real character and principles before the public. Paine was, in his words, 'incorrupt, straightforward, sincere', and his book substantiates this. Unfortunately it was only a sketch, made in 1811, of the larger biography Rickman had planned but had to abandon; but it remains a valuable work on which all later Paine writers have drawn. Further sympathetic biographies followed, culminating in Moncure D. Conway's monumental two-volume 'vindication' in 1892. Conway was an abolitionist who had supported Lincoln in the Civil War (Lincoln was deeply aware of the debt Americans owed to Paine). When living in London he became a friend of Carlyle and minister of South Place Chapel, the meeting place of the South Place Ethical Society (the site now of Conway Hall). Although his work went too far in sentimentalizing Paine, it is still the most valuable and fully documented source-book for writers on the subject.

I have been greatly indebted for my new material to a study of the Lewes eighteenth century records at the Town Hall, shown and explained to me by Mr Leslie Davey, and also unexplored records of the St Michael's Vestry which I discovered in the County Record Office at Lewes. Further new material has been obtained from the library of books and press-cuttings belonging to the Paine collection of the late Ambrose Barker, bequeathed to Norfolk County Library. For access to these and other books I must thank Mr J. R. Akam, Branch Librarian at Thetford; Mr D. P. Mortlock, F.L.A., County Librarian at County Hall, Norwich; and Mr Philip Hepworth, M.A., F.L.A., City Librarian of the Central Library in Norwich. Mr Christopher Brunel, Chairman of the Thomas Paine Society, has been particularly helpful in the loan of rare books and illustrations from the Paine collection of his father, the late Adrian Brunel, the film director; and Mr R. W. Morrell, F.L.S., F.G.S., the Society's Secretary, has also provided useful information. I am grateful in addition for books, information or illustrative material to Captain R. A. Midgley, M.A., custodian in 1971 of Bull House, Lewes; the Reverend Ralph Viney, a minister of Westgate Chapel, Lewes; Mr D. G. C. Allan, M.Sc.(econ.), F.R.Hist.S., F.S.A., Curator-Librarian, the Royal Society of Arts; Miss Brigid Brophy and her husband, Mr Michael Levey, Keeper and Deputy Director at the National Gallery; Mrs V. B. Lamb, Hon. Librarian of the Sussex Archaeological Society at Barbican House Museum, Lewes; Mr Ashton Booth, A.T.D., A.M.A., Curator of Farnham Museum; Hampstead Public Library; Mr T. R. Sobel, News Editor of *Sussex Life*; Mr Peter Cotes; Commander Trevor James; Misses Freda and Mary Tester; Miss Florence Pillepich; Mrs G. F. Willson; and Miss Janell M. Mac-Arthur of New York City. I must also thank my cousin Mary Tester for driving me to and around Lewes and its environs in quest of Paine, and Major Eric Rickman, whose genealogical researches into the two English families of Rickman have provided some new and interesting background material on Paine's friend.

A bibliography, including some major collections and articles, is listed at the end of the book, and these and other sources are on occasion also specified within the text. Full details, mainly dates, of a few items, taken from the Ambrose Barker collection, I have unfortunately been unable to obtain. I must thank publishers for permission to quote passages from some of the works listed, and also the photographers concerned with the illustrations.

Audrey Williamson

London
1971–2

CONTENTS

ILLUSTRATIONS

I

THE CHILD OF NORFOLK

A man is born of his time, and only in rare cases will he break through
the barriers and conventions of his age and send out signals to the future.
Almost always in such cases he will suffer persecution and misunder-
standing, for the world does not like to be jerked out of its comfortable
patterns of privilege and power, its sense of security which is so often
merely stagnation, a quality that no civilization can afford without
danger.

Such a man was Thomas Paine, born in the small country town of
Thetford, Norfolk, on 29 January 1737. In a sense the time was ripe for
him, although it would take his country, England, more than a century
fully to realize it. It was an age of transition, from the old world of the
Stuarts and the 'glorious' 1688 Revolution to the new one of Hanoverian
rule, agricultural change and industrial expansion. The enclosure of the
common lands, ruinous to the small farmer or peasant without capital,
was nevertheless within a few years of Paine's birth to enable modern
forms of agriculture and grazing permanently to reduce the mortality
rate, providing fresh unsalted meat throughout the winter for the first
time in history. Between 1720 and 1745, five of London's great hospitals
were founded, and in 1745 Captain Coram's foundling hospital, to
which Handel gave an organ and Hogarth a painting, was opened,
heralding a new humanitarian sense of responsibility to poor children.
The English deists, Toland, Tindal and Collins, had produced in
France their more influential disciple, Voltaire, and soon, when Paine
was still a young man in his early twenties, Jean-Jacques Rousseau was
to publish his *Social Contract*, with its rebellious and world-echoing cry:
'Man is born free; but everywhere he is in chains.'

Yet although the stirrings of social reform were there, they were still
fettered by class privilege and the iron chains of political rigidity. The
gin palace, the one comfort of the desperately poor, was still for some
time to produce scenes of appalling town squalor and hold back the
rise in population, and reduction in the death rate, stimulated by rural
change and urban medicine. The franchise was severely restricted
and its distribution was uneven and disgracefully corrupt. 'Rotten' or
pocket boroughs in the gift of local dukedom or squirearchy sent up
to two members to Parliament; such a one was the small town of
Thetford, controlled by the Dukes of Grafton, who made sure its

thirty-two voters supported their party, the Whigs; and such a one was the tiny non-village of Old Sarum, with only three houses, which also returned two members. The county of Yorkshire, with one million inhabitants, had only the same number of M.P.s; while the growing manufacturing town of Manchester—population 60,000—was allowed no Parliamentary representation at all.

With such a system political justice was as impossible as legal equity. The poor literally had no voice, nor had as yet the middle classes, who by the end of the century were to emerge in some cases more tyrannically than their aristocratic predecessors as employers in the fire-new factories. Oppression was consolidated, and privilege maintained, by a barbaric code of penal law under which a child could be hanged for minor theft and the prisons were sinks less of iniquity than degradation, breeding disease, despair and yet more crime which could so easily be expiated on the gallows. 'Throughout the century,' wrote Trevelyan in his *Illustrated English Social History*, 'Parliament went on adding statute after statute to the "bloody code" of English law, enlarging perpetually the long list of offences punishable by death; finally they numbered two hundred.'

For the rich and the elegant, however, there were all the beauties and the graces of a civilized society: costly and architecturally noble country mansions; carriages with teams of England's superb horses; the music of Handel in the early years of the century and of Mozart in the later; some of the most exquisitely designed furniture ever produced by the craftsman; one of the greatest actors of our stage, David Garrick, in the (somewhat adulterated) works of Shakespeare; the stentorian philosophizing of Dr Johnson; and other works of literature disseminated freely through the circulating libraries. Those with wealth, leisure and sporting instincts could take advantage of Queen Anne's lovely inspiration, Ascot Racecourse, the even older emerald spaciousness of Newmarket, where Charles II had ridden in races, and the sweeping gallops of the Epsom Downs, where the first Derby was run in 1780 and where Paine's Thetford contemporary, Augustus Henry Fitzroy, third Duke of Grafton (known as 'the Sporting Duke' and a great-grandson of Charles II by Barbara Villiers), was late in life to carry off the rare Turf feat of winning the race three times with his horses Tyrant, Pope and Whalebone. (The Quaker-born Paine, by then back in America after the dangers, exhilarations and disillusions of the French Revolution, would not have been impressed; though as owner of an American horse named Button, after whose wellbeing he constantly inquired in letters from France, he was not indifferent to horses.)

Even the poorer classes, denied a free education, could enjoy the delights of Vauxhall Gardens, the fireworks and the cockfighting that mingled prettiness with cruelties. Gambling houses thrived, and a politician like Charles James Fox, later in the century, could lose a fortune in a night. Yet the green fields and what Wordsworth was to call the 'little bits of sportive wood run wild' of the English countryside still lapped the edges of the towns, within reach of most of those inhabitants who wished to savour unpolluted, grass-scented air of a Sunday.

The ghostly clang of the coming age of iron and steel was, in 1737, unheard in the country towns; cottage industries still provided a livelihood of sorts without contaminating the smokeless atmosphere. Descartes in the previous century had referred to 'the natural light of the mind', which indeed had been irradiated by the foundation of the Royal Society and Greenwich Observatory, the invention of the lens and the study of the stars. Science was on the move, modern experiment replacing the medieval pursuit of the philosopher's stone; but it was still largely confined to the laboratories, from which later in the century it was to burst like an electric fireball, illuminating the dawn of a new world.

For a boy born in a country town like Thetford, with a population of scarcely 2000, the life, though restrictive, need not be unpleasant. The dry yet well-watered soil of the 'brake', now known as the Thetford Breckland, was rich in wildlife and flowers, river and grassland. The young Paine could have plucked the tall-stalked, blue-flowered Viper's Bugloss, the musk thistle and wild mignonette, and watched the flight of innumerable birds, including the Great Bustard who long ago left our shores. He could have wandered along the green banks of the Little Ouse, crossed its single-arched Town Bridge (built 1697) to school, and explored its other bridges and papermill and the place where it merged, not far away, with the River Thet. And for the boy with a yen to travel, what more exciting than the numerous stagecoaches which stopped to change horses at the early Tudor hostelry, the Bell, on the Norfolk side of the Town Bridge, which he daily traversed to reach the local Grammar School.

All these things helped to form the older Thomas Paine, with his rosy country complexion and brilliant, intelligent eyes (so often remarked on), his wanderlust and his gift for scientific enquiry. And the sense of history which is a necessary ingredient of political knowledge was nurtured prolifically by his surroundings. The most distinctive feature of the little town is its artificial Mound, sometimes called Castle Hill although there is no record of a castle, only defensive earthworks at the base. According to the *History of Thetford* of Paine's contemporary, Thomas Martin (1696–1776), 'no one knows what race of men raised this heap of chalk', rising abruptly for 100 feet from the wreck of the old fortifications. It has been ascribed to the Normans and to the Danes, who earlier swept across East Anglia, wintering in Thetford head-quarters in A.D. 870. (Guildhall Street was until recent times known as Heathenman Street.) Perhaps it was to the fiery Viking hordes that Paine owed his ancestry: his name derives from the Saxon for 'pagan', a not unfitting title for the author of *The Age of Reason* and questioner (though as a deist not an atheist) of the Christian/Jewish faith. Not far away, Grime's Graves, famous even in Paine's time, mark a flint mine in use from the Stone Age, 'Grim' being Scandinavian for the Devil; and of local black flint, mingled with stone, much of the town was built.

Theodford (the People's Ford) had been founded as long ago as the eighth century, a seat of priories whose ruins still bespatter the town. Its church of Mary-the-Great (mentioned in Domesday Book) for nineteen years became the town cathedral until the Bishop's See was transferred to Norwich in 1094. Up to the time of the Crusades the town flourished in trade; its three kilns produced storage jars and cooking pots, its Mint, even earlier, silver coins which found their way as Danegeld to the Stockholm Museum. By the time of Paine's birth the town had sunk in status, but the ploughs of Thetford still churned up archaeological treasures. The fifteenth-century house in Bridge Street (now White Hart Street) which Paine must have passed daily as he walked down the hill to school is now the town's 'Ancient Museum', commemorating its historical past as well as its celebrities: Sir Joseph Williamson who built its Guildhall, edited England's first newspaper, the *London Gazette* (propaganda for the Government), and represented Thetford in Parliament in the time of Charles II; the Reverend Francis Blomefield, the great Norfolk historian, Paine's contemporary; and Sir Robert Cotton, Thetford's M.P. in Elizabethan times, whose collection of MSS at the British Museum is still a mine of information for historians. Paine himself boasted in a letter that he went to the same school as Blomefield.

He was the son of a Quaker staymaker, Joseph Pain (the 'e' seems to have been used only later, although Thomas's looped signature had always suggested it and probably settled its final use). His mother, Frances Cocke, was a Protestant, the daughter of a Thetford attorney and eleven years her husband's senior. The names of both Pain (or Payne) and Cock were prominent in Norfolk history, and it is tempting, as Paine's biographer Moncure D. Conway pointed out, to trace the genealogy of the author of *Rights of Man* back to that Thomas Payne of Norfolk, who in 1650 was awarded £20 by the Council of State 'for his sufferings by printing a book for the cause of Parliament'.

Joseph and Frances were married on 20 June 1734, in Euston Parish, where the following year the third Duke of Grafton, the Derby-winning 'Sporting Duke', was born; but they seem to have set up house and shop immediately in Thetford town centre, at the top of the little hill then known as Bridge Street (the other side of Town Bridge, which in Paine's time was in Suffolk, is still known as Bridge Street). Joseph Pain also worked a small farm, but whether on the same site is not certain.

It is a pleasant elevated spot with a view, now bordering the London-Newmarket road and with the modern Thomas Paine Avenue curving off beside it. The street dips down within a few minutes' walk to the Town Bridge, then flanked by two inns, the Bell, near St Peter's Church on the Norfolk side of the little river, and the Tudor-built Anchor on the other. Both are now hotels. Almost opposite the Anchor stands the Boys' Grammar School, with its proud inscription boasting its 'Pre-Conquest Foundation'. Except for the addition of shining windowed extensions, it is much the same as when Thomas Paine was a pupil there.

Paine would not have known, at least in his schooldays, the square tower of St Peter's at the foot of the hill; it was added in 1789, the year of the fall of the Bastille, so momentous to Paine and many of his contemporaries. It seems rather strange, as St Peter's was in Bridge Street, that Paine was apparently baptized, like his baby sister who died, at St Cuthbert's, a longer walk away beside the Guildhall, at the top of King Street. The choice may have been made because St Cuthbert's was nearer the old Quaker meeting house in Cage Lane, where Thomas was taken to worship in his childhood. The church baptism, unrecorded owing to missing pages in the register, and the boy's later confirmation by the Bishop of Norwich, seem to have been a gesture to his mother's religion, although it appears from a letter from Joseph to his son that by 1787, at least, Frances Pain had joined her husband as a member of the meeting house. The Quaker's was the faith in which the boy was largely brought up, and the chill of it early entered his soul. '. . . if the taste of a Quaker could have been consulted at the Creation, what a silent and drab-coloured Creation it would have been!' was his comment, half a century later, in *The Age of Reason*. 'Not a flower would have blossomed its gaieties, nor a bird been permitted to sing.'

There were shadows, then, across the sun and Thetford was not all fields, river and warm summer air. In winter the salt winds from the Wash and the plunging North Sea blew icily across the town, scurrying amid the maze of little streets in which even today strangers complain of constant lost directions. While, at the end of the century, John Constable explored the summer richnesses of Suffolk foliage and millstream, the Norfolk painter and water-colourist, John Sell Cotman, saw his county's skies split and bruised with rainstorm, riven by lightning, and looming like a threat above the Yarmouth beaches and galliots. Charles G.

Harper's *The Newmarket, Bury, Thetford and Cromer Road*, published in 1904, contains a striking Pollard print of 'The Norwich Mail in a thunderstorm on Thetford Heath', the front horses rearing with flying manes as forked lightning rips the darkening sky. This tumult of nature and animal, in and around a town which was a centre for stagecoaches, must have impressed itself early on the imagination of the boy Paine.

There were darker pictures still. On the same side of Cage Lane as the Quaker meeting house stood the town stocks and 'cage', doubtless often inhabited by prisoners; for Assizes were held at Thetford, and the Thetford-Norwich road carried prisoners in wagons to be tried there or in Norwich. The March Fair at Attleborough, a few miles from Thetford and held when the Assizes were in progress, was popularly known as 'Rogues' Fair'.

But although their meeting house struck the child as gloomy and its surroundings were almost gruesome, the Quakers themselves formed a peace-loving, mild community and Paine to his death carried many marks of their influence. His condemnation of the wastefulness of war, his humane concern for the individual and even animals, and his total sobriety in dress, all seemed to reach back to his Quaker inheritance. It is very difficult to eradicate habits of mind and manner instilled in childhood, and Paine seems in addition to have been attached to his father. Not only were they closer in age, but there appeared to be no special *rapport* at all with his mother, described by Chalmers (and there is some indication he may have been right here) as a woman of 'sour temper and eccentric character'. If true, it may have been from his mother that Paine inherited the strain which formed his talents. His temper was convivial, but eccentricity is often allied to genius, and Paine could be contentious in an argument. In some ways he and his mother may have been too alike for comfort, and his greater sympathy with his father derived from the attraction of opposites.

The fact remains that although he provided for his mother in old age —she lived to be over ninety—Paine hardly ever referred to her in his writings, and it was an affectionate letter from his father that brought him back to England from America, after the end of the War of Independence. It was a sadness to him, no doubt, that on his arrival (he had delayed *en route* in France) he found Joseph had died several months before.

The Quakers, or Society of Friends, founded by George Fox the previous century, had ceased to be an evangelistic group of dissent but had settled down into a thriving lower middle class of tradesmen and artisans, conventional in all but their religion. Later in America, Paine was to find them a strong Tory element particularly opposed to the secession from England. His father's shop—whether for the actual making of ladies' corsets or the insertion of their steel or whalebone ribs, or both, is still disputed in Thetford—was a typical example of Quaker enterprise, and although Joseph was made a freeman of the town in the year of Thomas's birth, it did not provide the kind of status symbol acceptable in higher social circles. Thomas, who for a few years followed his father's profession, found it gave much food to the snobs who politically opposed his writings, and the satiric Thomas Carlyle, in his monumental *French Revolution*, refers to him disparagingly throughout (in singularly meagre references) as 'the rebellious Needleman'. The otherwise vivid documentation of Carlyle's great work shows how deeply, therefore, the corrosive governmental campaign against the author of *Rights of Man* had eaten, like acid, into the minds of both public and historians, even forty years after its publication, when Carlyle was gathering material for his book.

The staymaking business was, however, successful enough for Joseph to be able to pay for his son's education at the Grammar School, although not, according to the son, without sacrifice. Probably because of this the boy left to be apprenticed to his father's trade in 1750, at the age of thirteen. There is little record of his schooldays, although George Chalmers (writing as Francis Oldys, A.M. of the University of Pennsylvania, both name and degree being fictitious) in his unreliable 'Life', published in 1791 to counteract the sales of *Rights of Man*, admits finding reference to him as a 'sharp' boy, although of 'unsettled application'. In the latter we may read already, perhaps, the diffuse nature of Paine's interests.

The school, founded on a legacy left by Sir Richard Fulmerston in 1566, was a good one, although Paine did not take Latin, to which the Quakers objected, doubtless mainly on the 'No Popery' principle as well as, according to the adult Paine, their moral objection to the Roman stories. Paine's later writings show that subsequent reading familiarized him with a number of Latin and Greek writers, though in translation. He had, he wrote, 'no inclination to learn languages', and in fact resembled many writers in this. 'I would rather write three plays,' Bernard Shaw wrote to Mrs Patrick Campbell, 'than ask my way anywhere in a foreign country.' Paine, although he learned to read French well, had difficulty even when living in France in following it in conversation, and always spoke through an interpreter when a Deputy in the National Assembly.

His mind, however, was stimulated by history, mathematics and science, and also rather surprisingly by poetry. He remained an occasional versifier throughout his life, starting with a pompously moral little elegy on the death of a crow, which he buried in his garden at the age of eight. 'My father being of the Quaker profession, it was my good fortune to have an exceedingly good moral education, and a tolerable stock of learning,' he later wrote. His principal teacher, the Reverend William Knowles, who was the school's Usher, not its Head Master, seems to have instilled in him in addition some lively interest in sea life, for he had served on a man o' war.

Solitariness, as an only child in an austerely religious home, perhaps kept the boy from expanding in his school life; he was, in spite of his 'sharpness', either a late developer or rather reticent. But the sea and ships of Knowles' experiences and perhaps the blood of Viking ancestors stirred romantically in his veins, and his first adventure, at the age of sixteen, was an attempted escape from staymaking to the decks of a privateer, *The Terrible*, at Harwich. Here, some thirty miles from Thetford, his anxiously pursuing and morally aghast father quickly rescued him from the arms of a Captain ominously named Death.

The young Paine, however, still had to work the beckoning North Sea out of his system. In 1756, when war was declared with France, he so far threw away his pacific Quaker teaching as to sign on another privateer, *The King of Prussia*, under a Captain Mendez. He mentions the episode in *Rights of Man* but there is no other record. The experience seems to have finally exorcized the magic of the sea from his soul. Perhaps it also solidified his later celebrated distrust of Kings.

This could have come, too, in part from his Norfolk surroundings. Norwich, one of England's three major cities in the eighteenth century, had long been a centre for liberalism and dissent, some of it dating back to the Levellers of Cromwell's time. In Paine's middle age it was to contribute much to the resistance against the government treason trials and censorship, and to the whole movement of reform down to the Chartists of the next century. The child of Norfolk with an independent mind and spirit could hardly fail to register some of the influences of his county's radicalism.

II

THE WANDERER

The break away from Thetford, at the age of nineteen, was to prove conclusive; except to visit his parents, and for some months to study for the Excise, Paine never lived there again. He early, however, abandoned the sea, a tough and savage calling for a youngster in pre-Nelson days, without losing his new restlessness and urge to keep on the move.

His sea adventure imprinted itself on his future in various ways. The fascination of astronomy for him may well, it has been suggested, have begun in those days at sea on *The King of Prussia*, when the youth who locked up his experiences of the lower decks within his soul could still, on starry nights, have dreamed his dreams by the ship's rail, and had a vision of those inhabited worlds in space which so prophetically intrude into his book of deistic dissent, *The Age of Reason*. A space traveller in the mind, and like so many of the men of his century passionately involved in the newly-opening world of scientific experiment, Paine near the end of his long life was still working out mechanical theories in connection with naval gunboats and fortifications, and published a treatise on them.

His American writings also show he kept a nostalgic eye on *The Terrible*, in which he had tried to sail as a boy almost a quarter of a century before. It was not necessary, he wrote in *Common Sense*, that in manning a fleet one-fourth part should be sailors. 'The *Terrible*, privateer, Captain Death, stood the hottest engagement of any ship last war, yet had not twenty sailors on board, though her complement of men was upwards of two hundred. A few able and social sailors will soon instruct a sufficient number of active landsmen in the common work of a ship.' The history of the American marine suggests his advice may have been taken to heart. And Paine was perhaps the first, in 1776, to point out that no power in Europe could rival America in its extent of coastline and internal supply of materials. 'Ship building is America's greatest pride, in which she will in time excel the whole world.' A fleet was a major necessity for naval protection, and the English navy three or four thousand miles off was of little use at any time and in sudden emergencies of no use at all.

Paine once said to Rickman that there was no time in his life during which he was not absorbing knowledge, and it is a fact that every experience from childhood onwards seems to have become embedded, like a pearl, in the multi-coloured oyster shell of his mind. So although, in *Rights of Man*, he could look back in middle age with distaste on the 'false heroism' of his schoolmaster that had inflamed the 'raw and adventurous' boy of sixteen, the life on *The King of Prussia*, bitter as salt but bright with stars, was not to prove infertile for the later writer. And it was in his feeling for the galaxies of the universe that Paine was to become nearest to creative vision.

His country backgrounds, too, at Thetford and among the undulating downs of Lewes, left an imprint on his writing that could not have been obtained from life in the larger towns. A meticulous naturalistic analogy of the industriously spinning spider occurs more than once in his pages; he refers to the old country custom of the 'horse-tie' by which two villagers with only one horse proceed to their destination by taking turn in the saddle and at the bridle; and Part II of *Rights of Man* ends with the hopeful allegory:

'It is now towards the middle of February. Were I to take a turn into the country the trees would present a leafless winterly appearance. As people are apt to pluck twigs as they walk along, I perhaps might do the same, and by chance might observe that a *single bud* on that twig had begun to swell. I should reason very unnaturally, or rather not reason at all, to suppose *this* was the *only* bud in England which had this appearance. Instead of deciding thus, I should instantly conclude that the same appearance was beginning, or about to begin, everywhere; and though the vegetable sleep will continue longer on some trees and plants than on others, and though some of them may not *blossom* for two or three years, all will be in leaf in the summer, except those which are *rotten*. What pace the political summer may keep with the natural, no human foresight can determine. It is, however, not difficult to perceive that the spring is begun.'

The optimism was characteristic of Paine, the idealist, dreaming of world revolution; but although change did come at last to the society he so wished to reform, he could hardly have foreseen at the time that it would be so retarded a spring.

When the young Paine returned from his war service on *The King of Prussia*, however, it was not to pluck twigs in a wintry landscape. In 1757, having either absconded from the ship or obtained his release, he appears for the first time in London, working for a staymaker named Morris in Hanover Street. Characteristically reticent about his private life and work, he recorded eagerly enough his first urban introduction to the world of philosophy and science. 'As soon as I was able I purchased a pair of globes, and attended the philosophical lectures of Martin and Ferguson, and became afterwards acquainted with Dr Bevis, of the society called the Royal Society, then living in the Temple, and an excellent astronomer.'

It was at Dr Bevis's, presumably, that he first looked through the most advanced form of telescope and saw so clearly, as he describes later in *The Age of Reason*, those many suns which must surely, like our own, have attendant planets supporting life, even though invisible as yet to the eye. What had been a distant pattern for dreams on the deck of *The King of Prussia*, suddenly leapt into sharper focus and became a field of scientific conjecture. The prophecy of space, like the prophecy of so many future developments, political and social, became a part of the Paine genius; the genius not of the creative artist, but of the man of prismatic vision who can see within multitudinous interests the seeds of a future society. That Paine's vision was never metaphysical, but redolent of the 'common sense' which he later took for a pseudonym, was perhaps the secret of its ultimate truth.

London in 1757 was both a lively and a brutalizing city, its slums still reeling from the gin palaces immortalized in Hogarth's 'Gin Lane' six years before, its public executions at Tyburn Tree (which is now the site of Marble Arch) very much a matter of public entertainment. The scandal of the small boy chimney sweeps was only one of the aspects of the growing abuses of child labour; Bedlam, the lunatic asylum, was open to visitors as one of the sights of London; and conditions in the jails were such that in May 1750, the court at the Old Bailey had succumbed to jail fever, 'killing judges, counsel and others to the number of forty'. Yet the playhouses thrived, mainly on meretricious plays (the great revivifying age of Goldsmith and Sheridan was twenty years in the future), although political satire was kept alive with revivals of Gay's *Beggar's Opera* and Fielding's *Tom Thumb*. London's shops with their wide glass fronts were the envy of Europe; famous clubs were the resort of aristocrats and politicians, gambling away the night; and the coffee houses provided humbler but pleasant surroundings for the writer and the middle classes.

It was the London of Boswell and Dr Johnson, who had published his famous Dictionary in 1755, and told Boswell he saw nothing against the common practice of duelling, on the grounds that 'if publick war be allowed to be consistent with morality, private war must be equally so'. It was a practice against which Paine, still hoarding his Quaker antipathy to war itself, was to rail with vigour in an American article; and there is no indication anywhere in his works that he was aware of Dr Johnson's stature in the community. To the youth of twenty, Newtonian science, not literature, was the key to the universe, and although Hogarth's series of pictures on the corruptions of electioneering appeared between 1755 and 1758, and may certainly have made an impact on him, Paine never gave any special indication of interest in painting or engraving. It is true the Royal Academy was not founded by Joshua Reynolds until a decade later, and the talents of its major members— one of whom, George Romney, was to paint a portrait of Paine in 1792 —were not yet in full bloom. William Blake, born in 1757 when Paine first came to London, was, however, by tradition to play a decisive rôle at a turning point of his life.

Of the Seven Years War then in progress young Paine could hardly have been unaware, having served in it; and recruiting was stimulated by the ballads of the time. The elder Pitt first came to office in 1757. He was a Whig (a party to which Paine certainly adhered when in Lewes eleven years later): and the crisis of April—when the King dismissed him from office, but a compromise was reached leaving Pitt in control of the war and foreign policy—must have been a lively topic in the coffee houses of the time. Doubtless public events were already building up slowly to form Paine's political mind. He was a boy of humble birth with latent abilities and ambitions, not easily fulfilled within the social fabric of the times. A great deal of what has later been termed his 'vanity' was, perhaps, not so much personal as a pride in achievement against odds, epitomized in his use of the phrase 'the republic of letters' when pressing for greater chances to be given to talent in all social classes. It was one of his major arguments against primogeniture. 'The greatest characters the world have known,' he wrote over-boldly in *Rights of Man*, 'have risen on the democratic floor.'

'Johnson,' wrote Boswell, 'was much attached to London: he observed that a man stored his mind better there, than anywhere else.' What this educative period in London did for the young Paine was to consolidate his scientific bent with a background of up-to-date knowledge, and by eager study to settle the 'unsettled application' which is said to have bedevilled his schooldays. It brought him for the first time in contact with a known scientific scholar, and paved the way for an easy fellowship, later, with some of the leading figures of his time.

It was, however, as brief as all these early incursions into the world. Whether the wanderlust again struck him, or his scientific enthusiasms interfered with his daily work for the staymaker, thus losing him his job, we do not know; but little more than a year later, in 1758, he was in employment with another staymaker named Grace in Dover.

Oldys, who later admitted he was paid well for his anti-Paine biography and that there were many lies in it, maintained that 'Miss Grace either won our author's heart, or our author attempted to win the heart of Miss Grace. And the father was thus induced to lend him twelve pounds, in order to enable our adventurer to set up as a staymaker at Sandwich. Yet it is certain, that he neither married the lady, nor repaid the loan.' As Oldys did his biographical snooping in Dover and Sandwich over thirty years after Paine left the towns, it is extremely open to question whether any gossip he heard, or pretended he heard, had any basis in fact or reliable local memory; but in spite of the apparent sexual abstemiousness in which, as in other things, he so resembled Bernard Shaw, Paine was never indifferent to women and like Shaw enjoyed their friendship and company. He was, in fact, one of the first to write an article sympathetic to women's rights. It is quite possible that as a young man of twenty-one he was attracted to his employer's daughter and she to him; and more than possible that the boy-and-girl romance blew over, as such romances will.

In any case in April the next year—whether with Mr Grace's help or his own savings—Paine set up as a master staymaker in Sandwich, a few miles to the west of Dover on the Kent coast. Sandwich like Dover was one of the original Cinque Ports, and the source of England's ships before the establishment of a permanent navy in the reign of Henry VII. Although after the Revolution of 1688 the choice of parliamentary representatives by the Lord Wardens had ceased, and the election system was introduced, privileges remained and the Cinque Ports were heavily over-represented in Parliament. It was not until the Acts of 1832 and 1885 that their number of M.P.s was reduced from sixteen to three.

Paine, therefore, must have been acutely aware of this injustice of Parliamentary representation which was to be a theme of his later writing. Tiny Thetford had also, through the influence of the Dukes of Grafton, been over-represented in Parliament in comparison with far larger, more important towns. What seems apparent is that Paine, country born, at this stage still preferred the environment of the small town and the sea to the closer-packed, gayer life of London, in which had he wished he could surely have remained.

In Sandwich, however, his mind was on other things than politics and history. Whether Miss Grace's charms had stirred his instincts we do not know; but in the September after his arrival he married an orphan girl, Mary Lambert, who had been a maid in the employment of the local woollen draper's wife, a Mrs Richard Solly. The marriage on 27 September 1759 is recorded in the Church of St Peter's, Sandwich, with a Thomas Taylor, Maria Solly and John Joslin as witnesses. It would appear from this that Mrs Solly took a friendly interest in the young girl's romance and settlement; and no shadow cast itself across the happiness of the little ceremony.

The desperation that sent the boy Paine running away to sea from the boredom of his father's trade of staymaker is, perhaps, the key to his continued lack of success in the business. The shop at 20 New Street did not thrive and within a few months the young people left for Margate, on the North Sea side of Kent. There, in 1760, Paine's young wife died. The circumstances are completely obscure. 'By some,' ventured the unspeakable Oldys, 'she is said to have died on the road of ill usage, and a premature birth. The women of Sandwich are positive, that she died in the British Lying-in Hospital, in Brownlow Street, Long Acre'— although what the women of Sandwich, where she no longer lived, could be expected to know about it thirty-one years later, and why the unfortunate girl should be in London instead of Margate, then her home, make the story as unbelievable as so much of Oldys' material. Paine's reputation—according to everyone who knew him at all intimately—as well as his written works, dispose of the subtle hint of cruelty, and Oldys' claim of diligent search of the registers of the Brownlow Street and other London lying-in hospitals produced, not unexpectedly, no evidence of a Mrs Pain there in the years 1760 or 1761. So he ends by contenting himself with a still more subtle innuendo, that some people told him Paine's first wife was still 'alive in obscure retreat'.

Paine left no record of his first wife. Whether the memory was one of painful bereavement, or the brief youthful marriage faded, quite naturally, from his mind with the passage of years, we do not know. He must have spoken of her to Clio Rickman, who mentions the marriage in his book; but Rickman gives us no clue as to the character of this ill-starred girl whose fate so evanescently crossed that of a young man destined for future fame, of which she could hardly have dreamed.

Her influence on Paine, however, was in one sense important. Mary Lambert's father had been an officer in the Customs and Excise, and this seems to have caught Paine's imagination. Perhaps there was still a faint call of the sea in his blood; perhaps, quite apart from his dissatisfaction with staymaking, Margate now held too poignant memories. In any case he was soon corresponding with his father on a project to become an exciseman, and during 1761 he spent some months in Thetford studying for the work at his parents' home. Another famous eighteenth century radical, the poet Robert Burns, was also an exciseman twenty years later, and equally contemptuous of the meagre pay (£50 a year), as well as the influence of 'great folks' needed to obtain entry. Paine, however, managed to get entry through a Mr Falkland, and was first appointed as a supernumerary, or unattached officer, on 1 December 1762. He was employed as a gauger of brewers' casks at Grantham, in Lincolnshire. There was no higher grade vacancy until 8 August 1764, when he was appointed to the Alford Out-Ride, also in Lincolnshire: a position entailing much horse-riding along the coast on the lookout for smugglers.

Throughout his life Paine enjoyed riding, and there is no doubt, until he 'found himself' as a writer, he preferred an open-air life. The work, however, was dangerous and he must have been aware of it. Smuggling, owing to the heavy and, it was believed, unfair taxes on certain imports, was in the nature of a national pastime, and considered by the population at large entirely venial. Important personages were often engaged in it, and their implication tended to be overlooked by the authorities. As in all crimes, however, there was a portion of hardened and unscrupulous desperadoes, and a few years later, in 1769, a Customs official named William Deighton was murdered in Halifax by counterfeit coiners he had helped to unmask in the course of his duties.

Paine escaped this risk, but he did not escape the other, dismissal for stamping a consignment he had not actually examined. The temptation was great, not because the Customs officer gained anything financially but because the extent of the consignments was sometimes too much for any one officer to handle. The profession was ill-paid and therefore understaffed, and the practice of stamping without examination was common, as the chalking of tourists' suitcases without opening them is common (but legally recognized) at Customs ports of entry today. Paine freely admitted his guilt by letter on 13 August 1765, and was discharged before the end of the month. The fault was not considered important enough, however, to exclude his successful application for readmission at a later date.

In 1766, therefore, Paine was back at the hated staymaking, with a master staymaker at Diss in Norfolk, not many miles from Thetford. This did not last long, and he seems to have returned on a visit to his Alford haunts in Lincolnshire, for in an essay called 'Forgetfulness' written many years later, he mentions visiting a widow in the Lincolnshire fens and while walking in her garden seeing a white figure moving in the distance. He pursued the ghostly apparition, wondering suddenly if his hand would 'pass through the air'. It was, however, no spirit but a young woman bent on drowning herself, as a reaction to the marriage of her lover. Paine and his (equivocal?) friend, the widow, comforted the girl and dissuaded her from suicide.

On 3 July 1766, Paine successfully petitioned to be reinstated in the Excise, writing a letter of such self-abasement and humility, for one of his strong views and independence of character, that one can only guess at the straits to which he felt reduced at the time. It should be noted, however, that he maintained: 'No complaint of the least dishonesty, or intemperance, ever appeared against me.' There was no immediate vacancy, and until Christmas that year he was working in London in a new profession, that of teacher of English in a school in Goodman's Fields belonging to a Mr Noble. Today this would have

B

been a rise in status; but the private schoolteacher, like the private governess, was often considered little more than a menial in eighteenth century England and salaried accordingly. According to his friend Rickman, Paine was paid £25 a year.

Perhaps understandably, in January 1767, Paine transferred to the school of a Mr Gardiner at Kensington. Oldys maintains Paine left Gardiner's school within three months and took to itinerant preaching, having unsuccessfully asked Noble to send a certificate of his qualifications to the Bishop of London. It is in many ways an unlikely story, although Conway accepted it on the grounds of its being too creditable to Paine for Oldys to have made it up! Much of Paine's religious writing, though, was pious in character although certainly anti-biblical, and it is possible, though not to my mind probable, he thus early began to preach the doctrine of a God whose greatness could be seen, not in the Bible, but the creation of the universe. That he could ever have contemplated ordination within the Church hardly seems conceivable, as according to himself his questioning of the Bible began at the age of seven or eight years; Wesleyan evangelism with its fervent hysterics was equally alien to him. Deism was already established to some extent in England, but it was not usual for deists to become itinerant preachers. They were the philosophers and writers of the religious world. Paine, moreover, had already applied to the Excise for reinstatement and was at this time awaiting a vacancy.

We have record, however, that he retained contact with at least one of his pupils at one of the London schools, for on 17 September 1783, he wrote to General Knox a letter of introduction: 'Old friend, I just take the opportunity of sending my respects to you by Mr Darby, a gentleman who was formerly a pupil of mine in England.' This, though hardly necessary, disposes of Oldys' Squeers-like picture of a Paine 'hated by the boys, who were terrified by his harshness'.

'I had no disposition,' wrote Paine of his younger days, 'for what is called politics. It presented to my mind no other idea than is contained in the word jockeyship.' This only too realistic picture of the corrupt politics of those heavily gambling days, as practised even by the major Whigs, must have been reinforced by what Paine heard in Thetford and the Cinque Ports, and by Hogarth's election lampoons during his earlier stay in London. It is hard to believe, nevertheless, that even though disgusted by the 'jobbery', he was unaware of what was going on. In 1765 his young Thetford contemporary, the Duke of Grafton, who had succeeded his father in 1757 at the age of twenty-two, became Secretary of State in the ministry of Lord Rockingham, and although he resigned in May 1766, in order to support the older Pitt, he was a few months later appointed First Lord of the Treasury, with Pitt nominally

Privy Seal but in actual fact Prime Minister. Pitt, the only minister of known integrity, became Lord Chatham in July 1766, and in his subsequent illness Grafton succeeded him as Prime Minister.

The disparity of achievement and opportunity—for the third Duke of Grafton was only two years Paine's senior—could hardly have failed to strike the other young man of Thetford, himself to date both penniless and unsuccessful and kicking his heels in London while he waited for a place in the Excise. It is understandable that the famous 'Letters of Junius' in the *Public Advertiser*, which began with an attack on Grafton two years later and in 1771 named the Duke as 'the pillow upon which I am determined to rest all my resentments', should have been attributed by at least one writer to Paine[1].

The still unsolved mystery of the identity of this acclaimed and often stylish pamphleteer, who provided a pattern on which much later polemical journalism was based, has provoked generations of amateur detectives to suggest a solution. Practically every leading political figure of the time, unless actually attacked by Junius, has been named as the possible writer. The candidates, all with optimistic supporters, have included Lord Chesterfield, Edward Gibbon, John Wilkes, Lord Chatham, Sir Philip Francis (for long odds-on favourite) and two men whom Paine later challenged as opponents, Edmund Burke and Lord Shelburne. In 1949 Cordasco published a memorandum by Shelburne found in Glasgow, naming his under-secretary Laughlin Macleane as Junius; but C. W. Dilke in *Papers of a Critic*, in 1875, had already discussed and eliminated Macleane on grounds—including his known political affiliations—which cannot be totally dismissed; and the mystery remains. Was Shelburne right, throwing dust, in collusion with Macleane, or simply mistaken?

In point of time—the last letter in the series appeared on 10 May 1772, two years before Paine left for America—Paine could be made to fit, and certainly some of the phrasing and ideas recall him. In the famous 35th Letter to the King, which ended in the prosecution of publisher and printer without discovery of Junius' identity, George III is warned that the crown 'as it was acquired by one revolution ... may be lost by another', a point made by Paine in his attacks on the King later; and one can hear an echo of Paine's views on the national debt in Junius' remark concerning Grafton, that 'the finances of a nation sinking under its debts have been committed to a young nobleman already ruined by play'. Coleridge assessed the Letters as 'suited to their purpose, and perfect in their kind ... they are plain and sensible whenever the author is in the right and, whether right or wrong, always shrewd and epigrammatic ... the key is hardly ever changed from that

[1] W. H. Burr: *Thomas Paine: Was He Junius?* (1890).

of sustained personal invective, of bitter, merciless sarcasm. But there is also a fine boldness and liveliness, an urgency and often a direct blunt eloquence which still arrest.'

Many of these things, including 'witty logic' and the effect of 'an honest, warm-hearted man', suggest Paine's style. But Paine rarely used personal invective or sarcasm of this kind, even in his wartime propaganda in the American *Crisis*, and it seems far more possible that he had read the Junius letters at the time and absorbed some of their ideas and methods. They were sensational and widely discussed. Conway quotes Paine's own reference to Junius, whose 'brilliant pen enraptured without convincing; and though in the plenitude of its rage it might be said to give elegance to bitterness, yet the policy survived the blast'. In view of Paine's protests that 'it was the cause of America that made me an author', we must assume, if he were Junius, a prolonged and deliberate subterfuge very alien to his personality.

There is no evidence, moreover, that Paine could have had at this time—writing, as he must have done, between Excise duties at Lewes— the internal political knowledge which, in most views, has placed Junius in a position within the government or civil service. Nor does it seem in his nature to have taken the secret of his identity to the grave. 'I am the sole depository of my secret, and it shall die with me,' wrote Junius, and time has proved him right. It is true he had to conceal his identity at the time, for prosecution would certainly have followed; but Paine, faced with a similar situation of seditious libel in respect of *Rights of Man*, shouted his responsibility to the house-tops, or more precisely to the Attorney-General. Throughout his writing life he presented his views, however dangerous or unpopular, without fear. This honesty was the very basis of his talent, and of his effect on events. The pseudonyms he used were the flimsiest veils, and half America knew the identity of Common Sense before the ink was dry on the first *Crisis*, if not before.

He was appointed to the Excise position at Lewes on 19 February 1768, having taken the risk of refusing a vacancy at Grampound, in faraway Cornwall, in order to wait for a more congenial post. Lewes was to prove the real foundation of his later career, with parochial, rather than wider political affairs, as practical experience.

III

LEWES: THE FORMATIVE YEARS

When Paine arrived in Lewes in February 1768, he took lodgings at the house and shop of Samuel Ollive, a tobacconist, and thus found himself at once introduced into the prominent parish life of the town. For Ollive was at this period one of the two Constables elected annually to take charge of town affairs, the other being Henry Verral, whose family until recently had been landlords of the White Hart Inn, which was the centre of most of the town's social activities. And on 15th September the same year, when Ollive and Verral surrendered their Constableship, Paine was present at the town meeting electing their successors for the following year, 1768–9, and his signature appears in the town record book.

The fact that Paine's major biographers this century have been American perhaps partly accounts for the fact that both his and Ollive's involvement in town affairs, and the Paine signatures (there are six at meetings over the next five years), have been totally overlooked until recently. Paine's general interest in parish matters is further evidenced by his signatures at the meetings of St Michael's Vestry, which have remained until now undiscovered. St Michael's is Lewes's principal and almost oldest church (with a rare example of a round Norman tower and steeple) and Paine was later married there; but as anyone who has studied the beginnings of English local government will know, the Vestry, which preceded the Town Council, was not specifically a Church organization but a town group convened regularly in order to administer grants to the needy, as well as to levy rates and provide for town needs such as roads and lighting. Bernard Shaw, in his early days as a Labour Councillor, was a member of the St Pancras Vestry which only later became known as the St Pancras Borough Council; so the term 'Vestry' lingered on for over a century after Paine's time.

In the middle of the eighteenth century, corporate local government was in its earliest stages. Private Acts of Parliament in 1761 and 1765 had secured for Westminster the right to levy house rates in return for paving and lighting, and as J. H. Plumb writes in *England in the Eighteenth Century*, 'the improvement in social amenities at Westminster was startling'. Birmingham and other towns followed; but Lewes, the County town of Sussex with quarterly Assizes, was too small and rural to have expanded as yet from a rather nebulous form of public spirit.

The annual elections of the two Constables and two Headboroughs, normally held at the White Hart Inn, were controlled by an organization called 'the Society of Twelve', of which Paine by his signature is shown to have been a member. The meeting consisted normally of the handing over to the new officers 'in the presence of the Jury', of certain town insignia and 'the several Deeds, Bonds, surenders, Writings and Evidences together with the several Books, Utensills and other things hereinafter mentioned belonging to the said Borough'. It dealt with mortgages and on at least one occasion attended by Paine agreed to 'make and Collect a Town Tax on all and every the Housekeepers within the Borough aforesaid at and after this rate of Three Pence in the pound for defraying the necessary Expences of the said late Constables during the Execution of their Office'.

The town insignia listed included a fine James I silver gilt steeple cup and cover, inscribed 'the gift of Thomas Blunt, 1611'. Known as the Blunt Cup, it is still part of the Lewes town regalia and is described and illustrated in Leslie S. Davey's *The Civil Insignia and Plate of the Corporation of Lewes* (1967). It was Mr Davey who found and brought to light the Paine signatures in the town records, when in 1966 the then Mayor, later Alderman A. C. Barber, invited the recently-formed Thomas Paine Society to the town and felt the occasion warranted some enquiry into Paine's parish activities.

The St Michael's Vestry meetings, quite separate, were sometimes held in the Parish Church, and sometimes at other addresses. They generally administered the payment of small weekly sums to widows, orphans or others in need, the amounts ranging from one shilling to five shillings (which was usually for a family). These recipients and sums were listed and were witnessed by Paine and others present. It was, in fact, a form of social welfare. Resolutions were passed on urgent matters such as adjuring the Church Wardens 'to as soon as convenient put the small House adjoining to the Steeple of the Church in good Repair', and payments for work done were agreed. In fact the Constables, Headboroughs and Vestry between them were responsible for a rudimentary form of parish administration which was later merged into the work now covered by the Town Councils.

Samuel Ollive and Henry Verral had previously held office as joint Constables in 1752–3, so they were experienced and prominent figures in the town community. It is now obvious why Thomas Paine, the exciseman—not a particularly well-regarded calling, and one often provoking actual hostility in the eighteenth century—so easily took a leading place in the social club gatherings at the White Hart. Ollive must have early realized his tenant's live mentality and propensity for political questioning, and introduced him naturally into the town's social life. And from Ollive, during the six months after Paine's arrival that he still held the office of Constable, Paine would have learned much about parish affairs and administration. Biographers' assumption that, outside the White Hart social club, Paine's later references to town affairs derived from his boyhood in Thetford has never seemed entirely credible. He was scarcely nineteen when he left his birthplace, and apart from a brief friendship with the Thetford Recorder, a Mr Cocksedge, during the short period he was with his parents studying for the Excise, he had no personal contact with its local affairs. Doubtless what he did hear contributed to his parochial knowledge; but his active adult life within an English town community was spent mainly at Lewes. It was certainly political enough in character, in the sense of town policies, to explain his rapid advance in journalism and public affairs when he emigrated to America. He already had at least some groundwork of practical knowledge.

Clio Rickman does not mention Ollive's position in the town as Constable or Paine's activities in Vestry and parish affairs; but biographers of Paine do not make it clear that Rickman was born on 27 July 1761, and therefore was under seven years old when Paine came to the town, and only twelve or thirteen when he left. His book was written from material gathered much later, from Lewes associates and from Paine himself, who stayed at the adult Rickman's house in London while writing Part II of *Rights of Man*. By then both had other political matters on their mind and except in nostalgia (to which Paine was not greatly given) the Lewes days are not likely to have occurred much in conversation, more particularly as Paine had known Rickman only as a child there.

Rickman got his nickname, Clio, from signing it on youthful poems printed in the Lewes local paper. He was undoubtedly deeply attached to Paine, and was described in a book called *Lewes Men of Note* as 'extremely well educated, a good classical scholar, and well acquainted with the French language'. In the last two qualifications he certainly outpaced Paine, although the several books of which he was author have hardly equalled his friend's in importance or staying power. He eventually made his living mainly as a bookseller and publisher (the two professions at the time frequently coincided), and brandished his political and literary sympathies boldly by naming his sons Paine, Washington, Franklin, Rousseau, Petrarch and Volney! Perhaps he never quite lost his small-boy enthusiasms, one of which grew into a close and loyal friendship which must often, in the difficult later years, have warmed Paine's heart. It may be partly from him that Paine picked up his knowledge of classical literature.

It was, of course, good business for landlords of local hostelries to take an active part in town affairs and the Verrals' was no isolated case in eighteenth century England. Although the family had relinquished the White Hart on the death of Henry Verral's brother William, its land-lord as their father had been, in 1761, Henry himself was proprietor of a Lewes Coffee House much used by Whigs informally, and the White Hart, with its spacious Assembly Room, remained the centre for larger gatherings and parochial meetings. Through Ollive, Paine knew Henry Verral well. They both signed one set of minutes of the St Michael's Vestry, and Verral was a witness at Paine's wedding (it is surprising no writers on Paine have linked this witness with the Lewes town constable of 1768 and the well-known Sussex family that, until only a short time before Paine's arrival in Lewes, had long been landlords of the White Hart).

The White Hart became a focal point in Paine's life. The first floor room with its large windows overlooked the High Street and was the centre of the men's social club, where politics were discussed, ideas exchanged, healths drunk and literary effusions produced. Rickman's account hereunder was partly obtained from a Mr Lee who was often present, and who wrote a poem at the time crowning 'Immortal Paine' as 'General of the Headstrong War':

'In this place he lived several years in habits of intimacy with a very respectable, sensible, and convivial set of acquaintance, who were entertained with his witty sallies and informed by his more serious conversations. In politics he was at this time a Whig, and notorious for that quality which has been defined perseverance in a good cause and obstinacy in a bad one. He was tenacious of his opinions, which were bold, acute, and independent, and which he maintained with ardour, elegance, and argument. At this period, at Lewes, the White Hart evening club was the resort of a social and intelligent circle who, out of fun, seeing that disputes often ran very warm and high, frequently had what they called the "Headstrong Book". This was no other than an old Greek Homer which was sent the morning after a debate vehemently maintained, to the most obstinate haranguer in the Club: this book had the following title, as implying that Mr Paine the best deserved and most frequently obtained it: "The Headstrong Book, or Original Book of Obstinacy." Written by * * * *, of Lewes, in Sussex, and Revised and Corrected by THOMAS PAINE.'

Among Paine's contributions to the Club were several poems, including an elegy on the death of General Wolfe which he published some years later in *The Pennsylvania Magazine*. It hardly suggests that at this time his feelings against Britain as an Empire-builder had strongly developed. He also received a three-guinea fee—a helpful windfall for a badly-paid exciseman—for writing an election song for the Whig candidate at New Shoreham, a Mr Rumbold. He was, in fact, beginning to write, to play with words and ideas, and his output included unexpectedly a drama, *The Trial of Farmer Carter's Dog Porter*, described by Rickman as 'a work of exquisite wit and humour'. This it was not; but the hanging of the dog on the erroneous charge of killing a hare—'Which treason was, or some such thing, Against our Sovereign Lord the King'—was certainly political satire, an antecedent of *Animal Farm* without Orwell's penetrating pity.

Another of Paine's sparetime activities was at the Lewes Bowling Green Club, founded in 1753. Paine must have paid its fee of five shillings for the season, plus sixpence each time he was present to play the game. According to William Sherwin's biography (1819), it was as the result of a casual remark here by Verral on the King of Prussia that he was inspired to write *Rights of Man*, as 'if it were necessary for a King to have so much of the Devil in him, Kings might be very well dispensed with'. Paine admitted making some such comment, and it is obvious from the nature of his book that Burke's *Reflections on the Revolution in France* was only partly its *raison d'être*, and that Paine must have been pondering some of these political problems for many years. The scope of his book was wider than Burke's and there is evidence Paine began it before his former friend's attack on the Revolution was published. If the seeds were sown in Lewes, however, they really germinated in *Common Sense* and the *Crisis* a few years later, for Paine's American writings anticipate ideas which he developed long afterwards in *Rights of Man*.

The White Hart and Bowling Green Club, nevertheless, were only the social trimmings on Paine's life. As an exciseman his work was demanding. In a passage on charter and corporation towns in *Rights of Man*, he suggested that the evils of the then system from the point of view of the population could only be eased by 'some circumstance in their situation, such as a navigable river, or a plentiful surrounding country'. He also believed the origins of such towns probably arose from their being garrisoned, and 'the corporations were charged with the care of the gates of the towns when no military garrison was present'. Lewes at the time Paine went there had preserved its West Gate, just beside the one-time Bull Inn, now Ollive's residence and shop, Bull House, where Paine went to live in the High Street. It was close to the famous ruined Norman Castle and Keep and the old town wall, and originally had marked the edge of the town beyond which no one was allowed to build. The rights of inhabitants were still, as Paine wrote, 'circumscribed to the town'. 'A native of England, under the operation of these charters and corporations, cannot be said to be an Englishman in the full sense of the word. He is not free of the Nation in the same manner that a Frenchman is free of France, and an American of America . . . This species of feudality is kept up to aggrandize the corporations at the ruin of the towns; and the effect is visible.'

The lack of individual freedom of movement Paine had personal opportunities of noting at St Michael's Vestry meetings: the record of one of them, signed by Paine and Verral on 2 August 1772, includes a resolution that 'the Parish Officers do immediately get an Order to remove Hanah Hood to the Parish she belongs to . . .'. The resolution was passed unanimously, but Paine stored the experience up in his mind, as an example of English restrictions on liberty which he was later able to compare unfavourably with American practice.

Lewes, however, had its 'navigable river', and its beautiful surroundings of rolling Sussex downs, pleasantly visible from the latticed windows of Sam Ollive's house at the crest of the High Street. At that time Newhaven's fine natural harbour had not been developed and the Lewes river was a busy waterway. The town and coast, only a few miles away, were as a result a haunt of smugglers. When I visited Lewes during research for this book, the local children in the bright May sunshine were still, under the guidance of a teacher, acting in the open air an extemporized play about smuggling. Local traditions die hard!

The river, another Ouse, must have reminded Paine of Thetford, but his task was not an easy one. His Excise area extended some ten miles to the coast at Brighthelmston, once a tiny fishing village but now a small health resort made popular by Dr Richard Russell's seabathing cure theories, although as yet it gave no hint of its later Regency brilliance as 'Brighton', under the patronage of the Prince Regent. The long downland rides took him through many other villages, full of history and treacherous muddy surfaces. At Wilmington the famous Saxon or prehistoric Long Man, 226 feet high and outlined in chalk between his two giant staves on the grass of Windover Hill, would have loomed over the passing rider, mysteriously eyeless, like Samson in Gaza. Paine is said to have liked music, and is recorded at least once at the opera; but the small Eley house at Glyndebourne, cradled in the downs outside Lewes, would have as yet brought to his ears no distant echoes of Mozartian melody. Nor could he have guessed, as he galloped through or by the little hamlet of Firle, that its distinguished Catholic family of Gage, one of whom had been in charge of the young Princess Elizabeth under 'Bloody' Mary, and one of whom had given his name to the 'greengage', a new plum brought back from his travels and planted at Firle Place, would in a few years' time provide the Commander-in-Chief of the British Forces in America, at the outbreak of the War of Independence.

This Thomas Gage, a son of the local Viscount, was to figure in Paine's *Dialogue between General Wolfe and General Gage in a Wood near Boston*, where he was briefly exhorted to resign his commission if he had 'any regard for the glory of the British name'; and oddly also in Robert Burns' ironic verses on General Sir William Howe's dubious 'victory' in taking Philadelphia:

> Poor Tammy Gage within a cage
> Was kept at Boston ha', man,
> Till Willie Howe took o'er the knowe,
> For Philadelphia, man.

Gage in fact was recalled soon after the Battle of Bunker's Hill, only two months after his epoch-making skirmish at Lexington had set the first match to the American conflagration. Trotting past Firle Place in 1768, Paine could have had no prevision of future strife with one of its faraway sons, or of a fellow exciseman in Dumfries who would join him, in verse, in recording his adventures, Elysian and actual.

It was a healthy, open air life and Paine probably enjoyed it. 'You can drive many downland roads and they are often glorious, but you are not on the downs until you take to your own feet,' writes Barbara Willard in *Sussex*. 'A horse is better still . . . there are miles of good riding country.' Paine, although he did not know it, was at the end of a transport era. In 1769, a year after he came to Lewes, Watt invented the steam engine, sounding the knell of Paine's loved horses in the service they had given to man for thousands of years. In the meantime, the eighteenth century roads were rough but the sea-sprayed Sussex air and streamlined downs, 'bow-backed' as Kipling called them, provided refreshing interludes between the more mundane duties in Lewes, when he walked the town with his cane covered with figures and ink-bottle hanging from his buttonhole, ready for measuring and receipts.

The fact that Paine preserved his popularity in Lewes, and was accepted so easily into its society, must have meant that he carried out his duties with a good deal of tact. Tea-drinking in particular had become a national habit, and a few years later, wrote Trevelyan, quoting Lecky's *England*, 'Pitt calculated that thirteen million pounds of tea were consumed in the kingdom, of which only five and a half millions had paid duty'. The good and respectable Parson Woodforde of Weston Longeville, in Paine's home county of Norfolk, in 1777 recorded in his diary that Andrews the smuggler brought him 'this night about 11 o'clock a bagg of Hyson Tea 6 pound weight . . . I gave him some Geneva and paid him for the tea at 10/6 per pound'. As Trevelyan remarks, the inhabitants of the rectory thought and spoke of 'Andrews the smuggler' just as one might speak of 'Andrews the grocer'!

Perhaps Paine did turn a blind eye to the activities of some of the Lewes inhabitants and accepted any cups of tea offered him philosophically, without comment. His general reputation in the Excise was good, if Rickman is correct that Mr Jenner, principal clerk in the Excise Office, London, 'had several times to write letters from the Board of Excise thanking Mr Paine for his assiduity in his profession, and for his information and calculations forwarded to the office'. Paine being the kind of man with an urge to put his point of view to authority, one has no reason to doubt Rickman's source here, especially as 'calculations' were to prove so prominent a feature in Paine's later writing. But that he undertook his duties with some moderation and compassion, if no more, seems indicated in the letter he wrote to Lewes after his return from America. It was in respect of a meeting about to be held there to protest against a royal proclamation suppressing 'seditious' writings: in our term, the imposition of a censorship. The contents, though, are very revealing of character and Paine's own life there.

'It is now upwards of eighteen years since I was a resident inhabitant of the town of Lewes. My situation among you as an officer of the revenue, for more than six years, enabled me to see into the numerous and various distresses which the weight of taxes even at that time of day occasioned; and feeling, as I then did, and as it is natural for me to do, for the hard condition of others, it is with pleasure I can declare, and every person then under my survey, and now living, can witness the exceeding candor, and even tenderness, with which that part of the duty that fell to my share was executed. The name of Thomas Paine is not to be found in the records of the Lewes justices, in any one act of contention with, or severity of any kind whatever towards, the persons whom he surveyed, either in the town or in the country; of this Mr Fuller and Mr Shelley, who will probably attend the meeting, can, if they please, give full testimony . . . Since my departure from Lewes, fortune or providence has thrown me into a line of action which my first setting out in life could not possibly have suggested to me . . . Many of you will recollect, that whilst I resided among you, there was not a man more firm and open in supporting the principles of liberty than myself, and I still pursue, and ever will, the same path.'

The 'Mr Shelley' mentioned, obviously known well to Paine, was one of the family inhabiting Shelley House in Lewes, a close branch of the influential Sussex line which at Horsham and Goring was represented by Sir Bysshe Shelley, grandfather of the poet. Percy Bysshe Shelley was born in 1792, a year after the publication of Paine's *Rights of Man*. His aunts lived at Lewes, and he was to prove one of Paine's most enthusiastic disciples of the next generation: the young generation in revolt (Byron was another) who never lived to see the passing of the Reform Bill in 1832, but who carried on Paine's work and—unsuccessful though their efforts seemed at the time—helped to change the climate of opinion. Shelley House is now the Shelleys Hotel.

Another notable town house, Southover Grange, now surrounded by a charming public park, belonged to the grandparents of the diarist John Evelyn, who lived with them in his Lewes schooldays and at the age of eight laid one of the first stones of the nearby South Malling church, built by his grandfather. The Reverend John Harvard was married in this church in 1636, emigrated to New England in 1637 and died a year later, leaving his library of over three hundred volumes and £779 to the new college in Cambridge, Massachusetts. It was named Harvard College in his honour, and is now Harvard University. It is doubtful if Paine knew of the Lewes connection, although it might have interested him, for seventeenth century Harvard was the first college to make the experiment of co-education of Indians alongside whites. John Evelyn's diary, of course (not published until 1818), would have been unknown to him although he certainly would have known the fine house.

In July 1769, Samuel Ollive died, leaving a widow, three sons and a young daughter Elizabeth who was accounted pretty. Paine then left the house, presumably for the sake of respectability, but he remained close to the family and joined the widow in running the snuff and tobacco business, which was expanded to include groceries. Because of inadequate pay, it was quite customary for customs officials to ease their situation by taking other part-time employment, as indeed Robert Burns did in Dumfries. Whether because he was at the time attracted to the girl, or whether because it seemed the obvious step in all the circumstances, Paine on 26 March 1771, married Elizabeth Ollive and returned to live at the house.

The wedding was at St Michael's Church, almost opposite the Ollive house, and a photostat of the marriage certificate is before me as I write. Presumably the curate, Robert Austen, is responsible for the misspelling of Elizabeth's surname as Olive, as both she and her brother Thomas, one of the witnesses, sign it with the double 'l'. The other witness was Henry Verral, Samuel's old friend and fellow Constable. What it is more difficult to blame on the curate is the fact that 'Thomas Pain' is described as a 'Bachelor'. Did he, in fact, conceal from the Ollives his marriage of twelve years before? And if so, why? The fact that Rickman knew of it does not suggest the concealment was complete. The brevity of the first marriage may have accounted for Paine's reluctance to bring up the matter; it was, after all, old history, and we do not know if Elizabeth ever knew of it. Oldys, of course, makes much of the heinous illegality of Paine's surely rather venial offence. It may be at the bottom of his totally uncorroborated suggestion that the first wife was still alive.

A point about the Ollives and the marriage that needs clearing up is the statement by all biographers, beginning with Conway, that Samuel Ollive and his family were Quakers. *The Story of an Old Meeting House*, published in 1916 by the Reverend J. M. Connell, the then minister at the Westgate Chapel and later author of a slim book on Paine, emphasizes that this meeting house, in which the Ollives worshipped and where Elizabeth's grandfather had been minister, had never at any time in its history been used by the Quakers. After the passing of the Act of Uniformity in 1662 many dissenting clergymen were ejected from their livings, including those of the churches of St Anne's and St Michael's in Lewes. With part of their congregation, and after some compromise with the government and Anglican church, they eventually formed non-conformist groups of worship, one of which settled at the Westgate Chapel. It was originally Calvinist in its theology, 'though even then perhaps moving in the direction of Unitarianism', writes Connell. It remains Unitarian today; the Reverend Basil Viney, who is a minister of the church and also an author on religious and musical subjects, has preached a sermon on Thomas Paine there and maintains that Paine's form of deism was close to the chapel's present unitarianism, which he calls 'theistic'.

The Quakers formed a meeting house in another part of the town, and Clio Rickman was one of their members. Whether this fact, in addition to the known Quakerism of Paine's father, misled Conway into his error one cannot now tell; but it also trapped him into building on it a totally invalid assumption about the possible reason for the failure of the marriage, based on some Quaker folklore about the bride's period of 'mourning'—or delayed consummation—which need no longer concern us. It was never a convincing psychological theory and Conway admitted it was guesswork.

The reason the marriage took place at St Michael's was that eighteenth century non-conformist ministers still had no legal right to marry couples in their meeting houses. Paine already had some connection with the parish church as a witness at Vestry meetings, as we have seen, but there is no evidence that he worshipped there, although he may have had Quaker friends and visited their meeting house on occasion. The Westgate Chapel of his wife's family was originally part of the mansion bought by Sir Henry Goring in Elizabethan times for £160. Bull House was part of the same mansion. In earlier days it had been the Bull Inn, a hostelry with space for coaches. When the Gorings, a prominent Sussex family who had represented Lewes in Parliament, sold the property it was converted to form the present Bull House with the Westgate Chapel adjoining. A Reverend Thomas Barnard opened the Chapel on 5 November 1700, and sold 'The Bull' separately to John Ollive and a Samuel Swayne for £100. John Ollive became minister of the chapel from 1711 to 1740, and was Samuel Ollive's father.

The house was restored to a great deal of its original Tudor character in 1922 and in 1936 it passed to the Sussex Archaeological Trust. It is now used as a Paine Museum and restaurant on behalf of the Trust. There is a large library upstairs in what was traditionally Paine's room. A small path leading off an area at the back, which must have been the original garden or inn coaching space, is now called Paine's Twitten (twitten is Sussex dialect for path).

It is a beautiful and surprisingly spacious house, with substantial oak ceiling beams and some breathtaking views of the downs, although two narrow windows in the library were added after Paine's time. There was plenty of room for the Ollive children to grow up and Paine was fortunate in his lodgings. Much of the house was already historic, and in one of the upstairs rooms a duel is said to have been fought between a cavalier and roundhead in the time of the Civil War.

The position at the corner of Bull Lane and the High Street is very central. Paine had only to walk downhill to the White Hart further along the High Street, and on 5th November, then as now, the town would have blazed with bonfires, and torchlit processions swept up the High Street below the Bull House windows. On such nights there would have been much drinking, entertainment, and social vivacity at the White Hart. The situation, however, is rather an Irish one. The Lewes bonfires, fireworks and processions on Guy Fawkes night, famous throughout Sussex, use the date for a double purpose. They had nothing originally to do with gunpowder, treason and plot but in fact were begun soon after the end of 'Bloody' Mary's reign, in defiant commemoration of the sixteen Lewes martyrs who were burned in the market place for their Protestant faith. They would hardly discourage Paine in any incipient disapproval of the whole business of the monarchy and the established Church.

IV

WINE, WOMAN AND EXCISE REFORM

Paine when he came to Lewes was thirty-one years of age, and by no means an unattractive man. His height seems to have varied in the eye of the beholder, as heights always do, and fluctuated between five foot nine inches and 'tall'. He was slender and not inelegant, with a bold nose, fresh complexion and uncommonly large, brilliant and animated eyes, of a 'deep blue'. His hands were said to be slim and well-formed (his portraits bear this out), and he was a courageous sportsman on ice and in the water, earning the nickname 'The Commodore'.

William Carver, who knew Paine here and later in America, described him as a lover of sport, literature, good talk, oysters and (significantly, in view of a later rather exaggerated reputation) wine. There is no doubt he expanded in the atmosphere of his improved circumstances, and among his new circle of friends. And Elizabeth Ollive, born on 16 December 1749, and therefore thirteen years his junior, may well have been charmed by the young man her father so obviously took to. Nevertheless, Conway's unqualified statement that Paine was 'her hero' is a romantic assumption, no more.

It is also, perhaps, the moment to question Aldridge's equally categorical assertion in the Introduction to his 1959 biography that Paine's manners were 'rough and ungracious' and that he had 'tasted only the rudiments of formal education'. All men of intellect are largely self-educated after the age they leave school, but education at a grammar school was in the eighteenth century quite extensive, a legacy from the Renaissance and Tudor times; and Paine's had already produced at least one scholar of note. (The same mistake has been made with regard to Shakespeare, also a grammar school boy in a country town.)

It is not to claim exceptional merit for the Thetford Grammar School to say that for his time Paine was well educated, particularly on the mathematical side, nor was he in any sense a true proletariat. His father was a master staymaker and his mother the daughter of an attorney, which would put him today in the middle classes, and the manners of a Quaker child of this class would be highly disciplined and polite. There is not the slightest evidence from anyone who knew him intimately that Paine acted like a lout in society, nor would one expect it with any knowledge of English social structures of the time. Rickman, a man of very good family, described his manners as 'easy and gracious'. When it

1. Statue of Thomas Paine by Sir Charles Wheeler, R.A., Thetford

2. Bull House, Le

The White Hart,
Lewes, 1971

3. View of Lewes, 1762. Contemporary print

4. Letter in Paine's handwriting re Bull House, Lewes, 18 July 1772

Part list of charity payments signed by Paine and others at meeting of St Michael's Vestry, Lewes, 16 April 1770 became not merely the fashion but a political and religious necessity to discredit Paine, his comparatively humble birth made him an easy target for this kind of suggestion; but it is necessary to remember that apart from a brief youthful period at sea Paine rubbed shoulders throughout his life with men of reasonable education and social standing at worst, and at best with those from the highest strata. Even had he been from a lower class, he could not have failed to acquire much of the polish which was a feature of the manners of the age.

For three years we have no indication that all was not going well with the Paines and Ollives at Bull House. Two small legal documents exist during this time, in Paine's handwriting and preserved among the Westgate Chapel papers. One admits himself under obligation to pay one shilling yearly to the Trustees of the Meeting House, 'as an acknowledgment for their suffering the droppings of Rain which fall from a New Building lately erected by me, to fall into a Yard belonging and adjoining to the North side of the said Meeting House'. This provision of a shilling umbrella—as it might be termed—for the congregation was agreed on 18 July 1772, but for what purpose Paine erected his outhouse we can only guess. Probably it was to house the tobacco mill or grocery stores. On the same date he issued a letter sidestepping a complaint from the same source about the filling up of a doorway, on the grounds that he is 'only Tenant in the House' and he had no right even of objecting should Mrs Ollive fill it up. 'Immediately, I cannot have any power to give any kind of answer in a Case which is entirely hers, not mine.'

The two attitudes are not entirely inconsistent; Paine is accepting responsibility for the outhouse as he personally built it or had it erected, but in other matters Mrs Ollive remains the owner of the house. The use of the word 'Immediately' does rather suggest some consultation as to his and Mrs Ollive's actual position with regard to the house is contemplated. On the face of it, he was still only a tenant, although her son-in-law and a partner in the business.

In April 1774 the business failed, and Paine was forced to sell his household furniture and possessions, including the tobacco and snuff mill and other contents of the shop. A poster appeared in Lewes announcing the Auction 'on Thursday the 14th of April, and following day' and listing the articles. The sale was to meet Paine's creditors, and apparently more than did so. 'Trade I do not understand,' wrote the future philosopher with engaging, and one feels not greatly repentant, candour. It is not an unusual situation when two employments are undertaken at the same time, for one is sure to suffer, and Paine during the preceding two years had been greatly occupied with another matter undoubtedly much nearer his heart.

His position in the town, as well as some rumours, perhaps, of his literary efforts, in particular the election song for the Whig candidate at New Shoreham, had won the confidence of the excisemen who were anxious to make their grievances known. How much this arose from Paine's appointing himself a kind of unofficial shop steward among them we cannot tell: the old medieval guilds of craftsmen had virtually disappeared under growing government oppression, and the age of the trade union had not begun. Nearly twenty years later, one of Paine's most controversial suggestions in *Rights of Man* was that workmen should be left free to make their own bargains. 'Personal labour is all the property they have.' And he reinforced this argument a few pages later by drawing on his experience in the Excise of low wages: 'The salary of the inferior officers of the revenue has stood at the petty pittance of less than fifty pounds a year for upwards of one hundred years.'

The excisemen's wage of £50 a year was, he had calculated, reduced to £32 if the annual cost of maintaining a horse were taken into consideration; and although Mr Noel Murless and Captain Ryan Price, reckoning out the expense of maintaining each horse in their famous racing stables today, might be tempted to rush back through the time barrier to acquire animals capable of surviving, well fed and well groomed, at a cost of £18 a year, the figure represented a frightening one off a low wage at the cost of living at that period. Paine's pamphlet, *The Case of the Officers of Excise*, was therefore composed to put this and other arguments before the authorities, rationally and clearly, in the hope of betterment of their conditions.

It was Paine's first burst into print on any scale. He was a delayed-action writer, thirty-five years of age when he began work on the pamphlet in the summer of 1772, and although his style was often, in the future, to show signs of carelessness, not dissimilar to the carelessness of Dickens when writing to meet a serial deadline, its forcefulness, clarity and grasp of apt imagery were to reach their target in a way impossible to the higher-born writers of the time, with their emphasis on classical quotation and long-drawn-out sentences, encrusted with unnecessary elegancies. A comparison of Thomas Paine's prose style, not merely with that of Edmund Burke, but also with that of Thomas Carlyle sixty years later, shows how modern and direct Paine was, a revolutionist as ahead of his time as a writer as he was as a political reformer.

He was always a writer with a cause, and the cause which launched him happened to arise from personal experience. This gave it force, but the force would have been useless without self-sacrifice. The pamphlet was issued at three shillings a copy and four thousand copies were printed; but although his fellow officers contributed some share of the cost, the main body of expense would have fallen on Paine, as in the case of his later works. This was an age when reliance on a publisher for appeals to redress social evils could never be assured, and a generation or more later Shelley was also to rely heavily on his own means, already decimated by charity to other writers, to get his largely unread and savagely criticized poetry into print.

Paine spent some of the winter of 1772–3 in London distributing copies, including to Members of Parliament and to Oliver Goldsmith, already a famous writer of many facets whose most celebrated play, *She Stoops to Conquer*, first appeared in 1773. He was admired by Paine, who accompanied his copy of the Excise pamphlet with a curiously mock-modest note requesting that Goldsmith should 'partake of a bottle of wine, or any thing else', with the author. In fact Goldsmith responded well, for *The Case of the Officers of Excise* was very well put, and likely to interest any humane man of liberal views. The cost to Paine, not only in connection with the printing but also the distribution and travel to, and expenses in, London, must have been considerable and the bottle of wine was probably a rash outlay for a good cause. How much the till of the Bull House shop contributed we can only guess, but it may be one clue to the failure of the business. Paine was not merely living, but doubtless *hoping* beyond his means.

The social structure of the period was weighted too heavily against the workers, including civil workers, for the pamphlet to have any effect, but the attempt showed courage as well as solid sense. Paine claimed the not unimportant job of customs officer, being poorly paid, was as a result poorly carried out, and in the long run better pay would produce better revenue for the state. It was an argument used constantly later by political advocates of social reform, but Paine was ahead of his time in using it, and his incidental pointing out of the plight of those on fixed incomes in inflationary periods carries an even more contemporary ring. He was also to show an awareness of the connection between poverty and petty dishonesty, if not actual crime, and therefore of alleviating circumstances, which the law of his day largely ignored. It was fundamental to Paine's compassionate understanding of psychology which runs like a thread through his works:

'Poverty, in defiance of principle, begets a degree of meanness that will stoop to almost anything. A thousand refinements of argument may be brought to prove that the practice of honesty will be still the same, in the most trying and necessitous circumstances. He who never was ahungered may argue finely on the subjection of his appetite; and he who never was distressed, may harangue as beautifully on the power

51

of principle. But poverty, like grief, has an incurable deafness, which never hears; the oration loses all its edge; and "To be, or not to be" becomes the only question.

'The rich, in ease and affluence, may think I have drawn an unnatural portrait; but could they descend to the cold regions of want, the circle of polar poverty, they would find their opinions changing with the climate. There are habits of thinking peculiar to different conditions, and to find them out is truly to study mankind.'

Paine's 'cold regions of want' still make inroads in the 'affluent society', where the gap between rich and poor widens daily; and the habits of thinking from which he studied mankind persist. It is no derogation of his perspicacity, so much ahead of his time, that his work still rings a bell in our social conscience. Such universality is found in the work of all major thinkers and reformers.

Although later in America Paine declared to the Committee of Continental Congress, 'in England I never was the author of a syllable in print'—apparently dismissing this early pamphlet as unimportant in the light of his later activities—it set the pattern of his life in one direction, the need for social reform and its interrelation with a study of economics. Paine's importance and influence as a writer were to rest in his ability to put this revolutionary concept—now an axiom of politics—into the kind of vigorous, unintellectualized prose which could be read by any literate 'man in the street'. More than any writer before him, he was to become the Man of the People writing directly to the People and not only to impress students and politicians.

Perhaps it was this first taste of print that, in addition to his financial position which could not have been greatly improved by this expense, brought to a head Paine's dissatisfaction with his career to date. He was again discharged from the Excise (8 April 1774) on the grounds that he quit without the Board's leave and had 'gone off on Account of the Debts which he hath contracted'. How much the material of his pamphlet influenced this decision by the Excise to cut off a rebellious limb remains equivocal. Years later William Cobbett was to write that this dismissal was the real cause of the American Revolution.

Another even more equivocal and final cutting off of Paine from the past followed his Excise dismissal within two months. How much the one derived from the other it is impossible now to say, but on 4 June 1774, Paine and his wife came to what appears to have been an amicable and final separation. A great deal of speculation on the reasons for this has been made and all totally without any confirmation, for Elizabeth herself refused to talk about it and in subsequent life got up and left the room if anyone criticized Paine.[1] And Paine's own answer to Rickman's query on the matter of his marriage was final: 'It is nobody's business but my own; I had cause for it, but I will name no one.' This is generally quoted as referring to the separation, but in fact on a close reading of Rickman's text I have the impression the men at the time were discussing Paine's non-cohabitation with his wife. In any case Paine made no further comment. According to Rickman he 'always spoke tenderly and respectfully of his wife and several times gave financial aid without revealing the source'. There seems some acknowledgment even in England—where his name came to be unmentionable outside reform circles without abuse—that in the matter of his marriage he was not blameworthy, for when Elizabeth died (only a year before Paine) on 27 July 1808, her newspaper obituary stated that abuse of her husband would be 'needless, ungenerous and unjustifiable'.

In view of Paine's record of apparent elimination of sex in his life after this marriage, impotency has naturally been inferred by a number of biographers. Certainly the charge brought by his biographer and enemy in America, James Cheetham, that the three sons of Madame de Bonneville, whom he more or less adopted when she came to America—leaving her young husband, Paine's sincere friend, behind in France—were Paine's own sons is palpably absurd and evaporated with a libel action. Madame de Bonneville was, in fact, for long something of a thorn in Paine's flesh and her character, as well as her financial need, not to count his regard for her husband, were reasons he felt impelled to accept responsibility for the boys. He was, by this time, an old man. But apart from the lack of children there is no real evidence that in fact Paine was not a normal man in this respect. Rickman, who claims to have spoken to a Lewes doctor about the matter, states clearly that the marriage was not consummated, but that to his definite knowledge this was not due to any physical defect on Paine's part. The similarity to Shaw's marriage with Charlotte Payne-Townshend comes to mind. Paine's concentration was on his interests, politics, writing, and he was probably celibate in the way Shaw ('the writing machine', as he called himself when querying his wisdom in marrying) was celibate for the bulk of his life, in spite of unquestionable early sexual involvements. The fact that Paine married a second time would seem to flout the impotency theory, although it is true the marriage with Sam Ollive's daughter may have been in part a gesture to respectability when Paine became involved in running the business.

Was Paine, in any case, totally celibate from the age of thirty-five

---

[1] Paine's biographer, Gilbert Vale (1841), acquired this information directly from an apprentice to watchmaking who long shared her and her brother's home, and it was confirmed by other residents of Cranbrook, where they lived.

years, if not before? After considerable if not prurient search by his various biographers there is, it is true, only one possible piece of evidence to the contrary. The incident occurred in 1781 when Paine had journeyed to France for the first time from America on the frigate *Alliance*, accompanying Colonel Laurens on a political mission. It was, in essence, an anecdote of Rabelaisian farce. His hostile interpreter, Elkanah Watson, recounted in his Memoirs the disgust with which Paine was received by social gatherings on landing, owing to his uncouth appearance and the peculiar smell which emanated from his clothes: '. . . as he had been roasted alive on his arrival at L'Orient, for the * * * and well basted with brimstone, he was absolutely offensive and perfumed the whole apartment'. He was induced to take a hot bath, seduced by a file of English papers to read, the servant being instructed in French (which Paine did not easily understand) to increase the heat until Paine was '*bien bouilli*'. Paine became 'so much absorbed in his reading that he was nearly par-boiled before leaving the bath'.

The meaning of the row of asterisks was considered clear by all subsequent readers: Paine's unmentionable disease can only have been venereal. Aldridge, however, took the trouble to read Watson's original MS from which the printed version was made and found the term actually used was 'scotch fiddle', a well-known term at the period for scurvy, or the itch. He deduced from this that Paine could be totally exonerated. Modern medical research, however, has recently suggested that certain irritant diseases of this time taken to be scurvy (a scourge which in the Middle Ages, when syphilis was unknown in England, and in particular much later in ships at sea, was caused by a diet deficiency of Vitamin C) may sometimes have been venereal in origin. The 'scotch fiddle' could, it is just possible, have been a variant with wider application, hence the asterisks; it is a slight possibility, but in this case Paine could still, at this time—seven years after the breaking up of his marriage —have been seeking some occasional relief, apart from the brandy bottle, from the pressures of his other activities. If so, no other incident has come to light, and for a man with so many political and social contacts and enemies, spread across three countries and two continents, this would argue either extreme discretion (not a regular Paine characteristic) and luck, or the fact that sex indeed ceased, if it had ever begun, to be a factor in his personal life. His Quaker background and strong moral views would make this not entirely unlikely.

The fact that in later life he produced some romantic-style verses alleged to have been written in youth to young women with whom he was in love is not really significant: it was a normal literary exercise of the time and sincerity was not necessarily a part of it. But Paine was no misogynist and there is no sign of mental abnormality in any of his approaches to, or references to women. He looked kindly and sympathetically on them as friends and wrote warmly, and perhaps a little wistfully, in January 1789, to Kitty Nicholson, the daughter of his friend, an American Commodore of New York, on hearing of her marriage:

'When I see my female friends drop off by matrimony I am sensible of something that affects me like a loss in spite of all the appearances of joy. I cannot help mixing the sincere compliment of regret with that of congratulation. It appears that I had outlived or lost a friend.

'Though I appear a sort of wanderer, the married state has not a sincerer friend than I am. It is the harbour of human life, and is, with respect to the things of this world, what the next world is to this. It is home; and that one word conveys more than any other word can express. For a few years we may glide along the tide of youthful single life, and be wonderfully delighted; but it is a tide that flows but once, and what is still worse, it ebbs faster than it flows, and leaves many a hapless voyager aground.

'I am one, you see, that have experienced the fate I am describing. I have lost my tide; it passed by while every thought of my heart was on the wing for the salvation of my dear America, and I have now as contentedly as I can, made myself a little bower of willows on the shore that has the solitary resemblance of a home.

'Should I always continue the tenant of this home, I hope my female acquaintance will ever remember that it contains not the churlish enemy of their sex, not the inaccessible cold hearted mortal, nor the capricious tempered oddity, but one of the best and most affectionate of their friends.'

It is difficult not to gain from this letter the impression that Paine had concealed from his American friends the fact that he was, in fact, already married, with a wife still living. This was the real reason he could not marry, and it is quite possible, given the religious outlook of the time, that his Quaker principles prevented his engaging in any other kind of union in the circumstances. As for closer contacts in younger days, the fact that he returned to Lincolnshire to visit a widow friend after he had left his employment there is suggestive, if nothing more. A haven, and perhaps something more, during his Alford Excise work cannot be ruled out, although it is always dangerous to make assumptions regarding the friendships with congenial women of men like Paine and Shaw. A passage on women in the American *Crisis*, however, could possibly have a personal application:

'No man attempts to seduce a truly honest woman. It is the supposed looseness of her mind that starts the thoughts of seduction, and he who offers it calls her a prostitute. Our pride is always hurt by the same propositions which offend our principles; for when we are shocked at the crime we are wounded by the suspicion of our compliance.'

The final suggestion of conscience about compliance has the psychological acuteness one often finds in Paine, and although the passage must be equivocal it cannot be overlooked.

One thing Paine was remarkable in always was in putting into practice wherever possible the beliefs about which he wrote. One of these was women's rights, born of the viciously unjust laws of the time by which any husband, automatically, became owner of all of his wife's income or property, making it practically impossible (in view of the rarity of work for women) for her to leave him or gain repossession of her money if he deserted her. It was to be one of the mainsprings of Mary Wollstonecraft's *Vindication of the Rights of Women* in 1792, and her and William Godwin's resistance to legal marriage. A document belonging to the Bull House makes clear that Paine gave up all such legal rights on his separation from Elizabeth:

'Soon after the Testator's death, his daughter Elizabeth married Thos. Pain from whom she afterwards lived separate under articles dated 4th June 1774, and made between the said Thos. Pain of the first part, the said Elizabeth of the 2nd part, and the Rev. James Castley, Clerk, of the 3d part, by which Articles, after reciting (inter alia) that Dissentions had arisen between the said Thos. Pain and Elizabeth his wife, and that they had agreed to live separate. And also reciting the Will of the said Saml. Ollive and that the said Thomas Pain had agreed that the said Elizabeth should have and take her share of the said Monies of the said House when the same should become due and payable and that he would give any Discharge that should then be required to and for the use of the said Elizabeth: The said Thos. Pain did covenant to permit the said Elizabeth to live separate from him and to carry on such Trade and Business as she should think fit, notwithstanding her coverture and as if she were a Feme Sole. And that he would not at any time thereafter claim or demand the said monies which she should be entitled to at the time of the sale of the said House in Lewes aforesaid, or any of the Monies Rings, Plate Cloathes Linen Woollen Household Goods or Stock in Trade which the said Elizabeth should or might at any time thereafter buy or purchase or which should be devised or given to her . . .'

Elizabeth went eventually to live with her brother Thomas, a watchmaker in Cranbrook, Kent, and in 1800 she was party to a property agreement in which it is stated:

'That the said Elizabeth Pain had ever since lived separate from him the said Thos. Pain, and never had any issue, and the said Thomas Pain had many years quitted this Kingdom and resided (if living) in parts beyond the seas, but had not since been heard of by the said Elizabeth Pain, nor was it known for certain whether he was living or dead.'

The large seals attached to the signatures of Ollive's three children on this agreement show the head of Thomas Paine as a young man. The long preservation of these is interesting. Was it sentimental on Elizabeth's part, and did she truly believe her husband dead and not connect him with the Thomas Paine so frequently mentioned (and often execrated) in the newspapers? It suggests if so an extraordinary indifference to public events. More likely this was a legal formality to avoid questioning her rights in the property.

Oldys prints a bitterly complaining letter to her, at the time of the separation, from Paine's mother. The theme is the ungrateful child for whom the parents made so many sacrifices so ill-rewarded. Such parental reactions are common enough, especially when a youth leaves home to try his fortunes elsewhere, but the letter goes so much beyond this in accusations of money borrowed and never returned, and viciousness of character, that it is difficult to believe that Oldys did not 'touch it up', at the very least, if he did not concoct the whole, as he is known to have done elsewhere. It rings untrue because we know how closely affectionate to his father Paine remained, although the complaint that he had not written home for two years may well have been true. One does not write when news is bad and Paine's pen had been very fully engaged elsewhere.

If the letter is genuine, either in whole or in part, the interesting query remains as to from whom Oldys obtained it. If from Elizabeth, it does not accord with her reported reticence on the subject, nor are we given any hint as to her reply, if any. In her Kent retreat, would she have known of Oldys' biography? If she did, and read it, the 1800 protest that she never knew what became of her husband was certainly invalid, for the book makes clear this Thomas Paine's connection with her.[1] It also accuses him of beating his wife, an extension, of course, of the 'ill-usage' of Oldys' gossiping Sandwich housewives in connection with the earlier marriage. Keeping an open mind, Elizabeth's silence is certainly rather odd.

Her part in Paine's life was sad and equivocal. Unjustifiably, I think, some have tried to read in some of his later writings on marriage—such

---

[1] However, Paine at this time was in France, in the Napoleonic aftermath of revolution, and Elizabeth may well have heard nothing of him for some time.

as the article, *Reflections on Unhappy Marriages*, in the *Pennsylvania Magazine*, which stressed the matrimonial difficulties when the woman, before marriage, professes to share interests and beliefs which after marriage she entirely drops—a reflection on Elizabeth herself. It could be, but no writer takes only from his own experience and Paine may well have written after listening to complaints from his husband friends. Elizabeth's hold on him obviously was not strong enough to subdue his wanderlust and his eagerness for new experience. And he can be said to be selfish in the sense that he did not appear to stop to consider the situation of a woman, still young, who throughout her life could never hope to marry again or live with any man, and have children, without ostracism. The pretty girl of Lewes was to live on until 1808, dying only a year before Paine himself. Did she suspect the source of the anonymous gifts of money which Rickman maintained Paine sometimes sent her? Her loyalty, at any rate, did not run to public complaint or chatter, unless we are to accept the unreliable Oldys as having obtained information from her direct. It is not possible to think of her without some compassion. Like the first wife, she is a shadowy figure obliterated by the sun of the far stronger character she married.

The full truth about Paine's relations with women is as shadowy, in the end, as the figures of his two young wives. How much he was addicted to the wine bottle is more arguable, and his enemies made much of it, as will appear. Yet even here there is no indication that it ever left him in a wholly intemperate state or dulled his faculties in any way. Certainly we must dismiss Dr Benjamin Rush's statement, quoted without question by Aldridge, that 'he was intemperate and otherwise debauched in private life'. Not only has there never been any evidence of 'debauchery' in Paine's life, but Rush wrote this on some prompting to Paine's virulent biographer, Cheetham, after Paine's death, when he admitted 'His principles avowed in *The Age of Reason* were so offensive to me that I did not wish to renew my intercourse with him'. Elsewhere Rush was less censorious: Paine, he wrote, often visited in the families of Dr Franklin and others, 'where he made himself acceptable by a turn he discovered for philosophy as well as political subjects . . . After the year 1776 my intercourse with Mr Paine was casual. I met him now and then at the tables of some of our whig citizens, where he spoke but little, but was always inoffensive in his manner and conversation.'

Rush's was a general reaction in puritanical America to Paine's book (which few of its attackers had actually read), and the favourite way of fighting any religious deviance has always been to link its advocates with gross immorality. When Rush first knew Paine he was a friendly supporter of his anti-slavery propaganda, and nothing in his relations with Paine in earlier life supports his assertion in old age. That his memory was failing is shown in other details and dates which are provably wrong.

It was a hard-drinking age, in which the formidable intake of Dr Johnson, William Pitt, Charles James Fox and others has passed without question. Like many writers, in fact, Paine used wine as a stimulant, which became a necessity to add brilliance and liveliness to his work, the lucidity of which never wavered even when he was a septuagenarian. In a passage in *The Age of Reason* he writes of the providential rarity of brain damage, robbing man of his most valuable faculty, mind. 'But we see it happening,' he adds, 'by long and habitual intemperance.' This was written in Paris in disillusion with the Revolution, the only period in his life, he told Rickman, when he drank to excess. The impression one gets is that the experience pulled him up short. His brain was Paine's most treasured possession, to the point of accusations of vanity.

During Paine's second marriage wine added to the convivialities and good talk at the White Hart in Lewes, and how much any failure in that marriage contributed we cannot know. Certainly men need stimulants, more especially men of great mental activity, and the most, perhaps, that we can tolerantly conjecture is that in the absence of sex, the outlet for most normal men, Paine had increasing recourse to the obvious alternative. If it helped him to stand up to the pressures of his work— and it obviously did—we, the democratic beneficiaries, are in no position to cast stones.

V

THE NEW WORLD

Paine's creditors were covered by the sale of his effects, and the property and his wife's share of everything inherited from her father remained with her as we have seen. When Paine arrived in London in June 1774, he may be said to have been fancy free but he was certainly not in an easy financial position.

Nevertheless he seems to have survived and taken with gusto to his earlier scientific pursuits. Politically, too, he was now increasingly aware. *The Case of the Officers of Excise* had shown him he could write, and write with political point; and in fact he was to incorporate some of its arguments and ideas into his later work (it is a not uncommon practice with writers). He had been in London during 1772 and 1773 when the great Robert Clive scandal had burst, concerning his massive fortune partly acquired after the Battle of Plassy in 1757, when he had accepted a gift of upwards of £200,000 from Mir Jaffar, now England's puppet, in return for ensuring he became Nawab of Bengal (Jaffar had promptly strangled his predecessor). The freehold rights of nine hundred square miles around Calcutta for the East India Company, and a forged treaty, had also been a part of this deal, which had set the pattern for England's control of the maharajahs and exploitation of the Indian peasantry.

The British conscience about this wealth among East India Company officials, 'displayed with the ostentation natural to an eighteenth century gentleman', was just beginning to stir, and the censure of the select committee appointed to investigate Clive—notwithstanding his 'great and meritorious services to his country', as the committee conceded—was not lost on Paine. The Warren Hastings impeachment, in which Paine's later friend and antagonist Edmund Burke played so crucial a part, did not take place until 1788, but long before then, in the *Crisis* addressed to General Sir William Howe, Paine was to show how much he had absorbed the lesson of British India: a theme, with the subjection of Africa, which was to recur more than once in his work:

'For the domestic happiness of Britain and the peace of the world, I wish she had not a foot of land but what is circumscribed within her own island. Extent of dominion has been her ruin, and instead of civilizing others has brutalized herself. Her late reduction of India, under Clive and his successors, was not so properly a conquest as an extermination of mankind. She is the only power who could practise the prodigal barbarity of tying men to the mouths of loaded cannon and blowing them away. It happens that general Burgoyne, who made the report of that horrid transaction, in the house of commons, is now a prisoner with us, and though an enemy, I can appeal to him for the truth of it, being confident that he neither can nor will deny it. Yet Clive received the approbation of the last parliament.'

'Approbation' is not entirely true, and Clive had committed suicide in November 1774, the month Paine arrived in America. But his indignant outburst at the examination of his affairs—'By heaven, Mr. Chairman, at this moment I stand astonished at my own moderation'— would not have endeared him to Paine or any American colonist resisting dominion from Britain. Paine's horror at the barbarity of execution by cannon has been echoed again nearer our own time, including in a play performed by the National Theatre in London; it was the kind of thing of which Victorian England, built on the apparent glories of Empire, was to be kept widely ignorant. Paine's reaction fits in with his declaration elsewhere in the *Crisis*: 'If I have any where expressed myself over-warmly, 'tis from a fixed, immovable hatred I have, and ever had, to cruel men and cruel measures.'

The Burgoyne named was, of course, 'Gentlemanly Johnny', the witty and civilized British general immortalized in Bernard Shaw's *The Devil's Disciple*.

1774 was also the year that John Wilkes, after a stormy decade of exile, prison, and battles with the government on the subject of seditious libel, became Lord Mayor of London and re-entered Parliament after an unopposed election in Middlesex. In spite of his gay and unrepentant immorality (he had been outlawed in 1764 for printing a permissive *Essay on Woman* and for 'seditious libel'), he was the radical idol of a large proportion of the populace, who had elected him as regularly as the government expelled him. The liberty of the press owes much to him, and he was a man of some learning and literary taste. Paine, it is said, had been a reader of his paper, *The North Briton*, and undoubtedly must have been influenced by Wilkes' proposed reforms which included enfranchisement of the lower classes, suppression of the 'rotten' boroughs and protection of individual liberty. Wilkes had also launched an attack on the King's corrupt advisers, a theme echoed even by William Pitt and other Whigs. London coffee houses in 1774 must have been buzzing with Wilkes' final triumph, and Benjamin Franklin said of him that if his moral character had been equal to that of the king he might have taken the king's place.

It was this Benjamin Franklin now who was to be the first guardian angel of Paine's life, launching him into the New World like a well-aimed rocket before its time. The launching pad was provided by one of Paine's scientific friends, George Lewis Scott. Scott was a member of the Excise Board and his continued association with Paine emphasizes that Paine left the Excise with a clean sheet, apart from his 'absence' which his discharge had given as reason. He had also been a subpreceptor during the childhood of King George III, which Paine's American biographer Aldridge has taken to mean that Paine acquired from him much personal knowledge of the King which caused him to single him out as a 'villain' later.

This does not seem to me very likely. George III's private life was not notorious, nor did Paine ever suggest otherwise, apart from a reference to the King's Quaker mistress before his marriage, Hannah Lightfoot, which he could not resist using to score a point against the American Quakers. His target was the monarch, and a monarch whom the whole Whig oligarchy knew to have started his reign in 1760 with the direct aim of stretching his personal authority to the utmost limits which the parliamentary institution would allow. For this purpose he had selected what might be termed a 'King's party' of friends wholly subservient to his wishes, and the government of Lord North, which was to precipitate by its intransigence the American War of Independence, was among their number. Against this George III/North cabal Pitt, Fox and Burke, friendly to America's claims, were to hammer for the next few years in vain. Knowing much more about the King's later madness now, it is possible to see—as Paine and his colleagues could not—in this monarchial ambition of the King an aspect of the 'delusions of grandeur' often associated with mental instability.

In introducing Paine to Franklin, however, Scott did put twin planets in conjunction. Still considered in America the supreme example of the 'self-made man', Franklin's beginnings as son of a tallow-chandler had not been dissimilar to Paine's. Early success in the printing business had enabled him to devote himself to science, and after nearly electrocuting himself to prove the identity of lightning and electricity, in an experiment with a kite in a thunderstorm, he had invented the first lightning conductor, which was promptly put in use by George III. He had been elected as a Fellow to the Royal Society in 1756, and was already a prolific writer. At the time of his meeting with Paine in 1774 he was acting as agent for Pennsylvania and other colonies in London, and his later political career was to be distinguished, including the post of chief American representative to France and a hand in the drafting of the United States Constitution. He was, however, a reluctant supporter of the bid for Independence, cherishing

America's ties with Britain, from where his family originally sprang and where he had lived and worked for a time in his youth. Much of the later American over-emphasis on money and success was to be derived from his moralistic writings.

In 1774, however, this difference from his new admirer did not appear. He was thirty years older than Paine and was delighted to find in so many ways a kindred scientific and political spirit. He was impressed enough to write a letter of introduction for Paine to his son-in-law, Richard Bache, in Philadelphia. Whether Scott had engineered the introduction to Franklin for this purpose, or whether the suggestion of emigration arose naturally out of Paine's present uncertain prospects and Franklin's appreciation of his talents and conversation, we do not know. Paine, later in the *Crisis*, was to write: 'I happened, when a schoolboy, to pick up a pleasing natural history of Virginia, and my inclination from that day of seeing the western side of the Atlantic never left me.' At least a hope on his part, when hearing of Scott's acquaintance with Franklin, seems indicated.

His interest in natural history has already been mentioned and this dates it from his Thetford childhood, when he not only studied the adaptable habits of the spider, which would make a home, he noted, under almost any conditions and almost anywhere except under water, but also the beauties of certain birds and insects, to which he referred in *The Age of Reason:*

'. . . A very numerous part of the animal creation preaches to us, far better than Paul, the belief of a life hereafter. Their little life resembles an earth and a heaven, a present and a future state, and comprises, if it may be so expressed, immortality in miniature.

'The most beautiful parts of the creation, to our eyes, are the winged insects; and they are not so originally. They acquire that form and that inimitable brilliancy by progressive changes. The slow and creeping caterpillar-worm of to-day passes in a few days to a torpid figure and a state resembling death; and in the next change comes forth in all the miniature magnificence of life, a splendid butterfly. No resemblance of the former creature remains; everything is changed; all his powers are new, and life is to him another thing. We cannot conceive that the consciousness of existence is not the same in this state of the animal as before. Why, then, must I believe that the resurrection of the same body is necessary to continue to me the consciousness of existence hereafter? . . . it is not more difficult to believe that we shall exist hereafter in a better state and form than at present, than that a worm should become a butterfly, and quit the dunghill for the atmosphere, if we did not know it is a fact.'

Intimations of immortality, however, were not part of his renewed ambition to see America. Like many before and after him he had found his own country restrictive and frustrating, without hope of genuine advancement or of the individual liberties for which his heart craved: not only on his own account, but for the nation at large, whose need was always in his political creed to take precedence over the government in power, of whatever persuasion. A new world beckoned, and the wanderer, once again, was ready to take wing.

He had with him, in Franklin's handwriting, a personal recommendation which must have raised his hopes high:

'The bearer, Mr. Thomas Paine, is very well recommended to me, as an ingenious, worthy young man. He goes to Pennsylvania with a view of settling there. I request you to give him your best advice and countenance, as he is quite a stranger there. If you can put him in a way of obtaining employment as a clerk, or assistant tutor in a school, or assistant surveyor, (of all which I think him very capable,) so that he may procure a subsistence at least, till he can make acquaintance and obtain a knowledge of the country, you will do well, and much oblige your affectionate father.'

He sailed on the *London Packet* in the last week of September, and any intimations of immortality were very nearly put to the test. For an epidemic, most probably typhus, broke out in the ship, which carried over a hundred indentured servants, and when Philadelphia was at last reached on 30th November Paine, who had caught the disease, was carried off the ship on a stretcher, more dead than alive. The provider of the stretcher was a Dr John Kearsley, who seems to have been aware a passenger recommended by the great Dr Franklin was on board, and in spite of his care it was six weeks before Paine recovered sufficiently to approach Bache. It was the first of two occasions in Paine's long life that he was to be dangerously ill, and only his iron constitution, country bred, probably saved his life.

When he recovered Franklin's note soon helped him to obtain work as a tutor, and he at last had an opportunity to savour his new surroundings. More, perhaps, than appeared on the surface, resembled conditions in the country he had left. The criminal laws were harsh, and many of the punishments capital; cockfighting, gambling, drinking and, in the South particularly, horseracing were practised on as heavy a scale; and only in the 1760s had 'witchcraft' ceased to be punishable by death. Reaction from the celebrated Salem witch hunt hysteria of the 1690s had done much to bring this about. Rough justice in the way of tarring and feathering was meted out to offenders not legally chargeable, and Paine was to protest vigorously against this when it was applied by the mob to loyalists to the crown later: 'every sensible man must feel a conscious shame at seeing a poor fellow hawked for a show about the streets . . . we dishonour ourselves by attacking such trifling characters while greater ones are suffered to escape.' 'Already in its quest for liberty,' as Nye and Morpurgo write in *The Birth of the U.S.A.*, 'the American people had begun to define freedom according to the wishes of the majority.'

Yet it was a country in which most of the prominent figures (Washington and Franklin apart) were lawyers and much of Philadelphia must have struck Paine as fresh and invigorating. As in England the taverns thrived as social and debating clubs, and the Indian Queen was to become for him the American equivalent of the White Hart. There were fine and elegant houses, among which that of Dr Franklin, designed by Philadelphia's most eminent architect, Robert Smith, was prominent. The streets of Boston, well-lit and patrolled by night watchmen, had been paved since 1715, although those of New York were not paved until 1785. Philadelphia, larger than either, had already a population of almost forty thousand, with tree-lined streets, numerous gardens, brick pavements in at least the main streets, and brightly-coloured shop-fronts. The population of this 'City of Brotherly Love' had originally been largely Quaker, but now it had extended and included a strata of high society, wearing silk and lace and riding in either sedan chairs or carriages.

The division between rich and poor was, nevertheless, not as wide as in England, and Paine was to write, 'I see in America the generality of people living in a stile of plenty unknown in monarchial countries' . . . 'The income of a common labourer, who is industrious, is equal to that of the generality of tradesmen in England.'

Nor was there a lack of reading material. A capacious bookstore, Bradford's, sold all the most fashionable London magazines such as *The Spectator*, *The Tatler* and Steele's *Guardian*. ('The Americans,' growled Dr Johnson, 'what do they know and what do they read?' The answer was much the same as Londoners, plus a particular passion for Locke, whose works are supposed to have influenced Paine although he himself denied having read them.) All the American cities aped London in fashion and dancing: the dancing master who had figured so prominently in the social preparation of Hogarth's Rake in 1735 was as indispensable a feature of American society, and even Washington, later so careful of his image as a 'leader' and noble gentleman, achieved in younger days the athletic feat of dancing three hours with Mrs Nathaniel Greene. The form of dancing, less elegant than that at Bath, was probably square-dance in character, and therefore not unimpressively energetic. It is possible the Commodore, so graceful on the Lewes

c

ice, would have appreciated this achievement like so many others of General Washington.

The greatest stimulant to his own emergence as a force in his new country, however, was the fact that Philadelphia supported no less than seven newspapers. He must have quickly made his writing bent, and capacity for political argument, known, doubtless at the Indian Queen; for when Robert Aitken, a printer, started a monthly periodical, *The Pennsylvania Magazine*, in January 1775, Paine wrote an introduction on the 'Magazine in America' for its first issue. It showed a fire-new enthusiasm for the new world (of which he must at that time have had slender experience) and contemporary times as compared with the old world and the ancient. Aitken immediately engaged him as Editor, and by March the subscription list had increased from six hundred to fifteen hundred.

That Paine's capacity for honesty was unimpaired, however, was shown in his article in March in another magazine, *The Pennsylvania Journal*, when he attacked negro slavery which was then practised by both North and South, a bulwark on which individual fortunes were being built. How, wrote Paine, the logician ever to the fore, could the Americans complain of their inferior treatment by the British, when they themselves practised the same form of injustice by making slaves of the negroes? Slavery was 'contrary to the light of nature, to every principle of justice and humanity', he wrote, and 'most shocking of all is alleging the sacred scriptures to favour this wicked practice'. It would, he considered, prophetic of Black Power, 'naturally fill them (i.e. Africans) with abhorrence of Christians', and he entreats Americans to consider whether they '*ought not immediately to discontinue and renounce the practice of slavery, with grief and abhorrence?*' (Paine's italics). Nor is he lacking in constructive criticism. He singles out in particular the way in which husbands, wives and children were heartlessly parted by being sold to new owners. Surrounding territories, he suggested, might be set apart for the liberated coloured races (a hint of segregation perhaps more apparent to us than to him, seeking to alleviate greater evils), and 'perhaps', he adds, 'some former masters might give them reasonable allowances for their labour so as all may have some property, and fruits of their labours at their own disposal. The family may then live together, and enjoy the natural satisfaction of excercising relative affections and duties, with civil protection, and other advantages, like fellowmen.'

Within a month after the publication of this article, the first anti-slavery movement—the American Antislavery Society—was founded in Philadelphia. Franklin was later its President. It is often overlooked that Paine's was the first voice to be raised in support of the negro as a free citizen—before Wilberforce (if one excepts Wilberforce's letter as a fourteen-year-old schoolboy, in 1773, to a York newspaper), and even before Thomas Jefferson, who suggested an anti-slavery clause in the American Declaration of Independence but failed in the courage to insist on its implementation. There is considerable evidence from its wording that Paine wrote this particular clause which was dropped, and certainly he must have inspired it. Nearly a century later, America fought a Civil War on the issue and Abraham Lincoln wrote: 'I never tire of reading Paine'. According to William H. Herndin, Lincoln's law partner and most intimate friend, 'Paine became a part of Lincoln from 1834 to the end of his life'. In condemning slavery Paine was once again following a Quaker precedent, for in England they had adopted a resolution to this effect as early as 1724.

The journalism here begun was to be the springboard for Paine's political and literary reputation. It was the first regular outlet for his fermenting ideas, hitherto tossed off to admiring gatherings in the White Hart and other haunts of seekers after lively and intelligent conversation. Paine, in the right society of appreciative friends (he was shy among strangers), was renowned as a conversationalist, and this ability to hold the hearer was transferred to the printed page. His gifts in the one direction stimulated and fashioned his style in the other, and on both sides of the Atlantic he was the first political writer to be read widely outside those actively engaged in politics or interested in them. He spoke to the people, in the people's own voice, and his influence was immense for this reason. Those who attempted to underrate his contribution to two revolutions, and derided his vanity about that contribution (and they were many, especially in England, the country he abandoned and against which forever he seemed to bear a grudge), were wrong for this reason. For the first time, the wrongs of the poor, the oppressed, those seeking or needing a readjustment of society for the common good, were shown the means to achieve this in terms they could understand. It was a literary revolution which provoked a political one: the democratic age (even though at the time he wrote universal suffrage was unknown) was upon us.

In *The Pennsylvania Magazine* which he edited, his articles, under varied but easily penetrable pseudonyms, were often less inflammatory and more scientific, including descriptions of a new electrical machine and a new method of building frame houses. He pressed for encouragement of scientific pursuits, as fostering the inventive spirit, together with the cultivation of more productive soil and labour-saving devices (in which, already, we recognize the true American!). More provocatively, he attacked duelling, protested against cruelty to animals—living creatures, he pointed out, who had a right to share the earth with us—advocated national and international copyright, and began his lifelong campaign against acceptance of royalty and aristocracy without question. 'The lustre of the Star, and the title of My Lord, overawe the superstitious vulgar, and forbid them to enquire into the character of the possessor: Nay more, they are, as it were, bewitched to admire in the great the vices they would honestly condemn in themselves.' In this, as so often, he showed psychological perception: man has constantly been held back politically by preconceived notions of prerogatives, as well as ingrained snobbery, the greatest handicap always to socialist parties in times of plenty, when the working class move up into the regions of the *bourgeoisie*.

In August 1775, Paine published a plea for women's rights entitled 'An Occasional Letter on the Female Sex'. It makes sympathetic points about their sufferings from polygamy, jealousy and often brutality, and their exploitation through constraint in the disposal of their goods and property after marriage, not to count through the men who dishonour them and then degrade them by emphasizing their consequent reputation. He also shows himself sensitive to the burden on women whose husbands and sons die before them, and deprecates the general low esteem in which they are held.

The article nevertheless hardly warrants the place in the literature of women's rights some of his biographers have given it. There is no suggestion throughout of any need for equality of opportunity in work and the professions, nor of the educational reforms which could help to rectify woman's lot both financially and in widened horizons. Less than twenty years later, in 1792, Mary Wollstonecraft's *Vindication of the Rights of Women* was to deal with both, and in addition with co-education, sex education, state schools, the provision of playgrounds for exercise, equality in custody of the children of a marriage and the father's responsibility in the case of illegitimate children. No doubt Paine and Mary, who were to meet several times on terms of friendship, discussed these things later, and Paine must have become very conscious of the limitations of his own early article on the question. Most of Mary's reforms, of course, like Paine's in other directions, were not to be achieved, or even widely raised again, for a century. At least Paine's effort was good-hearted and enlightened.

In the autumn of 1775 he left Aitken's magazine because of poor pay and a disagreement over its increase. Aitken noted Paine wrote with the aid of brandy in order to get his copy out on the deadline, but appreciated the effect: 'What he penned from the inspiration of the brandy was perfectly fit for the press without any alteration or correction.' This is confirmed by Paine's other manuscripts. In fact, he wrote with some care, and refused to allow alterations with the fierceness of the true professional writer as opposed to the literary 'hack', even in his journalism. Years later, he was to break with an editor who attempted to alter his work, thus again anticipating Bernard Shaw who, on discovering his art criticism rewritten by an editor, threw the dust of *The World* off his feet even though this left him, at a time when he was still an unknown writer, with only £2 a week income from journalism to fall back on.

But the times, for Paine, were propitious. The unbending attitude to the American colonies of Lord North's administration under George III had led to the famous Boston Tea Party eleven months before Paine's arrival, and while he was editing *The Pennsylvania Magazine* the battles of Lexington and Concord, the true beginnings of the American War of Independence, took place. Paine at first was not altogether enthusiastic. 'I thought it very hard,' he complained in a letter to Franklin, 'to have the country set on fire about my ears almost the moment I got into it.' But Lexington changed his mind. 'No one was a warmer wisher for reconciliation than myself before the fatal nineteenth of April, 1775,' he wrote. In January 1776, his *Common Sense* (anonymously published as 'Written by an Englishman'), set the American cat among the English pigeons with a vengeance, and thereafter he was wholly involved.

VI

THE WRITER AND MAN OF ACTION

America had been in a ferment about taxation for some time. The Stamp Act, passed by the British Parliament in 1765, had had to be repealed a year later owing to the violence of the American opposition. Franklin had been largely instrumental in this repeal. But it is a feature of colonial empires that their governors rarely learn from their mistakes. England in 1773 was suffering particularly heavy taxation as a result of her wars in France and India, and there was a feeling that the Americans, who also had the use of a British army for frontier protection against the less friendly Red Indians, should pay towards the cost. In May 1773, the Tea Act was passed, and in December the same year American radicals, disguised as Red Indians, boarded British vessels in Boston Harbour and as a gesture of defiance threw the taxed tea overboard.

It was the climax of a situation which had been combustible in Boston ever since the British army of occupation had fired on a mob on the Boston Rope Walk, killing a negro, the first victim of his race. Although the army to an extent acted in self-defence, the Boston 'massacre' of March 1770 still rankled in men's minds, and agitation mounted. Lord North's threepenny tea act, in itself apparently trivial, was the spark for which the agitators had waited. Within a few months Paul Revere was riding to New York and Philadelphia for aid and Washington, in Virginia, realized that the moment had come which would settle whether the Americans would sit 'supinely, and see one province after another fall to despotism'.

The first inter-colonial congress was called, and appeals to George III followed. They were ignored. On 19 April 1775, at Lexington, Massachusetts, the first shot was fired, after that indefatigable horseman Revere had once again set out, this time to warn the militia. The British and American armies were now facing each other, and as always in such cases, the responsibility for the first shots is disputed. In any case, seven men lay dead. The American War of Independence had begun.

It was not a matter of tea, but of the whole question of Britain's right to tax a colony to which she allowed no representation in Parliament. America was prosperous, but she laboured under difficulties of trade that threatened, in time, to impoverish her. She was allowed no direct trade with Europe, but had to send all exports from her farms and growing industries to England, from whence they were again exported to the enrichment of the British middleman. In converse direction, America could herself only purchase European goods through English merchants at a price from twenty-five to forty per cent higher than if she had bought the goods in the free market. Her smaller farmers suffered, and when their living was threatened they were not allowed to settle on land west of the Alleghenies, a great tract stretching from the eastern seaboard colonies to the Mississippi. These fertile lands were, in fact, reserved for the Indians, and, remembering the later devastation of the buffalo herds and Indian tribes in the great nineteenth century drive to the West, today one can sympathize with Lord Dartmouth, Secretary of State for Foreign Affairs, who in 1774 proclaimed the promotion of Western settlements 'a gross indignity and dishonour to the Crown and an act of equal inhumanity and injustice to the Indians'.

Looking ahead, however, they were in many ways necessary to America as a nation, and in most things the American colonies had a good case. In England there was much support for them. Wiser and more liberal measures, as Burke wrote, 'would have averted all the mischief that ensued'. But George III stood firm, totally unwilling to yield an inch and supported by Lord North (though with some secret reluctance) to the point of colonial suicide. And on this monarchial rock all hopes of conciliation foundered.

The hopes were genuine, and few Americans openly talked of secession. 'I happened to come to America a few months before the breaking out of hostilities,' wrote Paine in the *Crisis* addressed 'To the People of England' in November 1778. 'I found the disposition of the people such, that they might have been led by a thread and governed by a reed. Their suspicion was quick and penetrating, but their attachment to Britain was obstinate, and it was at that time a kind of treason to speak against it. They disliked the ministry, but they esteemed the nation. Their idea of grievance operated without resentment, and their single object was reconciliation . . . I viewed the dispute as a kind of law-suit, in which I supposed the parties would find a way either to decide or settle it. I had no thoughts of independence or of arms. The world could not then have persuaded me that I should be either a soldier or an author . . . But when the country, into which I had just set my foot, was set on fire about my ears, it was time to stir. It was time for every man to stir. Those who had been long settled had something to defend; those who had just come had something to pursue; and the call and the concern was equal and universal.'

Common Sense was the first open declaration calling for independence from England—an appeal written for the common man, farmers, merchants and their like. The generals Washington, Greene and Lee, the politicians Franklin, Rush, Adams and others at Philadelphia, may already have been thinking along the same lines; but Paine's was the first open statement to the American people. It attacked bad government and condemned the eternal 'balance of power' theory of the military which set the throats of nation against nation and debilitated all countries in continual wars. 'Society in every state is a blessing, but government, even in its best state, is but a necessary evil; in its worst state, an intolerable one . . .' He stigmatized George III as the 'greatest enemy this continent hath, or can have'. 'Of more worth is one honest man to society and in the sight of God, than all the crowned ruffians that ever lived.' He struck, in fact, at the basis of the continued belief in the Divine Right of Kings, never wholly dispersed even by Cromwell, emphasizing that moral and intellectual characteristics were not inherited and (fundamental to much of his later theory) 'no generation has the right to impose its choices upon posterity'. This last was to prove a key to his later vision of democracy. Paine believed passionately that whatever government or form of society was right for one generation might be totally unsuited to the differing needs of another. His understanding of what we call 'the generation gap' never wavered and still has not entirely been absorbed.

The issue, as he stated, was 'whether we shall make our own laws, or whether the King . . . shall tell us, *There shall be no laws but such as I like*'. In free countries the law ought to be King, and there ought to be no other. It was not, he pointed out, 'in the power of Britain to do this continent justice; the business of it will soon be too weighty and intricate to be managed with any tolerable degree of convenience, by a power so distant from us, and so very ignorant of us'. The weight of Britain's wars, moreover, was ruinous to America without in any way being her affair: 'any submission to, or dependence on, Great Britain tends to involve this continent in European wars and quarrels, and set us at variance with nations who would otherwise seek our friendship, and against whom we have neither anger nor complaint.' 'In this extensive quarter of the globe, we forget the narrow limits of three hundred and sixty miles (the extent of England), and carry our friendship on a larger scale; we claim brotherhood with every European Christian.'

Paine's vision of a European/American community based on peaceful trade and the brotherhood of man was to be the basis of a philosophy which anticipated both the United Nations and the Common Market. From Locke—consciously or unconsciously—he echoed the spirit of free trade, and with some truth urged: 'We have boasted of the protection of Great Britain, without considering that her motive was *interest*, not *attachment*.' 'It is the commerce and not the conquest of America by which England is to be benefited; and that would in a great measure continue, were the countries as independent of each other as France and Spain; because, in many articles, neither can go to a better market.'

What Paine envisaged was a peace in which trade connections with Britain would still thrive but at the expense of neither country, and without restriction on commerce elsewhere. Although many of Britain's wars had been commercial wars, Paine was never able to conceive of such a necessity: to him commerce was the antithesis of, the answer to war, against which all his Quaker instincts revolted. 'Our plan is *peace for ever*. We are tired of contention with Britain and can see no real end to it but in final separation.' But although war in his eyes was 'murder', as he was later to write, there was a case for a war of defence. 'Beneath the shade of our own vines are we attacked; in our own houses, and in our own land, is the violence committed against us.'

The echo of Cranmer's speech over the infant Elizabeth in Shakespeare's *Henry VIII* is interesting:

> . . . 'good grows with her:
> In her days every man shall eat in safety,
> Under his own vine, what he plants; and sing
> The merry songs of peace to all his neighbours.'

Paine was to revert to it in the last *Crisis*, at the end of the war: 'She (i.e. America) is now descending to the scenes of quiet and domestic life. Not beneath the cypress shade of disappointment, but to enjoy in her own land, and under her own vine, the sweet of her labours, and the reward of her toil.' There was an earlier reference I have quoted to Hamlet's 'To be or not to be', and in later years, particularly in *The Age of Reason*, the habit of literary reference and quotation grew on him, so that the final impression is of a man quite widely read. Cervantes, Homer, Cicero, Bunyan, Swift, Voltaire and Milton as well as Shakespeare were to occur in his pages, and in spite of his commonsensical style his rhythms show biblical origins and his prose sometimes leaps into imagery. 'Government, like dress, is the badge of last innocense; the palaces of kings are built on the ruins of the bowers of paradise.' Already, in *Common Sense*, we have that sense of the apt metaphor that often turns on a dramatic image, although the reading here is obviously less wide.

That he was already reading political books is shown by a key quotation from the *Virtue and Rewards* of Dragonetti: 'The science of the politician consists in fixing the true point of happiness and freedom. Those men would deserve the gratitude of ages, who should discover a mode of government that contained the greatest sum of individual happiness, with the least national expence.' Did this quotation from 'that wise observer on governments', as Paine called him, have some influence later on the 'pursuit of happiness' clause in the Declaration of Independence?

Paine strongly challenged the British mistrust of 'the ripeness or fitness of the continent for independence'. 'The time hath found us,' is his reply. Those who support Britain, he points out, have not had their house burnt, their property destroyed or a child killed. He calls not for revenge but a reshaping of the system, 'securing freedom and property to all men; and, above all things, the free exercise of religion, according to the dictates of conscience'. It cannot be found under kings: 'monarchy and succession have laid, not this or that kingdom only, but the world in blood and ashes'; and he is only too aware of the psychology of power: 'Men, who look upon themselves as born to reign, and on the others to obey, soon grow insolent; selected from the rest of mankind, their minds are easily poisoned by importance, and the world they act in differs so materially from the world at large, that they have but little opportunity of knowing its true interests.' His solution is a republic, 'a large and equal representation' and, above all, a constitution. 'If we omit it now, some Masaniello may hereafter arise, who, laying hold of popular disquietudes, may collect together the desperate and discontented, and by assuming to themselves the powers of government, may sweep away the liberties of the continent like a deluge.' History has shown in other countries how prophetic this passage was, and his sense of the importance to the future of the present struggle:

'The sun never shined on a cause of greater worth. It is not the affair of a city, a country, a province, or a kingdom, but of a continent . . . It is not the concern of a day, a year, or an age; posterity are involved in the contest, and will be more or less affected, even to the end of time, by the proceedings now. Now is the seed-time of continental union, faith and honour. The least fracture now will be like a name engraved with the point of a pin on the tender rind of a young oak; the wound will enlarge with the tree, and posterity read it in full-grown characters.'

His vision is of a new world, no less. 'We have it in our power to begin the world over again . . . The birthday of a new world is at hand, and a race of men, perhaps as numerous as all Europe contains, are to receive their portion of freedom from the event of a few months.'

If the vision afterwards went awry, and began to show many of the corruptions and evils of European civilization, the fault was not Paine's. The American Dream is still dreamt, and his important contribution to it increasingly understood.

In a corrupt society he at least was to prove incorruptible. 'I am not induced by motives of pride, party, or resentment, to espouse the doctrine of separation and independence. I am clearly, positively, and conscientiously persuaded, that it is the true interest of the continent to be so.' And he supported his claim, now and later, by refusing to gain financially from his writings for the cause. In this, again, he resembled Shaw, who also refused payment for his political work and prolific writings for the Fabian Society, at a time when he was still receiving little money for his plays or journalism.

Paine was an 'original' as a writer, or as he said himself, 'What I write is pure nature'. Although he certainly read a good deal more than is often realized, and was certainly not—as has been maintained by some disciples—the first in all of his ideas, his style, fresh and clear in its time and essentially modern even today, was very much his own. Writing came easily to him: the phrases still leap from the page. And *Common Sense* was new and epoch-making for its time. As George Trevelyan wrote in his *History of the American Revolution*: 'It would be difficult to name any human composition which has had an effect at once so instant, so extended and so lasting . . . It was pirated, parodied and imitated, and translated into the language of every country where the new republic had well-wishers. It worked nothing short of miracles and turned Tories into Whigs.'

Paine agreed to cover the printer, Bell, for any loss, and a first edition of one thousand copies sold in two weeks. Bell apparently attempted to cheat (he had been promised half the profits, the other half to go for mittens for the troops in Quebec) and maintained there were no profits. Paine estimated there should be £60. Two other printers were therefore given an enlarged edition with an Appendix and Address to the Quakers, who had issued a proclamation of their loyalty to the English crown. Six thousand copies were sold and Bell printed a second edition without permission. In 1779 Paine was still nearly £40 out of pocket, but for whatever reason he made this a source of pride and believed 150,000 copies were sold in America. It was read by all ranks in the army and its influence was immense. Washington wrote that in Virginia it was 'working a powerful change in the minds of many men'. The influence was felt in France, and Latin America, and it started off independence movements in Venezuela, Mexico and Ecuador.

The pseudonym was fairly easily pierced. A month after publication Franklin, who had landed in Philadelphia from London on 5 May 1775, wrote General Lee that Paine 'is the reputed and, I think, the real author of *Common Sense*'. Franklin undoubtedly must have formed a shrewd idea of Paine's ideas and abilities from his conversation with him in London, and probably Paine (never a light under a bushel) had scattered plenty of hints, if nothing more, among journalistic circles in Philadelphia. His knowledge of Paine's authorship of *Common Sense* could in any case have been gained from association with Paine in October 1775, when Franklin, as Paine wrote later in the *Crisis*, 'proposed giving me such materials as were in his hands, towards completing a history of the present transactions . . . I had then formed the outlines of *Common Sense*, and finished nearly the first part; and as I supposed the doctor's design in getting out a history, was to open the new year with a new system, I expected to surprise him with a production on that subject, much earlier than he thought of; and without informing him what I was doing, got it ready for the press as fast as I conveniently could, and sent him the first pamphlet that was printed off.' Paine later was to be dogged by the wish to write a full history of the American Revolution and it is a pity the project, for many reasons including matters of time and finance, never got off the ground.

Common Sense had coincided with the King's speech at the opening of Parliament, which was as violently intransigent as Paine could have wished to convert Americans to the principles of his pamphlet. Paine, having made his literary gesture, seems to have been seized with the conviction that words should be backed by action. In February 1776 he visited the troops in New York and dined with General Lee, who perceived 'the genius in his eyes' (once again Paine's luminous eyes had impressed an influential contact). He enlisted in July 1776, with the 'flying camp', a mobile body of one thousand men forming the militia of Jersey, Pennsylvania and Maryland. Paine was attached to the Pennsylvanian division. He served first as volunteer secretary to General Roberdeau and then at Fort Lee, on the western bank of the River Hudson, as aide-de-camp to General Nathanial Greene, holding the rank of Brigade Major. In a letter to his wife, Greene was to give an engaging and characteristic picture of his new officer: 'Common Sense (Thomas Paine) and Colonel Snarl, or Cornwell, are perpetually wrangling about mathematical problems.' It was Greene who first introduced Paine to Washington, a man of iron reticence and at the time deeply depressed by events.

Paine was, in our modern terms, in part a war correspondent, enlarging in his series of pamphlets called *The Crisis* (December 1776, to December 1783) on the ideas and principles first sketched in *Common Sense* and which had crystallized, at least in part, in the colonists' bold Declaration of Independence on 4 July 1776. They began at a genuine moment of crisis for the American troops. In the summer of 1776 the American army retreated across the Hudson to New Jersey. Hatred of the British army ran high: they were, as Paine was to note with corrosive propaganda point, in many cases not even British, of the Americans' kith and kin, but as Shaw's General Burgoyne was to admit, 'Hessians, Brunswickers, German dragoons, and Indians with scalping knives'.

(The British incitement and bribing of the Indians to join their side was one of Paine's bitterest complaints in the *Crisis*.) In January 1777, he was to be at the Council at Easton, seeking an Indian treaty. Here he met Indian chiefs, braves and squaws for the first time, being paid £300 for his services.

Washington, not without cause, was uncertain and distressed. On the Delaware, although now joined by General Williamson's and the Philadelphia militia, he could muster only five thousand men against the British General, Sir William Howe's whole army. He had been pressed back along the Hudson while Howe occupied Manhattan, Long Island and Staten Island, and he wrote dispiritedly to his brother in December: 'Your imagination can scarce extend to a situation more distressing than mine. Our only dependence now is upon the speedy enlistment of a new army. If this fails, I think the game will be pretty well up, as from disaffection and want of spirit and fortitude, the inhabitants, instead of resistance, are offering submission and taking protection from General Howe in Jersey.'

The distresses of his army, in fact, as he had informed the President of Congress, were 'extremely great, many of 'em being entirely naked and most so thinly clad as to be unfit for service'. It was a bitter and icy winter, the Arctic winds piercing like arrow heads across the snow-covered wastes, and penetrating the men's scanty clothes and feet wrapped in rags, owing to the lack of shoes and supplies. In November Fort Lee had been surprised and Paine with the rest had retreated in haste, abandoning the boiling kettles and much-needed food baking in the American ovens to the British, who fell with enthusiasm on their unexpected meal. It was in this atmosphere of retreat, at Newark, that Paine began to write his first *Crisis*: silently, by the camp fires at night, garnering the courage that was to turn the tides of war. Physical courage he had found, to his relief, he did not lack: in one of the earliest *Crises*, addressed to Howe, he was to write with typical sympathy of psychological divergencies:

'We cannot alter nature, neither ought we to punish the son because the father begot him in a cowardly mood. However, I believe most men have more courage than they know of, and that a little at first is enough to begin with. I knew the time when I thought the whistling of a cannon ball would have frightened me almost to death; but I have since tried it, and find that I can stand it with as little discomposure, and, I believe, with a much easier conscience than your lordship.'

There is no reason to doubt his sincerity. At Trenton, while with the Pennsylvanian navy board, he was to urge the setting fire of the British fleet on the Delaware and was restrained with difficulty from personally carrying out the project. And Washington's great Christmas victory at Trenton, a turning point of the war (though it was to heave to and fro for several years yet) was achieved by troops heartened and inspired by Paine's first *Crisis* with its celebrated opening line:

'These are the times that try men's souls.'

VII

CRISIS AND FOREIGN AFFAIRS

Throughout the next six years Paine was to produce a steady stream of thirteen *Crisis* pamphlets, all to some extent inspired by the fluctuations of the war as well as internal policy, but making as a whole a contribution to political literature not irrelevant today. America moved during this time through the invigorating victories of Trenton and Princeton to the final and crucial rout of the British under Lord Cornwallis at Yorktown on 19 October 1781. Peace even then was still two years away, but in spite of interim victories on both sides Britain really lost the war when General John Burgoyne surrendered with the British army at Saratoga in October 1777.

Burgoyne, whose humanity had been aroused by British oppression in India, as Paine accurately reported, was not unsympathetic to the American colonists, but he had accepted a commission, unlike many of his compatriot officers, out of a quirk of patriotic sentiment. 'While we remember that we are contending against brothers and fellow subjects,' he said in the House of Commons, 'we must also remember that we are contending in this crisis for the fate of the British Empire'. His crisis was the same crisis as Paine's, seen from a different angle; and his defeat at Saratoga after marching south by Lake Champlain from Canada was— though few knew it at the time—not his own fault but that of a Lord George Germain in London. Germain, who as Lord George Sackville had himself failed as an officer at Minden (and in Chatham's eyes was not fit to be a Minister), forgot to dispatch orders to General Howe, in New York, to march north and effect a conjunction with Burgoyne's army at Albany. Burgoyne, hopelessly outnumbered and without the expected reinforcements, had no option but to surrender, while Germain in London, who had been going on holiday at the time of his fatal blunder, continued for a number of years to be sheltered by the British government. Burgoyne, with a slur on his name that political 'jobbery' refused to clear, in the end resigned his commission and took to playwriting. 'Your friend the British soldier,' as he says to Major Swindon in Shaw's play, 'can stand up to anything except the British War Office.' His tragedy, which his temperament and talents were able to turn to comedy,[1] was foreshadowed in Horace Walpole's *dictum*, at a time of

---

[1] Burgoyne's *The Heiress*, produced in 1786, was to prove one of the most successful comedies of the time.

parliamentary recess, that the Lords could not be expected to lose their pheasant shooting for the sake of America.

Had Paine known all this at the time we can imagine what republican capital he would have made of it. But he had material enough from his knowledge of British politics and what he had called parliamentary 'jockeyship', and always maintained that this knowledge, undoubtedly widened during his years in Lewes and shorter periods in London, was his principal value to the Americans; many of whom, although of British stock, had never been outside their own country.

The first *Crisis* was published a few days before Washington's attack on Trenton, and its effect on the troops has never been denied. Before the battle 'they were called together in groups to listen to that thrilling exhortation', as Conway puts it. 'Tyranny, like hell,' wrote Paine, 'is not easily conquered; yet we have this consolation with us, that the harder the conflict the more glorious the triumph: what we obtain too cheap we esteem too lightly; 'tis dearness only that gives everything its value.' Charles Biddle said later that Paine's opening lines were 'in the mouths of everyone going to join the army'. Words do not win battles; but they can hearten soldiers. And Washington's army was never again to be in the mood of defeatism that had assailed it, together with its general, during this bitter winter of 1776 when the brave professions of liberty in Jefferson's Declaration of Independence seemed about to evaporate in the harder tests of hunger, tattered equipment, and desertion.

It was Paine's unswerving spirit that continued to challenge aggression, and keep bright the lamp of independence. 'If the grievances justified the taking up arms, they justified our separation: if they did not justify our separation, neither could they justify our taking up arms.' He hammers again on the anvil of trade: 'it is impossible that any country can flourish, as it otherwise might do, whose commerce is engrossed, cramped and fettered by the laws and mandates of another . . . The increasing importance of commerce, the weight and perplexity of legislation, and the entangled state of European politics, would daily have shown to the continent the impossibility of continuing subordinate.' Peace, not war, is the ideal of a civilized community: 'By having Britain for our master, we became enemies to the greatest part of Europe, and they to us . . . By being our own masters, independent of any foreign ones, we have Europe for our friends, and the prospect of an endless peace among ourselves.'

He is particularly incensed by the British government's resistance to the American alliance with France on the grounds that the French are 'our natural enemies', an outlook that devastated Europe for centuries although even now the phrase is not forgotten: it has been brought up on the question of Britain's entry into the Common Market. 'There does not exist in nature such a principle,' writes Paine. 'The expression is an unmeaning barbarism, and wholly unphilosophical, when applied to beings of the same species, let their station in the creation be what it may . . . The Creator of man did not constitute them the natural enemy of each other. He has not made any one order of beings so. Even wolves may quarrel, still they herd together.' It was to be nearly two hundred years before philosophers would begin again to make this parallel of man and animal, and point out that in waging war and killing his fellows man is almost alone among the earth's species.

In war, wrote Paine, 'the conquerors and the conquered are generally ruined alike', a truth which again was not to be widely expressed until after the 1918 Armistice. War is throughout for him basically an anachronism and a degradation of humanity. 'When we take a survey of mankind, we cannot help cursing the wretch, who, to the unavoidable misfortunes of nature, shall wilfully add the calamities of war. One would think there were evils enough in the world without studying to increase them, and that life is sufficiently short without shaking the sand that measures it . . . To see the bounties of heaven destroyed, the beautiful face of nature laid waste, and the choicest works of creation and art tumbled into ruin, would fetch a cruse from the soul of piety itself . . . If there is a sin superior to every other, it is that of wilful and offensive war.'

Nevertheless, 'Those who expect the blessings of freedom, must, like men, undergo the fatigues of supporting it', and for this uncorrupt government, too, is necessary. '. . . the support of our independence rests, in a great measure, on the vigour and purity of our public bodies.' He was to return to the theme with a warning in the last *Crisis*, when the war had been won. 'Character is much easier kept than recovered', and in this situation, he adds, may America 'never forget that a fair national reputation is of as much importance as independence. That it possesses a charm that wins upon the world, and makes even enemies civil. That it gives a dignity which is often superior to power, and commands reverence where pomp and splendour fail.' We have, he adds characteristically on one of his favourite themes, 'established an inheritance for posterity'. 'We are a young nation, just stepping upon the stage of public life, and the eye of the world is upon us to see how we act'.

As propagandist in the thick of war Paine hit out boldly at profiteering—the men who 'make a market of the times'—and at inflation and rising prices. 'Men are daily growing poor by the very means that they take to get rich; for in the same proportion that the prices of all goods on hand are raised, the value of all money laid by is reduced . . . it is not the number of dollars a man has, but how far they will go, that makes him either rich or poor.' It is one of the many passages in Paine's works that seem to cross a bridge from his own time to ours, often to the very day we read it. In fact he sat on the Committee studying profiteering and problems of currency inflation, which resulted in a change in the American currency; and in October 1780, his *Crisis Extraordinary* was written to convince the American people that taxation was necessary and preferable to debt and financial chaos.

He appeals to the English people constantly (the pamphlets were shipped across the Atlantic to radical circles, as *Common Sense* had been before them), pointing out that though the British army in America does not care how long the war lasts, 'the case is very different with the labouring farmer, the working tradesman, and the necessitous poor in England'. The first point may be disputable (not all the soldiers in the British army were content, as he put it, to 'fatten on the folly of one country and the spoils of another'), but the second was acute: it is the people who suffer in war, although it took the appalling, useless blood-shed of trench warfare between 1914 and 1918 to waken up humanity to the reality behind the jingoistic patriotism of the generals. The pressures of taxation, not personal destruction, were of course what Paine meant, and he drove a keen knife through the complacency of the distant and untouched, whether they be American colonists well away from the firing lines or Englishmen at home. 'Like fire at a distance you heard not even the cry.' The British public, he adds, are fed on propaganda. 'They are made to believe that their generals and armies differ from those of other nations, and have nothing of rudeness or barbarity in them . . . There was a time when I felt the same prejudices, and reasoned from the same errors; but experience, sad and painful experience, has taught me better.' So might today a soldier write on returning from the war in Vietnam, and an American citizen reeling from the shock of the massacres at My Lai. If there was nothing on this scale in the American War of Independence, there was enough in the way of the burning of property and hangings of civilian rebels and militia, when caught, to justify Paine's bitterness.

When a riot took place in Philadelphia against some profiteers, on the other hand, ending in the near-lynching of a group of Tories who had fortified themselves in a house and fired on the mob, Paine was far from condoning his own side, although he pointed out the provocation. It is possible that he felt some responsibility because of his recent propaganda against profiteering.

It would not have been in the nature of the *Crisis* pamphlets to avoid the question of the loyalists, those colonists who still clung to their wish to remain attached to Britain. Paine, according to the desperations of the hour, waxes hot and cold, but rarely loses his essentially humane outlook. In April 1777, he for the first and only time mentions 'the jail and the gibbet' ('When one villain is suffered to escape, it encourages another to proceed'), but immediately after this he is recording for the Council of Safety in Pennsylvania a meeting of Philadelphians professing liberality of sentiment to all men, upholding liberty of conscience, and stating: 'We persecute no man, neither will we abet in the persecution of any man for religion's sake; our common relation to others being that of fellow-citizens and fellow-subjects of one single community; and in this line of connection we hold out the right hand of fellowship to all men. But we should conceive ourselves to be unworthy members of the *free and independent state of America* were we unconcernedly to see or to suffer any treasonable wound, public or private, directly or indirectly, to be given against the peace and safety of the same.'

The utmost of penalty he had ever suggested was confiscation of loyalists' property, and then only to compensate those supporters of independence whose own property had been destroyed by the British army. He had also proposed a tax on the property of those who refused to take an oath of allegiance. It would bring potential traitors out into the open, he thought, or encourage them to support the cause of independence (Paine was not blind to men's motives, and knew well there must be many 'sitting on the fence' until the winning side should appear). After the war many loyalists left the United States for Canada or England, but there is nothing in Paine's writings to suggest he approved of any post-war persecution. 'We fight neither for revenge nor conquest' he had written in his *Epistle to the Quakers* in 1776.

There were naturally retaliations and excesses during the war, which troubled Paine's conscience when he observed them. His protest at the tarrings and featherings has been noted. He was strongly critical of what he believed—and many radicals since have echoed him—to be the selfishness and avarice behind many men's support of a society oppressive to others, although useful to themselves; but men were never to him good or evil, according to their views:

'I am not for declaring war with every man that appears not so warm as myself; difference of constitution, temper, habit of speaking, and many other things, will go a great way in fixing the outward character of a man, yet simple honesty may remain at bottom. Some men have naturally a military turn, and can brave hardships and the risk of life with a cheerful face; others have not; no slavery appears to them so great as the fatigue of arms, and no terror so powerful as that of personal danger. What can we say?'

Psychologically he was a liberal, as he was in politics; and when the Quakers in Philadelphia, or a section of them, issued their 'Testimony' declaring their loyalty to the crown, he was less incensed than regretful at their want of logic: to support one side in a war against another was, as he pointed out, hardly consistent with the Quaker rejection of war, which should have ensured their neutrality. And he ends his Epistle to them: 'And here without anger or resentment I bid you farewell. Sincerely wishing that, as men and christians, ye may always fully and uninterruptedly enjoy every civil and religious right; and be in your turn, the means of securing it to others: but that the example which ye have unwisely set, of mingling religion with politics, *may be disavowed and reprobated by every inhabitant of AMERICA.*' As for the Tories, they were, he wrote, 'rather a mistaken than a criminal people'.

It was Paine, in the third *Crisis*, who first used the phrase '*The* UNITED STATES OF AMERICA'. And before the end of the war it was common currency. Confederation of states was always his solution for strength, peace and security, and he was later to envisage a confederation of countries in the manner of the United Nations. Today on the base of his statue in Thetford is inscribed his own words: 'My country is the world. My religion is to do good.'

Where was Paine all this time? He was never the kind of man with whom writing and action were incompatible: he lived life as vivaciously and sometimes as combustibly as he wrote about it. Rickman has noted that the Lewes exciseman seemed always in a hurry when going about his duties, and 'Bustle! Bustle!' Paine might well have cried with Shakespeare's Richard III as he set about the business, in Dick Dudgeon's words in the Shaw play, of making America a nation. As author of *Common Sense* and the *Crisis* he had gained, for the first time in his life, prestige and position. He was no longer on the sidelines of political action, but actively within the maelstrom. It was to whirl him briefly into the office of America's first Secretary of State for Foreign Affairs, and twice across the Atlantic to France and back again. But rolling stones gather no moss, and Paine was to remain not far from the edge of poverty to his death. One disadvantage of proclaiming one's incorruptibility, and giving the proceeds of one's work to a cause, is that people, and particularly nations, are only too eager to take one at one's word. America never fully repaid Tom Paine for his work on her behalf. He survived, and it is difficult at times to understand quite how he did it, for in spite of all the calculations on political economy that bespatter the pages of his books and pamphlets, he left no personal accounts (it is true many of the papers preserved by Madame de Bonneville after his death were destroyed in a fire). Paine, like a Norfolk sparrow, seems to have had a natural capacity for survival.

After Washington's victory at Trenton the British took time in resuming the war. Paine left the army and at 'Second Street, opposite the Quaker meeting' wrote the *Epistle to the Quakers*, which was appended to an edition of *Common Sense*. In September 1777, Philadelphia fell to the British (to catcalls from Robert Burns, as we have seen), and Paine, with Washington at Valley Forge, received a letter from the President of the Pennsylvania Assembly saying that it had proposed and adopted a plan for obtaining more regular intelligence of the proceedings of Washington's army. 'Everyone agrees that you are the proper person for this purpose.' The Assembly had 'agreed to make you a reasonable compensation for your services in this business, if you think proper to engage in it, which I hope you will; as it is a duty of importance that there are few, however well disposed, who are capable of doing in a manner that will answer all the intentions of it . . .' He adds (a certain bait for Paine) that the correspondence may give Paine the opportunity of giving the Council 'some important hints that may occur to you on interesting subjects.'

The invitation shows how completely Paine had now established himself as the leading writer on the war and America's aims in it.

In April the same year he had returned to 'civvy street' and been unanimously elected to the Committee of Correspondence of the Whig Society of Philadelphia. Having been nominated by John Adams, he was now also Secretary to the Committee for Foreign Affairs. By October, however, while still holding this office, he was back as war correspondent with the army under Washington, doubtless as a result of the above letter, and writing official dispatches. It was at this time that he took up the case of General Burgoyne, writing from 'Headquarters, fourteen miles from Philadelphia' to the Hon. Richard Henry Lee expressing his concern that Burgoyne's terms of surrender might not be met. These had been 'That the Officers and Men shall be Transported to England and not serve more against North America during the present War'—or 'words to this effect' as Paine put it. Paine's concern was justified, for in fact Washington, seeking time for England to ratify the articles of capitulation, asked Congress to delay in every possible way the return of the prisoners to England 'since the most virtuous adhesion to the articles would not prevent their replacing in garrison an equal number of soldiers who might be sent against us'. This seeking of military advantage at the expense of honour caused Burgoyne, after long delays on various pretexts, to protest 'the publick faith is broke'. Congress promptly suspended the embarkation of the troops until Britain ratified the Convention of Saratoga. Burgoyne only was allowed to return to England, and his troops were retained.

As Conway points out, Paine had expressed his concern at the terms of the treaty and this potential injustice, but when it happened he remained silent. The *Crisis* pamphlets were American propaganda, and we must accept that Paine did not consider it part of his job to record things discreditable to America on the military side. Nevertheless, he was to intervene privately in another case of injustice, this time successfully. In 1782, near the end of the war, an American officer in British hands, Captain Huddy, had been taken one night by a band of British soldiers and hanged, apparently for no other reason than pure sport and devilry. The murderer in chief, a Captain Lippencott, was traced and Washington demanded the British surrender him to American justice. He was not given up, and Washington and his generals directed that in retaliation a British prisoner of war of Huddy's rank be chosen by lot for execution.

A young Captain Asgill was the unlucky selection, and quite apart from the moral question involved there was one of military honour, for Asgill had capitulated with Cornwallis, whose army was relieved from liability to reprisals by Article 14. Paine did not know this last point, which was still a military secret; but he heard of Asgill's plight and at once wrote to inform Sir Guy Carleton, the British commander, expressing horror at Huddy's fate and warning him that by withholding the true murderer he in effect was signing Asgill's death warrant. At the same time he approached Washington: 'For my own part, I am fully persuaded that a suspension of his fate, still holding it *in terrorem,* will operate on a greater quantity of their passions and vices, and restrain them more, than his execution would do.' He adds his usual concern for American reputation in the future. Washington, it must be conceded, had three months before shown in a letter to the Secretary for War, General Lincoln, some slight doubts of conscience about the legality of this discreditable business, but it was only after Paine's letter of 7th September that he first, on 30th September, actually made a move to Congress for Asgill's release.

This was finally effected in October, when a letter from the French Minister of Foreign Affairs, Count Vergennes, inspired by Marie Antoinette to whom Lady Asgill had appealed, reached Congress. It pointed out the military obligation, and settled the matter which Paine had already questioned on moral grounds. If Paine knew of Marie Antoinette's intervention in this case (and he seems always to have had extensive sources of political information), it can only have supported the later instance in which he acknowledged gratitude to the Queen. Gratitude, with Paine, was a matter of honour, although he was to receive little of it himself. He never forgot helpful actions by the King or Queen of France, even at the height of the French Revolution; and his plea for the King's life was almost to cost him his own.

Early in 1778 Paine was back in civilian life, working with a fellow enthusiast, William Henry, at Lancaster on the theory of applying steam power to vessels. But his political activities continued. He met the opposition to the Constitution with vigorous arguments that what was good for the poor man was good for the rich as well, as the poor were consumers of the goods supplied by the merchants; and he added the pertinent point that if freedom was dangerous (as had been protested) in the hands of the poor from ignorance, it was equally dangerous in the hands of the rich from influence. He had himself, in 1776, been instrumental, with Franklin and others, in framing a Constitution for Pennsylvania.

On 8 January 1779, he was forced to resign from the position of Secretary of the Committee for Foreign Affairs: a step he took when it became clear he was not to be granted a full hearing on the point at issue. The reason was the curiously involved affair of one Silas Deane, who had been operating as an American agent (alongside Benjamin Franklin) in France and whose honesty was coming into question. Paine, convinced of his guilt, published an indictment of Deane which the government took it into its head to regard in the light of the publication of a state secret.

Paine's *Crisis* included a strong plea for openness in government as a necessary adjunct of democracy. 'A government or an administration, who means and acts honestly, has nothing to fear, and consequently has nothing to conceal.' He was writing specifically of public expenditure and receipts, but he must now have reflected ruefully on the vagaries of governmental interpretation of what should be made public, and what not.

The affair of Silas Deane has never been wholly unravelled, although its incidental complexities read like something out of the adventures of Figaro, whose creator, Beaumarchais, in fact was heavily involved. Certainly there seems to have been chicanery of some kind. Deane had been sent in 1776 on a mission to France which included the obtaining of arms and ammunition for the hard-pressed American army. The negotiations had to be secret as France at the time was rather uneasily at peace with England. It was, however, obviously in her interests to support the cause of American independence, for war between England and France was almost a constant historical factor and France had already suffered reverses in her new world colonies, including Canada. The plan was evolved for a commercial firm, Hortalez and Company, to be established, owned by private exporters: arms could therefore be sent under cover of legitimate export trade. The head of this organization was to be Caron de Beaumarchais (original name Pierre Caron, the son of the official watch and clock mender to the royal palace). A handsome and talented charmer, he had inherited a country estate called Beaumarchais from his first wife and was both a courtier and established satirist and playwright (*The Barber of Seville* had been produced in 1775, although *The Marriage of Figaro* did not follow until 1784).

'The shifty but not over-scrupulous author', as one historian described him, entered into his under-cover activities with aplomb, the amassing of a fortune never having been a negligible part of his ambitions. In 1775 he was sent to London to contact Arthur Lee, representative of the American colonies there, and they met at a dinner given by the Mayor, our old friend John Wilkes. Lee then wrote the Secret Committee in Philadelphia that according to Beaumarchais the King of France had decided to send five million livres in arms and munitions (actually the matter was still under consideration, and the amount was two not five: half to be subscribed by France, the other half by Spain). In June 1776, Louis XVI approved one million francs to go through Beaumarchais in the form of arms, to be shipped *via* Hortalez and Company.

Was it a gift to America, or a loan? This was the whole basis of the later case against Beaumarchais and Silas Deane, who arrived in Paris in July 1776, as commercial agent for the colonies, having been appointed by the Secret Committee without the knowledge of Congress. His mission was to establish credit, and he was to be paid his expenses and a commission of five per cent. This commission was only to be received if Beaumarchais was not providing the goods as a gift, but on sale. Lee informed Deane that Beaumarchais had no financial interest: the arms were a French gift. Beaumarchais maintained, on the contrary, that in fact the French aid was on loan and his own agreed payment was ten per cent. With an eye on his own five per cent, Deane chose to believe Beaumarchais and forwarded his bills for payment to the Committee.

It was March 1778 before the Committee learned that the French government did not expect repayment, as the original letter containing this information was lost en route. Deane was ordered to return to 'report on the state of affairs'. He arrived in May without vouchers or records and found Lee had written accusing him of dishonesty. He appeared twice before Congress and published a virulent attack on Lee and his own treatment by Congress. It was to this attack that Paine, as Secretary to the Committee for Foreign Affairs, replied in his 'Letter to Silas Deane' in *The Pennsylvania Packet*. He strongly criticized Deane for attacking Lee when Lee was thousands of miles away and unable to reply, and asserted he believed the French arms were a gift to America. The inference was clear that the French government had given aid to the American Congress while at peace with England. Actually this was already widely known or suspected, but Paine was in an official position and there is no doubt his Letter, though meeting his own demands of truth in public affairs, was tactless from the government's point of view.

He was advised to resign by friends and did so, in a letter protesting not without dignity:

'My wish and my intentions in all my late publications were to preserve the public from error and imposition . . . I have betrayed no trust because I have constantly employed that trust to the public good. I have revealed no secrets because I have told nothing that was, or I conceive ought to be, a secret.'

Paine did not know that a Gouverneur Morris, whom years later in France, to his cost, he took to be a friend, had written to Congress before his resignation labelling him 'a mere adventurer from England, without fortune, without family or connections . . . a man who has been just now puffed as of great importance'. It is often forgotten that in republican America, no less than monarchial Britain, snobbery and the bitchiness attendant on it could be vicious when one of the 'lower orders' attained some degree of success. Both friends and enemies of Paine clashed in Congress over his resignation, and the enemies were not silenced.

Deane's actual culpability in supporting Beaumarchais was virtually unestablishable. He had been suspected by some as being a double agent, in the employment also of the British, and his later behaviour in England did not make this seem unlikely. His career ruined, he died in comparative poverty, but after his death his descendants received some compensation ($35,000) from the American government.

The buoyant and irrepressible creator of Figaro was rich enough by the 1780s to build a large and ostentatious mansion on a site now known as the Boulevard Beaumarchais. A supporter of the Revolution, he was in charge of the razing to the ground of the Bastille after its fall but was later imprisoned as a suspected embezzler and Royalist agent. Released with the help of his mistress in the time-old, indeed prehistoric, fashion (seduction of his accuser), he went to Holland to purchase muskets for sale to the revolutionaries. In his absence, he was denounced before the Convention on suspicion of actually selling the Dutch arms to the reactionary armies then invading France. He was in England when he heard that his property in France had been confiscated and his wife and daughter put in prison. Resisting all attempts by his English friends to restrain him, he returned, banners flying, full tilt to France, where he pleaded his cause with such effect that his speech was received with thunderous applause, the decree against him was rescinded, his property was returned to him and his wife and daughter released!

He died in his sleep in 1799, outliving by eight years the young musical genius, Mozart, who was to immortalize and internationalize his Figaro on a scale his own dramatic talents could never have achieved. After his death, it was learned that in the early days of the Revolution he had given away 900,000 francs for the relief of artists, writers and others impoverished by the times. In his Will he bequeathed his claim against the United States to his daughter, and in 1835 Congress settled it in full, to the tune of 800,000 francs. The claim remains unproven; but with Beaumarchais living dangerously seems almost always to have met with uproarious success.

Thomas Paine left no heirs, and no claims. And he died in comparative poverty and obscurity, ignored by the great whom he had helped to found a nation.

VIII

SLAVERY, FRANCE AND PEACE

What the Silas Deane affair proved above all things was that Paine already had bitter enemies as well as staunch friends, among whom of course Richard Henry Lee, brother of Arthur Lee, was prominent. Deane had the support of many Tories and, inevitably, among the merchant class affected through their vested interests by Paine's propaganda against the profiteers; and soon after Paine's resignation a band of these is reported to have attacked him in the wet streets of Philadelphia and thrown him into the gutter. The whole business was to have repercussions on his later career, and he did not improve matters by continuing to worry it, like a dog with a bone, in a series of articles after he left official service. That he was proved right on Deane in the long run, when Deane's attacks on America from the safe shores of Britain were intercepted on the high seas, did not appreciably mollify his enemies. Being proved wrong is never a welcome stimulant to the human psyche; nor does it instil a sense of forgiveness towards the man proved right.

To his credit Franklin, whose association with Deane in France had naturally come under fire—although not by Paine—does not appear to have lessened in his regard for his protégé; although he was the following year to declare Arthur Lee, whom Paine supported, 'the most malicious enemy I ever had'. Lee suspected his complicity in the Deane affair, and perhaps in Deane's personal attack on himself: certainly he stirred up trouble for Franklin in France, where in 1780 he and Franklin were also involved in a bitter controversy over the command of the frigate *Alliance*. It was this that provoked Franklin's remark. Franklin certainly left Europe with a fortune and it is a measure of the times that a certain amount of money-making on the side was not considered generally culpable, but part of the acceptable 'perks' of office. For his period, Paine's rather prickly incorruptibility was the more remarkable. He himself maintained it was a necessity, if his work against corruptions in government and war was to carry any weight and not be discredited. Consciously or unconsciously, he had set out to disprove Robert Walpole's aphorism, 'Every man has his price'. In *Rights of Man* he certainly showed knowledge of the saying, although he did not ascribe it to Walpole.

There is, of course, no specific evidence that Franklin was aware of

Beaumarchais' and Deane's irregularities. In February 1779, a month after the storm causing Paine's resignation, he received notice of his appointment as sole minister plenipotentiary at the Court of France. He was thereafter deeply engaged in obtaining more aid for America, and in March that year, through a directive to armed ships in European waters, he was instrumental in securing a safe passage for the scientific expedition of Captain Cook, who had been killed on the voyage, returning from the Pacific. For this in 1784, after the war, the Royal Society once again honoured him with a medal struck in honour of Cook. One of Cook's officers, Lieutenant John Rickman of *The Discovery*, was a close relative of Clio Rickman, whose family was a distinguished one and has been traced back to 1480 by a descendant, Miss Rickman, in our own times. It also included among Clio's younger contemporaries the ecclesiastical architect, Thomas Rickman, and another John Rickman, born in 1771, who as Clerk of the House of Commons in 1801 was to organize Britain's first census. He was a friend of Southey and Lamb.

Franklin's cordiality towards Paine withstood not only the feud with Arthur Lee but also the onslaught of his daughter, Sarah Bache, who, sharply conscious of the implications of her father's involvement with Deane, wrote acidly to him in France in 1781: 'there never was a man less beloved in a place than Payne is in this, having at different times disputed with everybody. The most rational thing he could have done would have been to have died the instant he finished his Common Sense, for he never again will have it in his power to leave the World with so much credit.' Presumably she had said as much to Paine, for she reports that since they had quarrelled over the Deane affair he had never even moved his hat to her. (The keeping on of hats was, it may be worth noting, a Quaker characteristic.)

Although of course she is wrong about Paine's total loss of friends, it is probably near the truth that he had at some time or other 'disputed with everybody'. His articles and letters show no inclination to hold his tongue when he disagreed with American actions. If Paine's advice was not taken, he certainly was not the type of man to eat humble pie and change his ideas for the asking; and we may gather from his reputation at the White Hart, Lewes, that he could be contentious in an argument.

A thorn in the side of both Congress and Paine in the whole matter of Silas Deane was the French Minister to the United States, Conrad Gérard. Although the truce with England had now virtually ended, the French government were still disturbed that their secret supplies to America should be disclosed. They acted as if unaware that as early as May 1777, the aged and ailing Lord Chatham, swathed in flannel, had dragged himself on a crutch to the House of Lords to warn them that

France was financing the colonies, that American representatives were in Paris, and that there was 'only a fleeting moment before France recognized the independence of the colonies and entered into a treaty with them.'[1] Congress to its shame eventually agreed under French pressure to declare openly that in fact there had been no supplies of arms, and this did not improve Paine's position. When approached by Gérard with an offer of money—reports, including Paine's own, vary from $700 to over $1000—to go along with Congress in this he prevaricated. He certainly had some sense of America's debt to France. But he did not take the money and Gérard seethed to find his articles still avoided any whitewashing of the affair.

Nevertheless a man must live, however much he may decline to profit directly from his major writings and however willing he may prove to donate their proceeds to help the hungry and ill-clad soldiers, as Paine did. His loss of the office of Secretary to the Committee for Foreign Affairs presented him with problems. It left him with no income and he worked diligently for a year as a clerk to Owen Biddle, with whom he collaborated on an address on economic policy. It was a small wage and Paine did not descend to it without bitterness. 'I think I have a right to ride a horse of my own,' he complained to his friend Henry Laurens, 'but I cannot now even afford to hire one, which is a situation I was never in before.' His long insecurity as a staymaker and schoolteacher in England was obviously something the celebrated author of *Common Sense* did not care to recall among his American friends.

He did not discontinue his articles, one of which urged that America should retain her Newfoundland fishing rights in the event of any peace treaty with England. Already Congress was preparing itself for possible feelers towards peace negotiations from England, and Paine emphasized: 'There are but two natural sources of wealth—the Earth and the Ocean—and to lose the right to either is, in our situation, to put up the other for sale.' The future employment of American fishermen was also part of his concern. Other literary projects were the reissue of *Common Sense*, and the long-suggested history of the American Revolution. He also wrote to the Executive Council of Pennsylvania urging compensation for his past services, pointing out the necessity to continue the propaganda still irregularly appearing under the 'Common Sense' signature in the *Crisis* pamphlets. Gérard, still annoyed by Paine's failure to produce his own requested propaganda, put paid to Paine's hopes by suggesting to the Council that Paine might not keep his side of the bargain, if paid.

It was a mean assumption, not supported by facts as Paine had not accepted Gérard's money. But help did arrive, in the form of a clerkship with the Pennsylvania Assembly. On the day that Paine took office—

[1] O. A. Sherrard: *Lord Chatham and America* (Bodley Head, 1958).

93

2 November 1779—an Act for the abolition of slavery in the state was introduced. Paine is believed by tradition to have been responsible for the Preamble to the Act, which connected America's preserved freedom with a duty 'to extend a portion of that freedom to others'.

'It is not for us to enquire why, in the creation of mankind, the inhabitants of the several parts of the earth were distinguished by a difference in feature or complexion. It is sufficient to know that all are the work of the Almighty Hand. . . . We esteem it a peculiar blessing granted to us, that we are enabled this day to add one more step to universal civilization, by removing, as much as possible, the sorrows of those, who have lived in undeserved bondage, and from which, by the assumed authority of the Kings of Great Britain, no effectual, legal relief could be obtained.'

The Act was passed on 1 March 1780, and the thankfulness at America's continued freedom was in the nature of a gesture of optimistic defiance.It had been a year of grave difficulties for the American armies in the South; all of Georgia had had to be abandoned to the British, and in May 1780, Paine as Clerk had to read to the Assembly a depressed and depressing letter from Washington, which was followed within a few days by the surrender of Charleston, South Carolina, and the American army there of five thousand men.

The effect of this defeat was catastrophic on the Assembly, and characteristically energizing on Paine. Currency was depreciated, wartime collection of taxes slow, and government credit at its lowest ebb, and he realized 'private credit, and the voluntary aid of individuals', could now be the only effective stabilizers. He therefore drew out his whole year's salary as Clerk to the State and subscribed one half ($500). He proposed it as the spearhead of a voluntary subscription among his friends, and the scheme was then communicated to Robert Morris and others of political influence. A permanent security-subscription was opened which later formed the foundation of the Bank of North America, which supported the army for the rest of the war.

On 4 July 1780, the anniversary of Independence, Paine was given the honorary degree of M.A. at the University of Pennsylvania, one of the few gestures of gratitude he was to receive from the state where he did so much for the American cause. In December the same year he fell foul of Virginia with a pamphlet, *Public Good*, which dismissed on historical evidence that state's claim that its southern boundary extended to the Pacific, and decisively maintained that the vast unclaimed territories of America must now be assigned to the United States as a whole, not to any one state. This was Paine's one truly historical work of research but it is obvious the contents of the sixteenth

94

century historical documents and charters he used for his argument were provided for him by others, as such documents could not be consulted in Philadelphia. Confederation and unity of resources were still his strongest wish for America, and the jealously-guarded prerogatives or annexation ambitions of individual states were always outside his political vision.

The History of the Revolution scheme did not progress, and not for the only time in his life he was accused of laziness. In view of his output and activities, lack of concentration on this large work would be understandable. A writer is found seated at a desk or table, apparently dreaming away the time—as happened to Paine once or twice in France and America—and indolence is habitually assumed. In Paine's work particularly, there had to be time for thought processes, although the fluidity of his style did not always make this obvious.

On 11 February 1781, he was allowed to sail with Henry Laurens' son, Colonel John Laurens, for France. (Henry Laurens himself, who in June was appointed alongside Franklin, Jay and Jefferson as commissioner in France, was to spend some time as a prisoner in the Tower of London, having been captured at sea by the British.) The mission was to report on America's needs and difficulties and to try to obtain further aid, if necessary directly from King Louis XVI. The twenty-six-year-old Laurens, appointed sole negotiator but nervously conscious of his youth and inexperience, had made his acceptance conditional on Paine's accompanying him. They sailed on the frigate *Alliance* on 11 February 1781, enduring a hazardous journey threatened by ice floes and including the pursuit of a Scots vessel which had illegally captured a Venetian merchantman. The *Alliance* officers insisted on the release of the Venetian crew, who had been put in irons, and their restoration to their ship, which the Scots were taking to Glasgow: an act of piracy as the merchant ship was not carrying contraband. Twenty years later Paine was to be eloquent on the freedom of the seas in his *Compact Maritime* pamphlet. Everything that happened to him was grist to the writer's mill. The story in a contemporary biography of Captain John Barry, that Paine's adventures on board also included a duel with a French officer, though often repeated, is surely unlikely in view of his writings against duelling and his Quaker aversion to personal violence.

Paine, with Laurens, proceeded to Nantes, where he was ferociously disinfected and parboiled, as has been recounted in Chapter IV. There is no reason to suspect this particular episode of the bath, which seems too circumstantial to be invented. Nothing is more likely than that Paine, after his long absence from Europe, would fall on the English newspapers with an eagerness oblivious to heat and bathwater. But the teller of the story, Elkanah Watson, a Philadelphian citizen who helped

Laurens and Paine as an interpreter, wrote his in other ways malicious account many years later, when religious and popular propaganda against Paine was at its height, and we must take with considerable caution his embellishments as to Paine's 'filthy appearance, and awkward and unseemly address'; both embarrassing, we are assured, to the spotless and literate Watson. In view of Paine's long experience as a government official and distinguished writer, moving among the top people in American affairs, both charges are unlikely, although like many people with their heads in literary clouds he was apparently sometimes careless, in a professorial way, about his appearance. In Nantes he had just arrived from aboard ship: the voyage had taken five weeks and frigates of those days were not luxury transatlantic liners, with laundry and dry-cleaning facilities.

Dispensing with the epithet, we might, however, accept as containing a grain of truth the obviously envious Watson's allegation that Paine showed himself 'a disgusting egoist, rejoicing most in talking of himself, and reading the effusions of his own mind . . .' As the Mayor and some of the most prominent citizens, on Watson's admission, were enough impressed by Paine's reputation to call upon him 'to render their homage of respect', it seems not unlikely that Paine, always enthusiastic about the crusading subject matter of his works, was encouraged to read from them or talk about them. But as Watson admittedly had to interpret for him it does not sound a very easy process or likely to be prolonged.

In Paris, according to Vergennes, young Laurens almost ruined their chances of help by his inexperience and imprudence; be that as it may, Louis XVI, wrote Lamartine, 'loaded Paine with favours'. At any rate a gift of two and a half million livres in silver, and two shiploads of supplies, were entrusted to Franklin and Paine, and Paine never forgot this loan and the King's part in it. He had little social life in Paris but met Franklin and other Americans. He had had some hopes of going on to England but was dissuaded from it owing to the possible danger of his arrest. The war was still dragging on. From Brest on 28th May he wrote to Franklin a letter of farewell, assuring him of any services he can give and entrusting to him a letter to be forwarded to Bury St Edmunds, a few miles from his birthplace. It would appear Paine had a friend there: at any rate, ten years later the local paper, the *Bury Post*, was to come out in vigorous support of Paine and his *Rights of Man*.

Paine and Laurens sailed in the French frigate *La Resolute* on 1st June. Their splendid convoy could not have come at a more welcome moment for the Americans. The silver was put on public show at the bank, and Washington's army received substantial arrears of pay plus new outfits and other supplies. On 19th October Washington and the army were to show their revivification by their conclusive success at Yorktown, Virginia, when Lord Cornwallis surrendered with his army. Virtually, this was to be the finalizing victory for America, and although the British still held the ports of New York and Charleston there was a general feeling the war was over, and celebrations accordingly.

Paine himself, who had accompanied Laurens at his own expense, was penniless. Over a period of years he was to claim these expenses from the government, in vain. In the meantime he was forced to write to Washington (30th November) on his lack of funds and the following February Washington signed an agreement to allow him $800 a year, as a fee for writing on the legislatures in the papers. The agreement was kept secret to conceal the propaganda element, but the job was in effect that of a press agent, without fixed hours.

He revived his ill-fated scheme of a history of the Revolution, and in 1783 he wrote to Congress asking for the position of official historiographer. The Committee approved the idea but took no action. On 3rd September this year a definitive treaty of peace between Great Britain and the United States was signed in Paris by Franklin and others, and on 10th September Washington, suddenly remembering how much Paine's work had contributed to the American success, wrote inviting him to visit him at Rocky Hill, near Princeton. 'Your presence may remind Congress of your past services to this country.'

Paine was living now on a new farm at Bordentown, New Jersey: a house with five acres of land near the Delaware River, which he took to be near a friend, Colonel Kirkbride. Probably its acquisition had taken the last of his resources, for he had to borrow clothes from Kirkbride for the visit to Washington. He nevertheless enjoyed himself, as always, once in the congenial atmosphere of discussion and renewed esteem. A class society, founded on the old British system with its social barriers, was however forming in the new United States, and there were still many who had secretly remained Tory and did not look on Paine too kindly. It was to be noticed later that Washington himself greeted people, at receptions, with something of the stiff formality of a prince in his own right. A brilliant general but a reserved man, he was always something of an enigma, unbending in public.

Paine had not been idle. In 1782, apart from his intervention in the affair of the unfortunate young Captain Asgill, he had also published a *Letter to the Abbé Raynal*, whose *Observations on the Revolution in America* so curiously echoed in its title Burke's *Reflections on the Revolution in France* nine years later. The main subject was the American-French alliance, which Raynal had attacked. Gérard's successor, La Luzerne, sent a copy of Paine's pamphlet to Vergennes with a letter claiming he had paid fifty guineas to Paine to encourage him to write further in support of the alliance. Altogether Paine received about $300 from the French and does not in this case seem to have considered it as a bribe. His answer to Raynal had, after all, been written entirely voluntarily.

In this thesis Paine argued for internationalism and a federation of world states, thus anticipating the League of Nations advocated by an admirer of Paine, President Wilson, in 1919. He was moving away from the purely national view: 'We see with other eyes; we hear with other ears; and think with other thoughts, than those we formerly used . . .' His prose has a natural rhythm distinctive of the practised writer.

In 1783 Paine had still not obtained the arrears of salary still owing to him from his position as Secretary of the Committee for Foreign Affairs, from which he had resigned four years before. However, on 3rd October Congress granted him $3000, a sum which must have considerably enhanced his enjoyment of the long rides on his favourite horse, Button, at Bordentown. On 16 June 1784, he was cheered further by the gift of a farm at New Rochelle by the Assembly of New York. The fact that it was the confiscated property of a loyalist does not appear to have disturbed him, and he gave a village fête to celebrate. A New Rochelle girl afterwards recalled 'he had something to say to everybody . . . he sat in the shade and assisted in the labour of the feast'.

The Congress grant had been accompanied by an adequate appreciation:

'The early, unsolicited, and continued labors of Mr Thomas Paine, in explaining and enforcing the principles of the late revolution by ingenious and timely publications upon the nature of liberty and civil government, have been well received by the citizens of these states, and merit the approbation of Congress.'

Washington, too, had written and spoken in support of his reward. Paine had reason to believe that at last things were moving his way.

In February 1786, he published *Dissertation on Government, the Affairs of the Bank and Paper Money*, having designated paper currency as 'both the bubble and the iniquity of the day', but singularly, down to our present day, without effect. This publication once again anticipated *Rights of Man* on the need for flexibility in government systems to meet the requirements of future generations. 'As we are not to live forever ourselves, and other generations are to follow us, we have neither the power nor the right to govern them, or to say how they shall govern themselves.'

He was coming to the end of his American adventure, for so, in many ways, it had been; and the future was casting its shadows before.

IX

THE BRIDGE MAKER

The New Rochelle farm pleased Paine as a gesture of governmental appreciation; it was his Oscar, as it were, the official award and recognition of outstanding work and service. In a letter to Washington in April he enclosed a 'new song for the Cincinnati', his spirits with peace and his presentation obviously rising to something of their former White Hart conviviality. But although he found the new farm pleasant as a retreat he did not make it his permanent home. Bordentown, close to his friend Kirkbride, remained the centre of his semi-rural activities, which now returned to science as naturally as in times of national stress they had turned to writing and public affairs.

The brief sojourn with William Henry was bearing effect, and the $3000 granted by Congress helped Paine to concentrate on his scientific hobbies. On 31 December 1785, he sent Franklin (the tallow chandler's son) a smokeless candle of his invention, the device being apparently to use the current of air in such a way as to separate the smoke and flame at each end of the candle. One of Paine's biographers, W. E. Woodward (1946), anxious to test the quality of Paine's invention, contacted the Candle Manufacturers' Association of New York City and was told the experiment had been tried many years before, but the candle thus treated had 'no advantage over the solid candle of standard manufacture'. It was the kind of experiment, however, that Franklin would himself delight in, and in March 1786, Paine's iridescent mind turned in another direction when he met John Fitch, the scientist, who was experimenting with steam navigation.

Paine had discussed these experiments and pointed out some improvements to Fitch's steamboat to his friend William Henry in 1778, and his mind now turned to another project which, a labour of love with financial prospects which never (as so often with Paine) materialized, was to occupy him increasingly on his return to Europe. The ice-packs on the Schuylkill River, he had noted, were heavy enough to crush the piers of any normal bridge. This problem began to exercise Paine's mind absorbingly and he conceived the idea of constructing a bridge composed of one single arch, comprising several separate sections. He envisaged the possibility of such a bridge successfully spanning the Schuylkill, and later planned to erect iron bridges over the Thames and Seine. 'A child of common sense', he described it, commemorating both his first important work and the American Revolution in its 'arch of thirteen ribs' representing the thirteen United States.

Paine was not the inventor of the iron bridge or single-arch construction, as has been occasionally claimed. The first cast-iron bridge had been erected in 1779 over the Severn at Ironbridge, in Shropshire, by Abraham Darby, one of the Coalbrookdale Darby family who had been experimenting in the application of coal-coke to the smelting of iron in place of wood-charcoal. These experiments and the development of the iron trade, particularly in South Wales, South Yorkshire and Tyneside where coal and iron were found together, were to form a spearhead of the Industrial Revolution which was already beginning, and was to transform England in the nineteenth century. Iron was the new, the fashionable material, and Paine like so many of his contemporaries was entranced by its possibilities. The Shropshire bridge, like Paine's, had a single arch, but its length across the narrow Severn was only one hundred feet, nowhere near that proposed by Paine, which was for a four hundred foot span, something never yet tested or proposed. According to Neal FitzSimons, M.ASCE, in an article on Paine's iron bridge in an American civil engineering journal in March 1969, the 'longest bridge in the world at the time appears to have been a Swiss timber arch of 390 feet'.

Paine set out at once to make a thirteen-foot model, with the help of an English mechanic named John Hall, who had emigrated to America and now lived as a boarder in the neighbouring house of Colonel Kirkbride. Here Paine (apparently cookless) took his meals, but he had a servant boy Joe who assisted Hall and himself. It is from the diary kept by Hall that we catch intimate glimpses of Paine's life and his own in 1785 and 1786, when the friends were building the model bridge. On 17 November 1785, Hall records: 'At dinner Mr Pain told us a tale of the Indians, he being at a meeting of them with others to settle some affairs in 1776.' (This was obviously the story of Paine's adventure as a member of the Council seeking an Indian treaty at Easton in 1777. We can assume he 'dined out on it' more than once in after years, and the actual date fluctuated, as dates do, with passing time.) Five days later Hall records a Paine aphorism, in which we may detect personal experience: it was to the effect that one should never 'give a deciding opinion between two persons you are in friendship with lest you lose one by it; whilst doing that between two persons, your supposed enemies, may make one your friend'.

In December, Hall named Franklin and Gouverneur Morris (apparently reconciled following Paine's vindication in the Silas Deane affair) among Paine's visitors, and at the end of the month he begins to spell Paine's name with the now customary 'e'. On the 14th he and

Paine had had the first inevitable falling out: Paine complained Hall's work on the model was faulty and was indignantly repudiated. But that Paine could have care for individual humans as well as humanity at large was shown by his provision, gratefully accepted, of 'warm cloth overshoes' and a 'wooden pot stove' for Hall's comfort.

Paine had begun his planned bridge with the idea of several arches, and Hall had built a model of wood with nine of them. In May 1786 the material was changed to iron, and in June Paine sent Franklin models in both wood and cast-iron. It was apparently on hearing of a rival bridge over the Schuylkill planned by the Agricultural Society that Paine switched to the completely original conception of a bridge with a single arch span of four hundred feet. In December, the model was taken through the snow by sledge to the garden of Franklin's house in Market Street, Philadelphia, and the day after Christmas Paine demonstrated the strength of it by inducing three visitors to stand on it. Franklin was impressed by the demonstration, and on New Year's Day, 1787, the model was exhibited at the State House and inspected by the Assembly and others of note.

Paine had hoped for finance from friends or the Assembly, *via* a subscription, but it was an expensive project for an invention of untried strength and perhaps understandably the Assembly fought shy of it. It was Franklin who advised Paine to submit his model to the Academy of Sciences in Paris, and so Paine left a second time for France on 26 April 1787, with little thought of Revolution, or volcanic upheavals of the future. The scientist had taken over from the politician, and he was enmeshed in an earlier passion.

The model of his bridge went with him in the hold of the French packet, but on arrival it was held up by the Customs at Le Havre and Paine had to proceed to Paris without it. En route he visited Rouen, very conscious of its historical associations with the English monarchy, and commented with surprised approval on the fertility and apparent plenty of the lands of Normandy: the people were, he wrote, 'very stout, the women exceedingly fair, and the horses of a vast size and very fat'. In Paris he was well received, dining with the Count de Moustier on 24th July, Thomas Jefferson being a fellow guest on that occasion and others later. Jefferson was then American Minister at the Court of Louis XVI, and shared Franklin's and Paine's invention interests. Paine was in contact with him continually on his mechanical as well as political schemes, and as Conway wrote, 'The portion of the "Jefferson Papers" at Washington written by Paine would fill a good volume'. Quite apart from the smokeless candle and the bridge, his contrivances had included a planing machine, a new type of crane, a wheel of concentric rim, and a device for using gunpowder to power a motor! Even the war, he noticed in a letter to Sir George Staunton, 'with all its evils had some advantages. It energized invention and lessened the catalogue of impossibilities.' The same has been written with truth of both the World Wars of our time, aeronautics and medicine in particular expanding to meet new horizons under pressure of military and healing needs.

Paine's model bridge arrived in Paris in June and was presented to the French Academy of Sciences on 21 July 1787. On 29th August the Academy endorsed the model as 'a new extension of the application of iron'. But their encouragement, as for so many of Paine's projects in America, was paper rather than practical, although Paine probably did not realize this when the next day he began his journey to London to visit his parents at Thetford. Paine's father, whose last letter had partly inspired his whole European trip, had died of smallpox on 14 November 1786, and it is uncertain if the news had reached Paine. His mother was now in her ninetieth year, and he settled nine shillings a week on her. She was to live until the age of ninety-four.

A return to France in December seems to have convinced Paine that the finance he needed to construct his bridge was not forthcoming there, and indeed the volatile and versatile Beaumarchais had bounced up again with a patent for erecting another bridge across the Seine, opposite the Tuileries. Paine had renewed acquaintance in Paris not only with Jefferson, but also the Marquis de Lafayette, a young French nobleman of radical views who had defied all efforts by his outraged family to prevent his crossing the Atlantic to serve in the American army in the War of Independence. He was not the only European officer to do so, and Washington had been impressed enough by one Prussian adventurer and mercenary, the Baron Friedrich von Steuben, to give over to him, in 1778, the drilling and training of his army at Valley Forge. The Baron's military rank and qualifications, although it is true he had served in the Seven Years War, had been given somewhat hyperbolic recommendation by Franklin and Silas Deane in Paris, and it is not surprising to find Beaumarchais and the notorious Hortalez and Company involved in the costs of his travel to America. His training of the tattered and half-frozen American army, though, had met with Washington's warm approval and he had been created Inspector General; Washington ordering the commanding officers of all brigades and regiments to 'discontinue exercising their Men by way of instruction, until the new (von Steuben) regulations shall be distributed'.

Paine must have known him and the other mercenary officers from Europe, such as the Poles Count Kazimierz Pulaski (killed at Savannah in 1779) and Tadeusz Kościuszko, who survived until 1817 and met Paine again in Paris after the Revolution; but the young Lafayette, who had been only nineteen when he arrived in America in 1776, was nearer to his heart, as he was to Washington's, and was to remain a most significant friend. Lafayette had won Washington's regard by replying, when the General apologized for the raggedness of his troops, that 'he was there to learn, not to teach', and that he was in America not so much to fight for an old enemy of France, as to serve the cause of liberty wherever it could best be served. And he had justified the high army rank given him on account of his birth by serving with courage throughout the war and with particular heroism at Yorktown. His love of liberty he took back again to France, and although Paine did not know it their paths were to cross in yet another Revolution. In the meantime, in 1787 and 1788 Lafayette joined with Jefferson in trying, although without success, to interest the French government in building a bridge across the Seine based on Paine's model. FitzSimons, in his article on Paine's bridge, points out that the French had attempted to build a cast-iron arch at Lyons in 1755 but had abandoned the idea because of cost. They did not erect a cast-iron bridge until 1803, the year after Paine finally left France.

It was in England that the project got more actively set in motion. Paine obtained patents for England, Scotland and Ireland and then consulted the Walker Brothers, who maintained an ironworks in Rotherham, Yorkshire. The firm agreed to build under Paine's personal direction. 'It was,' wrote FitzSimons, 'a complete bridge with a span of 110 feet and a dramatically low rise of only five feet. Apparently, the patient Paine had even taken the trouble to test a pair of 90-ft. arch ribs to double their own weight prior to the Liston-Grove (*sic*) demonstration'.

This reference is to the bridge's later erection in London in the region of Lisson Grove, near Paddington, which was then a tiny village built around Paddington Green. According to the English writer and mathematician, Professor Charles Hutton, writing in a tract on *The History of Iron Bridges* in 1812 and quoted by FitzSimons, the 'arch was set up in a bowling green at the public-house called the Yorkshire Stingo, at Lisson-Green (London) in the year 1790'; a statement that provokes the conjecture that Paine, back in England, had reverted to his Lewes recreations of the bowling green and local tavern! Paine had earlier written a detailed description of his methods in a sixteen-page letter from Rotherham, Yorkshire, dated 25 May 1789, and addressed to Sir George Staunton, Bart, who had, it appears from Paine's letter, already seen the original American-made model. The following April Staunton sent the letter for publication to the Society of Arts, of which he was a member. 'The Subject is highly curious,' he wrote, 'and the writer whose name is already celebrated in the political World, seems to possess a Genius for Mechanics, that promises much Benefit to Mankind.' Both letters are still in the archives of what is now the Royal

Society of Arts, who however never published Paine's letter, although the matter was discussed by the Committee of Mechanicks on two occasions, the last at a meeting on 10 November 1791, when after a sympathetic reference to Paine's full account it was resolved 'to recommend to the Society to return Thanks to Sir George Staunton for this Communication and that He be requested to favour the Society with such drawing as he may be possessed of relative to Mr Payne's Bridge.' The fact that the matter was taken no further is probably due to Sir George's being sent, in 1792, on a long-term mission to China with Lord Macartney. He was a widely travelled diplomat with distinguished experience in the West Indies and India, and Paine may have known him through his intimacy with Burke.

Paine in his beautiful, even script, certainly presents a great deal of explanatory material, including, in French, a quotation from the Judgment of the Academy of Sciences at Paris. 'My intention, when I came to the Iron Works,' he writes, 'was to raise an Arch of, at least, two hundred feet span, but as it was late in the fall of last year, the season was too far advanced to work out of doors, and an arch of that extent too great to be worked within doors, and as I was unwilling to lose time, I moderated my ambition with a little *Common Sense* and began with such an Arch as could be compassed within some of the buildings belonging to the Works.' A long technical description follows of the building and testing of strength, and the stowing away of the dismantled bridge in pieces 'during the winter in a corner of a workshop'.

'I returned to the Works in April,' continues Paine, 'and began to prepare for erecting. We chose a situation between a Steel furnace and a workshop which served for Butments.' Later, 'the days begining to be warm and the nights continuing to be cool, I had now to observe the effects of the Contraction and Expansion of the Iron.' The result, according to Paine, established the truth of the French Academy of Science's opinion that the effects would be 'a matter of perfect indifference to the Arch or to the Butments'. He adds that the Academy 'may have taken in part the observations of M. Peronnet Architect to the King of France, and a Member of the Academy, as some ground for that opinion'. In fact, in April 1788, Ethic de Corny, who had been commissioner for war during the American war and was now Syndic of the City of Paris, had written to Peronnet on behalf of Lafayette trying to arrange a meeting between Paine and the royal architect. This was at the time when Paine was still hoping for erection of the bridge across the Seine.

Paine mentions later in his letter to Staunton, not surprisingly from observations of his favourite insect, that 'I took the Idea of constructing it from a Spider's Web of which it resembles a Section, and I naturally suppose, that when Nature enabled that insect to make a web she taught it the best method of putting it together'. Other ideas came from 'the Bones of animals, quils of Birds, reeds canes etc. which were they solid with the same quantity of matter would have the same weight with a much less degree of strength'. Living up to a certain posthumous reputation for vanity, he quotes a letter from a 'Member of the former Parliament for this County, who in speaking of the arch says, "In point of elegance and beauty it far exceeded my expectations and is certainly beyond anything I ever saw" ';[1] supplementing this with the information that 'it is much visited and exceedingly admired by the Ladies, who, tho' they may not be much acquainted with Mathematical principles are certainly Judges of Taste'.

Having loosed his little arrow of gallantry he ends, however, with more practical claims:

'A method for extending the Span and lessening the height of Arches has always been the desideratum of Bridge Architecture. These points are accomplished by this Construction. But it has other advantages. It renders Bridges capable of becoming a portable Manufacture, as they may, on this Construction be made and sent to any part of the World ready to be erected: and at the time that it greatly encreases the magnificence elegance and beauty of Bridges it considerably lessens their expence, and their appearance by re-painting will be ever new— and as they may be erected in all situations where Stone Bridges can be erected—they may, moreover, be erected in certain situations, where, on account of Ice, infirm foundations in the Beds of Rivers, low shores, and various other causes, stone Bridges cannot be erected. The last convenience, and which is not inconsiderable, that I shall mention is, that after they are erected, they may very easily be taken down, without any injury to the Materials or the Construction and be re-erected elsewhere.'

Paine's ingenious use of the 'pre-fab.' principle enabled his bridge to be transported by ship with reasonable ease in May 1790, from York-shire to London, where it was erected under his own supervision following a minor accident to a worker. It was proposed to erect a complete bridge spanning the Thames and to put it up for sale, but this grandiose scheme, based on expectation of credit raised in New York, never materialized. For a year it remained a Paddington entertainment: for the charge of a shilling visitors were allowed to walk and stamp on it, and it may well be the ladies of the south showed themselves no less 'Judges of Taste' than their northern sisters. In a letter to Jefferson in Paris, Paine had already recorded more illustrious visitors to the bridge

[1] The compliment so pleased him that he also quoted it in a letter to Jefferson.

at the Rotherham Works, including Edmund Burke who came with Lord Fitz-William, heir to the Marquis of Rockingham (Lord Rockingham, the Prime Minister who had succeeded Lord North and made the first overtures of peace to America, had died in 1782). This governmental interest shows the political and social circles in which Paine, as a famous unofficial emissary from America, was accepted on his return to England.

The bridge was taken down after a year on view in London and although it could have been erected elsewhere, there was no call for it. Once again Paine's always active, never successful, dreams of money-making failed. When he was in France, following the bankruptcy of his business partner in the venture, a former Philadelphia merchant named Peter Whiteside, the materials of Paine's bridge and most of its principles were used to erect a bridge over the River Wear near Sunderland. This was cast in the Walkers' Rotherham works and supervised by William Yates, who had been in charge of the 1789 erection at Rotherham under Paine's direction. One of Paine's influential friends, Sir Robert Smyth, attempted in vain to get him some reimbursement: the indebtedness to Paine was acknowledged, but perhaps genuinely, in view of Whiteside's liquidation, it was pointed out that the financial arrangements did not allow for any payment to the original designer.

Professor Hutton, in his 1812 tract on iron bridges, describes the Sunderland Bridge as having been completed in August 1796 (it had been begun in 1793 but been delayed for various reasons), with a single segmental arch span of 240 feet and weighing about one ton per foot span as compared with Darby's 1779 Ironbridge in Shropshire, where the weight was $1\frac{3}{4}$ tons per foot span. The Sunderland bridge has not survived to our time, but it was famous enough to have figured on Victorian mugs, apothecary's jars, jugs, plates and tea caddies, among other objects. In Sunderland pink lustre, they are now collectors' items.

When Paine returned to America in 1802, FitzSimons writes in his 1969 article, 'the Schuylkill was still being crossed by a planked, floating log bridge, but construction of Timothy Palmer's three-span (150 ft.–195 ft.–150 ft.) timber arch truss was under way and it was completed in 1805'. Paine had to content himself, in 1803, with a postscript to what he humorously called his 'pontifical works' in the form of a memoir on the history of iron bridges, designed to put his knowledge of the subject at the service of Congress. His work was not, however, without posthumous professional tribute. In his Presidential Address in 1905 to the American Society of Civil Engineers, the eminent structural engineer, Charles C. Schneider, stated: 'Paine's experimental bridge became the prototype of the modern steel arch.'

Paine could be said, in fact, quite literally, as well as metaphorically, to have erected bridges to the future.

X

REFLECTIONS ON REVOLUTION

In the meantime, there had occurred an event that was to inspire Paine to his most famous and influential work, and redirect his pipedreams from iron bridges to the more brightly furnaced forges of politics. In November 1790, Edmund Burke, a parliamentary orator who had appeared earlier to be a more liberal influence at Westminster, and was certainly known to the grateful Paine as an active opponent of North's policy in America, produced his attack on the French Revolution; and these reactionary *Reflections on the Revolution in France* stung Paine into a reply which was to go down in history not simply as an answer to Burke, but as a document of human rights which was to sound the tocsin for Chartism and the Reform Bill forty years later, and for universal franchise and social security in our own time.

Burke was not unknown to Paine. In 1788 they had been close enough to tour the northern iron foundries together, and Paine spent a week at Burke's estate in Buckinghamshire. 'I am just going to dine with the Duke of Portland,' Burke had written to John Wilkes the same year, 'in company with the great American Paine.' He had also, as we have seen, visited the Rotherham ironworks to inspect and admire Paine's bridge.

In one sense the men were not too widely divided in background. Burke, like Paine, was a self-made man, of classical education but without influential family connections to aid the advancement his talents and ambition craved. Born in Dublin in 1729, and therefore eight years senior to Paine, he had early attracted literary attention and in 1759 had produced the first volume of the *Annual Register*, which was to continue as a journal of political and literary note until 1788. In 1765 he had become private secretary to the Marquis of Rockingham and the same year was returned to Parliament as Whig member for Wendover. In 1770 his *On the Causes of the Present Discontents* had seemed a liberal contribution to the Wilkes controversy, and speeches on American taxation and conciliation in the House in the following years consolidated his stand against the King's and North's intractability. In 1781, he had even introduced a Reform Bill, including a scheme for the civil list whose effect would have been to prevent the King from spending large sums on Parliamentary corruption. When Lord Rockingham was recalled to office in 1782, Burke became Paymaster of the Forces and the Bill, earlier rejected, was passed. Although the Whig ministry fell the following year, Burke regained prominence in 1788 when he opened the trial of Warren Hastings with a speech long celebrated for its eloquence.

Little, therefore, in Burke's political background prepared Paine and indeed others (for Charles James Fox was equally stunned) for his sudden savage attack on the still infant and liberal political upheaval across the Channel. The attack began in a speech in Parliament on 9 February 1790, and although there was foreknowledge of the forthcoming book this did not immediately appear. Paine began to feel Burke was retreating in the face of Whig disapproval; so that when the *Reflections* were published in November, his own *Rights of Man* was well on its way. His book, in fact, on its political and social sides had long been projected; the Burke outburst merely twisted its immediate direction, so that Part I became in essence a reasoned report of the progress of the Revolution and a refutation of Burke's inaccuracies and philosophical assumptions.

Something needs to be said about both the English and French backgrounds to this confrontation. The England Paine returned to after his long years in America was different in some ways from the country he had left in 1774. In spite of his interest in the revolutionary new uses of iron, he could only, as yet, be remotely aware of the magnitude which the industrial revolution was soon to attain. His economics, like those of William Pitt, as Professor Gwyn Williams has claimed, were inevitably based on a part-rural society, and his visit to Thetford would have done little to enlighten him. The ironworks of the north were looming, but they had not yet engulfed society and produced the Black Country in its more widespread manifestation. The chimneys smoked, but had not blotted out the blue of the sky or filtered the light of the sun. Mrs Montagu, a founder of the bluestockings, was at the end of the century to be perturbed by the conditions of the human labour at the colliery she owned, enough at least to instigate meat suppers for her employees; but she did not question her basic responsibility or alter the hours and heaviness of the labour. Paine himself, only briefly back in England at the end of the 1780s, gave no indication of knowledge of the serfs in the coalpits of Scotland, where the children began to work at seven years of age and their mothers, naked to the waist and with lighted candles in their teeth, carried burdens of coal weighing one-and-a-half hundredweight from the bottom of the pit to the top: totalling thirty-six hundredweight a day for a wage of 8d a day.

He would have been more aware of the contrasts of the great country mansions and the wages of London's workers. Saltram, built for John Parker by Robert Adam, cost £10,000 at a time when labourers earned no more than 1s a day; and at Thetford the Dukes of Grafton lived in a style beyond the dreams of industrious master craftsmen like Paine's own father. These things he could understand, for they were of his world. Few at the time, although aware of transition, could truly estimate economically the extent of the scientific revolution which would transform England. Foremost in the mind of Londoners were the political controversies in their midst: the triumph of Wilkes, the secession of the vast colony of America, the growing Indian Empire and impeachment of Warren Hastings, the subtle transformation by which William Pitt the Younger, avoiding comparison with his father's unassailable reputation as a minister of war, and concentrating his vigorous mentality on internal policies, had turned from Whig to Tory almost without conscious intention.

Although Fox, Burke and Richard Brinsley Sheridan, late playwright and present parliamentarian, remained disillusioned supporters of the old-style Whig party, Pitt's régime as Prime Minister was by no means unenlightened and he had taken enough note of the disaster of the North administration, which had ended in American independence, to make a liberal grant of responsible self-government to another colony, in his Canada Bill of 1790. Paine could have approved his attitudes (not always enforceable) to commerce and the slave trade, and his counter-action against smuggling by the lessening of the tax on tea and spirits.

Still less would Paine have found himself in general opposition to the Duke of Grafton, the subject of Junius' envy and perhaps his own in the years before he left England. Augustus Henry Fitzroy had resigned in October 1775, because he could not convince his colleagues of the need to conciliate America, and not wage war on the colonists. He had become Privy Seal under Rockingham in 1782 and remained in office under Lord Shelburne the following year, when he finally gave up politics for his far happier, lifelong interest in field sports and the racing of horses. He was sometimes vacillating and obstinate as a politician, but basically a moderate and amiable character, who in his Memoirs notably refrained from recriminations, even of his opponents. As they were confined to his political life, they do not mention his fellow-townsman Thomas Paine, for they end in 1783 with his resignation from the government; although the edition edited by Sir William Anson in 1898 includes letters from Fox (acknowledging kindly gifts of venison from the Sporting Duke) as late as 1798 and 1800.

By 1798 Fox, an old and disillusioned political crony, was writing:

'I will certainly get Porson's Orestes as well as his Hecuba, and indeed this is the sort of reading I now take most delight in, politicks are too bad to be thought of with patience, and I confess I see no remedy; and so, why should one not consider one's own ease, and do nothing? However if any plan can be struck out that holds out any rational prospect of restoring substance and energy to the constitution of the country, or of saving us from the certain ruin which the continuance of the present expense must bring with it, I shall always be ready to give my assistance. But while what we used to call the *exploded* principles of tyranny seem acquiring even a sort of popularity, and no countenance is given in any one part of the world to sentiments of moderation, liberty, and justice; I own I completely despair, and feel myself quite excuseable in giving more attention to Euripides than to either House of Parliament.'

And in 1800 the famous Whig was acknowledging, 'I am not much versed in Locke', a statement which would seem to support Paine's own assertion of ignorance on the subject. Locke's works, apparently, were by no means read even by all prominent politicians in England at the time, although Grafton himself admitted basing his political studies 'on the sound system of Mr Locke'.

It is therefore probable that Paine would have heard little but good of the contemporary Duke of Grafton from his political associates, who included Shelburne and Fox, in spite of his holding in fee the 'rotten' borough of Thetford; and his tolerant views on marriage and separation are not likely to have made him critical, as some were, of the Duke's notorious but affectionate liaison with the lovely Nancy Parsons, and divorce from his first wife. It is significant of Grafton's liberal reputation that in November 1766, the ebullient Wilkes had written to him announcing his return to England, although still outlawed, and beginning his letter:

'It is a very peculiar satisfaction I feel on my return to my native country, that a nobleman, of your Grace's superior talents and inflexible integrity is at the head of the most important department of the State. I have been witness of the general applause which has been given abroad to the choice His Majesty has made, and I am happy to find my own countrymen zealous and unanimous in every testimony of their approbation.'

This unexpected, and indeed rather fulsome, announcement of a returning Hamlet 'set naked upon your kingdom', and request for rehabilitation, had created difficulties for the harassed Grafton, who had shown the letter to the King and Chatham, who 'on reading it', says the Duke in his *Memoirs*, 'remarked on the awkwardness of the business'. Grafton had, nevertheless, deprecated Wilkes' imprisonment and been one of those who had tried to see him and been refused, as he recounts with almost radical disapproval in his autobiography.

It seems doubtful if the Duke could have been unaware, at least in later years, of his Thetford contemporary, even more notorious for his political opinions than he himself was for his private life, especially after the action against Paine for seditious libel had underlined his dangerous importance from the Tory government's point of view. In view of their common political associates and horror of war, he may not have been totally out of sympathy with the local staymaker's son. Was it by accident, or slightly ironic design, that he named his 1810 Derby winner 'Whalebone'? Paine's death in America in 1809 was widely reported in the English papers, and Whalebone, a three-year-old in 1810, would have been foaled in 1807 and named at latest, as a two-year-old racing colt, in 1809.

In some ways London had changed for the better. The gin palace was on the wane, and agricultural and medical knowledge improved. The old London Bridge, with its shops and houses, which Paine would have known when he first came to London, had been demolished in 1760, and the growth of local government and rate-collecting had brought improvements throughout the country in road-travel and public amenities. Pitt had even tried to discontinue public executions at Tyburn, although Queen Victoria was to be twenty years on the throne before the hanging of criminals in public finally ceased. In 1776 Adam Smith had published his *Wealth of Nations*, showing a concern for political economy that was to grow in the succeeding century; and the same year Jeremy Bentham's *Fragment on Government* seriously challenged Blackstone's admired and widely read *Commentaries on the Laws of England*, which had in 1765 suggested the English law was fully adequate, static and unchangeable, much as Burke in his *Reflections on the Revolution in France* was to proclaim the irrevocability of the English system of government.

Poverty in the towns remained a desperate and largely unheeded problem (in the country, as Paine pointed out in *Rights of Man*, there was less death from starvation, because in smaller communities individual distresses were quickly known, and eased by well-wishers: a fact he had learned from his work on the charitable St Michael's Vestry in Lewes, as well as in his small home town of Thetford). John Wesley's evangelism had helped to lessen drunkenness among the poor and aroused a sense of selfless personal discipline; but it had also, like the charity schools for poor children, instilled a belief that the lower classes were created as such by providence and must accept unquestioningly their place in society. Methodism therefore became an ally of the rich and a weapon against the poor which was wielded by the poor themselves. From the point of view of Paine and his fellow reformers its rapid growth was responsible, as much as anything else, for the public apathy towards politics and the antipathy to rational thought which was ultimately to defeat the 'enlightenment' in England and pave the way for Victorian labour conditions and religious hypocrisy. Wesley's own narrow Toryism, hatred of political radicals and direct belief in Hell and the Devil were grafted on to the movement. So were his views on education, which were limited to a child's knowledge of the Bible and capacity for hard and constant work, to avoid endangering its soul. As J. H. Plumb has written[1]:

'Wesley more often than not was preaching in districts with an ever-growing demand for child labour. At the beginning of the century there had been a vigorous movement for primary education, which, if supported and strengthened by Methodism, might have survived the increased pressure from industry. But it got no support at all, and education and the children suffered. The successful Methodist could regard his overworked children with a complacent heart.'

The Government was only relatively less corrupt than in Paine's earlier days in London. In 1780 an outburst of 'No Popery' riots, fomented by the unbalanced but popular young Lord George Gordon, a relative of Lord Byron, had shown religious intolerance still boiling, like a volcanic spring, beneath the surface of the Age of Reason. Dickens was to deal with the Gordon Riots in *Barnaby Rudge*, and William Blake had been an onlooker when the mob attacked and burned Newgate Prison, setting free three hundred prisoners. The only light note in the disturbances was said to have been provided by the popular licensed clown, Grimaldi, who instead of the customary protective 'No Popery' mark on his door effectively implied 'A plague on both your houses' by displaying the sign 'No Religion!'

It is true the riots had got out of hand, not for the first or last time in history, through the activities of a few of the rabble bent on destruction for its own sake; and they had hardened the government against anarchy and aroused the fears of respectable citizens. Certainly they became a source of Tory propaganda. As the Duke of Grafton wrote in his *Memoirs*:

'. . . all spirit and shew of firmness possessed by our rulers, were reserved to be displayed on the other side of the Atlantic; while, by a strange pusillanimity, this riot was left to increase to a length of many days; and to be quelled at last by the effusion of much blood. These riots, however, disgraceful as they were to the nation, served to prop up for a time a feeble Administration, and the dread of any thing like to anarchy, would have driven the men of property to support any

---

[1] *England in the Eighteenth Century (1714–1815)* (Pelican, 1950).

Government, and to look up to a military force alone for their protection. The pains taken, and the stories propagated, in order to insinuate that the riots were a deep scheme laid by the Opposition, would hardly now be credited; though such vile reports did then meet with belief, from men, who ought to have been ashamed of such credulity.'

Governmental retribution had been savage, and little boys under fourteen years of age were hanged in a row. 'I never saw boys cry so,' wrote the Member of Parliament, George Selwyn. It was an age of barbarity to children, in particular children of the poor. Many years afterwards, when the Nottingham frame-breakers were hanged in spite of Byron's passionate plea in the House of Lords, the victims included a retarded boy of sixteen, who had merely acted as 'sentry' for the Luddites during the destruction of the machines, and on the scaffold cried out in panic for his mother.

This was the society Burke's *Reflections* held up as a pattern set for all time and an example to revolutionary France. And his book was by no means written with prophetic foreknowledge as has often been suggested to justify its palpable inaccuracies. It was these inaccuracies—'reflections on supposed facts distorted into real falsehoods' as Paine put it—as much as its illiberal sentiments, that Paine was concerned to disprove. He had been in France: not sixteen years previously, as in the case of Burke, elegantly sentimental in his recollections of the young Marie Antoinette, 'decorating and cheering the elevated sphere she had just begun to move in, glittering like the morning star, full of life and splendour and joy'; but both before and since the Fall of the Bastille on 14 July 1789. And as an intimate of Lafayette, then one of the most prominent figures in the Revolution, he considered, and rightly, that he was currently in a better position to judge the state of French affairs.

The Revolution, as even Burke grudgingly admitted, was a popular revulsion from years of autocratic misrule in which the throne, aristocracy and clergy dominated the country to an extent unknown in England. It had begun with strict legality: the meeting of the States-General at Versailles, for the first time since 1614, on 4 May 1789. The country was in financial crisis verging on bankruptcy, and a *Parlement* of 144 chosen notables had failed to resolve it. There was no question of the King's dethronement, although within six weeks the States-General had become the National Assembly, in which nobles and clergymen were now outnumbered by the Commons, a Third Estate drawn largely from the insurgent provinces and consisting of many lawyers, including the young Maximilien Robespierre from Arras as well as intellectuals such as Volney and the astronomer Bailly. Leaders such as the Comte de Mirabeau and Lafayette showed the movement for reform included aristocrats and property-owners, who were certainly not anti-mon-archial: and the vast, Rabelaisian, energetic figure of Mirabeau was to hold the country together until his death in 1791, bridging the widening gap between the King's party and the revolutionaries.

The first schism in the bridge began to show as early as July, when the King appointed a reactionary chief minister, and his bodyguard at a regimental party trampled the tricolour, the new symbol of reform, underfoot. The people, fearing a counter-revolution, stormed the Bastille, murdering its hated elderly governor, de Launay, but otherwise achieving this surprising breach of assumed impregnability with hardly any bloodshed. The great days of the Bastille and the *lettres de cachet*, incarcerating prisoners without trial and often for life, were in any case over. The mob found only a handful of prisoners to release: it was the destruction of a symbol of power, rather than the thriving reality. But the symbol was potent, and the victory driven deep into the hearts of Frenchmen. Paris elected a town council with Bailly as mayor, and organized a National Guard, a form of armed citizen-police, to safe-guard public order. Lafayette, military hero of the American Revolu-tion, was symbolically and actually its inevitable Commander.

The first and, from the counter-revolutionists' point of view, most dangerous demand of successful revolution had been met: the vital element recognized by every revolutionary leader from Cromwell to Lenin and from Mao Tse-Tung to Che Guevara. 'According to the Marxist theory of the state,' as Mao writes, 'the army is the chief component of state power. Whoever wants to seize and retain state power must have a strong army.' This army the French reformists now had, the answer to Louis XVI's Swiss Guards; and the fact that it was there to control the people as well as the nobility did not yet occur to the celebrating mob. It had occurred to Lafayette; and his position, as time passed, was to become more and more equivocal.

In the meantime the Assembly, on 4th August, abolished feudal privileges, serfdom and tax exemptions; and the clipping of the wings of the wealthy priesthood (wealthy at the expense of the church's numer-ous poorly-paid members), and the arrangement of a democratic election of bishops by the rank and file, were among the reforms which in particular aroused Burke's ire. Partly, no doubt, this ire was calcula-tion, like so much of the indignation behind his book; any questioning of religious practice could be used to arouse particular violence of reaction among the superstitious public, as Paine's *The Age of Reason*, finally disastrous to his reputation, was to prove a few years later. But the special bogeyman Burke was to invoke in his attack, the spearhead of his playing on the fear of mob anarchy and murder, was the march of the women of Paris to Versailles on 5th and 6th October. Burke's luridly painted picture of a murderous, uncontrollable mob storming Versailles and carrying back the King and Queen, in fear of their lives, to Paris amid a forest of blood-dripping heads on pikes, was challenged point by point by Paine in his sober narrative, personally obtained from Lafayette as he points out. Paine's description has, of course, been largely substantiated by other historians later.

The Versailles march had been, in the beginning, not a menacing impulse, but one born of the rising price of bread in Paris and the ever-present fear of counter-revolution. It was felt the King and Queen should be in Paris, at the centre of government; and although the Hotel de Ville had seemed momentarily in danger it 'suffered', as Carlyle wrote in *The French Revolution*, 'comparatively nothing. Broken doors; an Abbé Lefèvre, who shall never more distribute powder;[1] three sacks of money, most part of which (for Sansculottism, though famishing, is not without honour) shall be returned; this is all the damage.' Cannon was seized and 'yoked with seized cart-horses: brown-locked Demoiselle Théroigne, with pike and helmet, sits there as gunneress, "with haughty eye and serene fair countenance"; comparable, some think, to the *Maid* of Orleans, or even recalling "the idea of Pallas Athene" '.[2]

Not all the 'amazons' in female clothes who marched on Versailles were, in fact, women; but the lovely, ill-starred Théroigne, of dubious profession (she ended her days in a lunatic asylum), who like the equally beautiful but virtuous Madame Roland so mesmerized the susceptible Carlyle, was a figurehead of the march, which was basically a protest and a supplication from half-starved housewives, and not at all an instrument of vengeance, in spite of the protective cannons. That there were disruptive elements (the men disguised as women) was suspected, and Lafayette followed the march with the National Guard; fearing in addition, as Paine says, that the King's *garde du corps*, who had so recently demonstrated their contempt for the revolutionary badge, might fire on the crowd. The demands put through Lafayette to the King were reasonable enough: the use of the patriot National Guard to protect the royal person; provisions for the starving Parisians; judges for the political prisoners in Paris; and 'that it would please his Majesty to come and live in Paris'. The terms were more or less agreed, and the rain-soaked Parisians settled down for the night.

It was at dawn that the disaster happened. One of the *garde du corps*, fulfilling Lafayette's fears, looked out of the Palace window on the

---

[1] The militant Abbé was half-hanged, but a Sansculotte apparently thought better of it and cut the rope. 'He lives,' writes Carlyle, 'long years after, though always with a *"tremblement* in the limbs".'

[2] Carlyle, quoting *Histoire de la Révolution Française, par Deux Amis de la Liberté* (Paris, 1792).

stirring multitude and fired; the arm of a sansculotte was shattered; and inevitably the peaceful mob, wet, hungry and half-asleep, awoke bent on revenge. The Palace was broken into, and no harm came of it (except to the *garde du corps*); but this is the explanation, carefully suppressed by Burke, of the supposed threatening of the King and Queen in their palace and the guards' heads on pikes that accompanied them back to Paris. One can understand the Queen's misgivings, melodramatically emphasized by Burke; but in fact the women treated the royal travellers with respect and there was no question of monarchial deposition.

The King and Queen were escorted to the Tuileries, and the National Assembly, holding its meetings in the Palace Riding School, on 2nd November confiscated the church lands; enabling the French government to pay its debts by treasury notes, or *assignats*, backed by church possessions—which were enormous—instead of gold. This, for the Burkeites, was the most unforgivable enormity; and this was the general position when Paine himself returned to France in the winter of 1789.

Like many English sympathizers, he wished to see the progress of the Revolution, and discuss it with his French and American friends in Paris. On 27th November he visited Gouverneur Morris, and he is mentioned again in Morris' diary on 5 January 1790, discussing a financial pamphlet to succeed his *Prospects on the Rubicon*. This had been published in 1787 as an attempt to discourage an English war with France, with its inevitable result of additional taxes falling heavily on the poor and bringing ruin to both countries. The pamphlet had not been anti-monarchial; it had, in fact, supported the view of the state as an alliance of the French King and the people against the nobility. As yet, in 1789, Paine no more anticipated the end of the French monarchy than the revolutionaries did. The Jacobin Club was still reasonably moderate, and the insurgent 'Mountain' that represented the extreme Left in the Assembly had not yet acquired its leaders and its power. Louis XVI, in effect, had become a constitutional king; and a cleverer diplomatist might have preserved that position to the end. Political tragedies can rarely be divorced from personal psychology; and the lumpish, slow-moving, obstinate Louis, clay in the hands of his advisers and his Austrian-proud Queen, lost his head, like King Charles of England over a century before, through a total inability to adapt gracefully to the circumstances in which he found himself.

In the Lafayette circle in Paris Paine met again his friend Jefferson, who had kept him posted with events and had written to him on 13th September: 'I think there is no possibility now of anything's hindering their final establishment of a good constitution, which will in its principles and merit be about a middle term between that of England

and the United States.' In July, in fact, three days before the taking of the Bastille, Lafayette had put before the National Assembly proposals for a declaration of rights; and this Declaration of the Rights of Man gave Paine the title of his book and Burke the spur for a bitter denial of men's equality of rights either civil or humanitarian, in property or in class. Burke's unlucky reference to 'the swinish multitude' did not appease his opponents, and not all the convolutions of his admirers since—and his own hasty and clumsy attempt to withdraw it—have eradicated its effect. Like his equally unfortunate suggestions of Jew-baiting—there are several references to Jews in the *Reflections*, all derogatory—it has consolidated his work's reputation, by no means undeserved, as a document so reactionary that in it can be traced the forewarnings of fascist state power as well as government based on class, in a form the English system has long since itself shed, at least in its obvious forms. 'We have prisons almost as strong as the Bastille, for those who dare to libel the queens of France' threatened Burke, making his position doubly clear; although in view of the ease with which the Bastille had been taken the threat was in the nature of a paper tiger.

Paine, in France in 1789, could not anticipate Burke's book, but there is much indication that he was already planning his own, while absorbing the sights and sounds of revolution. Apart from his other friendships he appears to have struck up an acquaintance with a Belgian baroness of the Lafayette circle, Cornélie de Vasse, who was authoress of two works including a frivolity with a title hardly likely to captivate Paine: *Confessions of a Woman of Gallantry.* How much the gallant lady, now in her fifties like Paine, expected of her celebrated new friend is not quite clear. She wrote a brief letter to Paine on 24 February 1790:

'I expect from your Friendship, you will be so kind to accompany me tomorrow afternoon at the marqs. La Fayette's, I have to talk with him about a business of moment, & importance, as it relates the welfare of the nation in general.
     I am my dear Sir your most affectionate Servant,
        La Baronne de Vasse.
I will call at your hotel tomorrow afternoon at five o'clock, an answer, if you please.'

This blameless missive signed as an 'affectionate Servant', requesting escort to a business discussion, has been taken by some of Paine's male biographers to betray coquettish overtures towards Paine. The obsession shown in this case would appear mainly to be one of masculine egoism. Paine's mind, in any case, was elsewhere: with iron bridges and the budding revolution. He had already tried to convince Burke of the good of the revolution, and proclaimed 'the Revolution in France is certainly a forerunner to other Revolutions in Europe': the kind of statement particularly calculated to dismay Burke, as he makes clear in his *Reflections*. Paine in his enthusiasms sometimes lost his usual perceptiveness as to character, although he was not the only liberal to misjudge Burke's reactions.

Paine returned to England early in the spring of 1790, bringing with him the key to the Bastille, given to him by Lafayette to forward to Washington. He wrote informing Washington of its coming in letters dated 1st May and 31st May (there had been some delay in shipment), describing the key as an 'early trophy of the Spoils of despotism, and the first ripe fruits of American principles transplanted into Europe'. It was no more than the truth: the effect of the American Revolution on the development of French ideals of liberty had been incalculable, although in the event the American system was inevitably remoulded by French needs and the inflammable Gallic temperament. Paine adds:

'I beg leave to suggest to your Excellency the propriety of congratulating the King and Queen of France (for they have been our friends,) and the National Assembly, on the happy example they are giving to Europe. You will see by the King's speech, which I enclose, that he prides himself on being at the head of the Revolution; and I am certain that such a congratulation will be well received and have a good effect.'

It confirms his friendly feelings towards the French monarchy, and he was not yet aware that Louis' apparent compliance with revolutionary aims was a mask for subversive activities outside France. Paine was an English republican, on principle, but ready to waive his principles in France while he believed the King and Queen to be co-operating in the Revolution. He was not alone in his naïvety; not even the Jacobins contemplated a republic at this stage.

Paine's bridge, then on the high seas between Yorkshire and London, was mentioned in the first letter, and its arrival was announced in the second. He gives it as the reason he cannot leave Europe and will not 'be able to see my much loved America till next Spring'. In the meantime, he shows his warm feelings towards the General with a little memento:

'In the partition in the Box, which contains the Key of the Bastille, I have put up half a dozen Razors, manufactured from Cast-steel made at the Works where the Bridge was constructed, which I request you to accept as a little token from a very grateful heart.'

Washington acknowledged the gifts and Paine's 'agreeable letters' on 10th August.

In London Paine began to gauge the true situation regarding Burke. On 4 November 1789, the anniversary of the 1688 Revolution, Dr

Richard Price, a prominent radical known to Paine, had preached a sermon, or 'Discours', at a meeting house in Old Jewry to the Society for Commemorating the Revolution in Great Britain. It was printed the same year, and provoked Burke's own attack on the Revolution in the House of Commons.

Price's is a name unjustifiably forgotten in comparison with those of Paine, Burke and Godwin but his influence in his own time was profound. His *Observations on the Nature of Civil Liberty, the Principles of Government and the Justice and Policy of the War with America*, had sold sixty thousand copies in 1776, the first year of its publication, and he has been called the 'father of' Life Insurance, a Sinking Fund for the National Debt, and Old Age Pensions, in which he anticipated Paine. It is totally without surprise, indeed with resignation, that we read he was also a Fellow of the Royal Society with a telescope, microscope and electrical machine in his laboratory (today he and his scientific-minded political friends, who included Franklin and Dr Priestley as well as Paine, would no doubt be building space rockets at the bottom of their gardens).

He had been given the freedom of the City of London and been made a Doctor of Law by Yale University, sharing the honour with Washington at the same ceremony. He was described as 'slim in person, and rather below the common size' but remarkably active; and the passionate concern with which not only Paine but Mary Wollstonecraft and others rushed to his defence, following Burke's attack, suggests a personality amiable and provoking loyalty. 'In reprobating Dr Price's opinions,' wrote Mary Wollstonecraft in *A Vindication of the Rights of Men*, taking a deep breath, 'you might have spared the man; and if you had had but half as much reverence for the grey hairs of virtue as for the accompanying distinctions of rank, you would not have treated with such indecent familiarity and supercilious contempt, a member of the community whose talents and modest virtues place him high in the scale of moral excellence.' Paine, more succinct, described him as 'one of the best-hearted men that lives'.

Price welcomed the Revolution with fervour:

'What an eventful period is this! I am thankful that I have lived to it . . . I have lived to see a diffusion of knowledge, which has undermined superstition and error. I have lived to see the rights of men better understood than ever; and nations panting for liberty, which seemed to have lost the idea of it.—I have lived to see THIRTY MILLIONS of people, indignant and resolute, spurning at slavery, and demanding liberty with an irresistible voice; their king led in triumph, and an arbitrary monarch surrendering himself to his subjects. After sharing in the benefits of one Revolution, I have been spared to be a witness to

2 other Revolutions, both glorious. And now, methinks, I see the ardour of liberty catching and spreading; a general amendment beginning in human affairs; the dominion of kings changed to the dominion of laws, and the dominion of priests giving way to the dominion of reason and conscience . . .'

(Price, like Dr Priestley and the reformed Duke of Grafton, was a Unitarian.)

He named the three aims of society as (1) the right to liberty of conscience in religious matters; (2) the right to resist power when abused; and (3) 'the right to chuse our own governors; to cashier them for misconduct; and to frame a government for ourselves': the last anathema to Burke, who maintained 'Our representation has been found perfectly adequate to all the purposes for which a representation of the people can be desired or devised'. 'I defy the enemies of our constitution to shew the contrary', he added rashly, giving the opening to Paine to point out the anomalies of unequal Parliamentary representation in respect of Manchester, Yorkshire and the almost non-existent Old Sarum.

The publication of Burke's book was delayed, and Paine, as soon as he reached London, called on the publisher Debrett in an attempt to get information. He also visited Fox and Lord Stanhope, both friendly to the Revolution. In October 1790 he was staying at the Angel in Islington: deliberately placing himself at a distance from his friends in central London in order to work without interruption. As Burke's *Reflections* did not appear until November, it would seem Paine's *Rights of Man* was already being written in anticipation of Burke's points, gathered from his speech in the Commons the previous February. That the book was near publication he would doubtless have known from Debrett.

Burke's thesis, of course, was presented with the rhetorical eloquence then particularly admired and for which he was already famous. It has been highly praised; but reading it today one is conscious of limitations, in particular in comparison with Paine's measured and patient argument. Burke is long-winded and repetitive, and slow in getting to the heart of his subject; basically, in fact, he has little to say, and the great emotional climaxes—'The age of chivalry is dead!'—are used to some extent to disguise the fact. 'He pities the plumage, and forgets the dying bird,' wrote Paine sharply of his lamentations over Marie Antoinette; and it is patent today how exclusive the Burkeian type of 'chivalry' was. It extended to Queens and aristocrats, not to the starving women of Paris, or those working like packhorses in the coal-pits of Scotland. Paine never wrote of the French queen except with kindness; he was conscious of past favours, and lacked the slightly feline quality of Mary Wollstone-craft's analysis in her *Historical and Moral View of the French Revolution.* But he knew just what this 'chivalry' was worth; 'the Quixotic age of chivalric nonsense' was his own description.

Burke's best passages are on social order and the dangers of anarchy; there is no doubt these were sincere, and justified by later events, although his theme is not, in fact, the breakdown of society in the future but bloody revolution and complete disorder here and now. In this he was wrong, and Paine maintained consciously wrong; for from Paine and others he really knew the truth about events in France, and deliberately distorted them. He was, of course, writing propaganda 'in the cause of the Gentlemen', as George III gratefully put it; 'he always sold himself in the best market' wrote Karl Marx, more bluntly. There was something in the charge, which Paine also made; for it is certainly true that Burke had been paid for contributions supporting American independence, and in 1795 he was granted a civil list pension of £1200 a year. His expensive home at Beaconsfield, always well beyond his means, and his personal attachment to his impecunious Irish relatives and family, laid him open to temptations it was not normal for the eighteenth century politician to resist.

'In his own writings,' writes Conor Cruise O'Brien in his Introduction to the Pelican edition of the *Reflections,* 'he is a conscious propagandist. He uses emotional language by deliberate policy'; and in spite of his general praise of Burke (which takes the form of omitting reference to Paine's penetrating counter-arguments and using only Mary Wollstone-craft's comments) O'Brien admits Burke's pamphlet has in our own time been a helpful source of propaganda by McCarthyites and others of the extreme Right. In 1790 and onwards, as Plumb writes, it was immensely successful in Tory circles, 'for it clarified in lucid language the fears and suspicions long felt towards radicalism by those with a large share in the ancient order of things'. Benjamin Disraeli may have been perceptive in stating that the book was in part Burke's revenge on Fox for taking the Whig leadership from him. As a Jew Disraeli could well have found the *Reflections* distasteful, although as a Tory he was not above trouncing Gladstone for formulating a Government which was 'no different from that of Thomas Paine'.

What seems clear now is that Burke, if not always 'an extreme conservative', as Harold Laski put it (many of Burke's previous writings give this the lie), had probably always been conservative by tempera-ment and outlook; and under the pressure of age and heavy financial commitments the thin crust of his liberalism finally cracked. His work became 'a classic exposition of the conservative attitude to politics from the 18th century down to the present', as Dr Henry Collins writes in his

Introduction to the Pelican edition of *Rights of Man*. His concern was for property and the 'natural' governing class, the mystique of royalty and the immutability of the established system. Almost everything was for the best in the best possible of worlds; and although minor changes might be admissible they must always be made within the long-accepted framework. The behaviour of the French aristocracy to the 'inferior classes' was good-natured and by English standards even familiar, he maintained; instances of 'ill-treatment of the humble part of the community were rare' (this statement would have greatly surprised 'the humble part'). Unjustifiably, then, the French have degraded their King to an executive machine, and put the government in the hands of incompetent provincial lawyers. Chaos is come again; for only the gentry know how to rule, and the rulers of the church how to educate. ('Along with its natural protectors and guardians, learning will be cast into the mire, and trodden down under the hoofs of a swinish multitude'.)

'We are not the converts of Rousseau; we are not the disciples of Voltaire' was another theme. In January 1790, he had written in a letter: 'Who ever dreamt of Voltaire and Rousseau as legislators? The first has the merit of writing agreeably; and nobody has ever united blasphemy and obscenity so happily together. The other was not a little deranged in his intellects, to my almost certain knowledge. But he saw things in bold and uncommon lights, and he was very eloquent.'

It is clear why Burke has always been a subject of special veneration in our public schools, and within the Conservative hierarchy. Many now reading him afresh might find even his literary reputation exaggerated. Our taste is for less rhetoric and dramatization, and certainly more accuracy of documentation. The passages of political perception, imagination and elegance of phrasing are fewer than reputation has suggested, and the sentence construction is, indeed, often involved by modern standards of clarity. It is Paine who speaks not only for his own time, the time of change, but for our own, in a language that spans two centuries.

XI

'RIGHTS OF MAN'

It is clear from Paine's Preface to the English edition of *Rights of Man* that his task was undertaken partly in accordance with a promise he had made his friends in France.

'At the time Mr Burke made his violent speech last winter in the English Parliament against the French Revolution and the National Assembly, I was in Paris, and had written him but a short time before to inform him how prosperously matters were going on. Soon after this I saw his advertisement of the pamphlet he intended to publish. As the attack was to be made in a language but little studied, and less understood in France, and as everything suffers by translation, I promised some of the friends of the Revolution in that country that whenever Mr Burke's pamphlet came forth I would answer it. This appeared to me the more necessary to be done when I saw the flagrant misrepresentations which Mr Burke's pamphlet contains; and that while it is an outrageous abuse on the French Revolution and the principles of Liberty, it is an imposition on the rest of the world.'

Paine's fears, he makes it plain, were centred in the possibility of renewed war.

'I had seen enough of the miseries of war to wish it might never more have existence in the world, and that some other mode might be found out to settle the differences that should occasionally arise in the neighbourhood of Nations. This certainly might be done if Courts were disposed to set honestly about it, or if countries were enlightened enough not to be made the dupes of Courts. The people of America had been bred up in the same prejudices against France, which at that time characterized the people of England; but experience and an acquaintance with the French Nation have most effectually shown to the Americans the falsehood of those prejudices; and I do not believe that a more cordial and confidential intercourse exists between any two countries than between America and France.'

This harmony, which he had hoped would now extend between England and France, could be disrupted by Burke's counter-revolutionary call.

'That there are men in all countries who get their living by war, and by keeping up the quarrels of Nations, is as shocking as it is true; but when those who are concerned in the government of a country make it their study to sow discord, and cultivate prejudices between Nations, it becomes the more unpardonable.'

Paine's anxiety was to be more than justified in the next few years, when counter-revolutionary forces from other nations were to invade France and, although successfully resisted, induce the panic that led in the end to the collapse of the Revolution through Terror. Burke's pamphlet, widely disseminated throughout Europe, in this sense achieved its object; it was a trumpet call to privilege and power, warning of the breaches in their fortifications, and its picture of revolutionary anarchy turned many potential liberals in a roundabout direction, fearful for hearth and home. Paine's cogent reply, a plea for human rights and the common people, reached even more readers, certainly in England and probably abroad; but its greatest impact was on the converted, and the poor who had neither the means nor the weapons to stake their claim. The law was on the side of the rich, as were all armies outside France; and America, although largely sympathetic, was in no position to cross the Atlantic and reciprocate even on the scale of France's overt aid to herself.

Yet the *Rights of Man* had its effect, both in the alarm it aroused in the Pitt government, invoking repressive measures and censorship of a kind England had not known for many years, and in its penetration of the hearts of men where the message, embedded like a seed, grew and flowered across the century to come. In this sense the confrontation led to victory for Paine; it is Burke's political system which has failed to stand the test of time. 'Tom Paine has triumphed over Edmund Burke,' as Shaw wrote; 'and the swine are now courted electors.'[1]

Paine's *Rights of Man*, Part I, was published by Joseph Johnson of 72 St Paul's Churchyard—the good friend, employer and publisher of Mary Wollstonecraft, William Blake and other radicals—on 22 February 1791, in a small edition. In March, reputedly owing to Johnson's fears of prosecution, it was taken over by J. S. Jordan and republished with some amendments. There seems no certain proof of the reason for the change of publisher, and one would not expect it of Johnson: that open-hearted man and friend of distressed radical writers, who published the Left-wing magazine, *The Analytical Review*, and regularly held dinners which not only provided stimulating conversation but often much-needed food for the hungry *literati*. (It was said he automatically greeted new acquaintances with the words: 'How d'ye do, sir? I dine at three.') Yet no other explanation but political pressure in the Paine case appears forthcoming; it is certainly true that the *French Revolution* written by Blake, also in response to Burke's *Reflections on the Revolution in France*,

---

[1] Preface, *Man and Superman* (1901–3).

although placed in Johnson's hands and put into print, was never published, possibly for the same reason.

William Godwin, later author of *Political Justice*, and Thomas Holcroft, the dramatist, saw the Jordan edition through the press, apparently because Paine wanted to return to Paris, where he was the guest of Lafayette in April, May and June. 'Hey for the New Jerusalem! The millenium! And peace and eternal beatitude be unto the soul of Thomas Paine' exploded Holcroft, histrionically, on receiving *Rights of Man* from the printing shop. The distribution was cautious owing to fear of government agents, possibly on the warning of Johnson's experience, and the dedication to George Washington was probably not without embarrassment to the American government, at that time investigating the possibility of a commercial treaty with England. Jefferson certainly found it so. He sent Paine's book to an American printer with the recommendation: 'I have no doubt our citizens will rally a *second* time round the *standard* of Common Sense', and this was published with the book. Under some pressure from the British government, Jefferson later denied he had given authorization for his note to be published. These diplomatic skirmishes would have hurt and baffled Paine; but at three shillings a copy his book had a phenomenally large sale.

Godwin's journal, a succinct but useful guide to his activities and those of his circle, records the publication—'Paine's pamphlet appears' —on 27th February, and in May adds that 'Scott, a believer in spiritual intercourses, lends Paine £40 to aid the publication of his pamphlet suspended for want of money', a normal Paine predicament where publication was concerned. The 'Scott' was possibly George Scott, who had introduced Paine to Franklin nearly twenty years before.

In November 1791, Godwin dined at the London Tavern with Paine, Horne Tooke, Dr Priestley and other radicals, at a meeting of the Revolution Society, and on the 13th he recorded a dinner at Johnson's, also with Paine and others, which certainly suggests that the transference of Paine's book to another publisher had been made without loss of goodwill on both sides. It is possible the whole transaction had been undertaken by mutual consent, so that the book could be got through the press in reasonable concealment, once it was known government agents had become interested in Johnson's activities. It was at this dinner that Mary Wollstonecraft, just emerging into literary and political society following a youth of great poverty and struggle,[1] annoyed

---

[1] It was, though, poverty of circumstance, not class. Her father, who inherited and dissipated a fortune of £10,000, had in her childhood been a close friend of Bamber Gascoyne, the Member of Parliament for Barking and a direct ancestor of the British author and television personality, Bamber Gascoigne, of our time. (The spelling of the ancestral name was changed in the next century.)

Godwin, who had never met her before, by talking so much that Paine, whose powers as a conversationalist he had looked forward to enjoying, lapsed into shyness and an unusual silence.

Paine's beguiling conversation, when he could be induced to speak in company, was often remarked on. 'His manners were easy and gracious, his knowledge was universal and boundless; in private company and among friends his conversation had every fascination that anecdote, novelty, and truth could give it. In mixed company and among strangers he said little, and was no public speaker.' This estimate, by his friend Rickman, is borne out by another contemporary portrait, that of Royall Taylor, who met Paine in 1790. He recorded his impressions, thinly disguised as fiction, in a book called *The Algerine Captive*:

'He was dressed in a snuff-colored coat, olive velvet vest, drab breeches, coarse hose. His shoe buckles were of the size of half a dollar. A bob-tailed wig covered the head which had worked such mickle woe to Courts and kings . . .

'He was a spare man, rather undersized,[1] subject to the extreme of low, and highly exhilarating spirits, often sat reserved in company, seldom mingled in common chitchat. But when a man of sense and elocution was present and the company numerous, he delighted in advancing the most unaccountable, and often the most whimsical paradoxes which he defended in his own plausible manner.

'If encouraged by success or the applause of the company his countenance was animated with an expression of feature, which, on ordinary occasions, one would look for in vain in a man so celebrated for acuteness of thought; but if interrupted by an extraneous observation, by the inattention of his auditory or in an irritable moment, even by the accidental fall of the poker, he would retire into himself and no persuasion could induce him to proceed on the most favourite subject.'

This tallies with Godwin's experience at the Johnson dinner a year later, when Mary's vivacious conversation was to overwhelm Paine into silence. It is worth consideration, I think, that Paine's extremes of mood and reticence in company, like his highly sensitive reactions to real or imagined slights, grew from his inner realization of his comparatively humble origins and the ambivalent attitudes he must have sensed, as a consequence, among some of his opponents (it is difficult to believe that the spite and sense of superiority shown in the references to Paine in Gouverneur Morris' secret diary did not seep through into their personal contacts, in spite of Morris' mask of apparent friendship; and doubtless

---

[1] Practically every other acquaintance described Paine as tall or of middle height: he was undoubtedly slim.

others were not so circumspect.) His so-called vanity in drawing attention to his works, as I have already suggested, could have sprung from the same source. It was his armour against the inferiority complex which, had he given way to it, might have been induced in him by the criticism of his views and overt reflections on his background. His refuge was the printed page, where he was no man's footstool and could most feel the quality of his own powers.

In the Godwin circle he was among friends of not dissimilar social class and largely identical radical opinions. Friendly towards women but not, perhaps, at his ease with them until he knew them well (the failed marriage cannot have been totally without psychological effects), Mary Wollstonecraft was obviously here the factor with which he could not contend. There is no record of what he thought of her, although he was to know her quite well two years later in Paris. He was perhaps dazzled as well as subdued by this red-haired, attractive young woman who could dominate the conversation of men, on the same subjects, which included monarchy, Voltaire and religion.

For Mary, her loquacity was a release. She was fairly new to this kind of literary society, where women were not expected to take second place, to be seen and not heard; and her own two books recently published— *Thoughts on the Education of Daughters* and *Vindication of the Rights of Men*, the first published answer to Burke—had revealed to her new powers of expression which only the tragic havocs of her personal life were eventually to constrict. Much later, Godwin was to fall under the spell of her beauty and charm, and provide for her a haven from the tempests of her unhappy experiences. It was his tragedy, perhaps more than hers ('Life is harder than death', as their son-in-law Shelley said with bitterness), that the haven was to be so brief. She died at the age of thirty-eight, giving birth to the daughter, Mary Godwin, who was to captivate Shelley (partly, it was claimed by Shelley's first wife, for her dead mother's sake) and share his exile until his own death, younger even than her mother, in Italy.

Godwin was to linger on until 1836, at the threshold of the Victorian age: a crumbling prophet and indefatigable borrower, only reconciled to his daughter after the fatal end to the elopement he had so bitterly resisted. Convention had come with age, along with the creditors; but the flame of his passion for Mary never left him. He altered the colder passages in *Political Justice*, deprecating the involvements of close relationships, under its influence.

None of this could have been sensed at the winter dinner in 1791 (unless the bachelor Godwin's reaction was an unacknowledged resistance to attraction). Mary sparkled like the century's new-minted electricity, and Paine's light diminished to candle power beside her glow. But the company was congenial and it is necessary to see Paine's opinions to some extent in its context.

His biographers and admirers have tended to overlook his fellow radicals, but Paine was original only within bounds. He was subject, like all political writers, to the climate of the times, and although he denied reading Locke, and with truth claimed a great deal of original political thinking, there is no evidence that he did not read the works of writers nearer his own period, indeed much to the contrary. Dr Price had anticipated him on old age pensions, as we have seen, and Paine's references to Montesquieu, Voltaire and Rousseau in *Rights of Man* show knowledge of their works, as well as a realization of their limitations due to forces they could not, at the time they wrote, wholly challenge.

Mary Wollstonecraft's *Rights of Men*, written in the heat of indignation within six weeks, could not have influenced him; apart from the time factor, she was still a comparatively inexperienced writer, whereas he was by now a man of fifty-four and a master of his craft, with political ideas formed and developed from a lifetime of mature experience in two continents. Godwin, though, was a different matter. His *Political Justice*, oddly echoing Paine in several passages, was not to be published until 1793—almost coinciding, in fact, with Paine's *The Age of Reason* written independently in France—but the men met a number of times and conversation is bound to have involved the interchange of views and ideas, subconsciously as well as consciously absorbed on both sides. Horne Tooke, Thomas Holcroft and Dr Joseph Priestley, among the circle, undoubtedly made verbal contributions. It is not irrelevant, I think, to consider these men and the background of their political beliefs.

'From the ashes of Rousseau's *Contrat Social*, burnt in Paris, rose *The Rights of Man*', wrote Conway, in an always striking *cliché* of the phoenix; but the rebirth was by no means so direct. Rousseau's *Social Contract* and equally influential *Discourse on the Origin of Inequality* were themselves not the first theories of society based on an original contract between the people and its governments: in effect this went back to classical times. But Rousseau gave a new and bold twist to the idea, with the object 'to inquire if, in the civil order, there can be any sure and certain rule of administration, taking men as they are and laws as they might be'. This was an advance on Montesquieu who, in the words of G. D. H. Cole,[1] 'took laws as they were and saw what sort of men they made: Rousseau, founding his whole system on human freedom, takes man as the basis, and regards him as giving himself what laws he pleases. He takes his stand on the nature of human freedom; on this he bases his whole system, making the will of the members the sole basis of every society.'

[1] Introduction, *Social Contract* (Dent *Everyman* edition).

In Rousseau's own words, 'the spirit of society, and the inequality which society produces . . . transform and alter all our natural inclinations'. It is 'contrary to the law of nature . . . that the privileged few should gorge themselves with superfluities, while the starving multitude are in want of the bare necessities of life'.[1] Paine's statement that man's 'natural rights are the foundation of all his civil rights' was in the Rousseau tradition; so was his theory that man 'is all of one degree, and consequently that all men are born equal': a theory which grew not out of a mistaken belief that all men were equal in mentality, but the religious conception (Paine's Quaker upbringing again) that all were created by God. He drew a careful distinction between 'that class of natural rights which man retains after entering into society and those which he throws into the common stock as a member of society', and echoed Rousseau directly on the social contract basis of government: 'The fact therefore must be that the *individuals themselves*, each in his own personal and sovereign right, *entered into a compact with each other* to produce a Government and this is the only mode in which Governments have a right to arise.' He merely turned Rousseau's thesis from the general to the particular when he added that 'Governments must have arisen either *out* of the people or *over* the people' and that the 'English Government is one of those which arose out of a conquest, and not out of society, and consequently it arose over the people; and though it has been much modified from the opportunity of circumstances since the time of William the Conqueror, the country has never yet regenerated itself, and is therefore without a Constitution'.[2]

In the *Social Contract*, written seven years after the *Discourse*, Rousseau extended his discussion to cover most aspects of society from war, sovereignty and civil rights to the arts and sciences. The influence of his book was immense and it has rightly been judged a major progenitor of the French Revolution eleven years after his death.

David Hume invited Rousseau to England, and Hume, Adam Smith and Bentham all had their influences on the Godwin circle. Paine in *Rights of Man* refers Burke to Smith's *Wealth of Nations*, by which 'he would have comprehended all the parts which enter into and, by assemblage, form a constitution'. And Bentham's saying, 'the greatest happiness of the greatest number is the foundation of morals and society', had in 1776 neatly dovetailed into the American Declaration of Independence, itself echoing the *Social Contract* but taking it a revolutionary step further, from theory to action:

---

[1] *A Discourse on the Origin of Inequality* (1755).
[2] This view of England's lack of a constitution was reasserted on 1 February 1972, by the Conservative M.P., St John-Stevas, who stated on television: 'We've got no constitution, for instance, only procedure.'

'We hold these truths to be self-evident, that all men are created equal, that they are endowed by their Creator with certain inalienable Rights, that among these are Life, Liberty, and the pursuit of Happiness. That, to secure these rights, Governments are instituted among Men, deriving their just powers from the consent of the governed, that whenever any form of Government becomes destructive to these ends, it is the Right of the People to alter or to abolish it, and to institute new Government.'

The immediate Godwin circle and the several British revolutionary societies to which its members belonged followed these principles and attempted to extend them to their own country. Dr Joseph Priestley was the scientist-theologian of the group (religious dissent—Priestley was a Unitarian—often led to questioning of the state as well as the church). According to Bentham, it was he who had first used the phrase 'the consideration of the greatest good'. Franklin (whose electrical experiments seem to have turned him into a magnet for scientific radicals) had supplied him with books which enabled him to write his *History and Present State of Electricity* in 1767, and in 1773 he accompanied Lord Shelburne on a continental tour. This was the Shelburne to whom Paine had addressed one of his American *Crises*, and whom he later knew as a friend, although expressing privately a slight distrust of his motives. He had led the Whig ministry in 1782 and 1783, which had ratified the peace negotiations with America begun by Rockingham before his death. In 1784, the year after the first manned balloon had successfully taken flight in France, Priestley was busily engaged on experiments to devise new methods of producing inflammable air for filling balloons. (It was to be a subject of apocalyptic satire by William Blake, and Horace Walpole was prophetic in a more practical way when he foresaw navigation of the air as a potential means of a new kind of warfare.) Priestley was the son of a cloth-dresser, the kind of middle-class background shared by so many English radicals. He also wrote a reply to Burke's *Reflections* which resulted, as in Paine's case, in his being made a citizen of the French Republic. His religious and political views led to a mob, probably government-inspired, breaking into his Birmingham house and burning its contents, books and scientific instruments.

John Horne Tooke and Thomas Holcroft were both to be among the accused in the famous Treason Trials of 1794, which came in the wake of Paine's own trial and condemnation, in his absence, for seditious libel. They were defended, like Paine, by Sir Thomas Erskine, tenth son of the Earl of Buchan and later a Whig Lord Chancellor. The brilliant and famous lawyer in this case secured acquittal, helped by a letter from William Godwin in the *Morning Chronicle* which caustically pointed out the illogicality of a trial for treason only inferred from the accuseds' other activities.

Tooke was a wit with an interest in philology and unquenchable resilience, as he showed in Court at his trial. When the gallery dissolved in laughter at one of his witticisms, the Judges reproved the gallery but not Tooke. Perhaps it was remembered in Court that he had been a law student at the Inner Temple.[1] After failing to get into Parliament as an independent he had finally achieved his object *via* a Rotten Borough, from which he was shortly evicted for being a Clerk in Holy Orders: 'a vocation', as Rosalie Glynn Grylls amusingly puts it, 'to which he seems early to have forgotten he was ever called'.[2] This was not surprising, as like so many sons of the time he had agreed to be ordained only on the insistence of his father. Like a later political wit, Bernard Shaw, he had an irrepressible 'Joey' which could not resist making mock even of the direst situation. He had also made some reputation with a book called *Diversions of Purley*, and had founded the Society of Supporters of the Bill of Rights to aid Wilkes and the cause of liberty.

Holcroft, literally like Shaw, was a radical playwright. The son of a London shoemaker, he had made his way up in the world from a youthful job as a stable-lad at Newmarket, where he gained the knowledge of the gambling world which was an ingredient—with the comic character of Charles Goldfinch, an ebullient horse-lover—of his comedy, *The Road to Ruin*, highly successful at Covent Garden in 1792. (It was revived as late as 1954, as the opening production of a season by the Bristol Old Vic.) A number of people at the 1794 trial attended, it was said, mainly to see the author of this popular play. He had been a schoolmaster and actor, and like Sheridan before him sought to introduce moral sentiment into the artificial comedy of manners. He had, in addition, a connection with that recurring revolutionary decimal, Beaumarchais, having in 1784 adapted and translated his *Marriage of Figaro* under the title, *Follies of a Day*. He had played the part of Figaro and had acquired his fluent knowledge of French when working in France as a correspondent for the *Morning Herald*.

Not only Godwin, but a young man named Samuel Taylor Coleridge and the attractive novelist, Amelia Alderson, of Norwich, followed this 1794 trial in Court. The radical-minded Amelia had been tentatively and unsuccessfully wooed by Godwin but instead married John Opie,

[1] Aldridge's description of him, in his *Man of Reason*, as a 'distinguished legalist' is unjustified, as Tooke never practised. Aldridge also confuses the radical Manchester cotton manufacturer, Thomas Walker, with one of the Walker brothers of Rotherham, associated with Paine in his bridge project.

[2] *William Godwin and his World* (Odhams Press, 1953). Nevertheless, all Tooke's applications for the Bar were turned down on the excuse of his having taken Holy Orders, although he had obvious legal talent.

who painted the portrait of Godwin's eventual wife, Mary Wollstone-craft, which is now in the National Portrait Gallery.

From the point of view of political literature, Godwin was the most considerable figure in the radical circle. He had been brought up puritanically and entered the ministry, but eventually, after much thinking and reading, gave up the church to turn agnostic and political philosopher. In a time of political graft, and although sympathetic to the Whigs, he refused financial offers to support the party as a writer. As with Paine, his religious upbringing had permanent effects on his moral attitudes. He was still a bachelor in his late thirties and a man, though appealing for the broader humanities and liberal thinking, without strong personal affections, withdrawn into himself. Only his lasting passion for Mary Wollstonecraft released the emotional springs lying dormant beneath the apparent ice-crust of the fine-eyed, long-nosed philosopher.

His *Life of Chatham* in 1783 had attracted attention and *Political Justice* was to bring him wider fame and his first and last experience of financial success. He received 700 guineas for the copyright and a further 300 guineas after the sale of 3000 copies. This was an outstanding sum in 1793. His novel, *The Adventures of Caleb Williams*, equally radical in sentiment and questioning the common moral code, in 1794 brought him further into prominence (it was even dramatized by Colman the younger, although not too faithfully, under the title *The Iron Chest*). He only escaped Paine's fate of government prosecution because it was reckoned that *Political Justice*, at three guineas a copy, could not reach enough people to be dangerous.

Although expressing more distrust of actual revolution than Paine ('I never for a moment ceased to disapprove of mob government and violence, and the impulses which men collected together in multitudes produce on each other'), *Political Justice*, like the *Rights of Man*, was a continuation of the lines of thought suggested in Rousseau's *Social Contract*. Rousseau, subject to continual pressures of prosecution, had been forced to present his subversive doctrines in not so much a diluted as a deviated form. 'In the eighteenth century it was, broadly speaking, safe to generalize and unsafe to particularize,' as G. D. H. Cole has written, and Paine, over a century before Cole, showed himself well aware of the restrictions on his predecessors:

'Montesquieu, President of the Parliament of Bordeaux, went as far as a writer under a despotic Government could well proceed; and being obliged to divide himself between principle and prudence, his mind often appears under a veil, and we ought to give him credit for more than he has expressed.

'Voltaire, who was both the flatterer and the satirist of despotism, took another line. His forte lay in exposing and ridiculing the superstitions which priestcraft, united with statecraft, had interwoven with Governments. It was not from the purity of his principles, or his love of mankind (for satire and philanthropy are not naturally concordant), but from his strong capacity of seeing folly in its true shape, and his irresistible propensity to expose it, that he made those attacks. They were, however, as formidable as if the motives had been virtuous; and he merits the thanks rather than the esteem of mankind.

'On the contrary, we find in the writings of Rousseau, and the Abbé Raynal, a loveliness of sentiment in favour of liberty, that excites respect, and elevates the human faculties; but having raised this animation, they do not direct its operations, and leave the mind in love with an object, without describing the means of possessing it.

'The writings of Quesnay, Turgot, and the friends of those authors, are of the serious kind; but they laboured under the same disadvantage with Montesquieu; their writings abound with moral maxims of Government, but are rather directed to economise and reform the administration of the Government, than the Government itself.'

Rousseau, like Voltaire, turned the generalization into a philosophical strength. But by the 1790s, under the stimulus of the French Revolution, there was room for more open criticism and harder hitting, and *Political Justice*, like the *Rights of Man* two years before, met the need of the time. It was anti-monarchial on libertarian grounds. 'Liberty strips hereditary honours of their imaginary splendour, shows the noble and the king for what they are—common mortals, kept in ignorance of what other mortals know, flattered and encouraged in folly and vice.' But although bitterly antagonistic to religion in its doctrinal forms, the ex-minister of it did not reject deism entirely. 'I believe in this being, not because I have any proper or direct knowledge of his existence. But I am at a loss to account for the existence and arrangement of the visible universe.' He was sympathetic to 'that religion that "sees God in clouds and hears him in the wind" . . . But accursed and detestable is that religion by which the fancy is hag-rid, and conscience is excited to torment us with phantoms of guilt, which endows the priest with his pernicious empire over the mind, which undermines the boldness of opinion and intrepidity in feeling . . . and haunts us with the fiends and retributory punishments of a future world.'

He anticipated Bernard Shaw in his nice distinction of the varied worth of men, but the social need to provide all of them with the necessities of living. The accumulation of private property was the main cause of human wretchedness: 'The present system of property confers on one man immense wealth in consideration of the accident of his birth . . . The most industrious and active member of society is frequently with great difficulty able to keep his family from starving.' Charity was not the answer, for it resulted in a degrading servility and sense of dependence by the poor towards the rich. 'The feudal spirit still survives, that reduced the great mass of mankind to the rank of slaves and cattle for the service of a few.' In his attitude to property Godwin was more socialist than Paine: as indeed was Mary Wollstonecraft with her sardonic flash: 'Security of property! Behold, in a few words, the definition of English liberty.'

Godwin's humanitarianism rejected not only physical violence but the forcing of ideas: men should never be reduced to 'intellectual uniformity', but every man taught 'to think for himself'. 'Beware of reducing men to the state of machines. Govern them through no medium but that of inclination and conviction.' Paine had much the same ideal of government; but he was infinitely more practical than Godwin and far more experienced in the intricacies of economics and employment. Godwin seriously believed that if labour were divided among all, half an hour per day 'seriously employed by every member of the community would sufficiently supply the whole with necessaries'. Production of 'trinkets and luxuries' should cease. There would then be 'ample leisure for the noblest energies of the mind'. In such conditions nothing could induce men to engage in war, and when inequalities of wealth were eradicated crime would automatically vanish. In spite of his belief in political justice and criticism of the accumulation of property, Godwin's miscalculations of economic possibilities and human nature invalidate much of his book today, whereas Paine's retains its authority and its relevance.

From the practical point of view, one of Godwin's most telling attacks was on the contemporary punishment of political prisoners by transportation: 'to shut me up in dungeons and darkness, or to transport me to the other side of the globe, that they may wreak their vengeance on me unobserved, is base, coward-like and infamous'. The convicts, in fact, were chained on the ship during the several months' journey, and the death rate by the time Botany Bay was reached averaged twenty per cent.[1] Godwin was perturbed, too, by the denial of books to prisoners, excluding them 'from all the means of intellectual pleasure and improvement, a reduction of men of taste and letters to the condition of galley-slaves'.

He was, perhaps, a little naïve in this: it is no part of the policy of authoritarian governments to allow access to works which may well be

[1] G. D. H. Cole and Raymond Postgate: *The Common People, 1746–1938* (1938). The figure has, however, been disputed.

subversive in their view. This is what the freedom of the press and its suppression are all about; and the world as a whole today is not greatly freer in this respect than in the time of Rousseau, Paine and Godwin. But Godwin, generally so cool as a man, was pierced as a writer and thinker by these rivulets of kindly sentiment. He was against marriage, partly because of its denial of rights to women, and supported divorce reform, but as his daughter Mary Shelley pointed out was 'utterly opposed to anything like vice or libertinism'. And his idealistic conception of the results of political reform are ironic to us of a later age. 'Give to a state but liberty enough,' he wrote, 'and it is impossible that vice should exist in it.' 'It may seem strange,' wrote his daughter again, 'that anyone should, in the sincerity of his heart, believe that no vice could co-exist with perfect freedom—but my father did—it was the basis of his system.'

To some extent, Paine shared the same naïvety. Both men were idealists of human nature, whom the Terror was to shock into only partial disillusion; and Franklin, writing 'mind will one day become omnipotent over matter', was not the only eighteenth century radical to anticipate Bernard Shaw and *Back to Methuselah*. Godwin himself made the strikingly Shavian comment that the term of human life may be indefinitely prolonged 'by the immediate operation of intellect'.

'France has not levelled, it has exalted,' wrote Paine, in answer to Burke, and in the wider sense of raising the lower and middle ranks of the population to some participation in political affairs he was, of course, right, as later socialist thinkers were right when they countered a similar criticism of the Soviet Union with a similar argument. As in China under Mao Tse-Tung, irrespective of the sacrifices involved (and any form of political reversal always means sacrifice for both sides), it was a case of the 'greatest happiness of the greatest number', at least in theoretic intention.

Paine's mapping of the course of the Revolution, from his own experience and the information he gained direct from Lafayette, Condorcet and other French friends, is still a valuable historical document. It is on several points a corrective to the diligent Carlyle, and even today remains a meticulous and rewarding study of events behind the contest for power. Nor, although putting it into perspective, does Paine minimize the incidental loss of life. 'There is in all European countries a large class of people of the description, which in England is called the *Mob*. Of this class were those who committed the burnings and devastations in London in 1780, and of this class were those who carried the heads upon pikes in Paris.' He also indicates the source. 'Examples are not wanting to show how dreadfully vindictive and cruel are all old Governments, when they are successful against what they call a revolt.' The people learn violence 'from the Governments they live under, and retaliate the punishments they have been accustomed to behold. The heads stuck upon pikes, which remained for years upon Temple Bar, differed nothing in the horror of the scene from those carried about upon spikes at Paris; yet this was done by the English Government.'

Paine was a boy of eight at the time of the Battle of Culloden, and the massacre that followed under the command of the victorious Duke of Cumberland, known as 'the Butcher', and he does not let this further example of British hypocrisy escape him. 'Among the few who fell (i.e. in France) there do not appear to be any that were intentionally singled out. They all of them had their fate in the circumstances of the moment, and were not pursued with that long, cold-blooded, unabated revenge which pursued the unfortunate Scotch in the affair of 1745.'

Looking from the specific to the general, he deepens the argument:

'If we look back to the riots and tumults which at various times have happened in England, we shall find that they did not proceed from the want of a Government, but that Government was itself the generating cause: instead of consolidating society it divided it; it deprived it of its natural cohesion, and engendered discontents and disorders which otherwise would not have existed . . . Whatever the apparent cause of any riots may be, the real one is always want of happiness. It shows that something is wrong in the system of Government that injures the felicity by which society is to be preserved.'

This analysis of the real and apparent causes of public revolt is strikingly applicable in our time to the disorders in Northern Ireland, which have been loosely labelled 'religious' although, as Miss Bernadette Devlin has pointed out in words remarkably similar to Paine's, their root is in social and governmental discrimination. It is a quality of Paine's political thought that it penetrates problems that remain constant in the history of the world's governments.

'It is power, and not principles, that Mr Burke venerates,' Paine adds caustically; 'It is not from his prejudices only, but from the disorderly cast of his genius, that he is unfitted for the subject he writes upon.'

Nevertheless, what distinguishes Paine from so many political writers is his genuine tolerance and common sense with regard to people of other views, taken as a whole. 'There never yet was any truth or any principle so irresistibly obvious that all men believed it at once,' he writes reasonably. 'He that would make his own liberty secure, must guard even his enemy from oppression, for if he fails in this duty, he establishes a precedent that will reach to himself.' And when he remarks that 'laws difficult to be executed, cannot be generally good', we are conscious, once again, of a mind which seems to reach out to problems and attitudes in our own century. The argument was being used, in 1971 and 1972, by opponents of the Industrial Relations Bill, which sets complex legal problems that defy easy solution.

The *Rights of Man*, although in essence a reply to Burke's anti-Revolution attitude and a defence of France and her aspirations, could also be regarded as a blueprint for a new society. Burke had maintained that the Revolution of 1688 had set the pattern of English government for all time, and that the nation could be ruled only by the privileged classes and the aristocracy, for only these had the necessary experience. To Paine this was a violation of democratic human rights, and he maintained, once again, that the privileges of aristocrats and monarchs should not be inherited. All men had equal rights to elect their chosen government, but they could not impose it on the next generation. 'There never did, there never will, and there never can, exist a Parliament, or any description of men, or any generation of men, in any country, possessed of the right or the power of binding and controuling posterity to the "end of time" . . . Every age and generation must be as free to act for itself *in all cases* as the ages and generations which preceded it. The vanity and presumption of governing beyond the grave is the most ridiculous and insolent of all tyrannies. Man has no property in man; neither has any generation a property in the generations which are to follow.'

'I am contending for the rights of the *living*,' was his theme, and he warned that the clauses brought forward by Burke 'serve to demonstrate how necessary it is at all time to watch against the attempted encroachment of power, and to prevent its running to excess'.

Rousseau's *Social Contract*, the springboard of French reform, had opened with the stirring line: 'Man is born free; but everywhere he is in chains.' Paine, analysing the origin of those chains, formulated the three historical bases of government: superstition (rule by priesthood); power (rule by conquest); and the common rights of man (rule by reason). Where the French Revolution was concerned, '*principles*, and not *persons*, were the meditated objects of destruction', although Paine has a perspicacious passage on the spreading tentacles of despotism that the revolutionists had had to destroy:

'When despotism has established itself for ages in a country, as in France, it is not in the person of the King that it resides . . . It has its standard everywhere. Every office and department has its despotism, founded upon custom and usage. Every place has its Bastille, and every Bastille its despot. The original hereditary despotism resident in the person of the King, divides and subdivides itself into a thousand shapes and forms, till at last the whole of it is acted by deputation. This was the case in France; and against this species of despotism, proceeding on through an endless labyrinth of office till the source of it is scarcely perceptible, there is no mode of redress.'

As an analysis of bureaucracy the passage is not without relevance today.

According to Clio Rickman, the first part of *Rights of Man* 'was written partly at the Angel in Islington, partly in Harding Street, Fetter Lane, and finished at Versailles'. A. O. Aldridge in his biography of Paine accepts the statement of William Cobbett, who never knew Paine, that Paine was in hiding in Fetter Lane while making arrangements for the publication of Part II, but this would seem to be a confusion with the writing of a portion of Part I in the Fetter Lane area. Rickman, who was a close friend of Paine throughout this period, maintains that Part II was written when Paine was living with him at No. 7, Upper Marylebone Street, where he resided and had a bookselling and publishing business, and he long preserved the table on which Paine wrote 'several of his invaluable works', with a commemorative brass tablet recording the fact.[1] It is possible, as Aldridge maintains, that Paine began working on this part in France but Paine's presence in France (*pace* Carlyle) at this period is doubtful and there seems no reason to doubt Rickman's word.

It is in this second part of the *Rights of Man*, published in 1792, that Paine gets down to the task of 'Combining Principle and Practice', as he headlines it. 'It is for the good of Nations and not for the emolument or aggrandisement of particular individuals, that Government ought to be established,' he writes, and is optimistic enough to add: 'I do not believe that Monarchy and Aristocracy will continue seven years longer in any of the enlightened countries in Europe.' This was, of course, the fear behind Burke's attack on the Revolution, and behind the amalgamation of other European countries later to make war on France and reestablish the old order. There was a parallel in modern times when White Armies actively supported by Britain and other nations joined forces to try and overthrow the Bolshevik government following the 1917 Revolution. In both cases the common people united to defeat what they looked on as a foreign invasion, and the figureheads used by the invaders—the royal family—lost their lives. The world does not learn from its history.

Paine supports the principle of Republican government while pointing out that a Republic can vary in its forms. 'Republican Government is no

[1] It is now in the collection of the Trade Union, Labour, Co-operative and Democratic History Society (T.U.L.C.).

other than Government established and conducted for the interest of the public . . . It is not necessarily connected with any particular form, but it most naturally associates with the representative form . . . Whatever the form or Constitution of Government may be, it ought to have no other object than the *general* happiness. When instead of this it operates to create and increase wretchedness, in any of the parts of society, it is on a wrong system and reformation is necessary.'

In the region of social welfare Paine, working on a strict economic basis, anticipates social reforms of a century and a half later. He advocates family allowances; universal education ('A Nation under a well-regulated Government should permit none to remain uninstructed'); and an extension of Dr Price's support for the aged, beginning with minor help at the age of fifty (when physical vigour begins to decline) which is increased to a proper pension at sixty. (The Inca civilization destroyed by Pizarro accepted fifty as an age for pension.)

'It is painful to see old age working itself to death,' writes Paine, 'in what are called civilized countries, for daily bread,' and he maintains, long ahead of his time, that these allowances should be *as a right*, not a matter of grace or favour. With the abolition of the Poor Law and indirect taxation, which falls heavily on the poor in the price of the goods they buy, he suggests a grant of £4 per year per head for each child under fourteen, and the payment of maternity benefit of twenty shillings to every woman who applies for it on the birth of a child. The £4 grant should help children under fourteen to be educated instead of being put to work, and 'the number of poor will hereafter become less, because their abilities, by the aid of education, will be greater'. The State should provide work centres for the unemployed, and levy graded estate duty on all estates of over £500 a year.

Paine was also rare in pointing out the curiously ambivalent nature of the class system, and in trying to awaken a sense of personal guilt in the aristocracy by drawing its attention to the fact that it was its own younger sons, grandsons and great-grandsons that, without patrimony, descended rapidly in the social class until descendants could be found among the lower-paid artisans and workers. Thomas Hardy, a countryman, was aware of the anomaly when he wrote *Tess of the D'Urbervilles*, but it is curious how often this legacy of the large, uncontrolled aristocratic families of the Middle Ages onwards is overlooked, even by social historians. In Paine's time the eighteenth century younger sons, in many cases, had nominal jobs and salaries created for them at Court, all putting a heavy drain on the public exchequer and the nation, as he pointed out, while the law of primogeniture ensured that the entire inheritance passed to the eldest son. The injustice, he claimed, was to the younger children themselves as well as to the people taxed to help support them.

The trade union, as a defence system for the workers, did not legally exist until 1824, when the Combination Laws which prohibited workers acting together were repealed. Paine realized the need when he wrote: 'Several laws are in existence for regulating and limiting workmen's wages. Why not leave them as free to make their own bargains as the law-makers are to let their farms and houses? Personal labour is all the property they have. Why is that little, and the little freedom they enjoy, to be infringed? . . . When wages are fixed by what is called a law, the legal wages remain stationary, while everything else is in progression; and as those who make that law still continue to lay on new taxes by other laws, they increase the expence of living by one law and take away the means by another.' The controversy of pegged wages, inflation and rising prices continues in our time.

How valid were Paine's figures? He based them on named financial sources and estimates, including those of his later hostile biographer, George Chalmers, in his 1786 publication, *Estimate of the Comparative Strength of Great Britain*, as well as those of Louis XVI's minister, Necker (father of Madame de Staël), in his *Administration of the Finances of France*. His calculations of the comparative figures, and reading, led him to the conclusion that forty-six millions of pounds sterling had vanished in England since the commencement of the Hanover succession; and he pointed out that the Crown of England, during this period, had been insolvent several times, 'the last of which, publicly known, was in May, 1777, when it applied to the nation to discharge upwards of £600,000 private debts which otherwise it could not pay'.

Was this investigation of the country's finances, and the disappearance of this vast sum, the concealed reason why Part II of *Rights of Man* was considered so much more dangerous than Part I? The heavy expense of supporting the Hanover kings and their numerous relations and Court followers was one target of Paine's attack, and both this and the corruptions involved had been widely mooted. For the first time, with Paine, facts and figures were examined and the deficit named: the suggestion was certainly made that millions had somehow been sifted away without explanation. The popular sales of Part I had given the government food for thought, but although it has been often assumed that Paine's schemes for social welfare were the main thing that alarmed the government, I do not think this is wholly tenable. He gave columns of figures to support his plans but the whole social security operation was largely an examination of possibilities and Paine himself, as a political realist, could hardly have expected its implementation by the Pitt government. It remained something of an Utopian ideal, even though he presented it as a viable project. Those who have challenged it economically have tended to overlook this, and the fact that Paine's economics were founded at least in part on the assumption of disarmament by arbitration treaties, another of his suggestions for the extension of monetary resources. He makes it quite clear, however, that many of the social reforms would save the government money in the long run (as in the case of education, reducing the number of illiterate poor who fall on the state and never realize their potential in value to the community).

The fact that social security has been made to work in our own infinitely more complex capitalist society proves that Paine's vision and figures were not beyond the scope of reason; but the government of his day would hardly have accepted this, within the framework of the established eighteenth century military and economic system. Paine's figures, nevertheless, were largely based on national estimates given in the works of economic writers, French and English, which at least arguably could be taken as authoritative.

It was the attack on the King as a hereditary monarch that laid him open to the charge of 'seditious libel', but Godwin's work, published a year later, was equally anti-monarchial. It is tenable, I think, that Paine was dangerous to the Hanoverian monarchy for financial, not purely political, reasons, as the rebel who produces facts and figures, and argues cause and effect, is always most dangerous to authority.

It should be added that Paine, like Rousseau and unlike Godwin, did not attack private property or land ownership, but he did suggest that the working people of the nation should share in its benefits. Rousseau had maintained that those who had only necessaries should not be taxed at all; those with superfluities should be supertaxed; and there should be a heavy imposition on all luxuries. Paine's system of graded taxation, according to income, was an idea he developed some years later in his pamphlet, *Agrarian Justice*, and he also forestalled Sir William Hardcastle by suggesting a tax on wealth in the form of death duties.

In *Rights of Man* he reached the frontiers of socialism without quite stepping over them (although Marx, unlike the so-called first socialist writer, Charles Hall (author in 1805 of *Effects of Civilisation*), acknowledged Paine's importance as an influence on the future). Socialism, from the point Paine left off, was to be a natural progression. In this Paine was a man of his time. For even Jean Paul Marat, 'the friend of the people', went no further than Paine and Rousseau in this, maintaining the right of private property as a necessary factor in civil liberty, but that 'nothing superfluous can belong to us legitimately as long as others lack necessities'.[1] Property tended to accumulate in the hands of the

[1] *Plan de législation criminelle* (1780). Reprinted by Marat, 1790.

few, wrote Marat, leaving the many in hunger and poverty; and in such inequitable conditions the people could not be obliged to respect the laws of society. If society wished to maintain the established order of things, it ought to provide food, shelter, medicine and clothing for the lower classes, establish public workshops for the unemployed, re-distribute ecclesiastical property and provide free public schools. 'His socialism, like Robespierre's,' writes J. M. Thompson in *Leaders of the French Revolution*, 'was of the old-fashioned kind that would leave the rich man in his castle and the poor man at his gate, but would tax the superfluities of the one to relieve the necessities of the other.'

If Paine's *Rights of Man* seems to echo Marat's book, which he almost certainly would not have read, it is because his ideas, like so many, derived from the whole reforming outlook of the time. It is worth noting that Marat, like Marx and Lenin after him, spent some formative years in London. As a physician, studying medical practice in various countries, he had lodged in St Martin's Lane in 1767–8 and at the London coffee houses professed himself a follower of John Wilkes. From 1774 to 1776 he was again in the British Isles, where he published *The Chains of Slavery* in 1774 and received the honorary degree of Doctor of Medicine at St Andrews University in 1775. 1774 was the year Paine left London for America, and there is no indication if he knew of Marat's work which was meant, at a time of Parliamentary election, to awaken the citizens of England to a sense of their civic duty. Marat's attack on the 'rotten borough' system, the power exerted by the King over Parliament through bribery, and the limited rights of suffrage owing to property qualifications, certainly reflected the whole tone of English reforming zeal some fifteen years later, but Marat still thought the constitution of England 'a monument of political wisdom if compared with others'. He was soon to acquire reasonable wealth (which he later exhausted entirely in publishing his revolutionary writings) as physician to the bodyguard of King Louis XVI's brother, the Count of Artois; but the groundwork of his passionate support of the rights of the people was already laid, only needing the torch of the French Revolution to ignite it.

Something in the temperate climate of England nurtures revolu-tionaries, yet suppresses revolution. Few of the members of England's active revolutionary societies in the 1790s could have realized this, and that their views were for export only. It was not only their fellow radical at Joseph Johnson's, William Blake, who saw the vision of a 'New Jerusalem'; it was part and parcel of the spirit of the age. Of this spirit *Rights of Man*, the name given to the French Declaration of Rights and adopted by Thomas Paine, was the most lucid and forward-looking expression.

XII

PARIS AND REVOLUTION

The success of *Rights of Man* with ordinary people sprang from the fact that it dealt with political problems clearly, in their own language, and without classical erudition or embellishment. It did not write down to them: on the contrary it paid them the compliment of assuming that they wanted facts and figures as well as an intelligible ideology, and could grasp the practical significance of a theory of government based on common sense and reason. As in America, Paine opened men's eyes to the possibilities of a better future, a future they could build with their own hands, and out of their own understanding. Its danger to the *status quo* resided in this. For the first time a book, widely read, pointed out the flaws in the establishment and suggested remedies which could be made both from within and from outside it.

It is not surprising that England's republican societies seized the opportunities that Paine's book offered for propaganda and reprinted 25,000 copies on their own account. Sold at nominal prices (Paine gave his proceeds to the Constitutional Society) these reached even the remoter sections of England and Ireland. The government, who had tolerated the societies as watchable, but probably harmless, examples of English eccentricity, was understandably alarmed. Not only the system, but the authority of the ruling class to control it, were being threatened. For what would become of privilege and the vast network of land ownership if every Tom, Dick and Harry in England began to fancy himself as a potential parliamentarian as well as voter? The revolution across the Channel had already shown how the dam of state could be burst by middle-class lawyers and journalists such as these, with the full flood of popular opinion behind them.

Knowing well that Paine intended a reply to Burke, it seems clear government agents had made some attempt to stifle Joseph Johnson. The tables had been turned by a rapid switch of publishers, enabling a second edition quickly to follow the first. The government brooded, but as yet without full knowledge of the impact of further editions through the societies. And in the spring, while Jordan's second edition still brewed in the printing presses, Paine returned happily and unmolested to France.

The year was 1791, and another climax of the French Revolution was about to explode. On Easter Monday, 18th April, the King and Queen had attempted to leave Paris for their royal residence at Saint-Cloud, supported by Lafayette and the National Guard. It was probably an innocent weekend excursion, an escape to the country and the royal sport of the racecourse, on which the English *jockés*, to Carlyle's contempt, had long been popular for their skill. The Saint-Cloud dinner was already cooking in the ovens, and the royal chapel preparing for the royal communion. But Paris this spring was buzzing with rumours, faint as yet but penetrating, that the King and Queen were planning to escape abroad: to the frontiers, in fact, where invading armies were preparing to restore them to full authority. The mob surrounded the royal carriage, and Lafayette, faced with a threatened mutiny by a section of the Grenadiers, was powerless to intervene.

It was his first open breach with the revolutionaries he had helped to form. 'Lafayette mounts and dismounts; runs haranguing, panting; on the verge of despair,' writes Carlyle, leaning heavily once again on *Deux Amis de la Liberté*. The King and Queen, reluctant and indignant, gave up the project, and returned to their now even more irksome confinement in the Tuileries; but the King rallied enough to complain to the Assembly. Lafayette, in a dramatic gesture, resigned his commission, and refused for three days to take it up again. 'National Guards kneeling to him, and declaring that it is not sycophancy, that they are free men kneeling here to the *Statue of Liberty*,' describes Carlyle. If royal flight was contemplated before it has now become an obsessive determination. Lafayette, once again in charge of the King and his family and beginning to show signs of divided loyalties, is aware of it; the public feels it in its very bones; and Paris waits with bated breath, murmuring with suspicion and rumour.

Paine arrived in Paris sometime before 7 April 1791, when Gouverneur Morris heard of his return. According to Morris' diary, he shared lodgings at first with a Mr Hodges, described by Morris as a 'fellow Traveller', although doubtless not intentionally anticipating the later political significance of the term. Morris, calling and finding Paine out, characteristically reports that Hodges described his fellow lodger as 'a little mad'. If the story is true it may be a reason Paine moved, for Rickman, who could only have had it from Paine, states that he was Lafayette's personal guest at this time. In any case Paine must soon have learned from Lafayette something of the situation. He was already in Paris at the time of Lafayette's abrupt resignation, and reinstatement, after the affair of Saint-Cloud.

How soon did he begin to realize that Lafayette's concern for the royal family was in conflict with his own basically more republican feelings? Lafayette had moved to an unhappy midway position between the people and the monarchy; he was, like Paine's other friend Sieyès,

Bridge over the Wear near Sunderland, built 1793–6 mainly from Paine's design

The National Assembly, Paris

(1)

Sir

Rotherham. Yorkshire
May 25th 1789 --

As I know you interest yourself in the
success of the Useful arts, and are a member of the Society
for the promotion thereof, I do myself the pleasure
to send you an account of a small experiment I have
been making at Mr. Walker's Iron Works at this place

You have already seen the model I constructed
for a Bridge of a single arch, to be made of Iron, and erected
over the River Schuylkill at Philadelphia; but as
the dimensions may have escaped your recollection
I will begin with stating those particulars

The vast quantities of Ice and melted Snow
at the breaking up of the frost, in that part of america,
render it impracticable to erect a Bridge on Piers.
The River can conveniently be contracted to four
hundred feet; the model, therefore, is for an arch of
four hundred feet span; the height of the arch in

the

6. First page of Paine's letter to Sir George Staunton describing the building of his bridge
   model, 25 May 1789

. Marquis de Lafayette

Thomas Jefferson

Robespierre

'Clio' Rickman in 1814

8. William Godwin in 1794, aged 38   Mary Wollstonecraft, by Opie

William Blake   Augustus Henry, third Duke of Grafton ('T
Sporting Duke')

increasingly unable to identify with the mob or its leaders, the Marats, the Dantons, and the Robespierres. The pattern of the American Revolution he had planned to reproduce in France was showing disconcerting signs of an individual reshapement, demanding something more than a replica Washington at its head. On 20th June, the royal family under his guard disappeared overnight from the Tuileries, and according to Rickman's story Lafayette burst into Paine's room the following morning with the cry, 'The birds are flown!'

It was a cry of distress, for whatever Lafayette's secret misgivings about the way the Revolution was going he was certainly the chief officer of the National Guard, and the royal family was entrusted to his custody. Suspicions of his loyalty by the populace were already beginning to stir, and he was a target for accusations of connivance, which indeed in some quarters were made.

Was this, for Paine, the moment of truth? He was, whether on the spot at the time or learning of his anxiety from Lafayette later, astonished at his old friend's attitude. For Paine, it was the best thing that could happen, leaving the way open for a republic, without the disagreeable business of having to decide what to do with a King now obviously disloyal to the Revolution he had pretended to support. The insistence of Lafayette and others that the King must be brought back seemed to him insane, and he is reported to have said so. Certainly, from this moment he was committed to a wholly republican view.

The flight to Varennes was doomed to failure from the start, but it had begun with a clever last-minute concealment in which Lafayette blundered badly, probably accentuating the suspicion of his involvement. When the royal preparations were at their height, at ten o'clock on the evening of the flight, he had called on the King and Queen in response to the general rumours and noticed nothing suspicious, although his unexpected call must have given them a considerable shock. Louis' natural phlegm, and the Queen's resourceful charm and *sangfroid*, carried them over the sudden hurdle; but the plan itself was fraught with absurdities and the amazing thing is that it ever got off the ground.

Although the flight depended on secrecy and disguise it was, of course, impossible for royalty to travel in ordinary, unobtrusive carriages; therefore two enormous and conspicuous berlins were ordered to be specially built. The passport was that of an authentic Russian aristocrat, Madame de Korff, and was held by the royal children's governness, dressed for the part. The King was to be disguised as a footman or valet and the Queen as governess. Nevertheless, both were to travel in unlikely juxtaposition with the children in the foremost carriage, and the Queen insisted on the inclusion of a splendid dressing-case specially made to hold her jewellery, makeup and trinkets. She had also ordered a large and expensive new wardrobe of clothes, presumably to cut a fashionable figure in whatever foreign court she eventually found herself. As a finishing touch, an almost sublime oversight, the great berlins were to be drawn by teams of six horses, a number allowed only to royal personages in France (four was the normal number).

The mind behind this master plan was partly that of Monsieur de Bouillé (who had at least argued for plain English diligences) but largely that of Count Fersen, the young Swedish diplomat known to be passionately attached to the Queen and believed quite widely (although there is no positive proof of this and it is not necessarily true) to be her lover. It seems likely his obsession blinded his judgment and that he was simply not positive enough a character, for all his daring, to induce Marie Antoinette to relinquish her luxuries. Even so, he himself showed extraordinary indiscretion; having acted as 'coachman' from the Rue de l'Echelle outside the Tuileries to the point on the outskirts of Paris where the party transferred to the berlins (even this scatterbrained group had realized that to bring the great new carriages to the doors of the palace would have evoked comment), he saw them on their way and, still dressed as a coachman, entered the carriage he had been driving and ordered the second coachman to drive him back to Paris (a passer-by witnessed and later recalled this democratic event with astonishment). Perhaps the romantic Swede's head was too full of parting's sweet sorrows to take even elementary precautions.

The imprint of failure was set on the whole adventure from the outset. The party of two children, governess, King and Queen left from the Tuileries in relays, on the strength of their disguises. The Queen, accompanied by a loyal young officer of the King's bodyguard, escaped in a fetching wide-brimmed gypsy hat and governess-type gown, but when the pair got outside they proceeded to take the wrong turning and lose themselves even on the short way to Fersen's coach, where the King and children were already waiting. Neither knew Paris well. The Queen, of course, hardly ever put her feet on its pavements, travelling on her rare visits from Versailles to the Opéra by coach; and her escort was either *distrait* by the nature of his charge or equally ignorant. The pair found themselves on the Rue de Bac on the quays and *had to ask their way*. They had almost brushed against Lafayette's passing carriage and been paces away from Danton, Camille Desmoulins and some friends, returning at eleven o'clock from the Jacobin Club.

It is an indication of Marie Antoinette's infrequent appearances in her capital that no one recognized her, even allowing for the bewitching hat. But her state of mind can be imagined: already romantic adventure was turning to frightening reality.

And now, safely berlined and abandoned to their fate by Fersen, they were on their way to the Netherlands frontier. The slow, lumbering berlins, moving like giant armoured snails over the summer landscape, took so long on the journey (including a precious half-hour's delay when the King insisted on getting out of the coach to enjoy the sun and walk alongside) that the body of Hussars waiting near Pont-de-Somme-Vesle to escort the berlins to the frontier gave up their vigil and went to quench their thirst in neighbouring village taverns. Their presence had already been remarked, and only weakly explained away by the story of their waiting to escort a 'treasure' of 100,000 crowns travelling towards the frontier.

At Châlons a friendly posting-master, Oudet, recognized the King and warned him to be careful. The carriages got away with difficulty after coping with fallen horses and an injured postilion. One of the crowd, too, had recognized the King and reported it to the Mayor, a royalist who turned a blind eye. At Pont-de-Somme-Vesle, where the berlins arrived at 4.30 p.m. instead of the arranged time of one o'clock, it was discovered that the Hussars had left with their commander, M. de Choiseul, and at Sainte-Menehould the posting-master, Drouet (a former Queen's Dragoon and ex-Deputy) also thought he recognized the King. He confirmed it by examining the courier's payment of the posting fee in assignats for fifty francs, which carried the portrait of the King. He at once went to the Municipal Council at the Town Hall and on their decision followed on horseback. At Varennes, the royal party learned the Hussars were in the lower town; but Drouet had by then aroused the citizens and stopped the berlins by the simple expedient of seizing a cart with furniture and overturning it in the middle of the bridge leading to the lower town.

Thus ended the celebrated 'flight to Varennes'; not by democratic anti-royalist feeling, as was after mistakenly assumed, but by a Procurator of the Commune named Sauce, Drouet and a crowd in no way abusive or ill-intentioned. 'The citizens opposed the departure of Louis XVI,' wrote M. de Bouillé, 'without however lacking in respect to him. The majority showed their deference openly . . . assuring him that they were compelled to obey the commands of the Assembly.'

In Paris, however, feeling ran high and in an infinitely less deferential manner. Outside Paris the party were met by three Assembly deputies, including Barnave, a lawyer, who travelled in the coach with the Queen and with the Dauphin playing on his knee. He was at once charmed by the Antoinette graciousness into a loyalty that was to cost him dear. The Queen, hated by the crowd who called her 'Madame Deficit' and later 'Madame Veto', and blamed on her most of the King's weaknesses and the country's ills, met adversity from now on with an unflinching dignity that quelled for ever her former frivolities: dredging up, from deep within her character, *genes* of her mother, the Empress Maria Theresa, that few could have suspected her of inheriting. That she could still use her charm as a weapon, the fate of Barnave proved.

The party arrived in Paris at eight o'clock on the evening of 25th June: dusty, exhausted and defeated, yet meeting the hostility of the Paris mob without show of fear. Lafayette met them at the Tuileries, and the mob, not likely to lose its truculence because of his and the National Guard's protection, was mollified to some extent by the young Dauphin, who blew kisses to the people from the carriage. But the Queen was conducted into the palace at some peril, and although the flight was glossed over by Lafayette and the constitutional monarchy continued in theory, the betrayal was neither forgotten nor forgiven.

Mirabeau, who had secretly advised the flight, had died on 2nd April, and been buried with great public ceremony and lamentation in the national Panthéon, followed by a crowd said to number 100,000. Four years later his remains were to be removed to make way for those of the new revolutionary hero and martyr, the murdered Marat, 'the people's friend'. The fissure in his reputation, and that of all the moderate royalist section, began with the arrest at Varennes. From 25 June 1791, when the King and Queen returned to Paris, the way was open for Paine's Manifesto for a republic and the entire holocaust that followed.

During the King's flight Paine had visited his friend Thomas Christie, who was staying at the Palais Royal, and with him and another companion, John Hurford Stone, had gone to the Tuileries, where they found the royal apartments full of people deeply concerned about the crisis but by no means, Paine emphasized, a wrecking or looting mob. 'I unseal my letter to tell you, with the cannon roaring and in the wildest commotion,' Madame Roland had written to Bancal, 'that the King and Queen have fled; the shops are closed, everything is in an uproar. It is almost sure that Lafayette is implicated. This means war.' The fear of war was a real one. 'Louis XVI and Marie Antoinette had been looked upon as hostages securing the emancipated nation from the vengeance of neighbouring monarchies,' as Madame Roland's biographer, Madeleine Clemenceau-Jacquemaire, comments. The invasion feared did indeed take place under a year later. But the immediate panic, like the tocsin, subsided, and Paris settled down to something like normal life and speculation.

The impression, fostered by Hollywood, that the Parisian public throughout the Revolution consisted entirely of bloodthirsty *sansculottes*[1] is an entirely false one. The people of revolutionary Paris were of all

[1] The name, literally 'without breeches', derived from the workers wearing of trousers, instead of the closely-fitting breeches and hose worn by the aristocrats and better-off citizens.

classes and largely what we would today call 'respectable', including the street crowds on all but abnormal occasions. Even the barbarous September massacres of 1792, in which aristocrats in, or being moved from, the prisons were brutally set upon and savagely murdered and mutilated in the streets, were prearranged politically by a handful of extremists, helped by the cut-throat element found in every society. Many aristocrats, as long as they did not meddle in politics, went through the entire Revolution, including the Terror, without harm; and Parisian night-life and gaiety went on a great deal of the time as if the guillotine did not exist. The cafés, brightly lit, stayed open and thrived, and although the theatres were closed in periods of crisis (as during the flight to Varennes), they continued to produce plays to meet republican taste and were often full.

In November 1789, France's greatest actor, François Joseph Talma, himself a revolutionary, made his name in Joseph Chénier's anti-monarchial play, *Charles IX*, quelling a reactionary demonstration in the Théâtre Français and then setting up a rival troupe of his own, the Théâtre de la République. This survived until 1799, when Talma's company reunited with the earlier one to form the Comédie Française. Chénier was to become a Member of the Convention and of the Committees of General Security and Public Safety, writing a play, among others, on Caius Gracchus, one of the two liberal Senator brothers of Republican Rome who were assassinated within a few years of each other: strangely anticipating the fate of the democratic Kennedy brothers in modern America.[1] Joseph Chénier, unlike his brother André, the poet, survived the Terror, although narrowly, like Paine, as he criticized its violence (like Paine he also suffered from hostile propaganda, being for long wrongly accused of bringing about his brother's death).

Another revolutionary dramatist, Fabre d'Eglantine, a former actor, was also to produce plays throughout the Revolution and be associated with Danton in his downfall. It was Fabre who invented the charmingly descriptive names of the months for the new French calendar beginning on 21 September 1792, the day the monarchy was abolished. He was theatrical even in politics. 'His head was one vast imbroglio,' said Danton, as robust in imagery as in personality and physique. On 15 June 1791, five days before the royal family fled, his *L'Intrigue Epistolaire*, a farce in the manner of Beaumarchais' *Barber of Seville*, was produced in Paris, with Talma in the comedy lead, Cléry; and in August he plunged into English history with *Isabelle de Salisbury*, a spectacular costume play set in the reign of Edward III.

---

[1] The historical parallel has not escaped a modern dramatist, Hans Keuls, whose play on the subject, *Confrontation*, was produced in 1971 by the Belgrade Theatre, Coventry, and performed in Norwich and London.

It was Talma, however, who revolutionized the theatre by the introduction of historical accuracy in setting and costume, beginning with a correct Roman toga and haircut in a minor rôle as Proculus in Voltaire's *Brutus*. This reform was to sweep its way later into England, where the great David Garrick and Mrs Siddons had continued performing Shakespeare, and indeed all plays, in the costume of the eighteenth century. As with most political upheavals, the French Revolution brought its sidekick of artistic reforms, and the topical emphasis on plays set in republican Rome gave Talma his opportunity. His great friend Jacques-Louis David, the artist of the Revolution, had educated him in the history of costume, and was later to set the neo-classic tone for Napoleon and the Empire. Talma's reforms went further, meeting the democratic needs of the times with a new realism of acting; 'grandeur without pomp, nature without triviality' as he put it.[1]

It is doubtful if Paine was greatly interested in these theatrical revolutions, although he must have been aware of the plays on the English monarchy, whose genesis had been caustically exposed in *Rights of Man*, soon to be translated into French. English kings were a popular anti-royalist target in the French theatre at this time. In 1791 Talma also appeared as King John, in a curious adaptation of Shakespeare by Ducis called *Jean Sans Terre*, and as Chénier's Henry VIII, with which he opened his new theatre on 27th April. Voltaire's *Brutus*, which Talma revived in May, with scenery by Boucher (an actor in his company) was a memorable production and particularly geared to revolutionary taste. Its anti-monarchial political thesis could be summed up in the lines in Act II:

> *Je porte en mon coeur . . .*
> *La liberté gravée et les rois en horreur.*

It is a curious fact that to many in France at this time Voltaire was known principally as a tragic poet-dramatist. Talma also played in his *La Mort du César* and on 6 July 1791, the part of Lasalle, the examining magistrate, in Chénier's tragedy *Jean Calas*, based on the famous contemporary case of injustice which Voltaire had publicized

Paine would certainly have known the dramatists d'Eglantine and Chénier later as Members of the Convention. His companion in the Tuileries in June 1791, however, was British like himself. Thomas Christie, a nephew of Dr Priestley, was one of the Joseph Johnson literary set, and in fact the Editor of the *Analytical Review* published by Johnson, a kind of eighteenth century *New Statesman*. Christie was later made a Citizen of France at the same time as Horne Tooke, and as a

---

[1] *Reflections on the Actor's Art* (Preface to Lekain's Memoirs), 1825.

friend of Danton he was chosen to translate the new French Constitution into English. It is possibly through him that Paine first met Danton.

On Mary Wollstonecraft's life he was to have a profounder effect: it was at the Paris home of Christie and his wife in 1793 that the author of *Vindication of the Rights of Women* first met her irresolute American lover, Captain Gilbert Imlay, and plunged disastrously from Women's Lib. into the chequered agonies of a love totally dependent on a man's whim, leading to attempted suicide and the near-collapse of her writing career.

It is from the unreliable Oldys that the widely-spread story derives of Paine's near-murder at the hands of the French mob at this time, when he is alleged to have omitted to wear the tricolour in his hat, but to have saved his life when threatened by drawing the badge out of his pocket and explaining it was an unintended omission. It is a good story, but of extremely dubious authenticity: perhaps invented by Oldys/Chalmers, among so much else, to emphasize the bloodthirsty nature of all Paris crowds of this time (it must be remembered his book was commissioned not only to counteract the *Rights of Man*, but to re-emphasize Burke's own picture of the Revolution). Of more authentic interest was Christie's statement, perhaps not word for word but near enough in spirit, that Paine at this time of the Varennes flight remarked to him: 'You see the absurdity of monarchial governments; here will be a whole nation disturbed by the folly of one man.'[1]

Paine, faithful in friendship, could not join Marat, in his paper *L'Ami du Peuple*, and those others who took the opportunity to demand the downfall of Lafayette. But he was ready enough to revive his Republican principles and actively work to disseminate them. He at once wrote and issued a Manifesto, translated by a young French friend, Achille Du Châtelet, who may have slightly altered the text, as it was signed with his name to meet the requirements of the law. It was then, on 1st July, pinned to walls in prominent places in Paris, including the door of the National Assembly. On 2nd July it was printed in full in Brissot's paper, *Le Patriote Français*, with some alarmed and derogatory comments by members of the National Assembly. Even now, the thought of a Republic did not come easily to many leading revolutionaries, in particular the Jacobins, who perhaps with jealous foresight feared the deposition of the King less than the possible rise of a dictator, from among themselves, to succeed him. Even Marat still favoured 'a very limited monarchy' and only supported the Republican party after the establishment of the Republic in September 1792.

It was the Girondists, usually labelled the 'moderate' party of the

[1] Letter in the London *Morning Chronicle*, 29 June 1791. It was written by Christie in Paris on 22nd June.

Revolution, who most clearly saw the dangers of a continued monarchy. Madame Roland, like Paine, had from the first considered the flight of Louis XVI 'far from being a misfortune, for the hatred of kings and the word Republic were yesterday voiced in every quarter'. She was dismayed at the Assembly's inertia, and easy acceptance of the old political position as soon as the King returned, for she foresaw that Louis would continue to obstruct the Assembly and would soon make use of the armies of France's enemies.

Brissot had proclaimed himself a Republican as early as 1787, and was to lead the Girondist party into power and finally into disaster. He had many qualities which Paine, like so many English and American radicals in Paris, must have found sympathetic. He had been in America, and was founder and first secretary of the *Société des Amis des Noirs*, formed to defend the negroes of the West Indies, and still very active in France. He and his followers also fraternized with 'the generous Quakers of England', as Bancal, now secretary of the *Amis des Noirs*, called them. Although he allowed contrary opinions in *Le Patriote Français* his own republican sympathies would have been with Paine.

In the journal of the *Société Républicaine* Paine on the same day published an article extending the ideas of the Manifesto. He attacked once again the principle of hereditary monarchy, and made history by referring to the King, for the first time, as 'Louis Capet'. Going deeper into his article, he challenged Montesquieu's theory that republicanism can only be successful in the smaller nations ('Liberty diminishes the larger the state becomes', Rousseau had also warned), and saw in a Constitution the remedy for French, as well as American, ills. 'Only when the French Constitution conforms to the *Declaration of Rights* can France be justly entitled to be called a *civic empire*; because then only will its government be the empire of laws based upon the great republican principles of Elective Representation and the Rights of Man.'

In fact, the King accepted a Constitution in September 1791: a gesture which did not convince many, remembering the flight to Varennes three months before. 'As to the personal safety of Louis Capet,' Paine had written, 'it is so much the more confirmed, as France will not stoop to degrade herself by a spirit of revenge against a wretch who has dishonoured himself.' The throne was to survive another year; but it was no longer safe. Paine's hand, and those of the four other members he declared later had formed the brief-lived *Société Républicaine*, had moved it fractionally near the abyss.[1]

Before his return to England, Paine in July engaged in a cor-

[1] The five members were not named by Paine and are not certainly known. Conway conjectured Paine, Du Châtelet, Condorcet, Brissot and Nicolas de Bonneville, another journalist and later Paine's close friend.

respondence-at-arms with Sieyès, who in a letter to *Le Moniteur* had defended the system of monarchy as compared with a republic. A trimmer of sails, who later was to explain his survival of the Terror with the succinct *J'ai vécu*, Sieyès had been preparing to take the place of Mirabeau in handling the vacillating King, when the King had devastated his plans by his flight, obviously long prepared. In 1796 Joseph Lakanal declared that Condorcet, who published Paine's *Le Moniteur* reply to Sieyès simultaneously in the *Républicain*, had told him that the correspondence was deliberately pre-arranged by Sieyès, Paine and himself to provide a further opening for republican propaganda. Lakanal as a result considered 'Condorcet, Thomas Paine and Sieyès as the first founders of the republic in France'.

Although not at first sight likely, Sieyès' complicity is possible if one considers it in the light of his disgust at the King's duplicity, at a moment he was giving him his support. In 1790 he had founded the '89 Club with Condorcet, whose republicanism was unquestionable. It was Sieyès who had named the 'National Assembly' and taken a principal part in establishing the new system, helped by his influential *Qu'est-ce que le Tiers-Etat?* in 1789. His later fading out of politics (he was to return to them actively in the clearing-up after the Terror) was not only the result of a well-developed sense of preservation, but a natural disinclination to sustain a battle in power politics. His intellectual approach and often quoted *bon mots* gave him a certain detachment: he was philosopher first, politician second, writing:

'The influence of reason is a phenomenon which few men are able to appreciate. The love of humanity, the desire for a perfect society, and the passionate attachment of the upright mind to objects of such grandeur as these, are beyond their mortal reach; they cannot believe in them. They do not even understand that political science (*l'art social*) can win the attention and rouse the enthusiasm of artists in philosophy just as the musician, the painter, and the architect are absorbed by the charm of painting, the taste for beautiful buildings, or the search for perfect harmony.'

Later, Napoleon was to sum up his support with his usual shrewdness: 'It may have distressed Sieyès to find me a stumbling-block in the way of his metaphysical ideas; but he came to realize the necessity that some-body should govern, and he preferred me to anyone else.'

An attempt to prosecute Paine and Du Châtelet within the Assembly soon petered out, and Paine left Paris in July for London, leaving his republican theories to simmer, suppressed but not forgotten, on the ovens of the Revolution, which were steadily increasing in heat.

XIII

THE LAST YEAR IN LONDON

Paine was accompanied on the journey to London by a young radical Scotsman, Lord Daer, and Etienne Dumont, a Genevan who had been Mirabeau's secretary. Dumont was sour on the subject of Paine and his *Rights of Man*:

'He believed that his book on *The Rights of Man* could take the place of all the books of the world, and he said to us quite sincerely that if it were in his power to demolish all the libraries in existence he would do it without hesitation so as to destroy all the errors of which they were the depository—and with *The Rights of Man* begin a new chain of ideas and principles. He knew by heart all his own writings and knew nothing else.'

The final tag gives away Dumont's own ignorance of Paine's work, which by quotation and discussion showed a good deal of serious reading. Paine, sincerely concerned about the errors of society his *Rights of Man* sought to check, may well have made some such remark as Dumont suggests, on the purely hypothetical basis of discussion(who brought up the subject of demolished libraries?). But it is necessary also to note that Dumont's literary plan to bring Mirabeau from the tomb to explain away the King's flight to the Assembly, and urge them fully to restore the King to power, had been frustrated by the publication of Paine's republican Manifesto. 'I determined, for fear of evil consequences to myself,' wrote Dumont in his *Souvenirs sur Mirabeau*, 'to make Mirabeau return to his tomb.'

Paine arrived in London in time for the commemoration of the fall of the Bastille arranged by the Revolution Society, on 14th July, at the Crown and Anchor Tavern, but he missed it on doctor's orders, due to exhaustion after the journey. Horace Walpole, whose *Historic Doubts* included one of the first attempts to dispel some of the Tudor propagandist distortions about Richard III, was not so prepared to question political propaganda of his own time. 'The villain Paine,' he reported, had returned from France specially to attend the Revolution Society's commemoration, but 'finding that his pamphlet had not set a straw on fire, and the 14th of July was as little in fashion as the ancient Gunpowder Plot, he dined at another tavern with a few quaking conspirators.' It is a statement that, in view of the facts, might well encourage a new volume of *Historic Doubts* on the tales told by Horace Walpole.

Paine did on 22nd July attend a meeting of the Society for Constitutional Information, a club formed in 1780 and now, under the stimulus of the French Revolution, probably the largest, most active and influential of the several English Jacobin-style societies. Horne Tooke was one of its most prominent members, and in April the Club had strongly supported Paine's *Rights of Man* and printed a cheap edition. On 4th August a meeting of the same Club to commemorate the abolition of the feudal system in France was prevented by government agents, who frightened the landlord of the Crown and Anchor into refusing the members admission. On 20th August another meeting was convened at which Paine gave an address, an ironic comment on the reduction in English taxes imminent if, as the English government maintained, the seventeen million pounds spent annually on military defence had been due to the aggrandisement ambitions of the French Court. The Revolution, he pointed out, had dismissed such ambitions and rendered the huge sums spent on defence unnecessary. It was published under the signature of Horne Tooke (the Club's chairman) as *Address and Declaration at a Select Meeting of the Friends of Universal Peace and Liberty, Held at the Thatched House Tavern, St James' Street, August 20, 1791.*

Some of it shows the lines on which Paine was already working in Part II of the *Rights of Man*:

'We are oppressed with a heavy national debt, a burthen of taxes, an expensive administration of government, beyond those of any people in the world.

'We have also a very numerous poor; and we hold that the moral obligation of providing for old age, helpless infancy, and poverty, is far superior to that of supplying the invented wants of courtly extravagance, ambition, and intrigue.

'If we are asked what government is, we hold it to be nothing more than a national association; and we hold that to be the best which secures to every man his rights and promotes the greatest quantity of happiness with the least expence. *We live to improve, or we live in vain . . .*'

Government suspicion of the Society for Constitutional Information was not without its reasons, for it had active and prominent branches in a number of industrial towns, notably Sheffield and Manchester. A review in the *Athenaeum*, on 15 June 1901, of R. E. Leader's *Sheffield in the Eighteenth Century* noted:

'Sheffield was foremost among the more democratic towns of the kingdom towards the end of the century in acclaiming, by ox-roasting, cannon-firing, and immense processions, the triumph of "our French brethren over despots and despotism". In 1794 "the Society for Constitutional Information", composed of those who saw in the French Revolution a summons to Englishmen to rise on behalf of liberty, grew bolder, and held a great meeting on Castle Hill, where the crowd sang to the tune of the National Anthem a song beginning "God save great Thomas Paine".'

For most of 1794 Paine was in a French prison, desperately ill and expecting execution, and the cheering news of Sheffield's acclaim could not have reached him. In the circumstances its expression of admiration for the French Revolution might have seemed to him ironic. But he would probably have known of, and been warmed by, the Sheffield Constitutional Society's declaration on 14 March 1792, that they had 'derived more true knowledge from the two works of Mr Thomas Paine, intitled "Rights of Man", than from any other author on the subject'.

In January 1792, a club more closely allied to the working class, the London Corresponding Society, was founded by Thomas Hardy, a shoemaker, and again *Rights of Man* was taken as an acknowledged inspiration. Universal suffrage and annual parliaments were among the reforms it advocated. Paine knew Hardy—who indeed was a prominent figure among contemporary radicals and a victim of the 1794 treason trials—but was not a member of the Society.

Hardy as a shoemaker seems not to have been irreproachable (perhaps the time spent on his political activities was at the expense of his craft). But many well-known radicals were loyally shod at his shop, and expressed their occasional sufferings, in private, with commendable resignation.

During this last period in London from 1791 to 1792, Paine lived mainly with Thomas Rickman. Rickman gives a pleasant picture of his way of life:

'Mr Paine's life in London was a quiet round of philosophical leisure and enjoyment. It was occupied in writing, in a small epistolary correspondence, in walking about with me to visit different friends, occasionally lounging at coffee-houses and public places, or being visited by a select few. Lord Edward Fitzgerald, the French and American ambassadors, Mr Sharp the engraver, Romney the painter, Mrs Wolstonecraft (*sic*), Joel Barlow, Mr Hull, Mr Christie, Dr Priestley, Dr Towers, Col Oswald, the walking Stewart, Captain Sampson Perry, Mr Tuffin, Mr William Choppin, Captain De Stark, Mr Horne Tooke, &c. &c. were among the number of his friends and acquaintance; and of course, as he was my inmate, the most of my associates were frequently his. At this time he read but little, took his nap after dinner, and played with my family at some game in the evening, as chess, dominos, and drafts, but never at cards; in recitations, singing, music, &c.; or passed it in conversation; the part he took in the latter was always enlightened, full of information, entertainment, and anecdote. Occasionally we visited enlightened friends, indulged in domestic jaunts and recreations from home, frequently lounging at the White Bear, Piccadilly,[1] with his old friend the walking Stewart, and other clever travellers from France, and different parts of Europe and America. When by ourselves we sat very late, and often broke in on the morning hours, indulging the reciprocal interchange of affectionate and confidential intercourse.'

He also quotes Tooke, the wit, on what must have indeed been a remarkable meeting, that between Paine and the celebrated Madame, or Chevalier, D'Eon, who dressed as a woman but about whose sex there was much speculative eighteenth century society gossip.

'I am now' (writes Tooke) 'in the most extraordinary situation in which ever man was placed. On the left of me sits a gentleman who, brought up in obscurity, has proved himself the greatest political writer in the world, and has made more noise in it, and excited more attention and obtained more fame, than any man ever did. On the right of me sits a lady, who has been employed in public situations at different courts; who had high rank in the army, was greatly skilled in horsemanship, who has fought several duels, and at the small sword had no equal; who for fifty years past, all Europe has recognized in the character and dress of a gentleman . . .'

The speculation was fully justified and Rickman adds a definitive if macabre personal note to this famous eighteenth century transvestite story:

'If this same Chevalier D'Eon had been lost at sea, burnt, or had in anyway left the world, unknown and unnoticed, all Europe would have believed he was a woman . . . and yet this was not so. In 1810, soon after his death, I saw and examined this mysterious character; and that he was incontestibly a man, a chevalier, and not a madame, is most certain . . .'

On 4 November 1791, Paine at a dinner of the Revolution Society at the London Tavern proposed the toast of 'The Revolution of the World'. The anniversary being commemorated was the 1688 Revolution and deposition of James II, and Paine's ringing phrase was to echo down the

[1] The White Bear was on the site now occupied by the Criterion Theatre and Restaurant.

centuries until and after the 1917 Bolshevik Revolution. The official response never differed: fear, propaganda, and often the suppression of workers' organizations or freedom of speech. By the time it was known a second part of *Rights of Man* was in the presses, government agents were on the alert.

The printer was this time a Thomas Chapman, to whom Paine had been introduced by Thomas Christie. But in the middle of January 1792, Chapman returned the MS to Paine and refused to continue. Paine made quite clear later that he considered Chapman had been 'got at' by the government, and reported Chapman had earlier offered him £1000 for the complete copyright. This Paine refused, on the characteristic grounds that it would have left him without control over any alterations to his original script, or indeed its complete suppression ('he would not alter a line or a word, at the suggestion even of a friend', wrote Rickman). His impression was that this offer was government-inspired. It was, in fact, the third offer, the first two being of £100 and £500 respectively: the stepping up of the offer to such a large sum was, of course, in itself suspicious. Later, after Paine had left for France, Chapman at his trial for seditious libel maintained he had refused to print the MS after Paine had insulted his wife and been in a 'rather intoxicated' state. It is significant this is the only accusation of Paine's being intoxicated up to this time and even Chapman added this was 'rather unusual'. Paine's hostile 1791 biographer, Oldys/Chalmers, does not mention his drinking to excess.

The general content of the book has been discussed in Chapter XI, but it must be added here that Paine's Preface to Part II, dated 9 February 1792, seizes with satiric emphasis on Burke's recent *Appeal from the new to the old Whigs*, which quoted ten pages from *Rights of Man* and then added that he would 'not attempt in the smallest degree to refute them'—'meaning', writes Paine, 'the principles therein contained. I am enough acquainted with Mr Burke to know that he would if he could. But instead of contesting them, he immediately after consoles himself with saying that "he has done his part". He has not done his part. He has not performed his promise of a comparison of Constitutions. He started the controversy, he gave the challenge, and has fled from it.' He naturally does not spare Burke on the matter of his overt threat that the book's principles could probably be contested '*if such writings shall be thought to deserve any other refutation than that of criminal justice*'. The warning did not daunt Paine, but in view of it his later prosecution could not have come as a complete surprise. His Preface anticipated this to the degree of becoming a passionate defence of freedom for the writer. 'Mankind are not now to be told they shall not think or they shall not read; and publications that go no further than to investigate principles of Government, to invite men to reason and reflect and to shew the errors and excellencies of different systems, have a right to appear.'

He was, though, expecting too much of the Pitt government if he imagined they would not act, and act decisively, to counteract a book whose Introduction stated: 'If universal peace, civilization, and commerce are ever to be the happy lot of man, it cannot be accomplished but by a Revolution in the system of Governments. All the monarchial Governments are military. War is their trade, plunder and revenue their objects. While such Governments continue, peace has not the absolute security of a day . . . Government founded on a *moral* theory, on a system of universal peace, on the indefeasible hereditary Rights of Man, is now revolving from west to east by a stronger impulse than the Government of the Sword revolved from east to west. It interests not particular individuals, but Nations in its progress, and promises a new era to the human race.' And authority thus reacting, would not take much notice of Paine's commonsensical note of caution: 'The danger to which the success of Revolutions is most exposed is that of attempting them before the principles on which they proceed, and the advantages to result from them, are sufficiently seen and understood.'

The Dedication to Part II (also written in February 1792) was to Lafayette, showing that Paine did not share French distrust of the General's monarchial motives. 'The only point upon which I could ever discover that we differed,' wrote Paine, 'was not as to principles of Government, but as to time.' Lafayette's time limit was to prove considerably more elastic than Paine's.

The *Rights of Man*, Part II, was taken over by another printer, in fact J. S. Jordan, who had similarly succeeded Johnson as the publisher of Part I. It was published on 16 February 1792, and was sold both by Jordan and Paine's old publisher friend, Joseph Johnson. Paine had 'covered' Jordan, at least in his own mind, by sending him a letter—presumably for production if challenged—naming himself as the sole author and publisher. He also instructed Jordan to contact him through Johnson or Horne Tooke in the case of any difficulties.

Nevertheless, proceedings were soon taken against Jordan and Paine, returning to London from a visit to Bromley, arranged an attorney for him. Jordan, apparently frightened and thinking acknowledgment of fault would help him, angered Paine's friends by pleading 'guilty'. On 21st May, the date of a royal proclamation against writing, printing and selling seditious works, the Government also began proceedings against Paine, and on 8th June issued a trial summons for seditious writings. Paine attended Court, but the trial was postponed until December.

On 25th May there was a debate in the House of Commons on the proclamation, which Fox opposed as a subtle step towards complete censorship not only of writings but of free political organizations. If it were aimed against Paine, he maintained, it should say so openly. Henry Dundas, Secretary of the Home Office, declared proceedings had been taken against Jordan because Paine could not be found: an announcement that stung Paine into a letter of protest. Dundas made clear the true source of the danger in the government's mind when he mentioned that the book's principles had been adopted by the revolutionary societies 'and sedulously inculcated throughout the kingdom in a variety of shapes'. The inevitable result of the publicity, of course, was to increase the book's sales.

Paine, still living with the Rickmans, does not seem to have been shaken out of his placidity, apart from his open letter to Dundas on 6th June. He remained with the Rickmans in Marylebone until he left for France on 12th September. His passage, nevertheless, had become stormy enough. In April he had been arrested at the London Tavern by a bailiff on behalf of a Mark Gregory and others, for a reputed debt of two hundred pounds. An hour later Joseph Johnson and another friend, George Wilkie, provided bail and the whole affair seems to have been a complex mistake which petered out. Although the *Morning Chronicle*, often giving space in its correspondence columns to radical writers, reported merely Paine's withdrawal from the meeting, after which 'his health was given', the rest of the press made much of the incident and by the time Paine left for France the country was ringing with anti-Paine propaganda, a lot of it inspired, of course, by Oldys' book. (Paine never apparently challenged this, although he showed himself contemptuously aware of its coming publication and rumoured authorship. The centre of an admiring circle of friends who well knew his true character, he never seems to have been much bothered by defamations of his enemies, perhaps accepting them as inevitable.) Effigies of Paine were burnt in Staines, Leeds, Camberwell and Bristol, and after he left for France the November newspapers still reported demonstrations: apparently, like the burning of Priestley's Birmingham house in July, led by a handful of ruffians in government pay.

A paper on 21st November threw out an amusing hint of Paine's involvement with the radical dramatist Holcroft:

'An Exciseman, *till unmasked,* is the best guide in the kingdom to shew JOHN BULL, if he is weak enough to follow him, the *sure Road to Ruin.*'

On 22nd November, a paragraph headed 'Chelmsford, Essex', reported:

'On Wednesday last, the Effigy of that Infamous Incendiary, Tom Paine, was exhibited in this town, seated in a chair, and borne on four

men's shoulders;—in one hand he held the "Rights of Man" and under the other arm he bore a pair of stays; upon his head a mock resemblance of the Cap of Liberty, and a halter round his neck.
    'On a banner carried before him, was written,
Behold a Traitor!
Who, for the base purposes of Envy, Interest and Ambition,
Would have *deluged* this Happy Country in
BLOOD!'

The effigy was hanged on a gibbet, forty feet high, and then fired, to the accompaniment of muffled drums beating out the Dead March.

Nevertheless, the final summing-up is interesting, for it does not suggest the crowds that gathered round these ceremonies were always necessarily in sympathy with them, or out of sympathy with Paine:

'This awful ceremony was conducted with the greatest decorum, and seemed to make a very different impression upon the minds of those who were assembled, than such spectacles are in general intended to produce, as the whole proceeding appeared to convey a testimony of steady loyalty and honest resentment, without the least indecency, confusion, or tumult.'

Certainly the report of the reticence of the crowd seems equivocal.

Paine's parting with Rickman on 12th September was not to be final, and they were to meet again in France. According to Rickman, Achilles Audibert came to the house expressly 'from the French Convention . . . to request his personal assistance in their deliberations'. In fact, Audibert came from Calais, which was one of four French constituencies (another was Versailles) to invite Paine to represent them in the National Assembly. On 26th August, the Assembly had conferred the title of French citizen on a number of distinguished foreign sympathizers, including Paine, Priestley, Bentham, Wilberforce, Clootz and Washington (Schiller was added soon afterwards). After Paine's arrival, it was to add, among others, three of Paine's friends, Horne Tooke, Thomas Christie and the American poet, Joel Barlow.

The accompanying invitation signed by Louvet and thirty-two others, representing nine communes, in respect of Paine's election as representative of Puy-de-Dôme must have deeply appealed to Paine:

'Your love for humanity, for liberty and equality, the useful works that have issued from your heart and pen in their defence, have determined our choice. It has been hailed with universal and reiterated applause. Come, friend of the people, to swell the number of patriots in an assembly which will decide the destiny of a great people, perhaps of the human race.'

F

Jean Baptiste Louvet was a young author made famous by his romantic novel, *Faublas*, and in 1791 his *Emilie de Varmont* (translated into English in 1798 with the sub-title *Divorce dictated by necessity; to which are added the amours of Father Sévin*) embellished the revolutionary scene with a complicated love story and plea for easier divorce. His own love life had been complicated by a young woman, the greatly romanticized heroine of *Faublas*, whose elderly husband refused to divorce her, although she was already in love with Louvet when her family forced her into the marriage at the age of fifteen. From 1789 she and Louvet lived together in indignant sin, but mutual adoration, until the death of the husband enabled them to marry and live happily ever after: to the disappointed surprise of admirers of Louvet's first novel, who found on investigation that the romantic originals of Faublas and his loved Lodoiska were in fact a distinctly plain-looking pair.

In May 1792, Madame Roland mentioned in her notebooks of accounts the payment of 500 francs to Louvet 'to draw up a newspaper under the title of *Sentinelle*'. It was to be a government propaganda newspaper or, as Madame Roland delicately put it: 'Roland paid for the printing from a small sum he had collected in the ministry for the formation of the public mind.' (Her husband was Minister of the Interior.) The first number of *La Sentinelle* appeared on 16th May, and the famous pink broadsheets did much to arouse public feeling against the Court. In September 1792, Louvet entered the Convention and had the supreme satisfaction of witnessing the passing of a divorce law aimed to dissolve marriages with exemplary speed.

The invitation to Paine that carries his signature was dispatched early the same month. But Calais had elected Paine on 6th September, two days before Puy-de-Dôme, and Paine had already responded to the personal invitation of Achilles Audibert.

This, and not the coming trial, was the immediate reason for his leaving England. Nevertheless, his departure was long said to have been precipitated by an overnight warning from William Blake that government agents were about to arrest him. This story originated with Frederick Tatham, who printed the illustrated 'Songs of Innocence and Experience', after Blake's death, from plates he inherited from Blake's wife Catherine. It was stated categorically by Dr Henry Collins in 1969[1] to be 'untrue', but his source for this denial, David V. Erdman's *Blake: Prophet Against Empire*, produces no evidence except the purely negative. As Erdman's monumental work of analysis of Blake and his imagery makes clear, Blake moved and worked in the Joseph Johnson circle and his radicalism, unlike that of many of the English revolutionaries,

---

[1] Introduction: *Rights of Man*. Pelican edition: one of the best analyses of Paine's political significance.

remained unshaken and staunchly Jacobin even after the disillusions spread by the Terror. Although there is no direct evidence, apart from Blake's own word in old age, it is inconceivable that he did not meet Paine, as all the rest did, between July 1791, and September 1792; and in fact Paine figures as Godred in his anti-monarchial allegory, *Gwin*, and also in Blake's *America* alongside Washington and Franklin. Paine was Blake's 'scribe of Pensylvania', the 'worker of miracles' able 'to overthrow all the armies of Europe with a small pamphlet' (i.e. *Common Sense*).

It is not by accident that Blake, like Paine, speaks to our own time with a voice, for all its complex prophetic imagery, that has a contemporary appeal. And the term he invented, 'Republican Art', is understandable in our age in which 'Pop Art' has become a recognized part of modern expression. In Blake's own time, he was thought to be mad; in ours, he is the subject of the art book, the critical biography, and National Theatre experiment.

Blake undoubtedly was a 'queer fish', as Shaw described another visionary, Saint Joan, but he and Paine had much in common politically and in outraged human feeling. The one may well have reacted on the other and there are a number of evidences of this in Blake's work. Both regarded the sadistic suppression of the negro slaves in San Domingo and Dutch Guiana with horror. In November 1791, Paine was writing to William Short, U.S. Chargé d'Affaires in Paris:

'We have distressing accounts here from St Domingo. It is the natural consequence of Slavery and must be expected everywhere. The Negroes are enraged at the opposition made to their relief, and are determined, if not to relieve themselves to punish their enemies.'

And in the same year Joseph Johnson, according to Erdman, 'distributed to Blake and other engravers a sheaf of some eighty sketches of the flora and fauna and conditions of human servitude in the South American colony of Dutch Guiana during some early slave revolts. With more than his usual care Blake engraved at least sixteen plates, including nearly all those which illustrate slave conditions.' These included the pitiful and horrifying 'Negro hung alive by the Ribs to a Gallows' which with the others eventually appeared in Captain J. G. Stedman's *Narrative of a five Years' expedition, against the Revolted Negroes of Surinam, in Guiana, on the Wild Coast of South America*. In blow-up form it has appeared with others of Blake's engravings of slavery as background to one of the most striking and moving scenes in *Tyger*, Adrian Mitchell's satiric 'celebration of William Blake' produced in 1971 by the National Theatre in London.

The common link with Johnson could have brought together Blake and Paine on this matter, for slavery and the Guiana situation had

deeply concerned Paine in earlier works. The French Revolution link—
with both men producing answers to Burke, both intended for publication by Johnson—and the American one (i.e. Blake's *America*) are
obvious. Erdman assumes that Tatham's 'Friends of Liberty' (an
apocryphal society at which Paine is supposed to have made an incendiary speech shortly before Blake's warning) must have been the Friends
of Universal Peace and Liberty, which is possible, but there is no ground
for his assumption that the speech referred to by Tatham was actually
the one given on 20 August 1791, and that Tatham mistook the year for
1792 and thus Blake warned Paine 'a month or so' (*sic*) before he left for
France. Tatham could have misremembered the name of the society,
partly or completely, and Paine could have spoken to any of the
republican societies at this time.

Erdman is not completely reliable on Paine; for instance, in quoting a
statement that Blake 'rebuked the profanity of Paine',[1] he questions it
only on the grounds of Blake's motto of this time, 'Damn braces. Bless
relaxes', but does not remark on the fact that Paine, the Quaker's son,
was never known to swear, and the story is thus doubly unlikely. Paine's
aversion to swearing is vouched for by several friends, including the
young painter Jarvis in his old age.

In one thing in 1792 Paine would not have pleased Blake, the anti-
Royal Academy artist. At Rickman's insistence Paine sat for George
Romney and Sharp's engraving of this portrait, published as frontispiece
in Rickman's book, was said by the author to be a wonderfully speaking
likeness of Paine, by far the best ever done of him. (William Sharp, a
friend of Rickman's, had been introduced into the Constitutional
Society by Horne Tooke, and probably knew Paine personally.)
Certainly Romney seems to have captured a personality as firmly here
as he had earlier captured the dew-fresh country bloom of the young
Emma Hamilton. With Paine, now fifty-five years old, he caught a face
thoughtful yet alert, full of maturity and character, with the large eyes
giving the whole intelligence and vivacity. The high forehead and bold
nose suggest mental capacity and vigour, and the unpowdered hair is
still quite dark, as indeed it remained until his death at seventy-two
years. Conway possessed a lock of hair taken from the skull preserved by
William Cobbett and given him by Cobbett's biographer, Edward
Smith. He described it as 'soft and dark with a reddish tinge'. An
American portrait of Paine in old age by his young painter friend, John
Wesley Jarvis, also shows hair of 'dark brown, shot through with grey'.

The best evidence against the Blake-Paine story is that Rickman, with
whom Paine was staying when he left with Audibert, does not mention

[1] A letter from Samuel Palmer in 1855, published in Alexander Gilchrist's *Life of
William Blake* (1863). Gilchrist also gives a full account of Blake's warning of Paine.

it; but this is not necessarily conclusive. The Gilchrist version has it that Paine left after Blake's warning, given at a gathering at Johnson's, without going back to Rickman's house in Marylebone, and that by the time he reached Dover the officers were at the house. It is made clear in this account that Paine was about to go to France in any case; it may be straight from the meeting which could have been a farewell one. It is interesting that Gilchrist adds that the artist Fuseli, a close friend of Blake's and well known to the Johnson-Godwin circle, affirmed Paine 'to be more ignorant of the common affairs of life than himself even'. Fuseli certainly knew both men. Godwin's image of the religion that 'sees God in clouds and hears him in the wind' is rather Blakean, perhaps deriving from contact with the poet or his work.

It is apparent there had been active agent activity around the Johnson circle, and Paine was being watched. 'The Intelligence Department was strengthened. A coast waiter named Charles Ross had absented himself since June from the shores of Spithead to watch Paine at the house of his friend Clio Rickman, and keep the government posted.'[1] Ross or another government spy may well have got wind of Paine's imminent departure and, in view of the coming trial, intended to stop him. Blake would not need to use his prophetic powers to stumble on this, or suspect it. The fact that his name—rather than that of any other of the radicals—is mentioned suggests there must have been a reason to connect him with Paine at this time. There is no direct evidence that Paine was pursued to Dover and only just got away, as has often been published, but it is true he and Audibert were subjected to long personal search at the Customs. The fact that he was allowed to leave in spite of the coming trial has always seemed surprising; and a certain amount of secrecy, or at least discretion, must have been exercised. It is possible that Rickman, writing in 1811 and publishing in 1819, when government censorship of radical material and persecution of publishers of it was still active, would not want to emphasize his own connection with any irregularity in Paine's departure.

Dr Collins thought any attempt of Paine to flee 'uncharacteristic'; but as he obviously intended to take up the French Convention offer, in preference to standing trial, it would be natural for him to hasten departure if there were any question of his being prevented from leaving. In the circumstances it does not seem logical to suggest his evasion of arrest showed lack of courage, whereas his acceptance of the Calais deputyship did not. It was a matter of sensible choice, in all the circumstances.

Paine and Audibert were accompanied by John Frost, a liberal

[1] P. A. Brown: *The French Revolution in English History* (Allen & Unwin, 1918: Frank Cass, 1965).

attorney,[1] and the search at Dover was described by another passenger, J. Mason, as well as by Paine himself in a letter to Dundas dated 15th September. The contents of Paine's trunk were not unimpressive:

'Among the letters which he took out of my trunk were two sealed letters, given into my charge by the American minister in London (Pinckney), one of which was addressed to the American minister at Paris, the other to a private gentleman; a letter from the president of the United States, and a letter from the secretary of State in America, both directed to me, and which I had received from the American minister, now in London, and were private letters of friendship; a letter from the electoral body of the department of Calais, containing the notification of my being elected to the National Convention; and a letter from the president of the National Assembly informing me of my being also elected for the department of the Oise (Versailles) ... When the collector had taken what papers and letters he pleased out of the trunks, he proceeded to read them. The first letter he took up for this purpose was that from the president of the United States to me. While he was doing this I said, that it was very extraordinary that General Washington could not write a letter of private friendship to me, without its being subject to be read by a custom-house officer. Upon this Mr Frost laid his hand over the face of the letter, and told the collector that he should not read it, and took it from him. Mr Frost then, casting his eyes on the concluding paragraph of the letter, said, I will read this part to you, which he did; of which the following is an exact transcript—"And as no one can feel a greater interest in the happiness of mankind than I do, it is the first wish of my heart that the enlightened policy of the present age may diffuse to all men those blessings to which they are entitled and lay the foundation of happiness for future generations." '

There is small doubt that the imposing nature of this correspondence helped to get Paine his clearance, and it is interesting to conjecture if the travellers had armed themselves with a legal adviser to meet just such a contingency. Frost certainly seems to have taken charge to some effect. If Paine and Audibert were prepared for trouble, this would give credence to the story of Blake's warning. The Washington letter was presumably the one in which he acknowledged, nine months later, Paine's gift of fifty copies of *Rights of Man*.

Mason's account in a letter the day after the packet sailed, 13th September, records more humiliating details of the search and shows

---

[1] John Frost had been an ally of Pitt in his reform days, and was now an associate of Horne Tooke. In June 1793, he was sentenced to six months imprisonment, and struck off the register, for his political activities.

obvious animosity towards Paine, probably fed by the press campaign against him:

'The packet was followed till out of the pier, which might be a quarter of an hour, by numbers of people to stare at Tom Paine as they called him. He was hissed a great deal, and many ridiculous speeches made relative to his trade (he has been a stay-maker at Dover). The crowd increased very much: the wind being slack the packet was obliged to be towed out: I believe had we remained much longer they would have pelted him with stones from the beach. Personally he is a very mean looking man. It is in my opinion a disgrace to them, rather than a merit, that a better representative cannot be found at home without having recourse to a foreigner like him. He is the very picture of a journeyman tailor who has been drunk and playing at nine-pins for the 3 first days of the week, and is returning to his work on Thursday. We arrived at Calais, and as soon as he was known to be on the shore, the people flocked to see him, and it was talked of saluting him with the guards as he passed the Place d'Armes. It rained hard, and I left him.'

This is the only English reference to drunkenness (if that is what Mason's ambiguous description meant), apart from Chapman's comment of an 'unusual' occasion of it at Paine's trial a few months later. It is noticeable that it is only almost complete strangers who refer to Paine as either slovenly or dirty. Rickman gave an attractive description of Paine at this time:

'Mr Paine in his person was about 5' 10" high; and rather athletic; he was broad shouldered, and latterly stooped a little.

'His eye, of which the painter could not convey the exquisite meaning, was full, brilliant, and singularly piercing; it had in it the "muse of fire". In his dress and person he was generally very cleanly, and wore his hair cued, with side curls, and powdered, so that he looked altogether like a gentleman of the old French school.'

It is the picture one would expect of a man who rubbed shoulders on equal terms with men of a high social level, none of whom ever endorsed the accusations of uncleanliness, boorishness or drunkenness that came with his notoriety. Rickman takes pains to disclaim bias: 'I am not disposed to advocate the errors and irregularities of any man, however intimate with him, to suffer the partialities of friendship to prevent the due appreciation of character, or induce me to disregard the hallowed dictates of truth.'

Rickman's own distinguished family background and classical scholarship are not likely to have made him an enthusiastic host, within his home circle, to the kind of man Paine's hostile passing acquaintances described. We must, I think, believe him when he writes that 'during his residence with me in London in and about the year 1792, and in the course of his life previous to that time, he was not in the habit of drinking to excess; he was clean in his person, and in his manners polite and engaging; and ten years after this, when I was with him in France, he did not drink spirits, and wine he took moderately . . . That Mr Paine had his failings is as true as that he was a man, but to magnify these, to give him vices he had not, and seek only occasions of misrepresenting and vilifying his character is cruel, unkind and unjust.'

Paine did not depart from England, however, without leaving behind a little bombshell in the form of a *Letter Addressed to the Addressors on the Late Proclamation*. It was an open appeal for revolution, all other attempts to change the system having failed, and it was published in the autumn after he had left to take his seat in the National Convention. He was not, of course, calling for 'bloody revolution' but for the by-passing of Parliament and the election of a national convention to establish a new Constitution: the electors to be every man of twenty-one years or over, irrespective of profession or property. This was a form of universal male suffrage not even conceived at the time. It is significant Paine does not include women: he was no real campaigner for women's rights. Only Mary Wollstonecraft, in *Vindication of the Rights of Women* (1792), dared even to 'drop a hint which I mean to pursue some future time, for I really think that women ought to have representatives, instead of being arbitrarily governed without having any direct share allowed them in the deliberations of government . . . But in order to render their private virtue a public benefit, they must have a civil existence in the state, married or single.'

Paine proposed the elected convention should re-examine the whole political and social system and review the nation's laws: disposing of the dead wood and retaining the best for the ultimate good of society. It was a theory of government in direct opposition to Burke, whose whole conception was based on the past with only the minimum of slow evolution.

Soon, in France, Paine was to see the dangers when the fabric of government is subjected to too great and insufficiently planned a strain of innovation, by men whose good intentions are not matched by unity of purpose. It is by no means certain that the course of revolution would have taken the same path in England; and in any case for over a hundred years English society was to be split, blood spilled and prisons and transportation ships filled, in the desperate resistance to change. Change came, but at a price paid heavily by workers and reformers over a prolonged period. Paine, the practical idealist, was not necessarily at fault in wishing to speed the process; he was, like so many students of politics, simply ahead of his time.

XIV

THE NATIONAL CONVENTION

Paine was to stay in France for an historic ten years, embracing the attempted reforms of the National Convention, the displacement of the Brissot government and Danton, the Reign of Terror, the fall of Robespierre, the Directory and the rise of Napoleon to a status which, within two years of Paine's departure, was to lead to his enthronement as Emperor. It was a decade that moved like a boomerang, cleaving through the ideals of liberty and equality that had grown out of the century of the enlightenment, and leaving standing, at the end of its curved flight, a few shaken men of the Revolution, solitary stalks of wheat in a harvested field. It was Paine's last period in active politics, the harbinger of an old age of journalistic activity, but basic neglect and disillusion. In some ways, those who fell in the Terror were luckier than those who remained; not even America was to fulfil Paine's hopes, for reaction extended across the Atlantic to create a new spirit of the nineteenth century.

Paine's idealism, like that of many others, was too apt to close its eyes to realities which did not fit into the glowing revolutionary picture. Paine arrived in France at the end of a summer torrid with fear and violence. War between France and Austria had broken out in April 1792, Prussia had joined Austria and the French attempt to invade the Netherlands had collapsed. Brissot and his party, known widely as Girondists because so many deputies came from the Bordeaux area, rose to power on the crest of the policy of war, fermented by the popular distrust of the Royalist emigrés, food shortages in Paris and rebellion in the provinces. The embittered Robespierre, leader of the pacifists, attacked Brissot's war, as he called it, in a series of speeches at the Jacobin Club; out of office, he was awaiting his turn to rise, a formidable, livid-skinned opponent, incorruptible and, as it proved, irrepressible.

Events were to play into his hands: indeed had begun to do so as long ago as 17th July the previous year, a 'bloody Sunday' when a peaceable demonstration petitioning for the deposition of the King at the altar in the Champ de Mars had been fired on by Lafayette's National Guard, and a proscription had sent Danton, Marat and Robespierre into momentary retreat. The 'Massacres of the Champ de Mars' were not forgotten when, on 28 July 1792, the Duke of Brunswick, commander of the Austro-Prussian forces, issued a proclamation (drafted by the

Queen's Swedish admirer, Count Fersen) threatening the destruction of Paris if the royal family were harmed. This was because in June the people had, in fact, invaded the Tuileries, on the rumour, among others, that Marie Antoinette had betrayed the French plan of campaign to the Austrians. They had been dispersed once more by the National Guard, but the only result of the Duke of Brunswick's Manifesto was the formation of an insurrectionary Commune in Paris and another assault on the Tuileries on 10th August, when the King's Swiss Guards were slaughtered almost to a man, in a demonstration of crowd vengeance which shook the forces of moderation.

The massacre was not one-sided; a number died, too, among the Marseilles volunteers who had made their epic march from the Mediterranean to the capital the previous month, singing the stirring new song composed and sung in April at a musical party of the Mayor of Strasbourg, by a young captain in the Corps of Engineers, Rouget de Lisle. It was a patriotic song aimed at the German invaders, not the royalists, as misinterpretation has sometimes assumed; nor were the Marseilles 'patriots' all heroic. The element of rabble struck fear in some places; but their achievement created wonder, their song stirred the pulses of all good *citoyens,* and their deaths were mourned by a public that had taken them to their heart, dancing with them the *farandoles* so popular in the streets of revolutionary Paris. Although some of them died the song went on, irresistible and deathless, until it became the French National Anthem on 14 February 1879. De Lisle made nothing from the song; he died in poverty in 1836, living on a tiny inadequate pension granted by Louis-Philippe.

Lucile Desmoulins, young and loving wife of the handsome revolutionary journalist and poet Camille, has left a vivid and touching account of the fears of that night of the 10th August, when her husband and Danton came and went on mysterious errands, leaving the two wives petrified, sleepless, and spasmodically alone. This was the domestic background to Revolution, the living humanity behind the politics and insurrections. The immediate result was the confinement of the royal family in the Temple and a new spirit of revolution in the National Assembly, calling for the revised National Convention to which Paine was elected in September. Danton, on 11th August, became Minister of Justice; and the three ministers recently unwisely dismissed by the King—Servan, Clavière and Roland—were unanimously re-elected. The Jacobin-Girondin collaboration, however, was uneasy; and the Jacobins were now tugging fiercely at the reins of power.

Worse, however, was to come in the new wave of panic in September, when the Austrians and Prussians invaded France, the Commune ordered mass arrests of reactionary suspects, and the massacre of these prisoners from 2nd to 5th September cast a shadow of implication upon Danton (who was not directly responsible, although Marat apparently was) which was never entirely dispersed. Ostensibly a section of the mob got out of hand; but the moving of the prisoners from the prisons into the streets was prearranged. Fear of royalist reprisals on their families when they left Paris to fight in the army was given as a cause by some participants, but it could not have been the whole truth of a massacre which passed all the bounds of barbarity. Somehow equilibrium was restored, and on 21st September, two days after Paine arrived in Paris, the National Convention declared a Republic. The calendar was eventually changed as from that date. It was no longer 1792; it was Year One of a new era.

For a moment party conflict was buried in relief; for on 20th September Dumouriez, ex-Minister of War and now supreme commander of the French northern army, had defeated the enemy at Valmy, 'the Thermopylae', as he called it, of the French Republic. The retreat of Brunswick and the Prussians, struggling north out of Verdun decimated by dysentery and famine, was described by Goethe who took part in the campaign: 'like Pharaoh through a Red Sea of mud, for here also lay broken chariots, and riders and foot seemed sinking around'. It was five weeks since they had entered the town from the south, spreading panic and massacre in Paris. Goethe had heard with a sense of 'a new era in the history of the World' the singing of the Marseillaise by the triumphant French troops, accompanied by massed army bands and the roll of drums.

The revolutionists could breathe again; though more than ever alert to the dangers of the King and Queen as figureheads of foreign attack.

When Paine reached Calais on 13th September invasion was still spreading alarm in Paris, in all wars too close to the frontier for comfort; and the blood of the September massacres was scarcely dry in the streets. The news of these massacres did not reach England until after Paine left and the shadow of invasion did not cloud his Calais welcome, which must have done much to bolster his ego. A salvo of guns saluted the arrival of the packet; soldiers lined up alongside the new deputy; and a pretty young woman set a tricolour cockade in his hat, accompanied by a speech of welcome. The crowd shouted '*Vive* Thomas Paine!' and at the Town Hall he was received and embraced by the Municipal officials, and edified by a speech from the Mayor. Paine replied to Audibert's translation of this to the effect that his life would be devoted to the service of the French people.

Paine lodged at an inn on the Rue de l'Egalité, and left for Paris on

16th September. On the 20th he attended the night meeting of the Convention; John Frost, who was present, described his reception as one of excitement and curiosity. Paine, he wrote, 'entered his name on the roll of parliament, and went through the forms of office with a great deal of nonchalance'. More English than he cared always to admit, he was, however, 'rather fatigued with the kissing'.

In spite of emotional displays of welcome, however, the French could not spend much time on their new foreign deputy. Lack of knowledge of the language, however, was not to deter Paine from participation, although inevitably the need for an interpreter was to hamper his activity and influence to some extent. Almost immediately, on 22nd September, he was to cross swords with Danton on a judicial issue: a not unheroic duel when one considers that Paine had no legal training whereas Danton had been called to the Bar in 1785 and was now the new Minister of Justice. The question was that of the election of judges, whom Danton had moved should be chosen from any section of the community irrespective of legal training or knowledge of the law. Paine, through a colleague, Goupilleau, resisted so revolutionary a measure on the commonsense grounds that justice could only be effectively administered by men of good legal knowledge and training, and that reforms in the law, if necessary, could only be effective if planned as a whole, not in sections.

Paine won his point, and Danton capitulated, probably because as a lawyer his fundamental instinct corresponded with Paine's. He countered Paine's objection with the suggestion that in general he agreed with him, he was not advocating that the system should be changed immediately, but felt the selection of judges should be widened. From the revolutionists' point of view, Danton's proposal was not as unwise as might at first sight appear; the judiciary was known to be obstinately anti-revolutionary and the problem was to replace reactionary judges with those at least more basically in tune with the new state. Paine, in fact, over-eager to put in his oar, was not truly conversant with French affairs and it may be from this moment that Robespierre, at least, began to look at the celebrated American republican with new, and colder, speculation.

Robespierre, destined to die at the age of thirty-six, was one of the oldest of this astonishingly young generation of revolution makers. Danton was a year younger: the new deputy Saint-Just, whose implacable doctrine and elegant good looks were to earn him the nickname of 'the Angel of Death', was just twenty-five, and would die, with proud and stoic loyalty, alongside Robespierre at scarcely twenty-seven years old. The old republican Paine could have been father-figure to these political descendants of the American Revolution; but as is the way with political father-figures his ideas were outdistanced by those of the younger generation they helped to form. The Girondist ministers were mainly maturer men; Roland an old man compared with his wife, who directed so much of his affairs, Dumouriez over fifty, Brissot approaching forty, and like the young Lafayette bred in milder American revolutionary ideals.

It was true that Jean Paul Marat, the fiery prophet of *L'Ami du Peuple*, was now fifty, and the spearhead of the most savage radical journalism. As long ago as 1774, as we have seen, he had written *The Chains of Slavery*, among many medical and scientific tracts, and he alone of the new Left (not even Danton, loved of the proletariat, ever seemed quite a part of it) not only embraced the cause of the people but became as one with them, flaunting his allegiance with the bedraggled locks and red cap of the genuine *sansculotte*. A small, monkey-like creature, who at one political crisis had proposed not inaptly to escape disguised as a jockey, he spread fear and repulsion in the hearts of many Girondists.

In October 1792, the month following Paine's arrival in Paris, he was to create alarm and despondency by gate-crashing a party held by Talma and his wife Julie, honouring the victor of Valmy, General Dumouriez, who had snatched a few days' leave in Paris to discuss the strategy of the war. Marat's and Dumouriez' account of their clash naturally varied in the telling, Marat's in the *Journal de la République Française*[1] of 17th October being conspicuous for puritanical contempt of theatrical bohemia ('I shall not mention a dozen fairies whose purpose was to decorate the feast. Perhaps politics was not the purpose of their presence there.') Additional scorn was heaped on 'all henchmen of the Federal Republic' indulging 'in orgies in an actor's house with ballet-girls from the Opéra'. 'Finally,' he wrote, though he used the word as loosely as Dogberry used 'sixth and lastly', 'I shall not mention the master of the house who in his stage costume mingled with them all.'

Julie Talma's *salon* rivalled that of Madame Roland in revolutionary Paris, although her background, until she married Talma and produced twins histrionically named Henri-Castor and Charles-Pollux, was somewhat less virtuous. She was some years Talma's senior, but deeply attached to him, and much liked for her sweetness of nature. Her twins were to die young of consumption, and she was later to lose Talma to a younger rival, but no hint of tragedy as yet dimmed the sparkle of her *salon*. Theatreland duly blazed at Marat's imperviousness to stage greatness and his use of the word 'orgies', which indeed libelled in this case a highly respectable political after-theatre party, its range extended by a marquee in the garden of the little Talma house in the Rue Chantereine. Nor were political feathers deruffled by the shouts of the

---

[1] His new paper had replaced *L'Ami du Peuple* on 25th September.

newsboys selling Marat's paper on the streets: 'Party given to the traitor Dumouriez at Talma's house!'

The 'traitor Dumouriez' was not a totally misleading description, as events later proved. Marat, like a scribe of Count Dracula, dipped his pen in the blood of his victims; but he was sometimes a shrewd as well as a ferocious journalist. Nor was he impishly unaware of the effect he created: 'I noticed that my presence disturbed the general gaiety; . . . I am the scarecrow of the fatherland's enemies.' Scarecrow perhaps; but the actress Louise Fusil was able to preserve enough detachment to see him with a painter's eye: 'I saw Marat for the first time in my life and I hope it will be the last. But, if I were a painter, I could do his portrait, so much did his face impress me. He wore the carmagnole and around his head a dirty red bandana handkerchief, in which he had probably slept for a very long time. Greasy hair slipped beneath it in strands and round his neck was a choker loosely tied.' The bath in which Marat nine months later met his celebrated death did not, indeed, represent a high Roman taste for ablutions but was his balm for the irritant skin disease from which he suffered.

The *sansculotte* front he presented to the world was, nevertheless, as much publicity image as nature. However much Marat despised the actors, even the actors of the Théâtre de la République, he had all the histrionic instincts for which the French revolutionary leaders were notable. And like so many of them, when he put down the tools of trade of the political orator and journalist, he lived in austere simplicity and inspired deep domestic devotion. In Marat's case this came from Simonne Evrard, a young woman whom he had married 'according to the rites of Rousseau' and who not only devoted her fortune to financing his writing, after his own resources were exhausted, but cared for him with complete self-abnegation. Like most of his colleagues, too, he worked with extraordinary concentration and almost without rest, giving on his own estimate only two hours of the twenty-four to sleep, and as much as six 'to listening to the complaints of a crowd of unfortunate and oppressed people who regard me as their defender, to forwarding their claims by means of petitions or memorials, to reading and answering a multitude of letters, to supervising the printing of an important work that I have in the press . . . and lastly to editing my paper.' (It was Marat's editing of his paper in cellars, often in hiding, that gave the movement of the radical Left its permanent soubriquet of 'Underground'. It became a legitimate description after 10 August 1792, when the Paris Commune presented him with the Royal presses, taken from the Louvre and set up for Marat in the cellar of the Convent of the Cordeliers.)

He adds that he has not taken a quarter of an hour's recreation for more than three years. Nor was this hypocrisy: 'I like Marat,' Napoleon told Gourgaud, 'because he is honest: he always says what he thinks.' Marat's concern for the poorest people was as genuine as his hatred of those who he believed oppressed them. And under the pressing burden of overwork the hatred exploded into neurotic vindictiveness.

To an extent this pressure of overwork was shared by most of the leading revolutionists: even Madame Roland worked at her husband's affairs as Minister of the Interior with unremitting intensity, allowing not even her newly discovered, disturbing emotional feelings for the handsome young Norman deputy, François Buzot, to divert her from her task. She kept her bloom; but it is patent that others did not. 'An account like this,' writes J. M. Thompson of Marat's confession in a psychologically perspicacious passage, 'suggests that not enough attention has been paid to the medical history of the Revolution. Marat's "yellow aspect" that we have already observed, and the skin disease that might have saved Charlotte Corday the trouble of killing him; Mirabeau's ruined eyesight; the paleness of St. Just; and Robespierre's "sea-green" complexion; are they not all symptoms of physical ill-health due to overwork, nervous strain, and lack of sleep and exercise? Do they not go far to explain the atmosphere of personal and party passion in which the early promise of the Revolution was unfulfilled?'[1]

Paine, who wrote much (far too much, throughout his life, for the occasional accusation of 'laziness' to be credible), still at fifty-five kept his country-bred, ruddy complexion and robustness; but Paine, in spite of Quaker inhibitions in some directions, knew also how to play, and to enjoy life in his own way. The virulent personal hostilities felt by Marat were unknown to Paine until, significantly, a long illness in the Luxembourg prison left him broken physically and for a time partly paralysed. It was only then that he launched into the bitter attack on Washington —who had made no effort to get him released as an American citizen— which was to cast a shadow on his name as a writer and surprise even the devoted Rickman into shocked regret. A healthy balance between duty and recreation may be the basic secret of political tolerance.

Danton, who seems to have liked Paine, was, like his friend the actor-dramatist Fabre d'Eglantine, a profligate in the sense that Paine never was; and if his enjoyments did not make him financially scrupulous they may have helped to preserve his comparatively easygoing outlook. Danton was fierce only when France as a nation was at stake; soon his patriotism was to lift him to the pinnacles of public confidence. Whatever his connections with the massacres of 10th August and early September, they were negative and indirect; a case of non-intervention, not deliberate planning, though he was not above reaping the benefits.

[1] *Leaders of the French Revolution* (1929: Basil Blackwell, Oxford, 1968).

His massive pock-marked ugliness was of the kind that attracted as well as repelled. Madame Roland shuddered fastidiously at 'this repulsive and atrocious face', as she referred to it, with its 'brutal passions . . . half-concealed under the most jovial of manners, an affectation of frankness, and a sort of simple good-naturedness'. His obvious, almost cheerful, corruption revolted her: he had, she recorded with puritanical incredulity, 'drawn 100,000 *écus* one day, 60,000 another, still more at another place, without giving any accounting to the Assembly'. Doubtless the face of this Titan needed lined pockets for support in amorous adventure; in the end, that was Danton's tragedy and downfall. The leap from poverty-stricken lawyer to a minister of power was too heady. Yet the face did not prevent his delicate first wife from nearly dying of fear for his safety, in Lucile Desmoulins' arms, on the night of 10th August; and the new young wife, Sophy, whom he married in the June before his death, accepted him gladly. He was, like Paine, a countryman, continually returning to his loved Arcis as to a refreshing spring of life. His retirement there with his bride in the autumn of 1793 was to lose him, fatally, his hold on the Convention.

It was Robespierre, when he returned, who had gripped the reins of power, and stamped his imprint on the Convention. Already, in 1792, he was a force to be reckoned with. Basically, he and Paine had curious affinities. Incorruptibility was one; dislike of war and the death penalty had been others. Both, moreover (with almost equal uncertainty), have been conjectured impotent with women. Their liberal moral code had a common key, and so had their attitude to priestcraft, which retained a belief in religion without superstition, of which Robespierre's cult of the Supreme Being was to be the strange outward manifestation. It was one of the numerous anomalies of Robespierre's enigmatic personality that he had, as a young Arras lawyer, given up a good position obtained for him by his patron, the Bishop of Arras, because it involved hearing the passing of the death sentence. When in Paris in May 1791, Paine had heard Robespierre's speech in the National Assembly proposing the abolition of capital punishment; it was, declared Robespierre passionately, punishing murder with murder. 'Since judges are not infallible, they have no right to pronounce irreparable sentences.' Soon Paine was to remind Robespierre of this 'humane and excellent oration', which had deeply impressed him.

But Robespierre's ascetic zeal for Rousseau principles, even his championship of the people whom he had found his most spellbound hearers, was not 'humane' in the sense that Paine's or even Marat's concern for them was humane. 'This man believes everything he says', Mirabeau had noted, and although it was true and Robespierre was in no sense a hypocrite, he was too inturned and withdrawn a personality to give himself to any fellow creature except in abstract principle. This was his philosophy; when it came to translating principle to action he was only, by supreme irony, to achieve it with the Terror.

If Paine's personality had suffered at all from denigration, it had only acquired ego in the form of pride in his works, those expressions of revolt against a political system so destructive to human happiness. His personal diffidence was expressed in his sober, even careless, form of dress, and his outgoing spirit in a capacity to make friends in spite of shyness in strange company. Robespierre's hatred of the same social system was equally intense, and equally sincere; but early ridicule by journalists of his high voice and inadequate delivery had bred a dangerous narcissism, which could be seen in his almost foppish retention of aristocratic clothes and powdered wig, and in the multiplicity of portraits and busts of himself which visitors were surprised to find lining his study. At the flower-decked Festival of the Supreme Being, which he arranged not long before his death, it was difficult not to get the impression that Robespierre himself was the object of worship, rather than the worshipper.

The neurotic twitchings that marked his oratory, and which he hid to some extent in the Assembly by wearing tinted spectacles (which some found even more frightening), are possibly psychologically revealing. Robespierre was an orphan whose mother died when he was seven and whose father deserted him. He had won a good scholarship and in his early practice as a lawyer was so proud of one of his legal successes, defending a client who had been sued by his neighbours for erecting a lightning conductor, that he sent a copy of the case to Franklin, that magnetic inventor of the conductor. He had never lacked a sense of duty and had conscientiously provided for his younger brother and sisters, as soon as he could do so. His brother Augustin was his devoted follower, and he was loved, before and after death, almost fanatically by the family of Duplay, the carpenter, with whom he lodged quite humbly in Paris. (He was said to be engaged to the elder Duplay daughter, Eléonore, although if so he was as undemonstrative as a computer. The younger daughter, Elizabeth, committed suicide when he and her young husband, Saint-Just's friend Lebas, were arrested, and her mother did the same. Eléonore survived, but never married.) People sometimes hate what they cannot understand; but they can also be magnetized by it, lavishing a love which seems to flower without watering.

Robespierre, like Paine, was wedded to his work; but the marriage became an obsession, which was to destroy many and ultimately himself. His small, pointed face with its greenish eyes often gave people the impression of a cat; and like a cat he was mysterious and inaccessible, locked in a world of his own. No one ever had the key, and how much his cult of virtue was a substitute for emotional or sexual inadequacies, no one can truly know. His sincerity burned like ice; but it was genuine, like his ideals. Saint-Just, his most fanatic disciple, had the same icy flame of conviction; but his moral integrity had been spread consciously, like a cloak, over his youthful libertinism. He rejected his mistress when she followed him to Paris; but at least he had a mistress to reject. Saint-Just assumed a virtue though he had it not; Robespierre's was not assumed, but innate to the man.

To Paine in 1792, Robespierre was the young fellow idealist whose speech against capital punishment had so won his respect the year before. Nor had Robespierre been indifferent to Paine's achievement. He had described Paine as 'one of the most eloquent defenders of the rights of humanity' and in June 1792, three months before Paine returned to France, he had mentioned the *Rights of Man* in his journal, *Le Défenseur de la Constitution*. This was in an article attacking Lafayette, who had dropped behind the times with his outlook and had on 16th June written a letter to the press uncompromisingly baiting the Jacobin Club. After the revolution of 10th August, he failed to persuade the King and Queen to accept his plan for their escape. The Queen, who had never forgiven his support of the Revolution, was said by both Malouet and de Moleville to have refused his help, and Madame de la Tour du Pin, who knew both Lafayette and Marie Antoinette well, wrote in her *Memoirs*: 'The Queen's unbounded hatred of him, which she showed whenever she dared, did however embitter him as much as his gentle, almost foolish good nature permitted.' He finally threw in his hand and left the country. Ironically, on crossing the frontier, he was promptly imprisoned in a succession of dungeons for five years by the Prussians and Austrians, who looked on him as a revolutionist and an enemy.

It is doubtful if Paine, on his return to France, knew of his plight. That Lafayette had at last rejected the Revolution, in its new phase, he must have known. Soon, he would begin to suspect why. At the moment he knew only that he was apparently in good favour in the Convention, and that *Rights of Man*, like *Common Sense* and others of his works, had been published successfully in translation by François Lanthenas, a friend of the Rolands and a Vice-President of the Jacobin Club. It was he who had introduced Madame Roland to Louvet, thus launching *La Sentinelle*; but the Girondists, since the 10th August, were no longer the dominating state party and Barbaroux, the Girondist from Marseilles, when writing in retrospect of a meeting with Roland and Lanthenas, was to refer to 'that Lanthenas who since then so odiously abandoned his friend and the cause of Liberty'.

The reasons were more complex than Barbaroux realized. Lanthenas had long been accepted by Madame Roland as a 'brother', lodging at one time with the Rolands and closely in their confidence, but the friendship on Lanthenas' side went deeper. He was, in fact, in love with her. Now Buzot had moved into her life and heart and Lanthenas' bitter jealousy had forced her to break with him. (He was far quicker to grasp the situation than her elderly husband, to whom, in fact, she remained faithful and devoted.)

Lanthenas by September was moving to the Left. Paine became his friend, and it is as wrong to associate Paine exclusively with the Girondists (as some biographers have done in trying to stress his 'moderation'), as to associate him exclusively with the Jacobins. The party lines were not always rigid, and Paine's ideology was in many ways Jacobin rather than Girondist. Perhaps Madame Roland sensed this, for she did not take greatly to Paine when she met him, and underrated his practical politics (it is also possible his association with Lanthenas aroused her distrust). Until Robespierre moved from normal Jacobinism into Terror, his doctrines and Paine's had many points of contact. Their political ideals remained much the same; it was the means, not the end, that opened between them a vast gulf.

The gulf was to yawn at Paine's feet far sooner than he could have realized. But his first 'Address to the People of France', translated and delivered before the Convention on 25th September, was both adulatory and optimistic. As that true citizen of the world he had always proclaimed himself to be, he welcomed the honour of his adoption as a Citizen of France and Member of the Convention, seeing it as a 'barrier broken down that divided patriotism by spots of earth, and limited citizenship to the soil, like vegetation'. He is encouraging on the war: 'The interference of foreign despots may serve to introduce into their own enslaved countries the principles they come to oppose. Liberty and Equality are blessings too great to be the inheritance of France alone.' He shows a sense of the unavoidable agitations and confusions following 'the great change' of the 10th August; but looks forward to the 'establishment of a new era, that shall blot despotism from the earth, and fix, on the lasting principles of peace and citizenship, the great Republic of Man'.

Was he perhaps aware, nevertheless, of some of the unleashed forces of suspicion—the coming 'Law of Suspects'—around him? It was a strange feature of Paine's work that it was so often prophetic of the future. 'Let us punish by instructing, rather than by revenge', he concluded. 'Let us begin the new era by a greatness of friendship, and hail the approach of union and success.' Disunity was to be the predominant feature of the Convention during the coming year, the quality above all others which was to destroy the work begun so auspiciously in 1789. Paine's sixth sense once again seems to have been on the alert.

His hopes, however, must have been high when on 11th October he was appointed to the Committee of nine formed to frame a new Constitution. By this new Constitution, he told Danton (a confidant perhaps principally chosen because Danton spoke fluent English), 'France must speak for other nations who cannot yet speak for themselves'. An internationalist by ideal and travel, already the citizen of three nations, he was supported by Anacharsis Clootz, a wealthy Prussian baron who was the only other foreign deputy to the Convention. Clootz envisaged a world republic and became a Jacobin extremist, which did not save him from the guillotine early in 1794.

Only three of this Committee of nine survived the Terror, Barère, Sieyès and Paine. It met for several months, and the new Constitution was adopted, after many amendments, on 25 June 1793. It was then suspended on account of the war.

As in America, Paine's practical work for a government, apart from writing, was destined to be brief and insignificant. The language barrier in France could not have helped. At the end of his long life, one has a sense of talents wasted, which in politics today, in the democratic framework, would almost certainly have been used more creatively. It was in America that his knowledge and intuitive grasp of political theory could have been most gainfully employed. In July 1791, Jefferson, Madison and Edmund Randolph had attempted to find a place for him as postmaster in the Washington administration. 'Besides the advantage to him, which he deserves,' wrote Madison, 'an appointment for him at this moment would do public good in various ways.' The idea was discouraged by unknown forces on the grounds that it would be difficult to keep a vacancy unfilled until Paine returned from Europe. Had he been approached, he might well have chosen to return to America in 1791, and the history of his last years been changed not only for the 'public good', but his own.

While Paine was becoming acclimatized in the Convention he did not neglect other political interests; and in October the Irish question, never long dormant in any age, intruded. The young radical Lord Edward Fitzgerald, who had fought in the British army in the last year of the War of Independence, had come to Paris hoping to seek French help in an Irish revolution to throw off the British yoke; and Paine's magic in making friends with much younger men still worked.

'I lodged with my friend Paine,' wrote young Fitzgerald to his mother, the Duchess of Leinster, on 30th October, '—we breakfast, dine and sup together. The more I see of his interior, the more I like and respect him. I cannot express how kind he is to me; there is a simplicity of manner, a goodness of heart, and a strength of mind in him, that I never knew a man before possess.'

This Celtic enthusiasm inevitably aroused Paine's will to help and he petitioned the French government to aid the revolutionaries, suggesting the gift of £200,000 sterling (to be returned in the event of the rebels' success) in preference to a landing of troops. But Fitzgerald, not the first Irishman with more optimism than judgment, had overrated the readiness of his own countrymen. Colonel Oswald was dispatched by the French to gauge the situation and possibilities and reported the country in economic chaos and disunity. His unfavourable comments extinguished the enterprise before it was begun, for the French had other and more immediate problems on their hands. Yet within six years the great Irish Rebellion of 1798 exploded, with Paine as one of the acknowledged heroes of the United Irishmen, led by Theobald Wolfe Tone, while France was moving away from revolution and towards military despotism. It was an irony of which the rebels, who included both Protestants and Catholics, were not yet fully aware: perhaps France was not yet fully aware of it herself. The revolution in France had seemed a beacon to many of the eighteenth century Irish, oppressed alike by British masters and Irish landlords; and the Jacobin influence was early seen in the short hair fashions adopted from the *sansculottes*. Belfast was illuminated to celebrate the execution of Louis XVI. But the expected help from France did not arrive in 1798 any more than in 1792, the United Irishmen movement was betrayed by spies, and the government search for arms, neither the first nor the last of its kind, finally broke up the movement with violence and torture.

Edward Fitzgerald, who had joined the rebellion in 1796, was among those mortally wounded. He died in captivity in 1798, aged thirty-five years. When the small French force eventually landed in the West there was little that could be done: it was too late. Mayo rose, but the French were soon captured and made much (as uncomprehending foreigners have often made much) of the general unreliability and fecklessness of the Irish. Disunity (and the intervention of the Orangemen) helped to quench the Irish revolution much as it had helped by now to quench that of the French. The age of enlightenment and reason was waning with the century.

XV

TWO TRIALS

Outside the Convention Paine led a pleasantly social existence, living at White's Hotel which was later known as the Hôtel de Philadelphie, as a tribute to the American and English colony domiciled there. Here he met again the American poet Joel Barlow, who had been a visitor to Rickman's house when Paine was staying there earlier that year. Barlow's *Vision of Columbus*, an enthusiastic poetic reconstruction of the War of Independence which many years later he expanded and retitled *Columbiad*, had won him an exaggerated reputation as America's first epic poet in 1787; its main interest today is that it directly influenced Blake in his *America*. Barlow was a well-known republican on both sides of the Channel; Joseph Johnson had published his *Advice to the Privileged Orders* and also his *Conspiracy of Kings*. He and his wife Ruth had now settled in Paris, where he was involved in some rather dubious merchant propositions, apparently including Customs evasions and the shipping of black market goods, with Mary Wollstonecraft's future lover, Captain Gilbert Imlay.

Both men advised Brissot on the Louisiana project, a scheme by which the French were encouraged to take over by force the Spanish colonies along the Mississippi. It never got off the ground, but like Dumouriez' advance into Belgium to 'liberate' its people it pointed one curious aspect of the French Revolution, in particular within the so-called 'moderate' party of the Girondists: its recognition of annexation under the thin disguise of ridding foreign peoples of their repressive forms of government. The word 'Empire' recurs with surprising and unquestioning frequency in the writings of Madame Roland and others. What began unmistakably as defence against the massing reactionary forces and royalist emigrés, slipped almost imperceptibly into a quest for satellite states. It was this ambivalent revolutionary attitude that was to provide the brilliant young military commander Napoleon with his opportunities and his vision of a United States of Europe (under French protection).

Dumouriez, totally out of sympathy with his instructions, was to revolt like Lafayette, and in March 1793, fulfilling Marat's designation of 'traitor', he threatened to turn his whole army round and advance on Paris. Only a recent defeat in Holland, now the object of French attack, and the failure of the republican artillery to give him their support, prevented Dumouriez doing just this and setting up a Regency with the young Louis XVII as King. He then deserted to the Austrians, bringing Danton as well as himself into a certain disrepute: for Danton as Minister of Justice had backed Dumouriez continually after the Valmy victory and in March 1793, he had been sent with Delacroix on a mission to the Belgian army. Although reporting his suspicions on his return to Paris, he had failed to dismiss Dumouriez, leaving him in command. Danton, as usual, was easygoing, but his failure to take a strong line could have had serious consequences, and it was to give a lever to his enemies later.

How much did Paine realize the slightly imperialistic turn of the war, and the Girondist responsibility? In a letter to Danton the following May, he was to write: 'I agree with your motion of not interfering in the government of any foreign country, nor permitting any foreign country to interfere in the government of France. This decree was necessary as a preliminary towards terminating the war. But while these internal contentions continue, while the hope remains to the enemy of seeing the republic fall to pieces, . . . the enemy will be encouraged to hang about the frontiers and await the issue of circumstances.' It would seem from this that he supported the Jacobin tendency to peace and neutrality, although alert to the possible dangers. His lack of knowledge of spoken French must have seriously hampered his grasp of subtleties in Convention debates, but a number of his friends spoke both languages well and he learned to read French with ease in time, as Madame de Bonneville confirmed after his death. His writing of some passages of it in his letter to Sir George Staunton, quoting the French Academy of Science's report on his bridge, certainly suggested he understood what he was writing in 1789. Doubtless he had been learning it ever since his first visit to France in 1781; but his mind had many other occupations and he was not a natural linguist. Fluency could only come from living in France among the people, but the habit of mixing so largely with English and American residents probably did not encourage Paine to persevere in spoken French.

It was Robespierre who had been most against the war in the first place and Paine's continued respect for him may have derived also from this.

The committee elected to frame a Constitution, however, did not include Robespierre: its members, apart from Paine, were Sieyès, Brissot, Vergniaud, Pétion, Gensonné, Barère, Danton and Condorcet. It was traditionally Condorcet who led the work, and Paine who produced its Declaration of Rights; and according to the historian of the Convention, Durand de Maillane, the failure to include Robespierre caused him, in resentment, to cripple its work as far as possible. The seeds of Jacobin-Girondist conflict were sown, and sown deep. Paine, like others, was ultimately to be a victim; but in October 1792 his illusions were still mainly intact.

Paine and Barlow now became close friends and on 7th November Paine presented to the Convention Barlow's printed pamphlet, *A Letter to the National Convention . . . on the Defects in the Constitution of 1791*. On 18th November Paine was warmed by a toast to himself in a celebration at White's Hotel sponsored by the Friends of the Rights of Man. It was a gay, even flamboyant, occasion, originally British in intention but attended by other nationalities sympathetic to the Revolution in Paris. The crowded gathering also included army officers and military bands, in a lavishly decorated hall. The *Annual Register* made reference to it and Lord Edward Fitzgerald and Sir Robert Smyth, a British banker domiciled in Paris, caused a sensation by renouncing their titles.

This was the Sir Robert Smyth who later, in 1796, petitioned on Paine's behalf in the matter of the Sunderland bridge. It was he who proposed the principal toast of the evening: 'The speedy abolition of all hereditary titles and feudal distinctions.'

It was a conspicuously topical toast, for on 13th November, five days before, there had begun in the National Convention a debate which was to sow the seeds of the downfall not only of Louis XVI but of Paine himself. It was the debate on the proposed trial of the King for treason, and it was rendered deadly by an indiscretion of Louis' as long ago as 22nd May, when a Versailles locksmith named Gamain had been summoned to the Tuileries to place a special iron door over a secret cupboard. On 19th November, Gamain went to Roland and told him of this royal hiding place. Roland, Gamain and the architect Heurtier at once went to the palace and removed with Gamain's help a packet of papers. These papers proved incontestably that Louis had been actively engaged in secret correspondence with France's enemies, the object being their successful invasion of the country and the replacing of himself on the throne as absolute monarch.

If there had been a possibility of Louis successfully defending himself at his trial, on the grounds of insufficient evidence, it vanished with the discovery of these papers. He might well have said in his defence (as Alexandre Dumas, personally retracing the whole ground of the Varennes flight in the 1850s, said for him) that both he and his Queen, like royalty throughout Europe, were of mixed race, with many relatives abroad; and they could not think of the matter as treasonable in the same way as the ordinary French citizen. Royalty was of its nature an international caste, closely inbred, and it is probable as Dumas wrote that Louis' 'people became to him *foreigners*, the enemy. The foreigner became his friend.' The tolerant view is possible now to us as it was to Dumas. 'History is a tribunal,' he pointed out, 'both for the

Cordelier Danton and King Louis XVI. Surely it is no more than just that each should be judged according to the caste in which he was born, the class among which he was brought up, the sphere in which he lived and moved; that Danton should be judged as a man of the people, Louis XVI as a man of royalty?'[1]

Louis, phlegmatic and easily led, was not built for royalty; he had a mechanical, not a political, mind, fascinated by clockmaking and clock-mending. Saxon on the mother's side, he had other gifts and other virtues. He spoke German and English, read the works of David Hume, and translated into French Horace Walpole's *Historic Doubts* on the reign of King Richard III. But whatever he absorbed from his reading, in practice he assimilated the wrong lessons. Catherine II had written in a letter to Marie Antoinette: 'Kings must follow their course without worrying about the cries of the people'; but Catherine could not transfer to her troubled fellow-monarchs of France the natural appreciation of the need for reform which had early kept the Russian Empress on a liberal equilibrium, so that when she was forced to grasp the reins of despotism, to stay on her throne, she could still keep to some extent the trust of her people (Voltaire himself had fallen into the trap of her deception and maintained a lively, almost obsequious, correspondence with her).

Neither Louis nor Marie Antoinette possessed the mental subtlety or political skill of Catherine the Great: they took her words at their face value, and never learned to strike a balance between public graciousness and despotic pride. The Palace of Versailles which Louis XIV had built to keep the nobility well away from affairs of state in Paris, had in the end encased his successors in an iron fortress, totally out of touch with their people.

If they were out of touch physically they were even more out of touch mentally; and they had learned nothing from the Revolution except the impossible dream of putting the clock back. The King's renegade cousin, the Duke of Orleans (the hated but liberal Philippe Egalité, as he was known as a deputy in the Assembly), had thrown in his lot with the revolutionists; it did not save him from the Terror, but his son, the Duke of Chârtres, who had been in Lafayette's National Guard and defected to Austria with Dumouriez in 1793, lived to become the last and most constitutional Bourbon King, Louis-Philippe: '*le roi citoyen*'.

Louis XVI, though an amiable enough private character, had all the forces of destiny against him. France, in a later century's phrase, had its back to the wall: in spite of the retreat of the Prussians, the pressures of foreign invasion were still felt, more were anticipated, and the reaction against the King, hitherto tolerated as a lion whose claws had been

[1] *The Flight to Varennes* (1856: trans. A. Craig Bell, Alston Books, 1962).

185

withdrawn, flared into new life. It was a reaction of fear as much as revenge, but Paine, the humane idealist who could never forget Louis' help to the Americans in their need, underestimated the driving force of the emotion and tried, by reason, to stem it. In a paper read to the Convention on 21st November he stated unequivocally:

'I think it necessary that Louis XVI should be tried; not that this advice is suggested by a spirit of vengeance, but because this measure appears to me just, lawful, and conformable to sound policy. If Louis is innocent, let us put him to prove his innocence; if he is guilty, let the national will determine whether he shall be pardoned or punished.'

He goes on to suggest that it is not only the King who is to be tried, but metaphorically a horde of fellow-conspirators in Europe, who have heavily taxed the unfortunate inhabitants of their respective countries to send armies to Louis' defence. The deaths of the soldiers on both sides lay at the door of these monarchial 'brigands', among whom he classes 'Mr. Guelph, elector of Hanover', a description of King George III which was not to endear him to the Prosecuting Counsel in his own trial across the Channel. The long-subsisting fear of revolution in England, he maintained, and the lack of credit, alone prevent the English Court from openly joining the operations of Prussia and Austria; but he warns the will is there.

'France is now a republic; she has completed her revolution; but she cannot earn all its advantages so long as she is surrounded with despotic governments. Their armies and their marine oblige her also to keep troops and ships in readiness. It is therefore her immediate interest that all nations shall be as free as herself; that revolutions shall be universal; and since the trial of Louis XVI can serve to prove to the world the flagitiousness of governments in general, and the necessity of revolutions, she ought not to let slip so precious an opportunity.'

His last sentence in this long speech has been overlooked, but psychologically (and without regard to its accuracy concerning Louis XVI) it may throw another light on the vexed question of Paine's reputation as a heavy drinker.

'If,' he writes, 'seeing in Louis XVI only a weak and narrow-minded man, badly reared, like all his kind, given, as it is said, to frequent excesses of drunkenness—a man whom the national assembly imprudently raised again on a throne for which he was not made—he is shown hereafter some compassion, it shall be the result of the national magnanimity, and not the burlesque notion of a pretended "inviolability".' If Paine considered himself in the least open to any charge of 'drunkenness', this is surely a most extraordinary criticism for him to make, in public, of Louis XVI?

In December not only Louis but Paine was on trial. Paine's trial in England took place on 18th December, following the burnings in effigy which later stretched as far afield as Pembroke in Wales, from where Mary Wollstonecraft's sister, Eliza Bishop, wrote to her other sister Everina: 'The conversation turns on Murphy, on Irish potatoes, or Tommy Paine, whose effigy they burnt at Pembroke the other day. Nay, they talk of immortalizing Miss Wollstonecraft in like manner, but all end in damning politics.' In Scotland, Robert Burns the exciseman, warned to keep his radical sentiments to himself, watched without comment, but inward anger, another anti-Paine bonfire and demonstration. It was with justice that Paine's defending counsel, Sir Thomas Erskine, was able to protest that 'this cause has been prejudged', and he instanced the threats of prosecution for publishing Paine's work 'even while the cause has been standing here for immediate trial', including the advertisement of 'a reward on the conviction of any person who should dare to sell the book itself'.

The trial had been prefaced by an 'Information', a grandiloquent vilification of 'Thomas Paine, late of London, gentleman, being a wicked, malicious, seditious and ill-disposed person, and being greatly disaffected to our said Sovereign Lord the now King, and to the happy constitution and government of this kingdom', with much reiteration of Paine's 'most wicked, cunning and artful insinuations' that the said happy constitution and government were 'contrary to the right and interest of the subjects of this kingdom in general'. Though brevity, also, was not the soul of the Prosecuting Counsel's wit, he eventually got to the point of stating to the Gentlemen of the Jury that this was 'a plain, a clear, a short, and indisputable case'. With respect to the matter, he adds, 'in all my conscience I call it treason' (the actual charge, rather different, was 'seditious libel'), and he is full of self-congratulation on having done his duty 'in bringing before a Jury an offender of this magnitude'.

The only actual evidence he produced, apart from generalizations of the subversive nature of the book, were Paine's letter of 16 February 1792, to the printer Jordan, giving him authority to name him as author and publisher of Part II of *Rights of Man*, and, more seriously for Erskine, who was given no prior knowledge of it, a letter said to be written from Paine in Paris on 11th November, 'First Year of the Republic', to the Attorney-General.

Erskine, long after the trial, maintained he still believed this letter (which he was not allowed to examine) to be a forgery; and certainly if Paine sent it without his Counsel's knowledge he stepped far outside the

bounds of legal etiquette and prudence. The fact remains that much of it
is characteristic of Paine, starting with the statement: 'As there can be
no personal resentment between two strangers, I write this letter to you,
as to a man against whom I have no animosity.' He goes on to explain
his absence owing to his being elected a member of the National
Convention of France, and that but for this he would have remained to
contest the injustice of the prosecution; 'not upon my own account . . .
but to defend the principles I had advanced in the work'. He questions
whether the prosecution 'was intended against Thomas Paine, *or against
the rights of the people of England to investigate systems and principles of
government*'. (Paine's italics, according to the later printed transcript of
the trial.)

So far, so good; but the following paragraph with its implied threat
was seriously injudicious:

> 'The time, Sir, is becoming too serious to play with Court prosecu-
> tions, and sport with national rights. The terrible examples that have
> taken place here upon men who less than a year ago, thought them-
> selves as secure as any prosecuting Judge, Jury, or Attorney General,
> can now do in England, ought to have some weight with men in your
> situation.'

The threat naturally stung the Attorney-General to the remark: 'If any
of his assassins are here in London, and there is some ground to suppose
they may be . . . Let him not think, that not to be an incendiary is to be a
coward.'

Worse, however, was to come: 'That the government of England,'
wrote Paine, 'is as great, if not the greatest perfection of fraud and
corruption, that ever took place since governments began, is what you
cannot be a stranger to . . . But though you may not choose to see it,
the people are seeing it very fast.' He goes on to question 'that the
capacity of such a man as Mr. Guelph, or any of his profligate sons, is
necessary to the government of a nation', and adds (doubtless with some
truth) 'you cannot obtain a verdict (and if you do, it will signify nothing)
without packing a Jury, and we *both* know that such tricks are practised'.

It will be noted, as an indication of the letter's probable authenticity,
that Paine here uses the same name for the English king—'Mr. Guelph'
—that he used ten days later in the Convention in supporting the
motion that Louis XVI should be put on trial.

Erskine quite rightly objected to not being given an earlier opportunity to know the contents of the letter, and naturally questioned if it
were a forgery. He was quick, too, to make the absolutely legitimate
legal point that the trial was based on Paine's *book* and the letter, 'if
written by him at all', was inadmissible in the circumstances. It could

only further prejudice a partly prejudged case, as he knew, and he strongly suggested to the Jury that 'the letter should be wholly dismissed from your consideration'. There was little likelihood of this, as he must have known in what was virtually a State trial, but he nevertheless launched himself into a defence which he honestly admitted would compromise his own situation as Attorney-General to the Prince of Wales; which indeed it did.

It has sometimes been stated or assumed by champions of Paine, who have not read a transcript of the trial, that this ambivalent position did affect the assiduity of Erskine's defence. This could not be more untrue. Erskine's defence was a strongly felt and highly cogent argument for the freedom of the press which could be used today in cases of censorship with equal force and relevance. 'The cause,' he said at the outset, 'resolved itself into a question of the deepest importance to us all, the nature and extent of the Liberty of the English Press'; and he disclaimed partiality by adding, 'I am, and ever have been, attached to the genuine principles of the British government.'

'The proposition which I mean to maintain as the basis of the liberty of the press, and without which it is an empty sound, is this;— that every man, not intending to mislead, but seeking to enlighten others with what his own reading and conscience, however errone- ously, have dictated to him as truth, may address himself to the universal reason of a whole nation, either upon the subject of govern- ments in general, or upon that of our own particular country:—that he may analyze the principles of its constitution,—point out its errors and defects,—examine and publish its corruptions,—warn his fellow- citizens against their ruinous consequences,—and exert his whole faculties in pointing out the most advantageous changes in establish- ments which he considers to be radically defective, or sliding from their object by abuse . . .

'In this manner power has reasoned in every age: government, in *its own estimation*, has been *at all times* a system of perfection; but a free press has examined and detected its errors, and the people have from time to time reformed them. This freedom has alone made our government what it is; this freedom alone can preserve it; and there- fore, under the banners of that freedom, today I stand up to defend Thomas Paine.'

After a further emphasis on the prejudice already attaching to the case (it had included press attacks on himself for undertaking the defence), he urged that Paine had written 'only what appeared to *him* (though it may not to us) to be the interest and happiness of England and of the whole human race'. He referred at length to Paine's own

Preface, and as a defence of the book pointed out that 'a writing can never be seditious in the sense of the English law, which states that the government leans on the UNIVERSAL WILL for its support'. This was taking up Paine's own argument about the nature of government with some courage; but Erskine went further: he launched into a panegyric of the American system of government—there was 'less to deplore, and more to admire, in the constitution of America, than in that of any other country under heaven', adding boldly: 'I wish indeed to except our own, but I cannot even do that till it shall be purged of those abuses which, though they obscure and deform the surface, have not as yet, *thank God*, destroyed the vital parts.'

'How, then, can it be wondered at,' Erskine continued, 'that Mr. Paine should return to this country in his heart a *republican*? Was he not equally a republican when he wrote *Common Sense*?—Yet that volume has been sold without restraint in every shop in England ever since . . . and contains every one principle of government, and every abuse in the British constitution, which is to be found in the *Rights of Man*.'

The revolution in France was, he added, the consequence of her incurably corrupt and profligate government and as for Burke, his 'officious interference was the origin of Mr. Paine's book'.

Having more or less, with only a few judicious reservations, put himself into the dock with Paine, Erskine went on to claim support for Paine and himself by quoting Paley, Archdeacon of Carlisle, the author of *The Principles of Political and Moral Philosophy*: 'Civil societies cannot be upheld, unless, in each, the interest of the whole society be binding upon every part and member of it . . . That, so long as the interest of the whole society requires it, it is the will of God . . . that the established government be obeyed,—*and no longer*.' He follows with Locke, Hume and Milton, the last-named both as an agitator against censorship and a warner of the consequences of attempting it ('a forbidden writing is thought to be a certain spark of truth, that flies up in the face of them who seek to tread it out'). He instanced the notorious Star Chamber as 'the first restriction of the press of England . . . but truth and freedom found their way with greater force through secret channels; and the unhappy Charles, *unwarned by a free press*, was brought to an ignominious death'.

Nor is he content with instances from the past. Lord Stanhope had, he pointed out, written: 'If our boasted liberty of the press were to consist only in the liberty to write *in praise* of the constitution, this is a liberty enjoyed under many *arbitrary* governments.' More tellingly still, he refers back to Burke's earlier *Thoughts on the Cause of the Present Discontents*, published in 1775, and even to William Pitt himself.

Erskine could hardly have done more: he compromised himself by so strongly supporting some of Paine's views. But it was a 'loaded' Jury and a 'loaded' trial, supported by a public campaign against Paine that made the trial little more than a prejudged formality. Paine was found guilty of the charge of seditious libel and outlawed from return to the country.

It must be pointed out that it was not a trial for 'treason' as such, but a similar trial to that of John Wilkes with a similar verdict, which had not prevented Wilkes from returning eventually to become a Member of Parliament and Lord Mayor of London. The mistake, however, is still often made. The general impression gained by the public from this has been that Paine was involved in some way in treasonable activities associated with the betrayal of his country to the Americans or the French.

For the cynic on politicians it should be added that William Pitt, the instigator as Prime Minister of the trial of Paine for seditious libel, privately commented, according to Lady Hester Stanhope: 'Tom Paine was quite right when he wrote *Rights of Man*.' He added: 'What am I to do as things are? If I were to encourage Paine's influence we should have a bloody revolution.' He circumvented this undesirable imaginary event by suspending Habeas Corpus (the statute which gave the accused legal rights) in 1794, and suppressing freedom of speech, through systematic prosecution and imprisonment of publishers of radical works, in a censorship which lasted almost without break over thirty years: the only period of its kind in English history. This is what Fox meant when he wrote to Grafton in 1798 about what they 'used to call the *exploded* principles of tyranny' seeming to acquire now 'even a sort of popularity', with no countenance given 'to sentiments of moderation, liberty, and justice'. So far had Pitt moved from the tentative liberalism of his early days of office.

That the trial of Louis XVI across the Channel was a trial for treason was, however, indisputable. The activities of the royalist *emigrés* abroad, including the King's two brothers, had already suggested the charge: Gamain's revelation of the secret cupboard in the Tuileries had provided the evidence needed. On 26th December, Louis drove to the Convention in the green carriage of the Mayor of Paris, and Mary Wollstonecraft, a newcomer to France, watched him mournfully from her window and intuitively sensed the shadows to come. Her letter, written the same day, to Joseph Johnson, her fatherly friend and publisher, was a vivid evocation of the scene and its effect on even her own radical sensibilities:

'About nine o'clock this morning the King passed by my window, moving silently along, excepting now and then a few strokes of the drum, which rendered the stillness more awful, through empty streets, surrounded by the National Guards, who, clustering round the carriage, seemed to deserve their name. The inhabitants flocked to their windows, but the casements were all shut; not a voice was heard, nor did I see anything like an insulting gesture. For the first time since I entered France I bowed to the majesty of the people, and respected the propriety of behaviour, so perfectly in unison with my own feelings. I can scarcely tell you why, but an association of ideas made the tears flow insensibly from my eyes, when I saw Louis sitting, with more dignity than I expected from his character, in a hackney-coach, going to meet death where so many of his race have triumphed. My fancy instantly brought Louis XIV before me, entering the capital with all his pomp, after one of the victories most flattering to his pride, only to see the sunshine of prosperity overshadowed by the sublime gloom of misery. I have been alone ever since; and though my mind is calm, I cannot dismiss the lively images that have filled my imagination all the day. Nay, do not smile, but pity me, for once or twice, lifting my eyes from the paper, I have seen eyes glare through a glass door opposite my chair, and bloody hands shook at me. Not the distant sound of a footstep can I hear. My apartments are remote from those of the servants, the only persons who sleep with me in an immense hotel, one folding-door opening after another. I wish I had even kept the cat with me; I want to see something alive—death in so many frightful shapes has taken hold of my fancy. I am going to bed, and for the first time in my life I cannot put out the candle.'

It is one of the rare passages in Mary Wollstonecraft's works in which we are reminded of the imaginative sense of terror of her daughter, Mary Shelley, when describing the frightening vision that provided the basis for her novel, *Frankenstein*. It is interesting that, prophetically, Mary assumes the King is going to his death: was all Paris so sure of the verdict?

The matter of the King's condemnation and the nature of his punishment was, however, one under considerable dispute. On this same 26th December, Buzot, the attractive Girondist who so stirred Madame Roland's heart, suggested plebiscites as a solution, but the referendum was not taken. Paine moved that delegates should print their individual views, and this being done, his own reasons for preserving Louis' life were delivered on 15th January. They began on a note that made his subsequent position clear:

'Citizen President,

My hatred and abhorrence of monarchy are sufficiently known: they originate in principles of reason and conviction, nor, except with life, can they ever be extirpated; but my compassion for the unfortunate, whether friend or enemy, is equally lively and sincere.'

He believed Louis should be tried because only thus could the world be made to realize the treacheries and corruptions of the monarchial system. But had Louis been born in obscurity, he could not believe he would have shown himself destitute of social virtues. He goes over the ground of the flight to Varennes and the Manifesto issued by himself and his friends of the *Société Républicaine*, indignantly torn down from the Assembly door at the time by Malouet; and he naturally does not resist a metaphorical 'I told you so'.

'There remains,' he adds, 'then only one question to be considered, what is to be done with this man? For myself, I seriously confess, that when I reflect on the unaccountable folly that restored the executive power to his hands, ... I am far more ready to condemn the Constituent Assembly than the unfortunate Louis Capet.'

It was a bold statement, and he followed it with another. He reminds the Convention of the support given to the struggling United States of America in their hour of need, partly through Louis' own generosity, and suggests:

'Let then those United States be the safeguard and asylum of Louis Capet. There, hereafter, far removed from the miseries and crimes of royalty, he may learn from the constant aspect of public prosperity, that the true system of government consists not in kings, but in fair, equal and honourable representation.'

He adds he considers himself a citizen of both countries, and submits the suggestion 'as a citizen of America, who feels the debt of gratitude he owes to every Frenchman ... I submit it also as a man who, although the enemy of kings, cannot forget that they are subject to human frailties.'

The arguments he gives to support magnanimity to Louis are not without acuteness. The royalist *emigrés* might well make the King's death an excuse to rally round his two brothers, and try with armed support to put one of them on the throne. While Louis himself remained alive this would not be possible. And he goes on to remind the members of their own original feelings on the death penalty:

'It has already been proposed to abolish the punishment of death, and it is with infinite satisfaction that I recollect the humane and excellent oration pronounced by Robespierre on that subject in the Constituent Assembly. This cause must find its advocates in every corner where enlightened politicians and lovers of humanity exist, and it ought above all to find them in this assembly.

G

'Monarchical governments have trained the human race, and inured it to the sanguinary arts and refinements of punishment; and it is exactly the same punishment which has so long shocked the sight and tormented the patience of the people, that now, in their turn, they practise in revenge upon their oppressors. But it becomes us to be strictly on our guard against the abomination and perversity of monarchical examples: as France has been the first of European nations to abolish royalty, let her also be the first to abolish the punishment of death, and to find out a milder and more effectual substitute.

'In the particular case now under consideration, I submit the following propositions: 1st, That the National Convention shall pronounce sentence of banishment on Louis and his family. 2nd, That Louis Capet shall be detained in prison till the end of the war, and at that the sentence of banishment to be executed.'

Paine had many on his side, but those against him included prominent Girondists as well as Jacobins. The matter was not a party issue, nor were the Brissotins all moderate in it. Fear drove men, as well as revenge and conviction. Danton swept aside a suggestion that the execution should require a two-thirds majority in the voting, as French law required: a simple majority was decided upon. The voting was remarkably close, but it was for death. There was an instant demand for a reprieve and time for appeal from twenty-five delegates, but on 18th January Tallien successfully quelled it on (curiously enough) humanitarian grounds. An appeal would only prolong the King's agony; and with this Robespierre agreed.

On 19th January Paine made his last effort, mounting the rostrum with Bancal, who read his speech in a French translation. Bancal had only read the words 'Very sincerely do I regret the Convention's vote of yesterday for death' when Marat, in a sudden attack of anti-religious fever, sprang up and denied 'the right of Thomas Paine to vote on such a subject; as he is a Quaker; hence his religious views run counter to the infliction of capital punishment'. While Paine, in the ensuing disorder, was reflecting on this unexpected resuscitation of his father's religion, Bancal managed to get a hearing for the rest of his speech. It was a good one: the appeal of experience, reason and common humanity.

'I have the advantage of some experience; it is near twenty years that I have been engaged in the cause of liberty, having contributed something to it in the revolution of the United States of America. My language has always been that of liberty *and* humanity, and I know that nothing so exalts a nation as the union of these two principles, under all circumstances. I know that the public mind of France, and particularly that of Paris, has been heated and irritated by the dangers to which they have been exposed; but could we carry our thoughts into the future, when the dangers are ended and the irritations forgotten, what today seems an act of justice may then appear an act of vengeance. (Murmurs.) My anxiety for the cause of France has become for the moment concern for her honour. If, on my return to America, I should employ myself on a history of the French Revolution, I had rather record a thousand errors on the side of mercy, than be obliged to tell one act of severe justice.'

Paine's most cogent argument, politically, is the effect on the world, and particularly the United States, France's ally. 'His execution will be an affliction to them, and it is in your power not to wound the feelings of your ally.'

Marat's defence was to denounce the interpreter. 'I maintain that it is not Thomas Paine's opinion. It is an untrue translation' (the fact that this conflicted with his previous accusation that this was indeed Paine's opinion, because he was a Quaker, seems in the excitement to have been overlooked, including possibly by the friend of the people himself).

'I have read the original,' countered Garran, 'and the translation is correct.'

This created a prolonged uproar until Paine, standing beside Bancal on the tribune, declared the sentiments were his. 'Ah citizens, give not the tyrant of England the triumph of seeing the man perish on the scaffold who had aided my much-loved America to break his chains.'

Marat now launched himself into the middle of the hall, crying, 'Paine voted against the punishment of death because he is a Quaker!' 'I voted against it,' said Paine, 'from both moral motives and motives of public policy.'

It was useless. Barère settled the King's fate in a speech about wasting valuable time when there were many important reforms to be passed by the Convention. Philanthropy was required elsewhere. In the ensuing vote, there was again a very narrow margin in favour of death without reprieve or conditions. Robespierre, not perhaps happy at the reminder of his former attitude to capital punishment, listened to Paine with unfathomable, green-eyed detachment. Fate, by an even narrower margin of time, was finally to decide which of these two would be destroyed first.

It was a strange feature of the growing extremism, this hardening of more sensitive attitudes. Marat himself, reputedly the most bloodthirsty of the Jacobin Left Wing, had only a few years before excused himself from attending a post-mortem, on grounds of squeamishness. Some of his colleagues, indeed, thought Marat's bark a good deal worse than his bite; his exaggerated language a journalistic trick, a trademark of his volcanic temperament. 'But he would be the first to protect with his own body the most criminal of the aristocrats,' wrote Panis, not entirely incredibly, for Barras maintained he saw Marat save an aristocratically-dressed unfortunate from the mob—letting him run free with merely a parting kick to humour the crowd—and it was not the only incident of its kind. 'I am the anger, the just anger, of the people,' cried Marat, and the wide range of his figures in demanding imaginary heads for the scaffold suggests there may be some truth in his alleged confession to Basire, a Girondist, that he gave the people what they were looking for, but 'my hand would wither at my side rather than write, if I were sure that the people would carry out what I tell them to do'. 'Words, words, words . . .' as Hamlet might have said of the leaders of the Revolution, and other political theorists before and since. How far would the Terror have advanced had Robespierre had to undertake personally the duties of Sanson, the executioner? No leading member of the Convention attended any execution but his own.

Louis XVI died in the Place de la Révolution on 21 January 1793. Clumsy, short-sighted and stout, he had not been a dignified man. 'He looked like some peasant shambling along behind his plough; there was nothing proud or regal about him,' wrote Madame de la Tour du Pin. 'His sword was a continual embarrassment to him, and he never knew what to do with his hat.' But in death he acquired a dignity denied to him in life. 'Frenchmen,' he began, 'I die innocent: it is from the scaffold and near appearing before God that I tell you so. I pardon my enemies; I desire that France . . .' The drums drowned his last words.

From his own point of view, he was no doubt convinced he was telling the truth. He was thirty-eight years old. Most of those who sent him to his death were to die even younger. It was a conflict, like so many, in which the flower of youth on both sides was to perish before the armistice.

XVI

1793: THE LONG HOT SUMMER

The British Court went into mourning on learning of the execution of Louis XVI. Inevitably, as Paine had warned, it turned foreign governments even more implacably against France and the Revolution. Pitt had counted on peace, and reduced the armed forces. But the French invasion of Belgium and the appeal for help of the Dutch Republic, who had an alliance with Britain, could not be totally ignored. Shortly before the King's execution, the House of Commons had voted to raise 20,000 naval recruits and passed an Alien Act, which threatened foreigners with deportation. The French government decided to anticipate attack and on 1st February declared war on England.

It was a desperate act, for the British commanded the seas, and the defection of Dumouriez soon put the whole French military position in jeopardy. Not only the Girondists, but later the more extreme Jacobins, were to transfer their alarm and resentment on to Danton, who had so signally failed to arrest Dumouriez when he visited Belgium. It could not be foreseen in that Spring of 1793 that a series of remarkable generals were to arise on the republican side and the flaming patriotism of an unprecedented army of one million recruits would make the French military forces the fear and wonder of Europe. At the moment there was only defeat and retreat, and the threat not only of invading armies but of civil war at home. The royalists of the Vendée revolted and the insurrection extended to Lyons and by the end of the year to other provinces. The centralization of government in Paris, the aim of the Jacobins whose great following was there, was beginning to be felt and resented in the more prosperous French districts (or 'departments' as they were known in the Convention), as the Girondists, always largely a provincial-based party, began to lose their grip. In America, Paine had well known the difficulties created for the government by states jealous of their prerogatives, as a later letter to Danton showed. In France, with split loyalties and a shortage of grain plus high prices in Paris (largely blamed on the provincial farmers), the issue was to explode the uneasy party peace.

As yet the Girondists were still in office, and had they joined with Danton the advance of the extremists of the 'Mountain' (so-called because they sat on a steeply-raised dais in the Convention) might still have been halted. Both parties were dependent on the deciding votes of the unattached deputies of the 'Plain', in the centre of the hall. Danton and d'Eglantine had made tentative overtures in visits to Madame Roland's *salon*, but her rooted and to some extent unreasoning antipathy to Danton made compromise impossible, even though Brissot, like Paine, would not have opposed an alliance. Danton, more attached to the Cordelier Club than the Jacobin, drifted into the other camp, only to be destroyed by it in the end, as it destroyed the Girondists. In the minds of Robespierre and the extremists he was tarred with the same brush. And Danton knew it. 'They would not dare!' he cried when, the following year, he was told he might be threatened with prosecution; but the very cry was an admission of the possibility.

In April 1793, however, the Committee of Public Safety was largely organized by Danton to replace the old Committee of Defence. A Revolutionary Tribunal had been formed with unchecked legal powers, and in the debates on the Constitution Robespierre, who was not elected to the Committee of Public Safety until 27th July, began to take a more dominating rôle, developing his ideology while still advocating 'the right of every citizen to enjoy and dispose of that portion of goods which the law guarantees him'. The law of property was still an integral part of Robespierre's socialism, though the Constitution he envisaged was to be a declaration of the people's rights. After July his hold on the Committee steadily strengthened, and he had the absolute support of the Paris Commune. Without sacrificing a fleck of aristocratic powder from his hair, or an elegant fold of his linen neck-ruffle or stock, he was to become an idol of the poor as formidable as Marat with his flamboyant red cap of liberty. For Robespierre, working day and night in the Convention and his humble lodgings, was not idly named 'the Incorruptible' and the public knew it. In a Paris in which starvation fought with inflation, and profiteering was rife and not resisted even among some deputies, Robespierre won the absolute trust of the mob and deserved their trust. If the power-lust gripped him, it never deviated from personal satisfaction to personal gain. The gain—and he was quite genuine in this—was to be for the people. He led the life of a recluse, shuttered from men's eyes except only on the political scene. There the sky-blue coat he eventually favoured was a symbol of his purity of motive.

He had once been somewhat courted by the Girondists: Madame Roland wrote him letters of extravagant praise which she and her party afterwards preferred not to remember. Now the slight, waxen figure, delicate but inflexible, was becoming dangerous: a candle about to burst into flame. They saw the danger, sidestepped and rushed headlong into another.

In April 1793, Marat and Hébert led a campaign against profiteering and food hoarding which showed signs of developing into a popular revolt. Marat also had warned the departments against a counter-revolution in the Convention, and accused the Girondists of supporting Dumouriez. On 13th April the Girondists arrested Marat on a counter-charge of incitement to murder, the advocation of a dictatorship (an old remedy of Marat's in time of crisis, although he always maintained it should be of limited duration, either from over-optimism or pretence) and plotting to overthrow the sovereignty of the Convention; and Paine's reputation with the Jacobins suffered a further tremor.

He had been lodging with two friends, one of them a young English doctor named William Johnson whose unstable temperament began to be unhinged by surrounding events. He attempted suicide, leaving a note saying he feared for Paine's life and accusing Marat of the betrayal of the ideals of the revolution. Brissot published this note on 16th April in his journal, the *Patriote Française*, and it was used in Marat's trial, although without effect as it by-passed the real issue, and Johnson's mental state was obvious.

Paine attended the trial and testified that he had spoken to Marat only once in his life, at the Convention; but he admitted reading the suicide note to Brissot, and added that 'Johnson gave himself two blows with the knife after he had understood that Marat would denounce him'. Marat intervened to say: 'Not because I would denounce the youth who stabbed himself, but because I wish to denounce Thomas Paine.' It was clear Marat at least realized that Johnson's suicide attempt had been out of fear for Paine's life, not his own, and Paine's comment was only that 'Johnson had for some time suffered mental anguish'.[1]

Marat had in fact recently attacked 'all those members (of the Convention) who had betrayed their duties in trying to save a tyrant's life', and it is ironical that Paine's apparent friendship with the American Minister Gouverneur Morris had added to his animosity. Morris was distrusted by the revolutionists and with reason: not only was he obviously intimate with the French Court, he had on the occasion of the massacre in the Champ-de-Mars by the National Guard deplored that there had been 'so little firing'. He had not increased the popularity of Americans in Paris, and Paine, since his stand for the King's life, was also suspect.

Marat was acquitted by unanimous vote, and 'the intrepid defender of the rights of the people', as the Tribunal Chairman had described him in his respectful speech dismissing the charge, was carried away in triumph on the shoulders of his supporters. Although it in no way affected the verdict, as some of Paine's biographers, inflating its import-ance, have stated, the incident with Paine at Marat's trial lingered in

[1] *Le Moniteur*, 24 April 1793.

men's minds, and was not forgotten. This became especially dangerous after July, when the murder of Marat turned 'the scarecrow of the fatherland's enemies' into a popular martyr and placed any apparent opponent of his at risk.

Before this brief holocaust Paine's life had been comparatively and uncommonly peaceful. He had left White's Hotel to share the ground floor of a private mansion at No. 63, Rue du Faubourg St Denis with the young doctor Johnson and a William Choppin. The house, which was said once to have belonged to Madame Pompadour, had rural surroundings and was a haven from the ebb and flow of Parisian street life, with its celebrations, its irruptions of anger, and its neighbourly feasts and festivals. Parisian frivolities, which had been stimulated rather than quenched by the Revolution, were not to his taste any more than to those of a slightly scandalized Mary Wollstonecraft, who in February, only a month after the King's death, pictured with serious-minded surprise the surface lightness of the Parisian scene.

'The whole mode of life here tends indeed to render the people frivolous, and, to borrow their favourite epithet, amiable. Ever on the wing, they are always sipping the sparkling joy on the brim of the cup, leaving satiety at the bottom for those who venture to drink deep. On all sides they trip along, buoyed up by animal spirits, and seemingly so void of care that often, when I am walking on the Boulevards, it occurs to me that they alone understand the full import of the term leisure; and they trifle their time away with such an air of contentment, I know not how to wish them wiser at the expense of gaiety. They play before me like motes in a sunbeam, enjoying the passing ray . . .'

She was among the many friends—the Marquis de Condorcet and his young wife, the Barlows, the Christies and others—who visited Paine at the Faubourg St Denis that uneasy summer of 1793, and Mary was no longer alone. Her works were also well known in translation in France, and she had become an accepted part of the Anglo-American liberal scene. She had soon entered the circle of the young English poet, Helen Maria Williams, who had formed a steady liaison with John Hurford Stone, the English radical with whom Paine and Thomas Christie had visited the Tuileries at the time of the flight to Varennes. Such alliances and friendships abounded among the closely-knit circle of English-speaking emigrants in Paris, and Mary had at last found happiness with her American lover, Gilbert Imlay, also a writer and a supporter of the Revolution. When living in the village of Neuilly just outside Paris she had met him many times at the barriers, and the child whom they conceived she was to call tenderly 'your barrier girl'. Fanny Imlay, the elder sister of Mary Shelley, was born at Le Havre early the following year, ill-starred, like her mother, whose brief happiness was to end in much grief and attempted suicide. She bequeathed the suicide urge to Fanny, and to Mary, Godwin's daughter, her intellect and literary gifts. But this torrid summer of 1793 she was bright with a new-found femininity, her glow unwilling to be tarnished by the disillusion that was beginning to haunt Paine. The fall of the Girondists, and particularly, in Mary's case, the deaths of Brissot and Madame Roland, were soon to devastate them both; but Mary, unlike Paine, still had a personal joy to cling to, muffling for some time yet the roll of the drums in the Place de la Révolution.

Already, on 20th April, Paine was writing to Jefferson, now Secretary of State in America: 'Had this revolution been conducted consistently with its principles, there was once a good prospect of extending liberty through the greatest part of Europe; but I now relinquish that hope.' His reference was not only to Dumouriez, threatening Paris with the Austrian army. He wished only to wait for the adoption of a Constitution, he wrote, before returning to America. But even that dream was shadowed the same month by the news that his house and barn at New Rochelle had been burned down, and he added a postscript to his letter to Jefferson giving him the news, which he had just received from General Lewis Morris: 'I assure you,' he added, 'I shall not bring money enough to build another.'

Late in the Spring Danton, Robespierre and Marat joined forces and moved decisively against the Girondists, whom they distrusted as possible accomplices of Dumouriez and the provincial rebels. Their government had been tolerant but incompetent, doing nothing to stop the combination of rising prices and monetary inflation. Against the sudden *coup d'état* they had no resources, and when, on 2nd June, they refused to resign, the Convention voted to suspend twenty-two of the Girondist leaders. They were put for the rest of the summer under house arrest. Lanthenas, Paine's translator, was one of three deputies saved from arrest by Marat's prolonged battle on their behalf. Lanthenas had voted for the King's death, saying he thought it for the good of France.

On 31st May Danton, always friendly to Paine, had stopped him outside the Assembly and warned him not to go in, speaking in English. Brissot, the particular friend of the Americans and English in Paris, was to be arrested and as a friend of his Paine might be included on the list of his associates to be arrested with him. 'Revolutions cannot be made with rose water,' Danton had told Paine, and the lawyer Vergniaud, who sat with Paine on the committee to form a Constitution, was soon, in a famous phrase, to compare the French Revolution to Saturn:—'it devours its own children'.

It is possible that Danton's respect for Paine, and wish to help him, arose from a long letter Paine had written him on 6th May, putting on to paper his misgivings about the course of the revolution and some practical ideas on improved government, drawn from his own experiences during the growing pains of the American Republic, over a decade before. Taine first brought this letter to light in *La Révolution,* and wrote of it: 'Compared with the speeches and writings of the time, it produces the strangest effect by its practical good sense.' Dr Robinet also, in *Danton Emigré,* believed it showed the workings of 'a lucid and wise intellect'. Passages from it are worth quotation, for it shows Paine's continued grasp, in the maturity of his experience, of the problems that beset revolutionary government and the dangers to liberty and survival in which the French now stood, facing a split between Paris and the provinces.

'Citoyen Danton:

As you read English, I write this letter to you without passing it through the hands of a translator. I am exceedingly disturbed at the distractions, jealousies, discontents, and uneasiness that reign among us, and which, if they continue, will bring ruin and disgrace on the republic. When I left America in the year 1787, it was my intention to return the year following, but the French Revolution, and the prospect it afforded of extending the principles of liberty and fraternity through the greater part of Europe, have induced me to prolong my stay upwards of six years. I now despair of seeing the great object of European liberty accomplished, and my despair arises not from the combined foreign powers, not from the intrigues of aristocracy and priestcraft, but from the tumultuous misconduct with which the internal affairs of the present revolution are conducted . . .

'. . . The danger every day increases of a rupture between Paris and the departments . . . I see but one effectual plan to prevent this rupture taking place, and that is to fix the residence of the convention, and of the future assemblies, at a distance from Paris.

'I saw, during the American Revolution, the exceeding inconvenience that arose by having the government of Congress within the limits of any Municipal Jurisdiction. Congress first resided in Philadelphia, and after a residence of four years it found it necessary to leave it. It then adjourned to the State of Jersey. It afterwards removed to New-York; it again removed from New-York to Philadelphia, and after experiencing in every one of these places the great inconvenience of a government, it formed the project of building a Town, not within the limits of any municipal jurisdiction, for the future residence of Congress. In any one of the Places where Congress resided, the municipal authority privately or openly opposed itself to the authority of Congress, and the people of each of these places expected more attention from Congress than their equal share with the other States amounted to. The same thing now takes place in France, but in far greater excess.

'I see also another embarrassing circumstance arising in Paris of which we have had full experience in America. I mean that of fixing the price of provisions. But if this measure is to be attempted it ought to be done by the Municipality. The Convention has nothing to do with regulations of this kind; neither can they be carried into practice. The people of Paris may say they will not give more than a certain price for provisions, but as they cannot compel the country people to bring provisions to market the consequence will be directly contrary to their expectations, and they will find dearness and famine instead of plenty and cheapness. They may force the price down upon the stock in hand, but after that the market will be empty.

'I will give you an example. In Philadelphia we undertook, among other regulations of this kind, to regulate the price of Salt; the consequence was that no Salt was brought to market, and the price rose to thirty-six shillings sterling per Bushel. The price before the War was only one shilling and sixpence per Bushel; and we regulated the price of flour (farina) till there was none in the market, and the people were glad to procure it at any price.

'There is also a circumstance to be taken into the account which is not much attended to. The assignats are not of the same value they were a year ago, and as the quantity increases the value of them will diminish. This gives the appearance of things being dear when they are not so in fact, for in the same proportion that any kind of money falls in value articles rise in price. If it were not for this the quantity of assignats would be too great to be circulated. Paper money in America fell so much in value from this excessive quantity of it, that in the year 1781 I gave three hundred paper dollars for one pair of worsted stockings. What I write you upon this subject is experience and not merely opinion. I have no personal interest in any of these matters, nor in any party disputes. I attend only to general principles.

'As soon as a constitution shall be established I shall return to America; and be the future prosperity of France ever so great, I shall enjoy no other part of it than the happiness of knowing it. In the meantime I am distressed to see matters so badly conducted, and so little attention paid to moral principles. It is these things that injure the character of the Revolution and discourage the progress of liberty all over the world . . .

'There ought to be some regulation with respect to the spirit of denunciation that now prevails. If every individual is to indulge his private malignancy or his private ambition, to denounce at random and without any kind of proof, all confidence will be undermined and all authority be destroyed. Calumny is a species of Treachery that ought to be punished as well as any other kind of Treachery. It is a private vice productive of public evils; because it is possible to irritate men into disaffection by continual calumny who never intended to be disaffected. It is therefore, equally as necessary to guard against the evils of unfounded or malignant suspicion as against the evils of blind confidence. It is equally as necessary to protect the characters of public officers from calumny as it is to punish them for treachery or mis-conduct. For my own part I shall hold it a matter of doubt, until better evidence arises than is known at present, whether Dumouriez has been a traitor from policy or resentment. There was certainly a time when he acted well, but it is not every man whose mind is strong enough to bear up against ingratitude, and I think he experienced a great deal of this before he revolted. Calumny becomes harmless and defeats itself, when it attempts to act upon too large a scale. Thus the denunciation of the Sections (of Paris) against the twenty-two deputies (Girondists) falls to the ground. The departments that elected them are better judges of their moral and political characters than those who have denounced them. This denunciation will injure Paris in the opinion of the departments because it has the appearance of dictating to them what sort of deputies they shall elect. Most of the acquaintances that I have in the Convention are among those who are in that list, and I know there are not better men nor better patriots than what they are.

'I have written a letter to Marat of the same date as this but not on the same subject. He may show it to you if he chuse.

Votre Ami,
THOMAS PAINE.'

The 'spirit of denunciation' was to find its legal support before the end of the year in the infamous 'Law of Suspects', unleashing all the private animosities and dangerous partialities, without serious investigation, that Paine feared. Similar government uses of denunciation have continued into our own time, and Paine's warning strikes a con-temporary ring here as well as on the ever-recurring problems of inflation and rising prices. It was a bold letter in the situation and Danton, a bold man, and one not unconcerned with the issues involved, does not seem to have resented it. It is probable he appreciated its basic common sense. Paine's letter to Marat has not been discovered. The Cobbett papers show that Paine kept a copy, but it was probably destroyed, with so much else relative to Paine, in the disastrous fire that destroyed the library of Madame de Bonneville's son, General Bonneville, long after Paine's death (Rickman also, to his sorrow and our possible loss, lost a number of Paine's letters to him written in 1792 and 1793, on his journey back to England from France after seeing Paine off on his last journey to America in 1802). The letter to Marat may have equally lulled Marat's suspicions and perhaps impressed him by its common sense and desire to help. There is indication from this time that Paine was no longer on Marat's notorious proscribed list, and when on 7th June Robespierre demanded a more stringent law against foreigners, the two foreign deputies to the Convention, Paine and Clootz, were excepted.

Marat, though, was soon no longer to be a danger to anybody. In the schism between Paris and the provinces, he was to become the chosen victim. During July a girl from Normandy, Charlotte Corday, made reiterated attempts to gain admittance to Marat's house, pleading personal unhappiness and saying she had messages from her district, Caen, important to the Republic. On 13th July Marat, who since December had been a sick man, agreed to see her, holding audience in his bath which was designed to enable him to work and hold interviews; and while he was taking down notes at her dictation she calmly stabbed him to the heart. He died after one cry for Simonne, who ran to his aid too late. Charlotte had travelled to Paris by coach, alone, to do it, convinced that with Marat gone the Revolution's excesses would cease, and the royalists and priests of her district would regain control. Some of the Girondists had already escaped there. By an irony she did not foresee, her action sealed the fate of the Girondists and opened the cage doors that released the Terror. Thereafter the Jacobins rode the tiger of revolution, and could never, as the proverbial saying warns, get off its back.

In the long hot summer of 1793 Paine kept away from state affairs and attended to his visitors and his garden. In a letter to Lady Smyth he described later both the solace of his surroundings and his unquiet feelings at the turn of events:

'The house, which was enclosed by a wall and gateway from the street, was a good deal like an old mansion farmhouse, and the court-yard was like a farm-yard, stocked with fowls,—ducks, turkeys and geese; which for amusement, we used to feed out of the parlour window on the ground floor . . .

'My apartments consisted of three rooms; the first for wood, water, etc.; the next was the bedroom; and beyond it the sitting room, which led into the garden through a glass door. I used to find some relief by walking alone in the garden, after dark, and cursing with hearty goodwill the authors of that terrible system that had turned the character of the Revolution I had been proud to defend . . .

'Pen and ink were then of no use to me; no good could be done by writing, and no printer dared to print . . .

'And as to softer subjects, my heart was in distress at the fate of my friends, and my harp hung upon the weeping willows.'

He and his visitors spent most of their time in the garden, he adds, playing games such as marbles, Scotch hops and battledores, 'at which we were all pretty expert. In this retired manner we remained about six or seven weeks, and our landlord went every evening into the city to bring us news of the day and the evening journal.'

It was a calm before the storm. 'I went but little to the Convention,' wrote Paine, 'and then only to make my appearance; because I found it impossible to join in their tremendous decrees, and useless and dangerous to oppose them. My having voted and spoken extensively against the execution of the King had already fixed a mark upon me. . . . I saw many of my most intimate friends destroyed, others daily carried to prison, and I had reason to believe, and had also intimations given me that the same danger was approaching myself.'

In October the Girondists were finally tried and condemned. Some of them had escaped their house arrest and fled to the more friendly provinces, first to Normandy and then the Bordeaux region, where they were hidden and succoured by well-wishers, at considerable risk. Most were recaptured and executed; two suicides were found in the fields at harvest-time, their faces devoured by wolves. One of these was Buzot, the handsome republican who had so deeply won Madame Roland's love. The news of her death reached him before he died. 'She is no more, she is no more, my friend,' he had written in anguish to Jerôme Le Tellier: 'The ruffians have murdered her. Tell me if there is anything left to live for! When you hear of my death, burn her letters.' Her letters to him from prison were not burned, but hidden and revealed long afterwards.

Condemned after trial, Madame Roland had died believing that 'Death would bring him (Buzot) the woman that life denied him'. The thought gave her courage. She had left the scene of her condemnation in a white dress, her long black hair hanging down her back like a cloud; but for execution her hair was cut, her hands tied behind her back. In prison earlier she had briefly dissolved in tears, more distressed at the broken revolutionary illusions than her own fate; but like so many on both sides, aristocrats and revolutionists, she met death calmly, asking only, as a last wish, that her turn to mount the scaffold should be put back, so that the desperately frightened man with whom she shared the tumbril should not be further distressed by the sight of her blood. The wish was granted. 'Like a white Grecian statue,' wrote Carlyle, 'serenely complete, she shines in that black wreck of things—long memorable.'

When Roland, who had escaped to Normandy, heard of her death he, too, committed suicide. The Marquis de Condorcet, who had been among Paine's visitors in the summer, also died by his own hand, in prison early the next year. Brissot escaped from Paris towards the south, but was recaptured and put on trial on 24th October. He and the rest, who included Paine's young friend Du Châtelet of the Republican Manifesto, were executed on 31st October. Only Louvet, like the hero of one of his own romantic novels, miraculously escaped detection; wandering as a fugitive up and down the country roads of France and hiding in a cave in the Jura mountains, more agonized, according to his colourful *Memoirs*, about the fate of his 'Lodoiska' in Paris than his own. He lived to be reunited with her and to become a conspicuously tolerant Member of the Five Hundred, formed after the death of Robespierre, and then a bookseller in the Palais Egalité. He died in his bed in 1797, at the age of thirty-seven, worn out by his efforts in the Revolution which had included a triumphant challenging of Robespierre's authority, famous in the history of the Convention.

On 16 October 1793, Marie Antoinette too had died, after a trial on charges of giving help to the enemies of France. Her hair when she went to the scaffold was prematurely grey and wispy under a plain cap; she made none of the ebony-and-ivory pictorial *éclat* of Madame Roland. Talma's friend, David, nevertheless sketched her as she passed in the tumbril, as he sketched so many of the guillotine's victims, friends and foes alike, with the merciless detachment of the dedicated artist.

It was the end of another era: the beginning of the Reign of Terror. In the summer of 1793 the executions in Paris averaged only three a week; in the autumn the number reached thirty; in June and July the following year they are estimated to have mounted to the frightful average of two hundred a week.[1] National security was menaced by war from without, and rebellion within, and the accelerating wave of panic and suspicion swept like a blood-red tide along the *sillons* of de Lisle's song. The revolts in the provinces were put down with particular ferocity. Carrier, a deputy of the Convention at Nantes, resorted to mass drownings (*'les noyades'*) of the Vendée rebels, to help out the over-worked guillotine, and at Lyons Fouché, later Napoleon's chief of police, and the ex-actor, Collot d'Herbois, ordered mass shootings. Toulon, which had been captured by the English, was retaken by republican troops on 18th December, and savage reprisals were inflicted on collaborators by Fréron and Barras. This was the Barras, a nobleman by birth, who was to become a member of the Directory and remain in office during the whole of its rule.

[1] The figures have often been inflated: these are based on ascertainable records.

On 3rd October André Amar, in the accusation against the Girondists, denounced the seventy-three representatives who in June had voted against their forcible expulsion, including 'the Englishman, Thomas Paine' in his indictment. In his plea for the King's life he had, Amar declared with heavy sarcasm, assured the Convention of the displeasure of the United States of America, 'our natural allies, which he did not blush to depict for us as full of veneration and gratitude for the tyrant of France'. It was Robespierre who intervened to say the number Amar accused was too large: 'The Convention must not multiply the guilty.' He maintained, and succeeded in establishing, that the accusations should only apply to the twenty-two Girondists themselves, not their sympathizers.

For Paine it was only a temporary respite. In November Pierre Manuel, a former schoolmaster who had voted with Paine at the King's trial and afterwards resigned from the Convention, was tried and executed, and Paine's name occurred in the indictment. The tumbrils could be heard louder, and the rumbling of the wheels intensified when on 25th December Barère, following a report by Robespierre on the principles of government, rose to protest that the Committee of Public Safety had expected its representative (Robespierre) to include a denunciation of the foreigners in the Convention, as harmful to the interests of the French people. He was supported by Bourdon de l'Oise, who specifically mentioned Paine: 'Since the Brissotins have left the Convention, he has not set foot in the Assembly.' He accused Paine of intriguing with 'a former agent of the Ministry of Foreign Affairs', an obscure reference, possibly to Paine's acquaintance with Louis Otto or with the French Minister to America, Genêt, who had annoyed the Americans and recently been recalled in disgrace (Paine's acquaintance with Genêt was of the slightest). A decree was thereupon made to exclude foreigners as deputies to the Convention. It was with cause that Paine had written that he had had intimations given him that the danger which was destroying his friends was also approaching himself.

Paine's companions Johnson and Choppin had already fled, with his help, to Switzerland. 'Two days after they were gone,' wrote Paine to Lady Smyth, 'I heard a rapping at the gate, and looking out of the window of the bedroom I saw the landlord going with the candle to the gate, which he opened, and a guard with muskets and fixed bayonets entered. I went to bed again, and made up my mind for prison, for I was then the only lodger.' It proved to be a guard to take Johnson and Choppin, but 'I thank God,' wrote Paine, 'they were out of their reach. The guard came about a month after in the night, and took away the landlord Georgeit; and the scene in the house finished with the arrestation of myself.'

Thomas Paine, 1792. Engraving by Sharp of portrait by George Romney

10. 'The scarecrow of the fatherland's enemies': Jean Paul Marat

'Mad Tom': anti-Paine cartoon 'published as the Act directs', 1791

Published as the Act directs, by W.ᵐ Locke Sept.ᵗ 1791.

MAD TOM.
or the MAN of RIGHTS.

11. 'The Last Moments of Tom Paine.' From *The British Workman, c.* 1861

Fragment of Paine's original tombstone, brought to England by Cobbett in 1819

12. Paine at window of house in Herring Street (now Bleecker Street), Greenwich Village. Nineteenth century print

Paine's marriage certificate. St Michael's, Lewes: 2 March 1771

This nineteenth —— Day of March —— in the Year One Thousand seven Hund
and seventy one} by me Rob Austen [Curat

This Marriage was { Richard Brothers
solemnized between Us { The M mark of Philadelphia Cooper

In the { John Gatton
Presence of { John Tebbott.

No 40

Thomas Pain of [this] Parish Batchelor and
Elizabeth Olive of [th
same Spinster

Married in this [Church] by [Licence]
this twenty six Day of March —— in the Year One Thousand seven Hund
and seventy one} by me Rob Austen [Curat

This Marriage was { Tho Pain
solemnized between Us { Eliz: Ollive

In the { Henry Verral
Presence of { Tho Ollive

No 32

John Blundell of [the] Parish of St Michaels
and Sarah Stows of [th
same Parish

Married in this [Church] by [Licence]
this third Day of September in the Year One Thousand seven Hund

XVII

PRISON AND THE TERROR

Before his arrest Paine had been advising Barère on a project for sending commissioners to the United States to try and get American aid for France in the war with England. It was, in a sense, a request for a return for the French help to America in her own time of revolution, in which Paine had also been involved. Paine, as was his wont, wrote Barère long and lucid arguments and informations and also spent a good deal of time taking up the matter of some American sea captains, whose vessels had been held up in Bordeaux because the French government feared (following seizures on the high seas) that if they allowed the American ships to leave port loaded with exports, they too, and their cargo, might be taken by the British. The captains came to Paine after appealing, as they thought in vain, to the American Minister, Gouverneur Morris. In fact Morris had written home for directions; but in the meantime Paine succeeded in persuading the French to allow the Americans to leave (he had advised a convoy).

It did not assuage Morris' jealousy of Paine which was to have serious consequences later. His own secret support and harbouring of royalists, and pro-English activities, only fully came to light from his diary long afterwards; but his Court sympathies were already enough known to the French authorities for them to have appealed to America for his recall. America did nothing about their disastrously unsuitable choice of Minister, who had been given the post without much confidence, on a very narrow margin of votes in Congress; and the fact, with the French recall and disgrace of their own Minister in America, Genêt, put Paine under a cloud, unwittingly, on both sides.

Morris quite erroneously (as Paine's letters of the time make clear) was convinced Paine was intriguing against him in order to succeed him. In fact on 5th September Paine, in a letter to Barère about the American captains, had written: 'I shall return to America on one of the vessels which will start from Bordeaux in the month of October.' He points out that 'Mr. Jefferson, formerly Minister of the United States in France, and actually Minister for Foreign Affairs at Congress, is an ardent defender of the interests of France,' and adds (which was already known to the French executive), 'Gouverneur Morris, who is here now, is badly disposed to you. I believe he has expressed the wish to be recalled.' But he emphasizes, 'It will be fit to have respect for Gouverneur

Morris, on account of his relations, who, as I said above, are excellent patriots.' (The General Lewis Morris who had written to Paine inform-ing him of the destruction of his house by fire was a brother of Gouverneur Morris, and a good friend of Paine.) It is obvious from this that so far from wanting Morris's position as Minister, Paine was still anxious and expecting to leave France and return to America, as 'my affairs in that country have suffered considerably through my absence'; and he was also unaware that it was not Morris himself, but the French government, who had asked for his recall.

Morris was, however, doing his best to discredit Paine. Two months before he had written to Robert Morris in America:

'I suspected that Paine was intriguing against me, although he put on a face of attachment. Since that period I am confirmed in the idea, for he came to my house with Col. Oswald, and being a little more drunk than usual, behaved extremely ill, and through his insolence I discovered clearly his vain ambition.'

As Conway points out, it was unlikely Oswald would have taken a tipsy man eight leagues to Morris' country retreat at Sainport on business, and Paine two years later wrote a thoroughly clear-headed account to Washington of the matters discussed at this meeting. But Morris was probably right that Paine was known on occasion to be drinking heavily at this time; he himself admitted it to Rickman and ascribed it to his disillusion with the Revolution. The period in which he let himself go must have been brief or very occasional, for his correspondence on political matters by the autumn was extensive and highly intelligible; and in addition he had also filled out the long summer days writing Part I of *The Age of Reason*. Already partly printed, it was much on his mind at the time of his arrest, and involved Barlow in the event.

Barère was chief committeeman of the Committee of Public Safety, to which Robespierre had only been elected on 27th July. Barère had held his pre-eminent position since the Committee's formation in April. Contrary to a popular misconception, it was Barère, not Robespierre, who instigated the Reign of Terror, presenting a report to the Conven-tion on 5th September which contained the words: 'Let us make Terror the order of the day!' And it was Barère, 'the Anacreon of the guillo-tine', who also made the speech leading to Paine's arrest. His later excuse to Paine was that he felt himself in danger and was forced to do it for this reason: a ludicrous statement in view of his powerful position on the Committee of Public Safety at the time. But Barère survived the Terror, and excuses were as rife as scapegoats among those still in a posi-tion to shift all the blame elsewhere: preferably on the dead, for the dead cannot argue.

In his *Memoirs* he did give Paine credit for obtaining the shipments of grain and rice which reached France from America in 1794, while Paine himself was in prison. Paine, he wrote, 'indicated methods, facilitated correspondence and worked long hours in the bureau of foreign affairs in order to bring about this massive purchase of provisions, so much the more necessary that without this aid our armies and the departments would have been threatened with dreadful famine'. It is not the picture of a man habitually the worse for drink, and the surprising thing is that Paine managed to do this and write a large part of *The Age of Reason*, all within a few months and under the cloud of his friends' imprisonment and death.

What was the real reason behind Paine's arrest? Morris had thrown out a hint about 'an overruling influence' on American and French affairs 'from the other side of the Channel', and it is curious that although Paine always claimed American citizenship he was indicted as 'an Englishman'—i.e. an enemy alien. As a supporter of Brissot he was naturally suspect, although he always disclaimed French party allegiance, but his American nationality should have protected him from the measure against 'foreigners' that did affect Anacharsis Clootz, the only other foreign member of the Convention, who was arrested at the same time. Robespierre, wrote Sampson Perry, a contemporary commentator, despised Paine because Paine had more faith in the pen than the guillotine. 'Robespierre said that method might do with such a country as America, but could avail nothing in one highly corrupted like France. To disagree in opinion with a mind so heated, was to incur all the resentment it contained.' Perhaps. But it was no move of Robespierre's in the Convention that got the foreign deputies indicted; he was accused of omitting that charge, and others took it up.

After Robespierre's death a memorandum was found among his papers reading: 'Demand that Thomas Payne be decreed accused for the interests of America as well as of France' ('*Demander que Thomas Payne soit décréte d'accusation pour les interets de l'Amerigue autant que la France*'). It was in Robespierre's handwriting, and it finally convinced Paine that Robespierre was the direct cause of his imprisonment, and planned his death. He did not know—indeed no one did at the time—that Courtois, who controlled the investigation after Robespierre's death, deliberately suppressed material in Robespierre's favour in order to throw as much of the responsibility for the Terror as possible on Robespierre's shoulders. There is surely a possibility, which I have never seen put forward, that the memorandum could have been a note made by Robespierre of *someone else's* 'demand' for Paine's accusation, 'for the interests of America as well as of France'. The equivocal nature of the last ten words has often been pondered. One inevitably thinks of Morris.

There is no record of Robespierre's personal hostility to Paine, other than this note; and their ideological aims for the underprivileged originally had much in common. Robespierre had certainly written of Paine, and the *Rights of Man*, in his journal with respect; although in the dangers of 1793 he had finally abandoned his own stance against war and the death penalty and written: 'Revolutionary government owes every protection to good citizens; to the enemies of the people it owes only death.' Morris, the obvious organ, as American Minister, for Paine's release, made only a perfunctory gesture in the matter. Morris' actual words, quite casually in a letter to Jefferson on 21 January 1794, were as follows:

'Least I should forget it, I must mention that Thomas Paine is in prison, where he amuses himself with publishing a pamphlet against Jesus Christ.[1] I do not recollect whether I mentioned to you that he would have been executed along with the rest of the Brissotins if the advance party had not viewed him with contempt. I incline to think that if he is quiet in prison he may have the good luck to be forgotten, whereas, should he be brought much into notice, the long suspended axe might fall on him. I believe he thinks that I ought to claim him as an American citizen; but considering his birth, his naturalization in this country, and the place he filled, I doubt much the right, and I am sure that the claim would be, for the present at least, inexpedient and ineffectual.'

This makes quite clear that it was Morris himself who denied the right of Paine to American citizenship, in spite of the fact that he had lived there for a dozen years and held the office of Secretary to the Committee for Foreign Affairs. Jefferson's acceptance seems strange, although it is true he was no longer Secretary of State (Morris could not yet have known this). On 1 January 1794, he had withdrawn from public affairs and retired to his estate at Monticello, and he may have considered himself no longer in a position to advise Washington, now in his second term as President. He could still, surely, have made some move in the matter as Paine's friend. Paine, who never knew of this letter, continued through his life to look on Jefferson as his loyal supporter, putting all the blame for American indifference to his imprisonment on Washington. Not knowing the full circumstances, Jefferson may perhaps have believed Morris that it might be better not to bring Paine to the attention of the authorities.

There was, though, some indication that the French executive made no further move with regard to Paine because they rather expected the

[1] This was, of course, *The Age of Reason*, which praised Christ for morality and philanthropy although it questioned his 'divinity'.

Americans to claim him as a citizen, and the criticism of Paine's biographer Aldridge that it was sheer self-conceit on his part to expect a busy President or his ministers to waste any time on trying to get his release is, to say the least, unreasonable considering all Washington had admitted America owed to Paine. Paine, after all, languished in prison ten months. Nor was Morris impotent. The French Minister for Foreign Affairs, Deforgues, had ambitions to succeed the disgraced Genêt as Minister in America, and was counting on Morris' favour. Had Morris pressed for Paine's release, instead of tacitly supporting his imprisonment as a French citizen, there is little doubt Deforgues would have made some effort in that direction. The fact that France at this time was greatly dependent on America for aid would also certainly have helped Paine had his case been more strongly urged. It is significant that the death of Robespierre, in July 1794, did not result in Paine's release. He obtained his freedom only three months later, after constant petition and after Gouverneur Morris had been succeeded as American Minister in Paris by James Monroe.

Paine never suspected Morris, having no knowledge, of course, of Morris' secret diary and suspicion towards himself. The man he blamed for not obtaining his release, and blamed bitterly, was Washington. In the circumstances he had some provocation, in view of his acknowledged services to Washington's cause at a time it was most desperately needed; although by storing up all his deep resentment against this one man, without knowledge of the feeble efforts of the middleman in making his plight known, he was to descend for the first time in print to personal ferocity, and put a blot on his name as a writer. In this sense, imprisonment destroyed Paine, more cruelly, perhaps, than the guillotine would have done. Like so many who live long, in deteriorating circumstances, he outlived his best fame.

The Committee of General Security had ordered the arrest of Paine and Anacharsis Clootz on 27 December 1793. Following the meeting of 25th December, 'I saw,' wrote Paine, 'I was particularly pointed at by Bourdon de l'Oise in his speech', and he was therefore prepared for his immediate arrest. For reasons of his own he decided to leave the Faubourg St Denis and take a trip to the centre of Paris; but meeting up with some Americans at the Hôtel de Philadelphie, and perhaps conversing too long and merrily, he decided to stay there that night.

The reasons were the need to put *The Age of Reason* into the hands of Joel Barlow. He had finished Part I with speed, he later wrote in his Preface to Part II, after hearing of Bourdon de l'Oise's attack. On the early morning of 28th December, between the hours of three and four, Paine heard a knock on his door at the Hôtel de Philadelphie. The document signed by two deputies of the Committee, two commissaries, a policeman, Thomas Paine and Achille Audibert, in the French National Archives, tells what happened:

'. . . seeing we could not be understood by him, an American,[1] we begged the manager of the house, who knows his language, to kindly interpret for him, giving him notice of the order of which we were bearers; whereupon the said Citizen Thomas Paine submitted to be taken to Rue Jacob, Great Britain Hotel, which he declared through his interpreter to be the place where he had his papers; having recognized that his lodging contained none of them, we accompanied the said Thomas Paine and his interpreter to Great Britain Hotel, Rue Jacob, Unity Section; the present minutes closed, after being read before the undersigned.'

The next report begins rather plaintively: 'And as it was about seven or eight o'clock in the morning of this day 8th Nivôse, being worn out with fatigue, and forced to take some food, we postponed the end of our proceeding till eleven o'clock of the same day, when, desiring to finish it, we went with Citizen Thomas Paine to Britain House, where we found Citizen Barlow . . .' It goes on to recount that this was a subterfuge of Paine's to get Barlow as a witness, and hand over to him the MS of his book, some of which he was already having printed and some of which remained at Paine's lodgings. There proved to be no papers of Paine's at Barlow's house, and the party went on to 63 Faubourg St Denis, with Barlow as witness: 'and after the most scrupulous examination of all the papers, that we had there gathered, none of them has been found suspicious, neither in French nor in English, according to what was affirmed to us by Citizen Dessous our interpreter who signed with us, and Citizen Thomas Paine'. The report was ended and signed by all concerned at 4 o'clock.

It is interesting to compare this official French account with another by Paine himself, discovered by Conway after his biography was published and printed in *The Athenaeum* under the title, 'Newly discovered writings of Thomas Paine'. Conway found these in the middle of an early and unique copy of Paine's *The Age of Reason*, Part I, in New York. It was otherwise substantially the first Paris edition published by Barrois in January 1794; and Paine's writing included the beginning of a Postscript in the form of a 'reply' to the denunciation of Bourdon de l'Oise. The additions, wrote Conway, bore intrinsic evidence of having been written soon after Paine's imprisonment on 29th December. He conjectured they were intended by Paine to appear in the first edition of *The Age of Reason* but were suppressed after this one example was printed.

[1] The police admission that Paine was an American is interesting.

After describing his visit to the Hôtel de Philadelphie in the Passage des Petits Pères, and his meeting with the Americans, he went on:

'About four in the morning I was awakened by a rapping at my chamber door: when I opened it I saw a guard, and the master of the hotel with them. The guard told me they came to put me under arrestation, and to demand the key of my papers. I desired them to walk in, and I would dress myself, and go with them immediately.

'It happened that Achille Audibert, of Calais, was then in the hotel; and I desired to be conducted into his room. When we came there, I told the guard that I had only lodged at the hotel for that night; that I was printing a work, and that part of that work was at the Maison Bretagne, Rue Jacob; and desired they would take me there first, which they did.

'The printing office, at which the work was printing, was near to the Maison Bretagne, where Col. Blackden and Joel Barlow, of the United States of America, lodged; and I had desired Joel Barlow to compare the proof sheets with the copy, as they came from the press. The remainder of the manuscript, from page 32 to 76, was at my lodging. But besides the necessity of my collecting all parts of the work together, that the publication might not be interrupted by my imprisonment, or by any event that might happen to me, it was highly proper that I should have a fellow citizen of America with me during the examination of my papers, as I had letters of correspondence in my possession of the President of congress General Washington; the minister of foreign affairs to congress Mr Jefferson; and the late Benjamin Franklin; and it might be necessary for me to make a *proces verbal* to send to congress.

'It happened that Joel Barlow had received only one proof sheet of the work, which he had compared with the copy, and sent it back to the printing office.

'We then went, in company with Joel Barlow, to my lodging. . . . It was satisfactory to me that they went through the examination of my papers with the strictness they did; and it is but justice that I say, they did it not only with civility, but with tokens of respect to my character.

'I shewed them the remainder of the manuscript of the foregoing work. The interpreter examined it, and returned it to me, saying, "it is an interesting work; it will do much good." I also shewed him another manuscript, which I intended for the committee of public safety; it is entitled, "Observations on the Commerce between the United States of America and France."

'After the examination of my papers was finished, the guard conducted me to the prison of the Luxembourg, where they left me as they would a man whose undeserved fate they regretted. I offered to write under the *proces verbal* they had made, that they had executed their orders with civility, but they declined it.'

In the Postscript Paine replies to de l'Oise's accusation of his intriguing 'with a former agent of the Ministry of Foreign Affairs':

'I know but one person in the office of foreign affairs. He is adjoint in the American department of that office. He is married to a citizenne of the United States of America, and consequently my acquaintance with him is very natural.'

Paine's reference was to Louis Otto, who had married a Miss Livingston of New York. He goes on at length to describe his conferences with Barère of the Committee of Public Safety on matters of American supplies and trade and also in connection with the proposed French Constitution, of which Barère, who was on the committee with Paine, had asked for a copy. This Paine provided, together with his opinions in writing on the subject of sending commissioners from the Convention to Congress, details about America which he thought such commissioners should know, and 'an account of the different parties in England for and against the war with France'. He also discussed the internal affairs of France and 'the best measures to be adopted'.

Barère, of course, was in a position of some power, and although he admitted to the help from Paine long afterwards, in days of safety, it is possible he would not have welcomed these revelations at the time. Conway suggests it was Barlow who may have had Paine's additions and postscript expunged from *The Age of Reason* after a single printing: partly in collusion with Morris who was working to other ends (he wished for an American alliance with England, not France), and whom Barlow needed to conciliate on account of his own slightly irregular speculations. It can only remain conjecture, but the additions are of interest in confirming Paine's activity in Franco-American co-operation during this summer of his discontent.

Within a few weeks of Paine's imprisonment, a group of Americans living in Paris presented a petition to the Convention, urging his immediate release. The group of sixteen included Joel Barlow and, unexpectedly, Peter Whiteside, who had been Paine's partner in his bridge project in England, and whose bankruptcy had left the Walker Brothers of Rotherham in virtual possession of the plans and material. An account was published in *The Morning Advertiser* on 8 February 1794. Considering the English government's campaign of propaganda against Paine, it was remarkably factual and restrained:

'In sittings of the French Convention, of the 27th of January, a deputation of Americans were admitted to the bar, and the orator requested the freedom of Thomas Paine, that Apostle of Liberty, who had been proscribed in England, whose arrest was a species of triumph to all the tyrants on earth—His papers had been examined, and far from finding any dangerous propositions, the Committee had traced only the characters of that burning zeal for liberty—of that eloquence of nature to philosophy—and of those principles of public morality, which had through life procured him the hatred of despots and the love of his fellow-citizens. They requested, therefore, with confidence, that Thomas Paine should be restored to the fraternal embraces of his fellow citizens, and they offered themselves sureties for his conduct during the short time that he should remain in France.'

The President, *The Morning Advertiser* reported, 'after a high compliment to the American People', applauded this generous devotion, but pointed out 'Thomas Paine was born in England—that was enough to subject him to the decree in the first instance, which our safety demanded by the revolutionary laws. The Convention will take into consideration your demand.' In fact the President, Vadier, had added (unreported) that although Paine had 'collaborated forcefully in the American Revolution', his mind had not 'perceived the nature of the Revolution which has regenerated France; he has conceived the system only in the light of the delusions with which the false friends of our revolution have surrounded it. You, like us, should have deplored an error hardly consistent with the principles which one admires in the highly estimable works of this republican author.' The reference is quite patently to Paine's Girondist associations, and nothing was done, especially as the signature of Morris, American Minister in Paris, was so conspicuously absent from the petition.

So Paine remained in the Luxembourg. His plight might have been worse. It was, in fact, a former Palace, with traces of grandeur still lingering, although bedraggled. After the execution of the Girondists it was used mainly for English citizens, both men and women, incarcerated because of the war with England. The need not to draw attention to her English nationality was one reason, when she formed the liaison with Captain Imlay, Mary Wollstonecraft became known thereafter in Paris as 'Mrs Imlay', and indeed Gilbert Imlay registered her as his wife at the American embassy. It was also why so much depended on Paine's claim to be an American citizen.

There were severe discomforts at the Luxembourg, especially in winter with lack of firing and candles. But Benoit, the keeper, was kindly and helpful and the prisoners formed into compatible groups, doing their own cooking and cleaning and paying for their own board. Supervision was loose, and it was rumoured the English ladies were learning much about *l'amour* from the French guards. Scandal gave the Luxembourg, as a result, the reputation of being the 'principal brothel in Paris'. It was to some extent a Parisian joke, but near enough the bone to goad the authorities into segregating the sexes. Nevertheless, a young man was reputed to have bribed his way into the prison in broad daylight to spend an afternoon with his mistress.

Paine's room on the ground floor was level with the earth in the garden and floored with brick. After a few months Paine was seized with a malignant and nervous fever, in Sampson Perry's words, which endured five weeks. 'At the crisis of this disorder the mandate for carrying a hundred and fifty prisoners to the revolutionary tribunal was put in force. Paine was delirious while the carts were loading with these victims; and he believes he owes his life to that very fever which appeared so near to take it away: for it seems his name was afterwards found in the proscription list'.[1] This would appear to be a reference to the note afterwards found in Robespierre's desk. Perry records that when the prisoners heard of an order to take away their knives and money, Paine removed the lock from his door and hid within it 'an English banknote of some value, and some guineas and gold coin'. When he recovered from the fever he found his money intact, but about three hundred of the prisoners missing, having been taken before the Revolutionary Tribunal and executed. During his illness he shared a room with three Belgians who devotedly nursed him: one of them, Joseph Vanhuele, later became Mayor of Bruges. Both the prison doctor and two fellow-prisoners who were doctors attended him, including the surgeon of General O'Hara who was also confined to the Luxembourg.

Among the executed was Clootz, whom an earlier visitor to the prison, a friend of Helen Maria Williams, had found in daily controversy with Paine on theological matters. Clootz was an atheist. Paine's continuance to support even a free and churchless form of religion irritated him; they had little in common, like so many of the disparate personalities thrown up by the Revolution. Clootz was executed on 24 March 1794, in a group including another total incompatible, the extremist Hébert.

For the Jacobin Club, now, was turning on itself. The enemies of the people, real or imagined, seemed to stretch in a never-ending stream. The end of the Hébertists meant, virtually, the end of Danton, the last giant left of the great days of Revolution. His influence on the people was still strong, but in the autumn of 1793 he had lost his political control when he stayed overlong in the country with his new wife, Sophie Gély. On returning from Belgium early in February 1793, he

[1] *Argus*. Register of Occurrences, Miscellany, etc., for 1796.

had found his first wife had died. A Catholic and monarchist, she had turned against him after the death of the King, and her feelings had never made his position easy. He had nevertheless received a letter of great compassion and consolation from Robespierre:

'February 15, Year II

My dear Danton,

If, in the throes of a grief which alone could agitate a mind such as yours, the assurance that you have a tender and devoted friend can afford you any consolation, know that it be true. I feel for you in this moment, as though it were myself who was bereaved. Do not close your heart to the voice of a friend who suffers all your pain. Let us mourn our friends together and make those tyrants who are the authors of public misfortune and of private woe, soon feel the effects of our profound grief. My friend, I had already addressed the sentiments of my heart to Belgium. I would have been ere now at your side, had I not respected the first moments of your justifiable sorrow.

Embrace your friend

ROBESPIERRE.'

It sounds heartfelt; probably it *was* heartfelt, at the time. But much blood since then had flowed under the Seine bridges, and Robespierre and his merciless young admirer, Saint-Just, had moved into the place in the Committee of Public Safety once held by Danton. There is little doubt that Robespierre, the narcissist, fell under the spell of Saint-Just's ice-pure integrity, and shed, not his principles, which remained as steadfast as ever, but something of his humanity under Saint-Just's hypnotic influence. For Saint-Just was a rarefied, even more fanatic reflection of himself; but more practical, more brilliant in oration, and burning white-hot in the zeal to rid the Revolution of every fleck of impurity: which meant, of course, most of its members.

They were not dictators, these men; the rule was still rule by com-mittee. And undoubtedly they could not have done anything without the full vote and co-operation of the other committee members. There were worse and more savage men in France, in particular the men who had put down the revolts in the provinces; but the very lack of cor-ruption of Robespierre and Saint-Just, their self-admiration on this point, made them deadly. The rule of 'virtue' became a fetish; and fetishes mean blood-sacrifice. Danton was a libertine, something Saint-Just had once understood, but rejected, while Robespierre had never understood it at all. Perhaps this is why he had once been able to feel for Danton, in his grief at the loss of a wife, while Saint-Just, with the zeal of the reformed, no longer dared to feel at all.

Nevertheless, even in the Terror one did not guillotine a man for his

219

morals; and a great deal of research has gradually revealed how deeply Danton was probably implicated in Fabre d'Eglantine's involvement in a fraud of the State through the re-constructed India Company. It was a time of bitterness against profiteering, when the people still lacked bread. Paine had known the same phase in the American Revolution. Saint-Just brought Danton's trial to a halt before the various defendants could bring their witnesses and the full charges be known; and Danton's great voice, booming through the stone walls across the river, in the hope the people would know his plight, was quickly stilled. But in the rehabilitation drive after the end of the Terror neither he, the greatest of all its victims, nor d'Eglantine were put back on their pedestals, and the significance seems clear.

Danton, with all his temptations, was a human being; he would turn a blind eye to other men's excesses, as he did to the September massacres, but he remained personally outside them and never lost his capacity to pity and feel. His return to Arcis in the autumn of 1793 was not only an idyll of marriage: it was a rejection of the mass condemnation of the Girondists. Garat, Minister of Justice, went to see Danton at this time, hearing he was ill, and he recorded the scene in his *Memoirs*:

'. . . I had not been two minutes with him when I saw that his illness consisted of a profound grief . . .

' "I shall not be able to save them," were the first words that left his lips and, as he spoke, all the vigour of that man who has been compared with an athlete seemed crushed; great tears rolled down that face which has been likened to a Tartar's.

' "Twenty times have I offered them peace," he cried. "They refused to believe me, so as to conserve the right of bringing me to ruin." '

Now the ruin had come. He was admitted to the Luxembourg early in 1794 and greeted Paine, it has been said, once again in English: 'What you have done for the happiness and liberty of your country, I have in vain tried to do for mine. I have been less fortunate but not more guilty . . . They are taking me to the scaffold; well, my friends, I shall go gaily.' He went gaily, in fact, on 3rd April, accompanied by Camille Desmoulins and others of his followers. Camille, who like Danton had failed in the end as the Complete Revolutionist, had helped to bring about the fall of the Girondists with his May 1793, pamphlet, *Histoire des Brissotins*; but in December he had attacked the Reign of Terror in his journal, *Le Vieux Cordelier*, and demanded the formation of a 'Committee of Clemency'. For him, there was no clemency, although his wife Lucile frantically haunted Robespierre's door. The tumbrils passed the windows of Robespierre's lodging: they were shuttered. It was a beautiful Spring afternoon, and the lilacs in the Tuileries garden were already in bloom. 'You must show my head to the people,' said Danton to the executioner. 'It is worth it.' The massive, uncouth republican with a classical education and a good library, who had played truant from college to see Louis XVI crowned at Rheims, had followed the King he had helped to depose just over a year after the King's execution.

In prison Paine had not been idle. One month after admission he had composed the dedication of *The Age of Reason* to his fellow citizens of the United States. In May 1794, he prepared a new edition of *Rights of Man*, designed for 'the Use and Benefit of all Mankind' rather than for English and French readers specifically. He wrote a new Preface and managed to get the MS sent to London to the printer, Daniel Isaac Eaton, who was later sentenced to eighteen months' imprisonment in Newgate for his pains, in addition to a session in the pillory.

After his recovery from illness he learned Robespierre had been executed on 28th July. Nemesis moved swiftly in the last year of the Terror. Robespierre and Saint-Just did not survive Danton and Desmoulins four months. Too much Virtue, too often proclaimed, can become a bore; and there were a number of atheists in the Convention who watched with ironic distaste and misgiving the Festival of the Supreme Being on 8th June, when Robespierre led the procession in a flower-decked Paris, two nosegays in his hands, and set fire to the straw effigy of atheism. Robespierre's puritanical dream had been of a society as flawless as a diamond, and he had been deeply disturbed by the Festival of Liberty and Reason (with a plump dancer from the Opéra as presiding goddess) on 10 November 1793, ordered by the Commune. By December he had managed to get the Convention to pass a law forbidding 'any violence or measure against religious freedom', and it was a part of the extraordinary ambivalence of this man that he was as concerned as Paine lest (in Paine's words in *The Age of Reason*) 'in the general wreck of superstition, of false systems of government, and false theology, we lose sight of morality, of humanity, and of the theology that is true'.

Had Robespierre read *The Age of Reason* at the time of the Festival of the Supreme Being? It is a strange but inevitable question. Although Robespierre's philosophy and Supreme Being derived from Rousseau, Paine's work could certainly have been a reminder. Robespierre disliked the Hébertists, the most violent and anti-religious of the extremists, as much as Paine; his vision of an ideal society, with concern for the poorest sector, was similar; but where Paine gave freely of himself and his emotions Robespierre's eyes always seemed to turn inward, and swept along in the tide of Saint-Just's forensic demand for state purification he remained detached from humanity, able to ignore the violent means for the sake of the shining, unattainable end. The Law of Suspects, encouraging the spirit of denunciation that Paine feared, had not cleansed the state, but incarnadined it; not only suspected aristocrats, but inoffensive seamstresses and Paris artisans had perished in its shadow.

On 10 June 1794, the last straw at which the arrested could clutch had gone, with the suppression of legal rights to a trial, one of the safeguards that Robespierre, the lawyer, in the early days of the Revolution would never let go. From legalization the state was turning to anarchy, in spite of the brave plans for public assistance and free education; and although the poor of Paris were provided, if not with bread, at least with circuses (Talma's theatre had to give one free performance a week for the underprivileged), censorship had raised its head alongside puritanism. Political censorship had always existed under the Revolution, not, curiously enough, so much against monarchism as against radical criticism of the Convention and its ministers. Hence Marat's frequent disappearances into hiding from the police. Now it attacked the theatre.

In September 1793, the whole company of the Théâtre de la Nation had been imprisoned. A play they wished to perform, *L'Ami des Lois*, had been banned as an obvious satire against extremism, and then been defiantly *read*, to an enthusiastic audience, by the company. The denouncer was the ex-actor, Collot d'Herbois, the infamous massacrer of the Lyons rebels. It could have been a case, too, of professional jealousy, the kind of exercise of a personal grudge which Paine from the beginning had feared in a Law of Suspects. Talma had no share in the eclipse of his rivals, one of whom generously cleared him on her release; but his own choice of plays was hampered by the demand for patriotic republican sentiments, and *sansculotte* applause did not make up for the fall of the Girondist friends who had been so welcome in his and Julie's *salon*.

Paris had got into the habit of glancing nervously over its shoulder, and Robespierre's enemies were mounting, not always with the highest motives. His Achilles heel was the fact that he was not a dictator, in spite of the support given him by the Paris Commune. Republican Paris was still governed by committee and the Convention, and although Robespierre's hold on the Committee of Public Safety was strong he had no control if it did not vote with him, and he had been elected, in his correct turn, as President of the Convention only on 4th June, under two months before his death. Until then his power there was uncertain and constantly challenged. There remained the Committee of General Security, the instrument of the police state, where his influence was weakest, and it is generally conceded that a threat to members of this implied in his last speech precipitated his own fall. It became a question of who struck first.

Robespierre and his friends were arrested, rescued by his *sansculotte* followers, and recaptured within one night. Robespierre was signing his name to a new appeal to the people ('Courage, patriots of the Section of Pikes. Liberty is triumphant . . .') when men of the Convention seized him. The paper was stained with his blood. He was shot in the mouth, probably by a gendarme (one named Méda boasted of it: the belief that Robespierre attempted suicide is no longer widely held, nor does it fit his timid character or the immediate situation). Late the same afternoon he was dragged speechless, with shattered jaw and bloodstained cravat, like a broken wax doll splashed with red paint, to the guillotine.

Others on the Committees of Public Safety and General Security shared his responsibility; how much is still disputed. The Reign of Terror had outlasted its moment, and there were signs of public revulsion. At least one biographer of Robespierre, Louis Blanc, has maintained that it was Robespierre, following his appeal for religious freedom, 'God and the immortality of the soul', who was planning to attack the hard core of terrorists on the Committees, and they seized the chance to reverse the rôles. It would not be the first time in history, and there is no doubt that in the subsequent self-whitening ablutions by Robespierre's collaborators all evidence in his favour was suppressed. Some of this has come to light since, but the enigma of personality, even schizophrenia, remains.

'The very word Dictator abuses liberty,' he had said. And again, 'There do exist pure and sensitive souls . . . a profound horror of tyranny, a compassionate zeal for the oppressed, a sacred love of one's country, and a love of humanity . . . without which a great revolution is no more than the destruction of a lesser crime by a greater.' The last line is very close to a comment by Paine on the responsibilities of revolution. If it was self-deception, it was not hypocrisy in the ordinary sense. But the bright, elusive target of perfectibility drew him into strange and terrible pathways, the labyrinthine means to an end which became a Minatour, not a God.

Yet fifty years after his death one of his few close friends wrote: 'I would have given my life to save Robespierre, whom I loved like a brother. No one knows better than I do how sincere, disinterested, and absolute was his devotion to the Republic. He has become the scapegoat of the revolutionists; but he was the best man of them all.' Napoleon, who knew well the ones who survived him, said much the same thing: that he was the victim of men without convictions, in most ways worse than himself. 'It is fifty years since he died,' added the friend, 'but I still treasure in my heart the memory of him, and the lively affection which he inspired.' Few men have inspired epitaphs showing such extremes of devotion and hatred. His mask, which Carlyle saw in a sea-green aura of incorruptibility, has a theatrical power to shift and change focus under the arc lights of history.

XVIII

RETURN TO REASON

Paine, by nature guileless about others until the shock of betrayal, was easily enough led to accept the general verdict on Robespierre, and attribute all his tribulations, and most of those of France, to the man who never attacked him personally and in fact shared many of his views. As Robespierre was dead the overflow of the prisoner's wrath descended on Washington. But in the meantime, incredibly, the death of Robespierre did not mean instant release.

Paine much later claimed he had only escaped the guillotine by an accident. On the night when so many had been marked down for the tumbrils, by a chalk cross on their prison door, Paine's cross had been marked on the inside, while open, by mistake. When the guards came to collect the victims his door was shut, and the mark invisible, so he was passed by. Whether he really was aware of this at the time, or was told it later by those who tended him in his illness, is not clear. He could even have dreamed it in his delirium, which Sampson Perry mentions as the main cause he was overlooked. If the tale is true, the note in Robespierre's desk belonged to the past, not the future: a demand already acted on, either by himself or others.

After the death of Robespierre the atmosphere of the Reign of Terror began, slowly, to evaporate. Paris had supp'd full of horrors, and the following year an effervescence of long-forgotten luxury, many balls and the new fashion for the classic style in dress and painting were to pave the way for Napoleon and the new Empire. In the meantime Paine's release was expedited by the appointment of a new American Minister in Paris to succeed Morris, James Monroe, later one of America's Presidents. Monroe took up his appointment in August, and on 10th September Paine wrote to him on the citizenship question in connection with his imprisonment. 'The question is simply, whether I am, or am not a citizen of America.' Monroe replied sympathetically on 18th September, accepting that Paine was American. 'By being with us through the revolution, you are of our country, as absolutely as if you had been born there; and you are no more of England, than any native of America is.'

It was not entirely unequivocal, and the question of Paine's official citizenship, in spite of his long residence, was to be raised again in America later, when he was actually refused the right to vote in his own district. Monroe added, however, that Paine was considered 'not only as having rendered important services in our own revolution, but as being, upon a more extensive scale, the friend of human rights, and a distinguished and able advocate, in favour of the public liberty'.

Paine had also petitioned the Committee of General Security through Vanhuele, his cell-mate at the Luxembourg, who had himself been released. According to Vanhuele, Paine's letter had enraged Bourdon de l'Oise, who had been, with Barère, directly responsible for Paine's imprisonment. Perhaps because of de l'Oise's opposition, the matter did not make headway, and it was not until 1st November that Monroe wrote to the Committee of General Security asking that the French government should either bring Paine to trial, if they considered him guilty of any criminal offence, or release him if not. He praised Paine with warmth and obvious sincerity, and four days later Paine was released. He had been in prison ten months, and it was over three since Robespierre had died.

The prisons had been slowly emptied: Paine was almost the last left at the Luxembourg. Not all, though, escaped the guillotine and executions, on a smaller scale, went on during 1794 and 1795. The 9th Thermidor, the day of Robespierre's death, was not a *coup d'état* of the moderates but 'a settling of accounts between extremist leaders';[1] but gradually the balance began to weigh towards reaction. In June 1795, the young Dauphin, Louis XVII, imprisoned in the Temple, was reported to have died, and there is no great reason to doubt it. It made little difference politically, as his uncle in exile, the Count of Provence, instantly proclaimed himself King as Louis XVIII, and both at the time and many years later, when he ascended the throne, he made little effort to discover the true facts of his nephew's death. From his own point of view, it was not expedient, and none of the numerous 'pretenders' succeeded in establishing a valid and accepted claim.

In the provinces, not unnaturally, the royalists led reactionary insurrections and at Lyons a White Terror replaced, for a time, Fouché's and d'Herbois' Red one. In Paris, the Convention carried on the revolutionary government in a less oppressive spirit, but this did not mean that it absorbed only those, like Sieyès, who had quietly dissociated themselves from the Terror, or been banished under it. In February 1795, ironically, the Convention restored freedom of worship (as long as the priests obeyed the laws), which had been Robespierre's aim just before his death, and although the plan of free schooling was never implemented, the Convention did carry out certain reforms in higher education. The price controls instigated by Robespierre for the benefit of the poor were quickly abolished (in December 1794) to meet the

[1] *Larousse Encyclopaedia of Modern History* (1964).

outcry of the bourgeoisie, the shopkeepers and the farmers; and as a result, by April 1795, there were hunger marchers besieging the Assembly. Inevitably, on this, there was an abortive attempt by a few Convention extremists to regain control. It was suppressed, but France as yet showed no wish to return to the old *status quo*, more especially while her revolutionary armies continued victorious in the field.

In August 1795, she formed instead, as a safeguard from future dictatorships, a bi-cameral form of government. It consisted of a Committee of Five Hundred, whose function was to initiate and propose measures to a Council of two hundred and fifty Ancients, who alone could pass or reject them. The basis of this legislature was a new Constitution with a Declaration of Rights, but differing to some extent from the more revolutionary Constitution on which Sieyès and Paine had been working in the past. Sieyès was actively concerned in the new one. In it voting depended upon property qualifications, a feature which needless to say aroused Paine's instant protest.

He had before its adoption mounted the Convention tribune to express his views on the new proposals through Lanthenas. The effects of the malignant fever he had acquired in the Luxembourg explained, he stated, his long absence from the Convention, but although obviously still weak and ill he maintained the magnitude of the subject demanded his presence. It is characteristic that he added that he was 'not persecuted by the *people*, either of England or France. The proceedings in both countries were the effects of the despotism existing in their respective government.' Equally characteristically, he added that even had his persecution originated in the people at large, it would not have changed his views. 'Principles which are influenced and subject to the control of tyranny have not their foundation in the heart.'

He had been re-elected to the Assembly on 7 December 1794, a month after his release, as a result of a petition by a minor member named Thibaudeau: 'I appeal in favour of one of the most zealous defenders of liberty, of a man who has honoured his century by the energy with which he has defended the rights of man . . .' The voting for his return was unanimous.

Paine was now nearing fifty-eight years of age, and was described at this time by a younger man, Charles Nodier, as an 'ageing Anglo-American', and 'professed revolutionary, naif, fanatic, monomaniac, full of candour . . . a man of virtue, bold in doctrine, cautious in practice; likely to deliver himself instantaneously to revolutions, but incapable of accepting their dangerous consequences'. Paine had undoubtedly aged through his prison illness, which was shortly to return, and the picture, in the nature of a shrewd snap judgment, was ambivalent as so many descriptions of Paine were throughout his life. He was a chameleon whose colours changed with the eye of the individual beholder, not constant psychologically even to himself, except in this one great virtue which was not merely to go down into history, but in a sense transform it: the virtue of care for humanity in the mass and in particular the rights of the poor and dispossessed.

France was prepared to honour her adopted champion, but shared with America a tendency to honour in word rather than deed. On 7 January 1795, Marie-Joseph Chénier, the dramatist, presented to the Convention a scheme for awarding pensions to citizens who had performed distinguished literary services. Paine was the first on his list in this forerunner of official recognition of the Arts, but he never received the pension. With the Americans, too, Paine's welfare and official status were of some concern. A treaty of friendship and commerce between France and America presented an opportunity to Monroe to propose that Paine should be appointed official envoy to carry the French proposals to America. The Committee put paid to this by saying his position in the Assembly would not allow this.

In the meantime Paine got to work on a reprint and adaptation of his *Dissertation of the First Principles of Government*, partly to criticize some points in the proposed new Constitution. He maintained the art of government should not be mysterious to the common man but understandable by all: an old theory revived. He urged the distinction between society and government and resisted the Convention's limiting of citizenship to those who paid direct taxation, pleading for universal suffrage as has been seen. In no country in the world (including America) was this to be realized for several generations.

When the new Constitution was adopted the Convention itself was automatically disbanded, and Paine lost his deputyship and became once more a private citizen. In September 1795, he suffered a return of his prison illness, including paralysis of the hands. He was now living with the Monroes and with the help of Mrs Monroe's devoted care, and his own iron constitution, he recovered with surprising speed and completeness, although neither the Monroes nor his visitors expected him to live. Even during his illness his writing continued, and in addition to *Dissertation of the First Principles of Government* he set to work in 1795 on Part II of *The Age of Reason*, and followed it later with a third Part. The whole work was to become internationally his most famous achievement after the *Rights of Man*; for *Common Sense*, so highly regarded in his own time, is now little known or read outside America. It was the crux of the enlightenment on the religious side as *Rights of Man* was the crux of it on the radical; and both books owe their survival to a line of thought which remains relevant in spite of some contemporary reference which has been superseded.

In *The Age of Reason* this is, of course, the minute examination of the Bible in matters of contradiction, false chronology, false identification with Moses and other writers, and general unreliability. Modern theological and archaeological research has reached a number of the same conclusions and carried them further than Paine: the outrage with which his examination was greeted sprang from the almost total acceptance of the entire Bible as the Word of God, his Revelation, among churchmen and their followers in Paine's own time and later. Many of the foremost figures of the age thought as Paine did; Franklin, Jefferson, Voltaire and innumerable others. But political reasons kept most of them either off the printed page or, as in Voltaire's case, reasonably circumspect. Paine's dangerous quality was to examine and particularize, here on the Bible as heretofore, in *Rights of Man*, on Hanoverian finances and hereditary claims.

The remarkable thing about his conclusions is that in so many cases they anticipated those of modern theologians: on the Book of Job, for instance, which he admired as what has been described in our time as 'wisdom literature', and which Paine like Spinoza attributed to a source outside Judaism. He grasps that the bible stories, where not direct Jewish history, are fabulous and incredible and it is understandable that his rejection of them, in a credulous age, should omit in many cases an appreciation of the symbolic nature of the myth and its poetic expression: a fundamental of more modern biblical scholarship. Paine was fighting a giant whose dominion over mankind had dethroned reason and worked to establish a superstition which was used, and had nearly always been used, to exert a socially disastrous influence over the underprivileged. 'All natural institutions of Churches, whether Jewish, Christian, or Turkish, appear to me no other than human inventions set up to terrify and enslave mankind and monopolise power and profit.' The anticipation of Karl Marx and his more celebrated phrase about religion being used as 'the opium of the people' is obvious.

It is in its general analysis of the spiritual basis of philosophy and religious feeling that *The Age of Reason* remains a potent and interesting work. Its remarkably prophetic and scientific examination of astronomy and the worlds in space, and its sensitivity to nature and the insect world, have already been quoted; and it is significant of Paine's breadth of moral conscience that he included the animal world in his list of human responsibilities: 'everything of persecution between man and man, and everything of cruelty to animals, is a violation of moral duty'. This was far more unusual in the eighteenth century than it would seem today. That this was seen by him as an imitation of the 'moral goodness and beneficence of God manifested in the creation towards all his creatures' shows how far he was from the attitudes of atheism in his time or some more questioning evolutionary scientists later. Darwin's reaction to the cruelties suffered by the lower orders of creation was one of horror, and totally without the spiritual blindness of Paine's more conventional religious attitude. Paine's way with evil in nature is largely to ignore it, ascribing it neither to his beneficent God nor to the Devil in whom he stoutly refused to believe. His horror is of man's inhumanity to man as evidenced in the tales of Jewish history: the slayings of the enemy, the rape and slaughter of civilians, both women and children, held up as a gory triumph of the Israelites chosen and directed by their God. This to him was palpably not God's work, and invalidated the Bible on moral grounds from being considered the revealed word of God.

How unwelcome such probings into the actualities of the Old Testament were at the time, and how few dared question the Bible publicly, is shown by the reception of *The Age of Reason* and the many 'answers' to it which were published. As Bertrand Russell pointed out, some of the replies to Paine by 'the most liberal' of his contestants, the Bishop of Llandaff, were curious. 'For example, *The Age of Reason* ventured to doubt whether God really commanded that all males and married women among the Midianites should be slaughtered, while the maidens should be preserved. The Bishop indignantly retorted that the maidens were not preserved for immoral purposes, as Paine had wickedly suggested, but as slaves, to which there could be no ethical objection. The orthodox of our day have forgotten what orthodoxy was like a hundred and forty years ago. They have forgotten still more completely that it was men like Paine, who in face of persecution, caused the softening of dogma by which our age profits.'[1]

Paine wrote Part I before his arrest in December 1794, in a France lapsing into atheism and therefore without, he points out, a Bible being obtainable for consultation. It was after his release that he wrote Part II, and with a Bible to hand particularized his ethical and archaeological attack on the work. This is why Part I is the more interesting today. He points out at the beginning that it had been his intention for several years past to publish his thoughts on religion, and that he was well aware of the difficulties that attended the subject. He undertook it now because of this growing atheism, and also because he anticipated that he himself was near death. And he early sets forth his own creed:

'I believe in one God, and no more; and I hope for happiness beyond this life.

'I believe in the equality of man, and I believe that religious duties

---

[1] *Why I am not a Christian* (Allen & Unwin, 1957). From the essay 'The Fate of Thomas Paine', written by Russell in 1934.

consist in doing justice, loving mercy, and endeavouring to make our fellow-creatures happy.

'But lest it should be supposed that I believe many other things in addition to these, I shall, in the progress of this work, declare the things I do not believe, and my reasons for not believing them.'

These included the professed creeds of all the extant systems of religion and their respective churches. 'My own mind is my own church.' The fact that this was exactly the form of heresy expressed unwittingly by Shaw's Saint Joan did not save Paine from a similar, if less physically painful, reaction, in spite of the passing of three and a half centuries since the fire was lit in Rouen. And in both cases, State and Church combined forces as against a common enemy, because attack on the one was automatically considered an attack on the other, so closely were the temporal and the ecclesiastical linked in established society.

What Paine was attacking above all was, as he expressed it, 'mental lying', by which he meant the acceptance of things which in an age of reason, without self-deception, should be questioned as exceeding the bounds of rational thought. In this he included the doctrine of the immaculate conception, the divinity of Christ as the literal Son of God, the miracles and church dogma; and when he compared these things with the fabulous nature of pre-Christian mythology (which in some respects, the mother-and-son theme, for instance, he noticed seemed to have been passed on from the pagan to the Christian religion), he was scarcely to be faulted in including the giants who proliferate in international legend. The historical basis of that particular myth has been accepted as a possibility on archaeological evidence since Paine's time, and at least one modern writer has suggested a connection, on not totally dismissible evidence, with the visitation of our planet in its early history by explorers from outer space; thus explaining the still unaccountable mental 'jump' by which man detached himself, in comparatively recent history, from the animal world.[1] To say that this is a theory that would have attracted and interested Paine, the astronomical peopler of invisible planets around the suns of distant galaxies, is only to emphasize the range and modernity of his questioning mind. Von Däniken's theory is, after all, no more far-fetched in our time than was Paine's deduction of these planets, not discernible through any telescope, and their possible populations, in the eighteenth century.

On Jesus Paine adds: 'Nothing that is here said can apply, even with the most distant disrespect, to the *real* character of Jesus Christ. He was a virtuous and an amiable man. The morality that he preached and

[1] Erich von Däniken: *Chariots of the Gods* and *Return to the Stars* (Souvenir Press, 1969 and 1970).

practised was of the most benevolent kind.' But he also adds that 'Jesus Christ wrote no account of himself, of his birth, parentage, or anything else. Not a line of what is called the New Testament is of his own writing. The history of him is altogether the work of other people; and as to the account given of his resurrection and ascension, it was the necessary counterpart to the story of his birth. His historians, having brought him into the world in a supernatural manner, were obliged to take him out again in the same manner, or the first part of the story must have fallen to the ground.'

As the resurrection is the key point of Christian theology, the dismayed reaction to Paine's book is understandable. Though most people today would respect his moral stance, Christians would still reject his view on this; and it was easy enough to turn people against his book by quoting its anti-church attitude, and leaving out its moral rectitude. Immorality was assumed, when not even deliberately stated, as a principle of the book and its author: and this assumption became even more rigid in Victorian times. If *Rights of Man* provided Paine's political enemies with a weapon, *The Age of Reason* was a gift in the nature of an atomic bomb. It was used as a weapon of destruction, quite deliberately, for political purposes.

'The only idea man can affix to the name of God is that of a *first cause*, the cause of all things' was his creed. And his view of the universe was scientific but still leaving a mystery, the wonder and inexplicability of its creation. Science and God in a sense were interdependent, in spite of 'the continual persecution carried on by the Church for several hundred years against the sciences and against the professors of science'.

'It is an idea I have never lost sight of, that all our knowledge of science is derived from the revolutions (exhibited to our eye, and from thence to our understanding) which those several planets, or worlds, of which our system is composed make in their circuit round the sun.'

Yet paradoxically, although he is conscious of a universal mystery, and explains it by God, the creator and Supreme Being, he opposes the concept of mystery with that of moral truth. The belief in God is a necessity from man's observation of the planetary systems and the rules they obey. Thus Paine rather ingeniously manages to provide himself with the best of both worlds, the scientific and the religious, while banishing superstition and dogma as unnecessary accretions. He disposes of the miraculous by comparison with magic, shrewdly noting that Moses' conjuring trick with the rod that turned into a serpent was acquired from knowledge of Egyptian skills of this kind and is preserved in magicians' circles; and he instances from his eighteenth century surroundings: 'There is now an exhibition in Paris of ghosts and spectres which, though it is not imposed upon spectators as a fact, has an astonishing appearance.'

There is a good deal of wit in *The Age of Reason*. 'How happened it that he did not discover America?' he writes of Satan's temptation of Christ by showing him all the kingdoms of the world, and in view of the threat and atmosphere under which he wrote Part I, the apparent lightness of some of his commentary is psychologically rather remarkable. It is a less solemn book than either *Common Sense* or *Rights of Man*, and suggests a character that maintained courage by drawing on the springs of a sense of humour. The young convivial Paine of the White Hart in Lewes returned to support the ageing, disillusioned Paine of Paris and the Reign of Terror. In assessing Paine it is necessary to remember the taverner as well as the political philosopher; and as in the case of many of the Irish it is probable that the habit of drinking—by which on the evidence I do not mean drinking to excess—came originally from an attraction to the conversation and company most easily found in the surroundings of the inn. Paine was in many ways a 'solitary', like other writers; and solitude needs relief, even if it is an ingrained part of nature.

By the late autumn of 1793 Paine's isolation was marked; too many of the visitors of that hot summer had vanished, some never to return. His only outlet was the printed page, and it is perhaps not surprising that the humours of lost conversations spilled on to it; a safety valve against the solemnities of the subject matter and the time. His characterizations, from the Bible as in life, could also be acute; the Book of Ecclesiastes he described as 'the solitary reflection of a worn-out debauchee, such as Solomon was, who, looking back on scenes he can no longer enjoy, cries out, *All is vanity!* . . . he was witty, ostentatious, dissolute, and at last melancholy; he lived fast, and died, tired of the world, at the age of fifty-eight years.'

It doubtless did not escape Paine's notice that his own age, at the time he wrote Part II of *The Age of Reason*, was exactly that of Solomon, but he was far from being tired of the world. When providence seemed about to see to it that he also died at fifty-eight years, he fought the illness that attacked him tenaciously. On the accounts given by Monroe and others, only supreme will-power could have conquered the imminent death Paine's companions took for granted at the time.

Psychologically his writing on Solomon is interesting, particularly in the light of his own broken marriage and patently negligible sex life. 'Seven hundred wives, and three hundred concubines, are worse than none,' wrote Paine with confidence if not actual alarm, 'and however it may carry with it the appearance of heightened enjoyment, it defeats all the felicity of affection by leaving it no point to fix upon; divided love is never happy . . . It is needless after this to say that all was vanity and vexation of spirit, for it is impossible to derive happiness from the company of those whom we deprive of happiness.'

It would be stretching assumption perhaps too far to see in this a direct reference to Paine's marriage with Elizabeth Ollive; but the implication cannot be ignored. Did Paine realize that he deprived Elizabeth of happiness, for whatever reason, sexual or in refusing to change his interests and ways of life; and know only too well that the fact contributed to his own unhappiness in the union? His assumption of lack of happiness for the inhabitants of Solomon's harem is doubtless more political in its reflection on the degradation of women. He had already glanced at this in America, and recent contact with Mary Wollstonecraft would have revived the thoughts in his mind.

Now in the philosophy of late middle age, he contemplates old age, too, with resignation.

'To be happy in old age it is necessary that we accustom ourselves to objects that can accompany the mind all the way through life, and that we take the rest as good in their day. The mere man of pleasure is miserable in old age, and the mere drudge in business is but little better; whereas natural philosophy, mathematical and mechanical sciences, are a continual source of tranquil pleasure, and, in spite of the gloomy dogma of priests and of superstition, the study of these things is the study of the true theology . . .

'Those who knew Benjamin Franklin will recollect that his mind was ever young, his temper ever serene; science, that never grows grey, was always his mistress. Without an object, we become like an invalid in an hospital waiting for death.'

Death had come to Franklin in 1791, in the natural course of his eighty-four years. The month before his death he had expressed a religious creed very similar to Paine's: a belief in one God, the Creator, who is best served by 'doing good to his other children'. On the question of the divinity of Christ, on which he confessed some doubts, he had added with a wry humour that he thought it 'needless to busy myself with it now, when I expect soon an Opportunity of knowing the Truth with less Trouble'.

Paine, like many solitaries, had it within his character to be happy and busy in old age; by an irony of circumstance life was to cheat him of much of this happiness, in part through this very book, *The Age of Reason*, written at a time when the enlightenment was about to pass out of men's grasp. For in the new century a new capitalistic society was to arise, dependent, for the overwhelming prosperity of the few, on binding the poor in religious chains that forbade too active questioning of their condition.

Only a comparative few were to notice the deterioration in free thought, once the radical books and publishers were driven underground by the repeal of Habeas Corpus and the long terms of imprisonment. Protest, after the passing of the Reform Bill, had to become 'respectable', and few openly challenged religion again. Socialism, to work its slow way into Parliament, had to conform, although it was still often connected with congregationalism and other types of religious dissent.

The Age of Reason was the last great expression of the enlightenment, which was a matter not only of religion but of a freer moral attitude to pleasure and the arts as well as social reform. 'Everyone knows (thanks to Tom Paine, who christened the enlightenment the Age of Reason),' wrote Brigid Brophy in *Mozart the Dramatist*, 'that the immediate duty of the emancipated Ego was to reason out its own moral judgments.' Paine was never the profligate his opponents afterwards painted, and his pleasures like Shaw's were mainly mental; but his attitude was one of tolerance, and moral censoriousness, except when current or past morality actually caused suffering to others, was never present in his nature or his works. He was a part of that dying century which Brigid Brophy crystallized when she wrote in the same book: 'Social emancipation is accompanied by the tremendous intellectual and emotional emancipation which is what we mean by the enlightenment . . . The enlightenment is characterized by a new attainment of self-consciousness; and the enlightened society is brilliantly illuminated by its members' own awareness of it and themselves.'

This awareness, expressed in diaries, memoirs, journalism and portraits on a profuse scale, is shown in the French Revolution, with its forest of conflicting personalities who could rarely be precisely fitted even into one political pigeonhole; and the very self-consciousness and richness of these varied psychological entities created the internal combustion that destroyed the Revolution. The enlightened society, as Brigid Brophy points out, 'outlasted the eighteenth century, in the strict numerical sense of *century*, by a couple of decades', and 'it withstood the shock of the French Revolution, though it was that shock which shattered it in the end'. When Paine wrote *The Age of Reason*, thinking it a culmination, he was really tolling the last bell of an era. It was his tragedy that he lived to realize it, and to experience the beginnings of an alien New World in both the political and the geographical sense.

XIX

RELIGION AND ECONOMICS

There would seem to remain some question as to the publication date of Part I of *The Age of Reason*. Paine in *Prosecution of the Age of Reason* gave the date as 1793, which would mean it must have been printed prior to his arrest, and giving of the last pages to Barlow, at the end of December. Lanthenas himself, in his appeal for Paine's release from prison, written in August 1794, stated that Paine wrote the book 'in the beginning of the year '93', that he translated it 'before the revolution against the priests' and it was published in French about the same time. The American expert on Paine, Richard Gimbel, in 1956 recorded in the *Yale University Library Gazette* the discovery in a Paris catalogue of a shorter version of the book, with Lanthenas on the title page as author, and although this was undated the omission of Paine's references to the anger against the priests, and of his 1794 dedication, suggested it could be the lost 1793 edition. Lanthenas wrote he submitted the book in 1793 to Couthon who was 'offended' with him for translating it, so it could well have been suppressed apart from this rare copy. Paine, however, in the account of his arrest gives no indication that there was already an edition, minus several chapters, translated and in print. The other rare edition described by Conway in *The Athenaeum*, with Paine's additions on Bourdon de l'Oise and his work with Barère, must obviously have been compiled after his arrest.

Although Supreme Being was a common term used by both deists and freemasons of the time, it seems possible that Robespierre, as already suggested, had read this Lanthenas translation published early in 1794 and the reasons given by Paine in the first chapter for writing the book. When Robespierre, in June, arranged the Festival of the Supreme Being, he proclaimed its necessity in very much the same terms as Paine. Where Robespierre failed, could Paine succeed? The immediate answer was yes and no. The reaction to the Revolution threatened a church restoration which was far from the type of theology Paine had envisaged in his book; but in January 1797, with five families in support, Paine helped to found in Paris the society of Theophilanthropy—a word, as he stated in a letter to Erskine, 'compounded of three Greek words, signifying God, Love, and Man'. (Erskine would hardly need the elucidation and Paine, like Shakespeare according to Ben Jonson, was rather inclined to parade his 'little Latin and less

Greek'. With a similar grammar school education to Shakespeare's, he probably shared the same psychological incentive, nettled by the hint of superiority detected in the more expensively educated.) A Quaker upbringing dies hard, and it is obvious Paine could never shake off some inner need both for belief and an organization of that belief. In his inaugural discourse he said: 'Religion has two principal enemies, Fanaticism and Infidelity, or that which is called atheism. The first required to be combated by reason and morality, the other by natural philosophy.' This discourse was published by his friend Clio Rickman in 1798.

Theophilanthropy was a forerunner of the ethical and humanist societies that proliferated later, and its tolerance was wide. There were readings from Chinese, Hindu and Greek authors as well as the singing of humanitarian hymns; and one of its four festivals was in honour of Washington, an extraordinary instance of how Paine could separate past achievement from his own present individual feelings, which were markedly antagonistic to Washington. In a sense this strange spiritual exercise was a reversion to scenes of childhood, a nostalgia which often assails the ageing. That the Quakers were in his thoughts, far from unsympathetically, at this time is shown in a letter he published to Camille Jordan, who had made the plea for a committee to reaffirm some national recognition of public worship in France, and the restoration of churches and bells to the priesthood. The Constitution, argued Paine, gives no privilege to any one religion and 'the churches are the common property of all the people'. No one should make a living out of religion and it is 'a want of feeling to talk of priests and bells whilst so many infants are perishing in the hospitals, and aged and infirm in the streets'. The churches should be sold, and the money invested as a fund for the education of poor parents of every profession, and for the support of the aged poor. 'The only people who, as a professional sect of Christians, provide for the poor of their society, are people known by the name of Quakers. These men have no priests. They assemble quietly in their places of worship, and do not disturb their neighbours with shows and noise of bells.'

The letter to Erskine needs explanation. In 1797 an action was brought by the English government against Thomas Williams for printing *The Age of Reason*, and Erskine, who had so brilliantly but ineffectually defended Paine in the case of *Rights of Man*, was now on the prosecuting side. How much this was ingrained antipathy to *The Age of Reason*, and how much the accident of a legal brief, is not quite clear. Paine wrote ironically 'it is difficult to know when a lawyer is to be believed', perhaps preferring this interpretation of Erskine's *volte face* to facing the fact that the attorney may genuinely, like so many, have been shocked by the work on religious grounds. Erskine, who never lacked ability, certainly put up a very convincing show of this being the case, as he had seemed equally to believe in freedom of speech politically in the case of *Rights of Man*. Paine published *A Letter to Mr Erskine* but although bouncily satiric it was hardly as persuasive as *The Age of Reason* itself. In the trial the Judge, Lord Kenyon, closed his peroration with the statement: 'Unless it was for the most malignant purposes, I cannot conceive how it was published.' The Jury dutifully gave a verdict that the defendant was guilty of publishing a blasphemous work.

Before leaving the subject of Paine and religion, it is necessary to consider the statement that has been made in some works that he was a freemason. There appeared to be no evidence of this, and on enquiring myself of the United Grand Lodge of England at Freemason's Hall I received the following reply from the Librarian and Curator:

> 'Although Thomas Paine wrote a book on Freemasonry,[1] there is no trace that he was ever a Freemason. In the absence of any record of his initiation it must, therefore, be assumed that he was not a member of the order.'

This was understandable, for British freemasonry was closely linked with the aristocracy and even royalty (the Duke of Cumberland was Grand Master, and on his death in 1790 he was succeeded by the future George IV). In France this also was true, although many aristocratic members were liberals such as Philippe Egalité, Mirabeau and Lafayette.[2] Since I wrote to Freemason's Hall it has, however, been claimed in America that Paine joined the Albany Lodge in 1785. If true, presumably this would have been under the influence of Franklin, who like Voltaire, Goethe and other influential eighteenth century Europeans belonged to the order. It was a liberizing cult certainly to some extent and believed widely to have had influence in promoting the French Revolution, but this influence has been exaggerated and it has never seemed likely that Paine, with his individualism and dislike of secrecy and ritual, would have been long attracted to it.

It had begun in Scotland and historically had its roots in the medieval guilds of the stonemasons and architects building the Gothic cathedrals; but this hint of trade unionism had early become obscured and it had developed as a religious secret society with international connections. In the eighteenth century, partly through the influence of a romance called *Sethos* by the Abbé Jean Terasson, published in 1731, freemasonry began to claim derivations stretching back as far as ancient Egypt. It was certainly an organization of religious tolerance, and

[1] *Essay on the Origin of Freemasonry*, published posthumously in 1811.
[2] G. P. Gooch: *French Profiles*, 'The Golden Age of Freemasonry' (Longmans, 1961).

perhaps for this reason it had earned the implacable opposition of the Roman Catholic Church, which issued Papal Bulls outlawing the movement under Pope Clement VIII and Pope Benedict XIV. These were largely ignored even by Catholics throughout Europe, and as some members were known to be sympathetic to, or active in, the revolutions in America and France, in December 1789, five months after the fall of the Bastille, the Vatican aimed a new blow. It arrested the mysterious Count di Cagliostro, who was known to be a prominent freemason.

Cagliostro had founded an 'Egyptian' lodge in Lyons and had held séances there, with a child as medium. He had also practised successfully in London, Paris and Strasbourg as a spiritual 'healer': without accepting money for his cures and relying largely, it would appear, on common sense, psychology, diet and herbal knowledge much ahead of his time, medically speaking. His prestige was enormous, taking him into the highest social circles, and although the source of his wealth gave rise to speculation (he was certainly humbly born), and there was undoubtedly chicanery somewhere along the line of his notoriety (his *Memoirs* were entirely fabulous, inspired by *Sethos*, and he encouraged stories of his success as an alchemist in discovering 'the philosopher's stone'), his powerful personality seems to have been exercised with the austerity associated with the masonic order, into which he had been initiated in London in 1776.

The Inquisition of the Vatican seized him in December 1789, and after a prolonged trial in camera condemned and imprisoned him for life in March 1791. The condemnation was specifically for heresy through freemasonry, and once again the Vatican issued direful warnings that 'the most grievous corporal punishment reserved for heretics shall be inflicted on all who shall associate or hold communion with, or protect, these societies'.

It was a direct move to discredit freemasonry, especially as many people distrusted Cagliostro's reputation and claims of mystical powers; and it is true the order never again acquired the political influence it had exercised in the eighteenth century. The effect of the Cagliostro trial and sentence can be seen in Mozart's opera *The Magic Flute*, which during its composition changed direction towards a more powerful, although necessarily overt and symbolic, vindication of freemasonry. Both Mozart and Schikaneder, his librettist, were freemasons. The original source of the society still survived in the freemason description of the Supreme Being as 'Architect of the Universe', a term used at the masonic service on Mozart's death. Paine also employed the term in *The Age of Reason* and elsewhere, although whether with a masonic connotation or, more likely, a scientific recognition of the structure of the universe, it is not possible to say.

He would certainly have known of the Cagliostro trial; and the Papal wording of the Cagliostro verdict was a matter of alarm and sensation to freemasons throughout the world. On 8 June 1791, when Paine was in Paris, *Le Moniteur* published an account from their Rome Correspondent of the posting of the sentence and the public burning of all Cagliostro's papers, books and 'masonic cordons'. Freemasonry in some of its aspects would undoubtedly have appealed to Paine. It preached tolerance and wisdom, reason and compassion, as the major human virtues, and its ideal of equality made it attractive to revolutionists. But the rites of initiation he would surely have classed as superstitious mummery, and the derider of Moses' 'magic' would hardly have been impressed by the rumours of alchemy and spiritualism (although that term for the séance only came into use later) associated with Cagliostro.[1]

His own essay, written in America, on the subject makes clear, to my mind, that he was not then a member but writing of masons from the outside, with the help of certain key works on the subject which he closely analyses. Quite naturally he dismisses with derision Samuel Pritchard's claim, in *Masonry Dissected* (1730), that masonry began with the building of the Tower of Babel, and equally that of Captain George Smith in *The Use and Abuse of Freemasonry* (1783) that it was coeval with the creation and formulated by God. He treats with more respect the oration of Dr Dodd, Grand Chaplain of Freemasonry, at the dedication of Freemason's Hall in London, which described the building of Solomon's Temple as 'an important era' in masonry and linked it with the religious ritual of the ancient Druids, a theory which in the end Paine accepts on the evidence of hieroglyphics and the sun and zodiac symbols of the freemasons, conspicuous on the ceiling of Freemason's Hall.

Paine's essay is more intelligent and scholarly than some of this might suggest; without apparently knowing of *Sethos* or the Gothic cathedral links, he goes with some knowledge into the principles of mathematical and geometrical history, notes the association of Masonry's high festival, St John's Day, with the summer solstice which was a centre of pagan worship, and makes an interesting point about the continued Irish custom of lighting fires on the tops of hills on that day,

[1] Since this was written and printed, I have received from the Grand Lodge of Masons of the State of New York the following comments:

'We are familiar with some of the claims (perhaps those you have seen) of Masonic membership for Thomas Paine, and also share your finding that they are apparently made without the benefit of factual evidence. We have never been able to find a membership record for him.

'One of our Lodges was once named in his honor: Paine's Lodge No. 27, organized at Amenia, Dutchess County, in 1792, but many Lodges have been named in honor of famous men not necessarily members. Paine's Lodge was renamed Hiram in 1797 and passed out of existence in the early 1830's.'

dating back to pagan or Druidical custom and only veneered later with Christianity. He quotes a Question and Answer catechism of mason apprentices (this was obtainable from books: the closely guarded secrets of freemasonry were given only after long initiation and study, to those who attained the rank of Master), and it is interesting to note that this includes a hint of masonry's architectural antecedents, describing 'the level and plumb rule about their necks to close the lodge, and dismiss the men from labour, paying them their wages'.

Paine does not appear to know that the first Lodges as such were formed only in the eighteenth century; but a good deal of the evidence he examines does contain so much connected with building craftsmanship, geometry and pagan worship that, although Paine's knowledge of the Druids by modern standards is questionable, there is still, after reading his essay, a query in one's mind as to whether masonry might have some basis for its claims to a tenuous link with the ancient world, preserved much as witchcraft has been preserved from the earliest history of mankind. Paine with modern materials might have made a good historian: from the Bible he had absorbed the fact that the Jews were not builders, like the Egyptians, but had to rely on the skills of Hiram of Tyre even for the building of Solomon's Temple, and he notes that 'the description that Josephus gives of the decorations of this Temple, resembles on a large scale those of a Mason's Lodge'. It is a surprising reference from Paine, the classically unread. His own interests from childhood were largely mathematical, and one would say from his bridge engineering project that his school groundwork was good. He retained through life a zest for mathematical applications in many directions, both fiscal and Euclidian.

The fact that on his release from prison Paine became so caught up in religious speculation is an indication of his disillusion with politics and his sense of helplessness now that his work in the Convention was finished. The sense of helplessness, however, was suppressed and chafed against, and once he had recovered from his illness he renewed his antagonism to the English government and bitterly opposed the proposed Jay Treaty between England and the United States. This put Monroe as American Minister in a difficult position, and in 1796 Paine left Monroe's house, finding it impossible to hold his tongue or his pen. The fact that Monroe continued his loyal admirer shows the extent of his regard. Paine's knowledge of French politics had, in fact, been of considerable help to him as Minister in his reports back to Washington, and the kindness Paine received from him and his wife at the time of his illness created a bond which was never entirely broken.

Paine, ill and fretting at the turn of revolutionary events, was not an easy person to deal with, and Monroe's forbearance was also exercised in the matter of Paine's attack on Washington, from which he tried in vain to dissuade him. Undeterred, and genuinely vindictive for perhaps the first time in his life, Paine sent his *Letter to Washington*, like a poisoned dart, across the Atlantic and the Channel. There is no doubt there was some cause for his resentment, and he may have suspected that Washington had sacrificed him in part to help his relations with England, signified in the new Treaty. Nevertheless, Paine's public attack on an old companion in arms, a man he had highly praised on many occasions, took a turn of venom which perhaps one can only ascribe to a deterioration based on ill health and excessive brooding. He not only now questioned Washington's ability as a soldier and general, he used the term 'hermaphrodite' which in those days, whatever Paine may have thought he meant by the taunt, was certainly flinging an equivocal form of mud which was likely to cling.

Washington had the self-control not to reply; but Paine had irretrievably undermined his opportunity for any official position on his return. That Washington never made any attempt to explain why America made no effort to obtain Paine's release, or claim him as a citizen, suggests there *was* no valid excuse and perhaps some conscience in the matter. The charge of ingratitude at least seems not uncalled for, though it does not justify the tone of Paine's attack. It was, it may be claimed, a savage journalistic age: Paine himself had certainly received more than he ever returned, in this respect. Suddenly he picked up the same weapons, and for a personal, not a political reason. It was a decline, and a portent for the future.

As a political writer and economist, though, Paine's force was still not spent. Two more works in France were to win him some permanent respect. These were *The Decline and Fall of the English System of Finance* (1796) and *Agrarian Justice* (1797). The first work in 1803 made a convert of William Cobbett, who in his *Papers Against Gold* wrote that Paine's essay 'in the space of 25 pages conveys more useful knowledge on this subject and discovers infinitely greater depth of thought and general powers of mind, than are to be found in all the pamphlets of the financiers . . . on the money system'. Today it is not so highly regarded as a piece of economic analysis. Paine assumed inherent unsoundness in the British economy, due partly to the system of financing wars through the accumulation of a National Debt, and predicted the insolvency and collapse of the economy within twenty years, owing to the fact that this debt would outpace the gold reserve. It did not prove an accurate forecast, partly because of factors outside Paine's knowledge, which included the immense growth in manufacture and trade in the wake of the ever-expanding Industrial Revolution. In effect, he was referring back to comments on the 'funding system' in *Rights of Man*, which in their turn possibly derived from the suggestions of Dr Price for a sinking fund for the National Debt in his *Observations on the Nature of Civil Liberty*. It is probable Paine's English economics were already becoming too retrospective, in spite of the grasp of fundamentals and ideas of reform which were so deeply to impress Cobbett, who had earlier been an unknowledgeable victim of anti-Paine propaganda.

If *The Decline and Fall of the English System of Finance* failed as a long-range forecast, its immediate impression was highly prophetic, as the following year the Bank of England was forced to suspend cash payments. 'From then on,' as Dr Henry Collins has written, 'the automatic discipline of a currency linked to the gold reserve was removed and inflationary pressure increased. As in America, the main sufferers were the self-employed artisans and wage earners to whom Paine was linked both by social origins and political outlook.'[1]

Always these were the basis of Paine's fears, and the root cause of his economic strivings for their protection. The English government apparently recognized this, and commissioned two 'replies' to Paine's pamphlet, one of them from George Chalmers, who as 'Francis Oldys' had similarly been employed to try and wreck Paine's reputation with a spurious biography and attack on *Rights of Man*. The French government, on the contrary, realized the effectiveness of *The Decline and Fall* as war propaganda, and arranged for its publication in England, America, Holland, Switzerland and Germany. There was shrewdness in the move, for the war against France was by no means unanimously popular in England, and in the autumn of 1795 the King had actually been assaulted by the crowd when he went to open Parliament. It is understandable the government was nervous of Paine's continued influence.

Agrarian Justice, although less immediately provocative, was to prove the work of most lasting value and one which still retains much relevance. It was an attack on the tendency of society, as it grew more affluent, to widen the gap between rich and poor, so that the poor became ever more wretched. In this it was certainly prophetic of the course of Victorian capitalist society and is true of much in England even in our own time, when the 'affluent society' and welfare state have failed conspicuously to keep the unemployed, the homeless or, in particular the aged on pensions, at a tolerable level of existence compared with the rest of society. Paine's thesis is clear:

'To preserve the benefits of what is called civilised life, and to remedy, at the same time, the evils it has produced, ought to be considered as one of the first objects of reformed legislation.

[1] Introduction, *Rights of Man* (Pelican, 1969).

'Whether that state, that is proudly, perhaps erroneously, called civilisation, has most promoted or most injured the general happiness of man, is a question that may be strongly contested. On one side the spectator is dazzled by splendid appearances—on the other, he is shocked by extremes of wretchedness; both of which it has created. The most affluent and the most miserable of the human race are to be found in the countries that are called civilised . . .

'Poverty is a thing created by that which is called civilised life.'

The life of a (Red) Indian was a holiday compared with the poor of Europe.

Although there is an echo here of Rousseau's cult of nature and the noble savage, *Agrarian Justice* bears stronger similarities to the *Progress and Poverty* of Henry George, the American Land and Tax reformist of whom Bernard Shaw, on hearing him lecture, became a disciple in the early 1880s, until Hyndman's Marxist Democratic Federation contemptuously dismissed George and advised Shaw that he had been superseded by Marx. Shaw promptly read *Das Capital* and returned to the Federation to announce his complete conversion. 'Immediately,' wrote Shaw, 'contempt changed to awe; for Hyndman's disciples had not read the book themselves, it then being accessible only in Deville's French version in the British Museum Reading Room, my daily resort.'

Later, although Shaw was to protest to Winston Churchill that in essentials he remained a Marxist, he came to believe, with Sidney Webb, that Marx was not always valid on capitalist political economy or on the law of rent: partly because of his lack of administrative experience. Paine anticipated George, not Marx, when he wrote that 'it is the value of the *improvement* of the land through agriculture only, and not the earth itself, that is individual property'. As Oscar B. Johannsen has pointed out, drawing the parallel with George: 'How many economists today recognise this simple truth that *only wealth is ethically private property and not land*?' 'Man did not make the earth,' wrote Paine, 'and, though he had a natural right to *occupy it*, he had no right to *locate as his property* in perpetuity any part of it; neither did the Creator of the earth open a land-office, from whence the first title deeds should issue.'

He anticipated George again in suggesting that every proprietor of cultivated lands owes to the community a *ground rent* for the land he holds. Paine's remedial measures included a taxing of one-tenth of estates on death, the idea in fact of a death duty; and the establishment of a fund to give each individual on attaining the age of twenty-one a sum of £15 as compensation in part for the loss of his natural inheritance. He also returned to the matter of old age pensions, suggesting £10 per annum during life to those of fifty years and over.

243

Paine was to continue writing pamphlets and articles until his death in 1809; all lucid and constructive but most of them now of minor interest, because they dealt essentially with topical matters of his time. *Agrarian Justice* was really his last work of true significance. Like so many men of distinction, he had reached and passed his peak. He was twenty years older than most of the revolutionists who had listened to him with respect as an elder, and then turned, as new generations do, to bolder and more extreme political methods. He had outlived them, but could not rebuild the world of reform their ruin had distorted in men's minds. By an irony of fate the reins of power had passed to men like Barras and Sieyès, both of whom had voted for the death of Louis XVI and now led a government of growing reaction. Sieyès resigned when it became apparent the new Constitution was not to meet his ideas, but Barras continued as a member of the Directory for the whole five years of its existence.

It is true the Convention had put down a royalist insurrection which attacked the Tuileries where it was in session. The rebels were dispersed with a 'whiff of grapeshot' by a young Brigadier General who had gained some distinction at the siege of Toulon. The young officer was a Corsican named Napoleon Bonaparte.

XX

THE DIRECTORY AND NAPOLEON

When Paine left Monroe's house in 1796 he spent a quiet summer in Versailles, partly as a guest of Sir Robert and Lady Smyth. He had met Smyth, the banker, at the White's Hotel celebration at which Smyth and Edward Fitzgerald had created a sensation by renouncing their titles; but he knew him now more intimately through a most unexpected link with his wife.

During his imprisonment, Paine had been beguiled by letters of sympathy and encouragement signed 'A little corner of the World'. Paine, through the friendly Benoit (who was afterwards replaced by a harsher jailer), contrived to answer these notes with others signed 'The Castle in the Air'. It was a strange correspondence, a little romantic in character, not from content but by implication, in view of the dramatic circumstances. Most of it was conducted in verse, a form of writing for which Paine since his schooldays had always considered he had certain gifts, and now returned to mainly as escapism; perhaps in some nostalgia, too, for the literary days of the White Hart in Lewes, where his effusions had often been in verse form. The threat of approaching death must have made these earlier times, before he began to take the weight of the world's ills on his shoulders, seem particularly pleasant in retrospect.

It was only now, in his new friendship with the Smyths, that he discovered his 'contemplative correspondent', as he had called her, to be Lady Smyth herself. Conway, on perhaps rather slender evidence, identified her with the English lady who shortly before his arrest had called on him in the Faubourg St Denis to request his help on behalf of an Englishman of rank arrested by the government. It was too late for this: Paine's influence in the Convention, which was believed to have been great, had ceased.

It would seem he had some reputation for helping distressed American and English exiles in Paris at that time, both by money, when he had it, or direct political intervention. 'He was,' wrote Barlow, 'always charitable to the poor beyond his means, a sure friend and protector to all Americans in distress that he found in foreign countries; and he had frequent occasions to exert his influence in protecting them during the Revolution in France.'

That Paine did still have some money at the time of his arrest appears to be confirmed by Sampson Perry's tale of his hiding it within the lock of his prison door. After recovering it, following his illness, he gave it to General O'Hara, to enable him to return to America. O'Hara, also a prisoner, had proved a staunch friend in common adversity, and Paine possibly was grateful for all his surgeon had done for him. It may be this generous gift was the reason Paine could not himself, after his release, easily take ship to America, and he was certainly in financial difficulties.

On discovering the identity of his prison correspondent, Paine promptly addressed a poem to her, called 'The Castle in the Air to the Little Corner of the World':

'In the region of clouds, where the whirlwinds arise,
  My Castle of Fancy was built;
The turrets reflected the blue from the skies,
  And the windows with sunbeams were gilt.

'The rainbow sometimes, in its beautiful state,
  Enamelled the mansion around;
And the figures that fancy in clouds can create
  Supplied me with gardens and ground.

'I had grottos, and fountains, and orange-tree groves,
  I had all that enchantment has told;
I had sweet shady walks for the gods and their loves,
  I had mountains of coral and gold.

'But a storm that I felt not had risen and rolled,
  While wrapped in a slumber I lay;
And when I looked out in the morning, behold,
  My Castle was carried away.

'It passed over rivers and valleys and groves,
  The world it was all in my view;
I thought of my friends, of their fates, of their loves,
  And often, full often, of you.

'At length it came over a beautiful scene,
  That nature in silence had made;
The place was but small, but 't was sweetly serene,
  And chequered with sunshine and shade.

'I gazed and I envied with painful good will,
  And grew tired of my seat in the air;
When all of a sudden my Castle stood still,
  As if some attraction was there.

'Like a lark from the sky it came fluttering down,
  And placed me exactly in view,

When whom should I meet in this charming retreat,
  This corner of calmness, but—YOU.

'Delighted to find you in honour and ease,
  I felt no more sorrow nor pain;
But the wind coming fair, I ascended the breeze,
  And went back with my Castle again.'

I have given it in full as it provides a rare glimpse of Paine in lighter writing vein. Not a great poem, unvarying in rhythm, but pleasing and mellifluous, and certainly above the average of many penned in the eighteenth century (which rather prided itself on this accomplishment), including those of Rickman.

Whether he had any genuine romantic feelings for his correspondent, either before or after her identity became known, it is impossible to say. On his record, it seems unlikely, in spite of the poem's romanticism and his occasional little gallantries to 'the ladies' on paper. This had not prevented an English newspaper, on 14 November 1792, unexpectedly ferreting out a supposed blighted romance:

'Citizen PAINE, we regret to hear from one of his friends, has been unsuccessful in his 1st attempt at Matrimony. He paid his addresses to a French *Mantua-maker*, and has been (O direful mishap!)—REFUSED.'

It was, at any rate, a change from the burnings in effigy, and suggests Oldys' book, putting Paine's two marriages in their worst light, was less known than the government had hoped.

The country air of Versailles, enabling him to indulge in his favourite exercises of walking and riding, gave Paine a certain solace and serenity, as well as a renewed physical vigour; although this was to prove somewhat ephemeral and the effects of his prison fever were to return in later life. The Jay Treaty did not make Americans popular in Paris, and there was some fear of imprisonment among the English-speaking colony. Paine on 13th August took the opportunity to repay the Smyths' kindness by writing a guarantee for the banker, requesting a passport for him:

'CITIZEN MINISTER: The citizen Robert Smith, a very particular friend of mine, wishes to obtain a passport to go to Hamburg, and I will be obliged to you to do him that favour. Himself and family have lived several years in France, for he likes neither the government nor the climate of England. He has large property in England, but his Banker in that country has refused sending him remittances. This makes it necessary for him to go to Hamburg, because from there he can draw his money out of his Banker's hands, which he cannot do whilst in France. His family remains in France.—*Salut et fraternité.*'

In 1801, when Jefferson became American President, Paine wrote to him recommending Sir Robert's firm as one highly dependable as a medium of American financial transactions in Europe.

In Paris, old friends were beginning to trickle back from exile. Lafayette and Bancal, from their respective foreign prisons, were among them. Bancal in March 1793, had been sent by the Minister of War to demand Dumouriez' submission, and had promptly been seized and delivered to the Austrians, who imprisoned him for twenty months in a dungeon at Olmütz. In December 1795, he was exchanged by agreement for Louis XVI's daughter, became converted to religion, yet managed to remain a staunch republican. Drouet, the old dragoon who had captured the King and Queen at Varennes, had also been taken prisoner by the Austrians in the war and was exchanged as part of the same deal, releasing the young Princess who alone remained alive of the royal family who had fled, in the great conspicuous berlins, across France only four years before. Now seventeen years old, she was taken to Austrian relatives in Switzerland and died long years later, in 1851, as the Duchess of Angoulême.

Lafayette, like Bancal, had known the inside of a dungeon at Olmütz, as well as four others far worse than the Luxembourg in Paris. His cell at Magdeburg, he wrote, was three paces wide and five and a half long, without sunlight and without any form of outside communication. He returned to Paris in 1797, released through the victory of the Republican Army in Italy and 'the guns and diplomacy of citizen-general Bonaparte'. The French had little sympathy for him, but Lafayette had really been misjudged to some extent, and Paine's loyalty to him in the Dedication to Part II of *Rights of Man* was justified when it became apparent that Lafayette, although he had opposed the Jacobins, had no intention of relinquishing the rather outmoded ideals of 1789. He voted against the Life Consulship offered Napoleon and retired to his estate surrounded by sentimental mementoes of his American and National Guard activities. In 1824, long after the death of Paine and others of his old companions, he paid a year's visit to America, travelled all over the United States, and was received everywhere with wild enthusiasm, a returning conquering hero of a time now passing into American history. 'France gave him birth, but America gave him Immortality,' appeared on the triumphal arches. For Lafayette it had all, in the end, been fabulously worth while.

Paine in Paris made new acquaintances as well as meeting old friends. One of these, early in 1797, was Theobald Wolfe Tone, the Irish republican leader of the coming 1798 rebellion. It was a case of two strong personalities striving, perhaps, for ascendancy: Tone described Paine as 'vain beyond all belief'. No doubt Paine tried to give him republican directions, and Tone, with his Irish independence, had certainly no wish to take orders from anyone. 'He converses extremely well,' Tone admitted in his diary. 'He seems to plume himself more on his theology than his politics, in which I do not agree with him.' He told Paine of Burke's inconsolable grief at the death of his son Richard, and Paine did not come out of this in a good light by replying that it was the *Rights of Man* which had broken his heart, and Burke was merely making the death of his son the excuse. '*Paine has no children!*' commented Tone, much as Macduff of Macbeth (or, as some Shakespearean scholars prefer to think, of Malcolm) in a similar situation.

Tone adds of Paine: 'He drinks like a fish, a misfortune which I have known to befall other celebrated patriots. I am told, that the true time to see him to advantage is about ten at night, with a bottle of brandy and water before him, which I can very well conceive,' From this it appears that Paine had resumed to some extent the drinking that had been interrupted by his imprisonment, although Tone's conclusion suggests, as so often with Paine, that the drinking was not to the extent of befuddling, but rather of stimulating, his wits.

An American sea captain, Rowland Crocker, met Paine the same year and described him, according to Freeman's *History of Cape Cod*, as 'a well-dressed and most gentlemanly man, of sound and orthodox republican principles, of a good heart, a strong intellect, and a fascinating address'. Paine's chameleon quality continued, according perhaps to the day and time as well as the eye of the beholder.

American contacts only stimulated Paine's longing to return. 'It is the country of my heart and the place of my political and literary birth,' he wrote to Rickman. 'I had rather see my horse Button eating the grass of Bordentown or Morisania, than see all the pomp and shew of Europe.' In late March 1797, he actually got as far as Le Havre, awaiting a ship to the United States. The long wait proved abortive: Paine, in fact, feared seizure at sea by an English cruiser, a not uncommon hazard to French shipping at the time.

Paine now went to live at No. 4, Rue du Théâtre Français, the house of Nicolas de Bonneville and his family. Bonneville was the young editor of *Bien Informé*, for which Paine often wrote, and Paine had known him at least since 1792 when de Bonneville had published Lanthenas' translation of Part II of *Rights of Man*. Thomas Holcroft had also lodged with Bonneville when in France and with his help had 'pirated' Beaumarchais' *Marriage of Figaro*. The fact that Bonneville spoke and wrote English made the arrangement a happy and useful one for Paine, although it once again ensured that he need not bother to persevere with his French. Bonneville gave up a study and bedroom for Paine's use, and Paine in the end stayed for five years, always hoping to return to America and, Micawber-like, waiting for something to turn up to get him there. He led a characteristic life now he was no longer actively concerned in politics: rising late, reading the papers, writing his ceaseless letters or articles on political matters and chatting to his heart's content.

On 4 September 1797, the members of the Directory, supported by the army, took over the administration and virtually became a dictatorship. The excuse was a royalist plot, and Napoleon had made the *coup d'état* militarily possible by sending troops from Italy to quell, most decisively, the reactionaries. It may at first sight seem odd to find Paine, champion of democracy and liberty, supporting this move; but like many others he retained active fears of the possible alternatives, a return either of the Terror or the Bourbons. He wrote a pamphlet published by Bonneville early in October: *Letter of Thomas Paine to the People of France, and the French Armies, on the Event of the 18th Fructidor,*[1] *and its Consequences.* It explained to the public the reasons for the step taken by the Directory and pointed out that at a time of crisis, even in America, 'Congress invested Washington with dictatorial power. At another time the government of Pennsylvania suspended itself and declared martial law.' Once again he attacked England as a source of counter-revolution and suggested there would be no peace until the Elector of Hanover was returned to that principality. England's financial situation was desperate, and Pitt preferred war to peace in order to excuse it. He also made the practical suggestion that neutral nations should form an unarmed association making clear that if their ships or goods were seized on the high seas they would as a body demand reparation and refuse all trade until they received it. It was, in fact, an idea of sanctions before its time.

Paine also corresponded with Barras on a project for invading England, for he states that from a memorandum he has received from that country, 'I see they have little or no idea of a descent being made upon them; *tant mieux*—but they will be guarded in Ireland, as they expect a descent there.' By the end of the year he was openly supporting in *Bien Informé* the plans for a maritime invasion of the British Isles with 10,000 men and gunboats to land on the English coast. In a letter to the Council of Five Hundred he sent a donation of one hundred livres 'and with it all the wishes of my heart for the success of the descent, and a voluntary offer of any service I can render to promote it'. He adds there will be no lasting peace for France or the world until 'the tyranny and corruption of the English government be abolished . . . the mass of the people are the friends of liberty; tyranny and taxation oppress them, but they deserve to be free'.

The letter was read out by Coupé to the Council on 28 January 1798

---

[1] 4th September. The revised revolutionary calendar remained in force.

with the comment: 'The gift which Thomas Paine offers you appears very trifling, when it is compared with the revolting injustice which this faithful friend of liberty has experienced from the English government; but compare it with the state of poverty in which our former colleague finds himself, and you will then think it considerable'. Paine supported the project further with a publication, *Observations on the Construction and Operation of Navies with a Plan for an Invasion of England and the Final Overthrow of the English Government*, a mouthful with as little practical effect as Operation Sealion one hundred and forty years later. It was agreed he should accompany the forces as political adviser, the prime object of the invasion being, of course, from Paine's point of view the establishment of a new form of government in England along French and American lines. 'The intention of the expedition was to give the people of England an opportunity of forming a government for themselves, and thereby bring about peace'; an intention the English people were to regard as suspect in 1797 as in all subsequent years. Paine meant well, by his own standards; but his sensitivity to ingrained English reaction to threat of any kind was not acute. Even more hopefully and hopelessly, he was to work out later a scheme for a direct attack on Ireland (naturally to liberate Fitzgerald's Irish) from the United States. This he published in the *Citoyen François* on 28 September 1801.

Even given Paine's views of world citizenship and democratic federations, it is very hard not to look with concern on the deterioration of his once strongly-held opinions on war as 'murder' except when it was a war of defence. There is an apparent callousness to the suffering and death of ordinary English people, inevitable in an invasion, that shows how much, with age, Paine's humanity (or perhaps simply his imagination) was wanting when put to the test. In spite of the lucidity and common sense of his practical arguments, there is a decline of character in these last years in France that does suggest the possibility that the mental fever he had suffered in prison had made permanent inroads on his judgment as well as his physique. Perhaps it was why he returned to drinking. Was it to help ballast his obvious self-deception? He professed humane care for the generality of people as warmly as ever, and did much kindness in his private life. But the core of *public* compassion had gone. Grievance against England, as against Washington, had grown with what it fed on, and brought him to a form of treason which would have been indisputable if he had not so obviously looked on himself as an American. He believed, or made himself believe, that he was working for a wider good, the liberty of all peoples; but Paine, like Robespierre before him, was beginning to put the end before the means, and blind himself to the forces he was letting loose to attain an elusive ideal.

Paine, unlike Robespierre, never had to face the result, either in psychological introspection or in history. Two hundred and fifty gun-boats were built, but the expedition, like later ones, was abandoned. In a letter to Jefferson Paine expressed the suspicion that it was 'only a feint to cover the expedition to Egypt, which was then preparing'. He was confirmed in this view by the British attack on Ostend, which failed but was said by its captured officers to be in search of these gunboats. He gained this information from Vanhuele, the fellow-prisoner in the Luxembourg who had become President of the municipality of Bruges. Paine had kept in touch with him and actually enjoyed a long winter visit to Bruges as Vanhuele's guest before he finally left France.

What Paine had left out of account, in his estimate of the mass of the English people, was their easygoing, if not apathetic, indifference to politics and liberty whenever their pride in England's naval supremacy was aroused. The French had overlooked it, too, to their cost in declaring war in 1793. And the rise of a seafaring hero had given English national pride as great a boost as the French were ever to experience on land, through Napoleon. Admiral Nelson, another son of Norfolk, never entered into Paine's calculations at all; but after the Battle of the Nile on 1 August 1798, when Nelson's small fleet annihilated the French armada, neither the Directory nor Napoleon had any illusions about the difficulties of invading England.

Napoleon, nonetheless, returned to France from his Egyptian campaign in triumph, but only to find disaster on other fronts. In his absence the French had withdrawn from Naples, Anglo-Russian forces had landed in Holland, and most of his Italian conquests had been lost. Victories in Switzerland at Zurich, and the withdrawal of the Tsar from the Coalition after a quarrel, had saved France, but the situation was disturbing and Napoleon had power practically thrust at him by all factions. He seized it in the *coup* of *Brumaire* (November 1799) which had been intended as a constitutional revision, using his name for prestige, but ended in the collapse of the Directory, with Napoleon made First Consul of three. His position was consolidated when a plebiscite in January and February 1800 gave an overwhelming vote in favour of the new Constitution. The popularity of generals, a factor in politics since the time of Rome, had once again outweighed the ideals of democracy.

It was claimed that Napoleon sought out Paine in consequence of his efforts in the English project, and told him that he always slept with a copy of *Rights of Man* under his pillow. If so, he doubtless spoke metaphorically, if not ironically, although there is no doubt Napoleon, before ambition took hold, had been a good soldier of the Revolution, and to some extent he retained some of its ideals. No one, as yet, could forecast the coming Emperor. *Brumaire* was followed by an amnesty for all emigrés, and some attempt to preserve the interests of the Revolution in nationally acquired property, including church lands; but it also restored Christian worship in the churches and political censorship. Many newspapers were suppressed, and the *Moniteur* became an official journal of the state. Liberals such as Bonneville came under suspicion, and only Paine's spirited defence temporarily lifted a ban on the publication of *Bien Informé*. Bonneville was, wrote Paine, 'a very industrious man—a good husband—a good Father—and a good friend'. Bonneville was later sent to prison for an article comparing Bonaparte with Cromwell: a comparison which when hinted at (as it sometimes was) had for some reason always sent the leaders of the French Revolution into a frenzy of indignant denial, in particular Danton.

Paine, when he returned to Paris from Bruges, was warned that the police had him under surveillance and that at the first complaint against him he would be sent back to America, his country. This was hardly a threat, and Paine might have wryly noted that his American citizenship, with the French government, came and went according to their needs of the moment. But he knew his articles in *Bien Informé* were suspected of subversion; he took the warning, and practically ceased journalism until his departure from France in 1802. In 1801, his theophilanthropy project too had to be ended owing to Napoleon's Concordat with Pope Pius VII.

His scientific interests had not waned, and in 1800 he wrote for a government official a paper setting out some suggested public improvements such as canals, bridges, and the means of financing them. This contained many of his ideas on economics, bridge construction and naval strategy; and he pointed out to the French that England's commercial supremacy was a direct result of the improvement in her manufactures.

In one of his inordinately long letters to Jefferson, in October, 1800, he mentioned the Iron Bridge over the Wear at Sunderland which had been erected from his model by the Walkers of Rotherham, and adds:

'I have now made two other models, one is pasteboard, five feet span and five inches of height from the cords. It is in the opinion of every person who has seen it one of the most beautifull objects the eye can behold. I then cast a model in Metal following the construction of that in pasteboard and of the same dimensions. The whole was executed in my own Chamber. It is far superior in strength, elegance, and readiness in execution to the model I made in America, and which you saw in Paris. I shall bring those Models with me when I come home, which will be as soon as I can pass the seas in safety from the piratical John Bulls.'

A visiting friend, Henry Redhead Yorke, in 1802 was shown these models and wrote:

'In shewing me one day the beautiful models of two bridges he had devised he observed that Dr Franklin once told him that "books are written to please, houses built for great men, churches for priests, but no bridges for the people". These models exhibit an extraordinary degree not only of skill but of taste; and are wrought with extreme delicacy entirely by his own hands. The largest is nearly four feet in length; the iron works, the chains, and every other article belonging to it, were forged and manufactured by himself. It is intended as the model of a bridge which is to be constructed across the Delaware, extending 480 feet with only one arch. The other is to be erected over a lesser river, whose name I forget, and is likewise a single arch, and of his own workmanship, excepting the chains, which, instead of iron, are cut out of pasteboard, by the fair hand of his correspondent the "Little Corner of the World," whose indefatigable perseverance is extraordinary. He was offered £3000 for these models and refused it. The iron bars, which I before mentioned that I noticed in a corner of his room, were also forged by himself, as the model of a crane, of a new description. He put them together, and exhibited the power of the lever to a most surprising degree.'

It is possible that Paine's account of the £3000 offer he had refused was hyperbolic, but from all accounts his pride in his engineering models and delicacy and accuracy of workmanship was not by any means misplaced. His letter to Jefferson also mentions his *Compact Maritime* in course of translation, and manuscripts of which he encloses. Jefferson, always actively ready to help Paine in American publication, wrote him on 18 March 1801, that these manuscripts had been sent to the printer to be made into a pamphlet. In the same letter he also told Paine of orders given to the captain of the Maryland 'to receive and accommodate you back if you can be ready to depart at such short warning'. On 9th June, Paine wrote back warmly congratulating America on Jefferson's election as President, and thanking him for the Maryland offer. He says, however, he will wait for the return of another vessel. He knew Jefferson had been attacked by his political opponents for making the offer, which they had distorted to mean that a naval vessel was actually being sent specially for Paine. Jefferson had denied this. To bring Paine back to America was not the specific object of the voyage, and he wrote Paine: 'With respect to the letter (offering the ship) I never hesitate to avow and justify it in conversation.' Paine, however, did not change his mind, and waited.

In the meantime, Paine's social life had continued. On St Patrick's Day in the fateful rebellion year of 1798 Paine attended a banquet of the Irish in Paris, and in June the same year he had presented to the Directory an appeal by a group of Irish patriots in Paris for men and guns, to be used to protect their fellow-countrymen in the event of premature rebellion and English vengeance. Another appeal by Paine followed in connection with reprisals on Irish officers in the French army, who had fallen into British hands and been hanged. He attended a dinner alongside Robert Fulton, inventor of the steamboat, Volney the deist (after whom Rickman had named a son), and General Kościusko, whom he had known as a mercenary officer in Washington's army.[1] He took an English visitor, Lewis Goldsmith, to see Tallien, breakfasted among others with Thomas Holcroft, the playwright victim of the 1794 treason trials, and dined at Barlow's with Lafayette, Volney, Fulton and Kościusko. Barlow was now a regular companion, and his loyalty to Paine remained constant long after his death.

In 1802 Paine was still said to be in a melancholy state about the collapse of the Revolution. He had apparently let himself go and the visitor from England, Henry Yorke, described the state of his room with some horror. 'The chimney hearth was an heap of dirt; there was not a speck of cleanliness to be seen.' It was, in fact, a typical study of the more neglectful professorial nature. Charlotte Payne-Townshend had expressed similar horror at Shaw's before their marriage, and described it in much the same terms. Possibly Paine, like Shaw, had forbidden anyone to dust it for fear of disturbing his work and papers. It contained three shelves filled with boxes used as filing cabinets, 'several huge bars of iron, curiously shaped, and two large trunks; opposite the fireplace, a board covered with pamphlets and journals, having more the appearance of a dresser in a scullery than a sideboard'.

Henry Redhead Yorke was an English revolutionary named Henry Redhead, who had changed his name to Yorke to avoid political pressures. In 1802 he visited France again from England, and his letters on this visit, first published in 1804, were considered of such interest as a picture of the times that they were edited and republished in book form just over a century later.[2] He records at length his visit to Tom Paine, whom he had known in England. He had been ushered into the house by a 'jolly-looking' woman (presumably Madame de Bonneville) and was received by Paine in a long flannel gown, a garment which seems to have emphasized to Yorke his present 'abject poverty'. Paine's memory seemed confused.

[1] In 1938, Poland issued a stamp commemorating the American Revolution, showing both Kościusko and Paine. It was the first stamp to picture Paine.

[2] *France in Eighteen Hundred and Two*; edited by J. A. C. Sykes (Heinemann, 1906).

'Time seemed to have made dreadful ravages over his whole frame, and a settled melancholy was visible on his countenance. He desired me to be seated, and although he did not recollect me for a considerable time, he conversed with his usual affability. I confess I felt extremely surprised that he should have forgotten me; but I resolved not to make myself known to him, as long as it could be avoided with propriety. In order to try his memory, I referred to a number of circumstances which had occurred while we were in company, but carefully abstained from hinting that we had ever lived together. He would frequently put his hand to his forehead, and exclaim, "Ah! I know that voice, but my recollection fails!" At length I thought it time to remove his suspense, and stated an incident which instantly recalled me to his mind. It is impossible to describe the sudden change which this effected; his countenance brightened, he pressed me by the hand, and a silent tear stole down his cheek. Nor was I less affected than himself. For some time we sat without a word escaping from our lips . . . He then enquired what motive had brought me here, and on my explaining myself, he observed with a smile of contempt, "They have shed blood enough for liberty, and now they have it in perfection. This is not a country for an honest man to live in; they do not understand any thing at all of the principles of free government, and the best way is to leave them to themselves. You see they have conquered all Europe, only to make it more miserable than it was before." '

On Yorke's hopeful remark that much might yet be done for the Republic, Paine replied: 'Republic! Do you call this a Republic? . . . I know of no Republic in the world except America, which is the only country for such men as you and I. It is my intention to get away from this place as soon as possible, and I hope to be off in the autumn; you are a young man and may see better times, but I have done with Europe, and its slavish politics.'

Yorke then mentioned *The Age of Reason*, 'the publication of which I said had lost him the good opinion of numbers of his English advocates. He became uncommonly warm at this remark, and in a tone of singular energy declared that he would not have published it if he had not thought it calculated to "inspire mankind with a more exalted idea of the Supreme Architect of the Universe, and to put an end to villainous imposture". He then broke out with the most violent invectives against our received opinions, accompanying them at the same time with some of the most grand and sublime conceptions of an Omnipotent Being, that I ever heard or read of.'

An English lady, 'not less remarkable for her talents than for elegance of manners', entreated an interview with Paine which Yorke contrived, although warning Paine against touching on religious matters because she was a rigid Roman Catholic. 'With much good nature he promised to be *discreet* . . . For above four hours he kept every one in astonishment and admiration of his memory, his keen observation of men and manners, his numberless anecdotes of the American Indians, of the American war, of Franklin, Washington, and even of his Majesty, of whom he told several curious facts of humour and benevolence. His remarks on genius and taste can never be forgotten by those present. Thus far everything went on as I could wish; the sparkling champagne gave a zest to his conversation, and we were all delighted. But alas! alas! an expression relating to his *Age of Reason* having been mentioned by one of the company, he broke out immediately . . .' Beginning with astronomy, Paine went on from there and nothing could stop him. 'In vain I attempted to change the subject, by employing every artifice in my power, and even attacking with vehemence his political principles. He returned to the charge with unabated ardour. I called upon him for a song though I never heard him sing in my life. He struck up one of his own composition; but the instant he had finished it he resumed his favourite topic.'

It reads amusingly; but it does suggest a certain variability of mood, from violence to enthusiasm, and a forgetfulness that support the idea that Paine after his imprisonment suffered from an emotional instability that sent him into extremes of vivacity and depression. There is again here an indication of wine acting as a mental stimulant, so that he was never more rational and brilliant than when under its influence. The corresponding depressions may well have been the reaction.

Walter Savage Landor also met Paine in Paris, according to a correspondent of Conway's, and said that he particularly admired Paine. He added that Paine was always called 'Tom', not out of disrespect, but because he was 'a jolly good fellow'.

Another visitor was Thomas Poole, who like Mary Wollstonecraft's sister had seen Paine burnt in effigy (in Bridgwater), and who had enough influence in Somerset to prevent a similar occurrence at Stowey. Poole had been converted to liberalism by reading *Rights of Man*, and he wrote from Paris on 20 July 1802, that he had called one morning on Thomas Paine. 'He is an original, amusing fellow. Striking, strong physiognomy. Said a great many quaint things, and read us part of a reply which he intends to publish to Watson's *Apology*.'[1]

The time in Paris, for Paine, was out of joint. He was becoming a 'character' on view to international visitors, and under his apparent self-conceit there was a hint of unease. He had written to Jefferson in dismay in 1797, on learning that John Adams, one of the most conservative and English-orientated of Americans, had been elected President,

[1] Mrs Henry Sandford: *Thomas Poole and his Friends* (Macmillan, New York, 1888).

and he had only been consoled by the fact that Jefferson was Vice-President. Adams, he wrote, 'has such a talent for blundering and offending, it will be necessary to keep an eye on him'. In fact, Adams had not always been unwilling to accede Paine's importance in American affairs. 'Washington's sword,' he wrote, 'would have been wielded in vain had it not been supported by the pen of Paine.' But on learning that a letter by Barlow to Washington on 2 October 1798, on the issue of peace, was written after consultation with Paine, he had dismissed Barlow with the words, 'Tom Paine is not a more worthless fellow'. He had, nevertheless, followed the letter's recommendations.

The emissaries he sent to Paris were understandably cool towards Paine and Barlow, and made Paine's situation much less easy on the American side than it had been in the time of Monroe. Monroe had been recalled as long ago as 1796, and Paine, whose loyalties were becoming with age as prickly as his enmities, had resented his departure, and the appointment of his successor, Charles Pinckney, as some form of heinous vendetta against his friend. (Pinckney, in fact, was deserving of Paine's sympathetic consideration. As delegate from South Carolina he had, unlike many, condemned in 1787 the proposed new American Constitution, which moved away from some of Paine's revolutionary principles, with the words: 'We have universally considered ourselves as the inhabitants of an old instead of a new country.') Now the Paris situation seemed further to have deteriorated, and Jefferson's offer by letter of a vessel was doubly welcome.

In other ways, too, France had become uncongenial. His suspicions of Napoleon were growing, all the ascetic idealism of the Revolution had changed, and for the ageing, Quaker-born Paine there was little attraction in the new permissiveness in the theatre. Yorke himself was shocked, and wrote with a hint of the coming nineteenth century prudery that the Paris theatres 'at the present time display such gross acts of licentiousness among the spectators, and such obscene dialogue on the stage, that it is impossible to accompany a modest woman to most of them'.

It was, of course, like most estimates of the moral tone of the theatre, not entirely true. Napoleon, a long-time friend of Talma, with a genuine interest in the arts, on 2nd July the same year had endowed the re-constituted Comédie-Française with an annual income of 100,000 francs. The Talma marriage had broken up, and Napoleon and Josephine had acquired and now lived in their little house in the Rue Chantereine, which had been the scene of Julie Talma's *salon* in the days of Girondist ascendancy. Talma and his new wife, the young and distinguished actress Caroline Petit-Vanhove, continued to enchant the public in a repertoire including Racine and Voltaire. But elsewhere, in the freer, Napoleonic society of easy divorce and *décolleté* dress which had thrown Robespierre's inhibitions to the winds, Yorke's strictures were probably not unjust. The Paris theatre had certainly moved on from the days of 1792, when Talma's Othello (in a rewritten version by Ducis) had shocked French theatre tradition, based on the Greek austerities, by murdering Desdemona in her bed on-stage.

Paine embarked for America on 2 September 1802. It was a not unaffecting departure. Two of Paine's English admirers, Sir Francis Burdett[1] and William Bosville, presented Paine with 500 louis d'or to settle his account (presumably board and lodging) with Bonneville and ease his travelling expenses. And Clio Rickman came from London to bid him farewell and, after a few days of reunion in Paris, accompany him to Le Havre.

These English farewells on French soil were made possible by the Peace of Amiens, which had briefly ended the war with England on 22 March 1802: Paine also was taking advantage of the relative safety of the seas. Rickman, indefatigable poetical champion and recorder of liberty, commemorated the occasion in *Stanzas, on the beach of Havre-de-Grace, on parting with Paine, 1802*. This publication, issued by Rickman himself, proudly recorded on a fly-leaf that the subscribers to it included 'His Royal Highness, George, Prince of Wales, Mrs Fitzherbert, Thomas Jefferson, President of the United States of America and Thomas Paine'. How this astonishing juxtaposition of personalities came about Rickman does not explain, and one can only speculate on Paine's reactions (if Rickman was ever unwise enough to enlighten him) to this unlikely personal association with one of George III's 'profligate sons' and his celebrated Common Law wife.

Paine landed at Baltimore on 1 November 1802. The wheel had come full circle, and he was back in the country in which he had first stoked the fires of revolution. Rickman's verses breathed a hope for the future:

> 'Thus smooth be thy waves, and thus gentle the breeze,
>   As thou bearest my Paine far away;
> O waft him to comfort and regions of ease,
> Each blessing of freedom and friendship to seize,
>   And bright be his setting sun's ray.'

Paine's American sunset was to last seven years, but brightness was not to be a conspicuous part of it.

---

[1] Burdett, a pupil of Horne Tooke, was elected M.P. for Westminster in 1807 and after a House of Commons conflict in 1810 was imprisoned in the Tower. A not unusual fate for Paine's followers. Angela Burdett-Coutts, the noted philanthropist, was his daughter.

XXI
AMERICAN SUNSET

Paine was now sixty-five years old, and the last seven years of his life were to be spent in lively but sporadic journalism, fighting old battles, and domestic periods of peace and upheaval. As always he was at the centre of controversy: enemies proliferated as well as friends. But fifteen years' absence had cut him off from opportunities of direct influence, and the sunset of his life was also to be a decline.

The America Paine returned to in 1802 had moved away from the early days of revolution and rebirth. Although few now questioned independence from England, or the principle of republicanism, there were many, especially since the bloodshed of the French Revolution, who retained fears of too wide a spread of democracy, and Washington, in two terms of office as President, had indicated that, like his passionate admirer Lafayette, he preferred the idea of democratic rule still largely controlled by aristocrats and those experienced in old-style government.

The Constitution of 1788 did not supersede the Declaration of In-dependence but it diluted some of the egalitarian principles that Paine, at least, had most strongly advocated, and under the influence of John Adams and Alexander Hamilton America moved towards what has been termed the 'government for capitalists', so strongly ingrained that it could not be diverted by the extensions of suffrage that occurred later in the nineteenth century. Money-making, too, had become a major national interest. Madame de la Tour du Pin noted that no matter how attached a man was to his house, farm, horse or negro, if he were offered a price one-third above the real value, he could be relied upon to sell. 'It was a country where everything had a reckoned value.'

Washington had died in 1799, and in 1801, when Jefferson defeated Adams in the election for President, there was still no suggestion of uni-versal suffrage, nor did he attempt such an innovation; but his agrarian policy and party had many active enemies, whose bitter opposition to the President spilled over his known friend and supporter, Paine. *Common Sense* and its enormous influence in establishing the American nation was now a dim light of the past; and the Federalists opposed to Jefferson were able to extinguish it by a concentrated attack on *The Age of Reason*. How completely they were able to transform the true nature of that work in the public mind is shown by the generally very appreciative passages on Paine by Nye and Morpurgo in *The Birth of the U.S.A.*

'. . . The span of the Revolutionary War, the years between the Declaration of Independence and the ratification of the Constitution, saw the decline of Paine's power over American ideology from its zenith to its nadir.

'It was, it is true, his theology and not his politics which finally ruined his reputation with his American contemporaries and their successors. Paine, the revolutionary, was at least respectable, but Paine, the deist, could never hold the respect of puritanical New England, Catholic Maryland, or Episcopalian Virginia. And his case was the worse for his thorny personality and his aggressiveness. Not for Tom Paine the thoughtful, patient deism of Jefferson or Franklin. God, to him, was an *aristo*, and *aristos* were best without their heads. Such vigour could but bring upon him the distaste of good Christians and the hate of men who called themselves good Christians.

'Yet, for *Common Sense* alone, Tom Paine deserved more than he ever received from the American people.'

All of this is fundamentally true except the continued confusion about Paine's attitude to the guillotine and to a beneficent God, which lingers on in this excellent book on American history, first published as late as 1955.

In fact, Jefferson's scientific deism, influenced by Locke and the Unitarian Dr Priestley, was like his politics basically close to Paine's in its humanitarianism and its moral attitude to Christ. As he wrote in 1803 to Dr Benjamin Rush:

'To the corruptions of Christianity I am, indeed, opposed; but not to the genuine precepts of Jesus himself. I am a Christian in the only sense in which he wished anyone to be; sincerely attached to his doctrines, in preference to all others, ascribing to himself every *human* excellence; and believing that he never claimed any other.'

The attack on Paine, and distortion of his similar views, were not, however, lost on Jefferson. He avoided, like so many other American deists, committing them to print, and showed nervousness for years afterwards at any suggestion of their being made public.

In every other way he was, at least until the last years of Paine's life when he ceased to contact him, a steady friend and admirer of Paine, and those who maintain Paine was so conceited about his own writings that he never read or admired any others overlook not only the content of his works but his unswerving devotion to Jefferson, which never had in it the slightest hint of jealousy. Yet Thomas Jefferson's claims as a political writer were considerable and his fame in this respect, in later years, greater than Paine's own in America. How much Paine's influence is to be seen in the Declaration of Independence, ascribed (though the degree has lately been disputed) to Jefferson, is not clear, but it was obviously present, and not confined to the clause on slavery which Jefferson was forced to drop. As with the English radicals, the influences were probably mutual, and how many of the ideas in the works of Paine and Jefferson sprang, consciously or subconsciously, from half-remembered conversations and vivacious exchanges of opinion in private can never be fully estimated. They were, to some extent, a part of the mental fabric of the times, and America was still much linked to Europe in its literature and ideas. It may be it was in conversations with Jefferson that Paine acquired some knowledge of Locke, whose works he denied reading (and certainly he never quotes from them) but whose relevance to his own has often been remarked.

The fact remains that Jefferson and Paine had a philosophical and political accord. Paine was always loyal to those who remained loyal to him; and if he did not easily forgive the opposite, he was hardly unique in that characteristic of mankind.

It was, of course, to the President that he turned immediately on landing at Baltimore. 'I arrived here on Saturday from Havre,' he wrote to Jefferson, 'after a passage of sixty days. I have several cases of models, wheels, etc., and as soon as I can get them from the vessel and put them on board the packet for Georgetown I shall set off to pay my respects to you.'

One of the continual sources of astonishment to the modern reader is the amount of luggage and bulky goods, including furniture, that eighteenth and early nineteenth century travellers, before the arrival of steam, managed to transport with them on their journeys. Madame de la Tour du Pin, an aristocrat escaping at risk of her life from the French Revolution with two tiny children and a sick husband, managed to board the boat for America with a piano, among twenty-five cases of possessions. As John Weightman wittily commented in his review in *The Observer* of a new edition of her *Memoirs*,[1] 'even the Scarlet Pimpernel would have faltered at the thought of a piano'. The ship, only 150 tons with a crew of five including the Captain, was one of the American vessels held up in Bordeaux for a year and released by Paine's efforts.

It would have taken more than a six-week journey on the high seas, in variable weather and a sailing vessel, to have parted Paine from his precious bridge models and the unspecific but curiosity-provoking 'wheels, etc.' After dispatching them, Paine visited Monroe in the new city of Washington, just catching him before he started on the journey back to France, where he was once again to be American Minister.

[1] *Memoirs of Madame de la Tour du Pin*, ed. and trans. Felice Harcourt (Harvill Press, 1970).

Paine sent *via* Monroe a letter to Rickman, to be dispatched from Paris by the son-in-law of Sir Robert Smyth, whose death the same year had greatly affected Paine. 'You can have no idea,' he writes to Rickman, 'of the agitation which my arrival occasioned.' Every paper, he adds, was 'filled with applause or abuse'. He also gives the happy, but perhaps in the event characteristically optimistic information, that his American property, taken care of by his friends, was now worth six thousand pounds sterling; 'which put in the funds will bring me £400 sterling a year'. It appeared Paine had no objection to a little capitalism in the form of wise investment.

Washington was a new city on the River Potomac, in the specially created District of Columbia. It had been nobly laid out, in a radiation of straight avenues, in 1791 by the French veteran of the War of Independence, Major Pierre L'Enfant, whose successor, Andrew Ellicott (insisted on by Jefferson on the grounds that the plan should be American in style), mainly followed L'Enfant's original conception. The President's house, designed by the architect Hoban, was first occupied by John Adams near the end of his presidency, and it and the town were so new and incomplete that the unfortunate Mrs Adams, commenting as a consolation on the 'beautiful situation', had written to a friend (under pledge of secrecy) of the miseries of housekeeping in the circumstances. Of the miseries of Jefferson's housekeeper (his wife had died young in 1782) we do not hear, though she followed hard upon, and Paine was doubtless masculinely unaware of them when he visited Jefferson in November and December The house was not yet named the White House; it only acquired that world-famous title in 1814, during the renewed war with England, when the British made an attempt to burn it down and the damage had to be covered with lavish new coats of white paint.

Paine's meetings with the President show that Jefferson had no intention of letting the barrages of criticism in the press affect his old cordiality towards Paine, nor the casual informality of their association. A William Plumer of New Hampshire called on the President and was somewhat disconcerted to find Jefferson in an old brown coat, soiled corduroys and slippers. While he was there 'Thomas Paine entered, seated himself by the side of the President, and conversed and behaved towards him with the familiarity of an intimate and an equal'. He added with disapproval that the Vice-President also invited 'that miscreant Paine' to his dinners, but no Federalists were asked to meet him. 'In this they show their prudence.'

Attacks in the press notwithstanding, Paine was soon plunging once again into the deep end of journalism, encouraged by the proliferation of American newspapers, which nearly doubled in number between 1800 and 1810, from two hundred to three hundred and seventy-five. To the *National Intelligencer,* which on 3rd November had welcomed his arrival and wished him 'undisturbed possession of our common blessings', he wrote saying he would not ask or accept any office. This was probably to save Jefferson embarrassment. He maintained his principal interest was in his mechanical projects; but this did not prevent his publishing eight *Letters to the Citizens of the United States,* just to keep his hand in, as it were.

On Christmas Day he wrote to Jefferson with a suggestion that the Americans should purchase Louisiana, a continuing bone of contention now Spain had conceded the territory to France, who on 26th November had closed New Orleans and the Mississippi against all American and foreign ships. War seemed a possibility, with the Federalists only too ready to support it, but Jefferson was able to inform Paine verbally, in strict secrecy, that privately negotiations were already about to be made for the purchase. Napoleon, in fact, with his European commitments, was finding the maintenance of this distant colony a dangerous strain, and although he struck as hard a bargain as he could, the deal went through in 1803. With the acquisition of this large territory and navigable river, dividing the Eastern seaboard from the West, the expansion of the United States was assured and the vast lands of the West opened up for exploration. Paine never lived to see the fulfilment, some of which might have stirred his conscience along with his sense of American pride, but he did know of the heroic voyages of Meriwether Lewis and William Clark which, undertaken with Jefferson's support between 1804 and 1806, discovered the long dreamed-of North-West Passage and laid the foundation of the country's extension and drive to the West, with the Ohio and the Mississippi as the great navigational centres of North American trade.

Paine's later advice to Jefferson included a long letter on the establishment of democratic government for the French and Spanish-bred peoples of Louisiana, who had never known it. He also suggested that America should act as a moderator between the Negro Republic set up in Haiti in 1804, and the blockading French, which threatened American merchant ships.

In February 1803, he returned to New York, stopping on the way in Philadelphia to see a model of his iron bridge in Independence Hall, a Museum of the American artist, Charles Willson Peale, who had painted eight portraits of George Washington and brandished his enthusiams in a similar way to Clio Rickman by naming his seventeen sons and daughters after Rembrandt, Rubens, Van Dyck, Titian and other artistic heroes.[1] Peale also painted a portrait of Paine. On 24th February

[1] Rembrandt Peale also became a painter. His posthumous portrait of Washington, known from its shape as 'the Porthole Portrait', was sold at Christie's in 1972 for £11,550.

Paine reached Bordentown to see his old property and visit his friend, Colonel Kirkbride. Another old friend, his assistant on his original bridge model, John Hall, rode over to greet him, and recorded in his diary: 'Had a ride to Bordentown to Mr. Paine at Mr. Kirkbride's. He was well and apered jollyer than I had ever knowne him. He is full of whims and skeams and mechanicall inventions, and is to build a place or shop to carry them out, and wants my help.'

Hall, since they last met in America, had revisited England. In 1791 Paine had corresponded with him when he was staying in Leicester, and the following year they had met in London when the interest in Paine's *Rights of Man* was at its height. Hall had dined with the Revolution Society in the London Tavern and been in Leicester again at the time of Paine's trial, of which he received an account from a London correspondent: 'Erskine shone like the morning-Star. Johnson was there. The instant Erskine closed his speech the venal jury interrupted the Attorney General, who was about to make a reply, and without waiting for any answer, or any summing up by the Judge, pronounced him guilty. Such an instance of infernal corruption is scarcely upon record. . . . At this moment, while I write, the mob is drawing Erskine's carriage home, he riding in triumph . . .'

The old friends therefore had much to talk about, but Paine's stay at Bordentown this time was short. It had its disagreeable moment when he drove with Kirkbride to Trenton to get a seat on the stagecoach to New York, and the proprietor refused to have Paine in his coach. The Federalist propaganda against the author of *The Age of Reason*—its object, of course, more to damage Jefferson than his friend Paine—was already having its effect. When Paine and Kirkbride switched to a chaise a mob is reported to have accompanied them with catcalls and loud drumming, with the object of frightening their horse. Kirkbride and Paine were both Republicans, and were known to have formed the first Republican Club in Bordentown.

When Paine arrived in New York on 2nd March he was given a warm welcome by the Republican element and a dinner in his honour at the City Hall on 18th March. One of the leading Republicans at that time was James Cheetham, an English radical journalist recently arrived. Politically, in America, Cheetham was to prove a leopard willing to change his spots: he became an active anti-Republican and enemy of Jefferson. For Paine, unknowingly, it was an ominous meeting.

Sometime in 1803, Madame de Bonneville and her three sons arrived at Bordentown. Paine had wanted the whole family to come to America with him in 1802, but the situation of Nicolas de Bonneville under the Napoleonic régime seems to have been restrictive of his leaving the country. In the end Madame de Bonneville and the boys travelled without him, but with the hope of his shortly being able to join them. It was felt the boys would have greater opportunities in the New World, and Paine had sent the money for the family's passage. 'I have written to Colonel Kirkbride, of Bordentown, in the State of New Jersey, who will expect your coming there,' he wrote, 'and from whom you will receive every friendship . . . Embrace the poor boys for me and tell them they will soon see me at Bordentown.' On hearing of their arrival he wrote to Bonneville in Paris, assuring him of the hopeful future of his sons and begging him to join them as soon as possible. Bonneville did not arrive in America in fact until after Paine's death, when he published an edition of essays expressing his gratitude to Paine for all he had done for his family.

The idea was that Madame de Bonneville should earn a living as a teacher of French, while Paine made himself responsible for the education of the boys. But she was still a young woman, a typical Parisienne, who soon found Bordentown an inexpressibly dull village and longed for the bright lights of New York City. Colonel Kirkbride died in November 1803, to Paine's deep regret (he could ill afford to lose, in the present American atmosphere, so intimate and staunch a friend); and in 1804 he one day returned to his New York lodging in Gold Street and found Madame de Bonneville there: in considerable financial distress and adamant on not returning to Bordentown. He paid some of her bills but appears to have refused to cover others, considering her situation was due to unnecessary extravagance (doubtless there was a conflict here between the Quaker and the Parisian views of what constituted 'extravagance'). Later, after he had left her for a time in New York, he was sued by the Gold Street landlord, Wilburn, for $35 for lodging expenses. Paine in court pleaded he was not responsible, and won his case; but in fairness to Wilburn afterwards saw that he was paid. He had, with Madame de Bonneville, taken on more difficulties than he had perhaps anticipated.

He tried to find her work as a French teacher in New York, but apparently she was not successful at it, for eventually she joined Paine at his New Rochelle farm, officially to act as housekeeper to himself and two of the boys (the oldest had returned to his father in France, perhaps for reasons of homesickness or his father's loneliness). Paine's godson, Thomas Paine Bonneville, was sent in December to a tutor of deistic views, the Reverend John Foster. Paine tried to get the other boy, Benjamin, to New Rochelle so he could have a similar education (he felt strongly they should share equally in the benefits of the New World); but Madame de Bonneville, still in New York at the time, resisted parting with him and Paine in the end had to have them both at New Rochelle.

It was an ephemeral arrangement, as Madame de Bonneville once again longed for New York City, and Paine found her more a liability than an asset as housekeeper. 'She would not do anything,' he wrote, 'not even make an apple dumpling for her own children.' He let her go back to New York after a position had been found for her as a governess, and Benjamin in the end rejoined his mother, while Thomas remained with Paine. 'He shall not want for anything,' wrote Paine, ex-Quaker, 'if he be a good boy and learn no bad words.' In the interim, while he had both boys, he had begun to enjoy his fatherhood by proxy, so late in life, and spent a happy and active time replanning his home, repainting and repapering his bedroom and another for the boys, and supervising their education. It was, nevertheless, a rather primitive and picnic-like existence, with little furniture and a diet mainly of 'tea, milk, fruit pies, plain dumplings and a piece of meat' when meat was obtainable.

Benjamin de Bonneville eventually became a general in the United States Army, a profession it is difficult to imagine Paine would have chosen for him, although he achieved enough distinction in it to merit a biography by Washington Irving. The legacy of Paine's care, and his selfless and distinctly chequered association with Madame de Bonneville, took the form of rumours that the General was a natural son of Paine. The legend of Paine's 'immorality' was so strong that as late as 1903, a century later, the great journalist W. J. Stead, editor of *The Pall Mall Gazette* for which Bernard Shaw wrote much of his criticism, was engaged in a prolonged journalistic argument with a Reverend Dr Torrey who, on the subject of Paine's immorality, had accused him of 'taking another man's wife with him to France and living with her'. On Stead's patient attempt to put right this garbled version of Madame de Bonneville's joining of Paine in America with her sons, including the New York legal case, after Paine's death, in which she had cleared her name of the libel, the Reverend Torrey had clung to his theme, pointing out that a legal dismissal for lack of evidence was not proof. Christian charity is not always a characteristic of clergymen, as with other Christians, and wishful thinking will dismiss all the evidence, when a political or religious prejudice needs to be sustained.

Paine's enemies, even when they were mainly Jefferson's enemies, sowed their seeds well, and the seeds germinated. And animosity had not finished with Paine yet.

There is no doubt, political and religious opinion apart, that elements in Paine's character, especially in old age, contributed to the legend. They were not, of course, immoral elements, but they did include increasing cantankerousness in an argument and a high-minded but unyielding refusal to back down on any point of contention. A passionate belief that one is in the right tends to aggravate contradiction, and contradiction was something that Paine, in old age and with a growing sense of neglect, was not able to bear. There is no doubt from accounts that his drinking now contributed to the legend of disreputability, although his continued flow of voluminous letters and journalistic articles, as well as all personal confrontations in political and religious thought, make it clear his drinking was still as much stimulant as consolation, and never sufficient to render him inarticulate either in conversation or prose. 'Paine's brandy is less to the purpose than Pitt's port, and much less to the purpose than Coleridge's opium,' wrote Leslie Stephen. '. . . his writings were the product of brains certainly not sodden by brandy, but clear, vigorous, and in some ways curiously free from passion.' But there were disappointments in the country to which he had longed so much to return; he dropped increasingly out of public affairs if not of the press; and his indiscretion in reading out Jefferson's letters, probably as a psychological bolster to his uneasy ego, was reported to the President and doubtless widened the gap between himself and governmental acquaintances.

His great work was past, and in his innermost heart he must have realized it. It was a time no longer of great events but of vicious party strife, reflected in his own increasingly denigrated reputation in the country which owed him so much. The Americans, as a political race, had become strangers to him, forging a kind of society based on individual wealth and capital which he had not envisaged, although it still fulfilled ideals of democracy more completely than in the Old World. As Lafayette noted, the gap between the classes was much narrower than in Europe, but there were still many who believed John Adams' theory that society should be constructed with 'decency and respect and veneration . . . for persons in authority'. As for the scurrilous polemical journalism and attacks so mindlessly and mechanically echoed in mob action, the Americans where politics were concerned were 'a rough, tough people', as Dean Acheson still described them in a B.B.C. television interview on 31 March 1971, instancing the violence of the attacks on Washington and Lincoln down to the present day.

Not that Paine did not hit back in kind on occasion. When in 1804 the Federalist Alexander Hamilton was sensationally killed in a duel with Aaron Burr, the Republican Vice-President, and his death was greeted with extravagant eulogies, including in the funeral oration by Paine's old enemy Gouverneur Morris, Paine launched an attack both on Morris and the way Hamilton's death was being misused for political exaggerations. (Hamilton personally he described soberly enough as 'a man of some private merit', although deploring the process of making an heroic martyr of him. The memory of the 'martyrdom' of Marat could not have been far from his thoughts.) He also, more discreditably, re-urged his willingness to go back to Europe to support Napoleon's invasion of England; but this particular acrimonious bee in his bonnet about the government of his native country was forced to settle and stop buzzing with time, as Napoleon's inaction, even after the death of Nelson, became more and more marked. The rest was certainly not silence, but the vigorous conduct of campaigns in print which, at least to European eyes, seem now of mainly ephemeral interest.

His religious writings continued to arouse opposition, and did nothing substantially to supplement *The Age of Reason*. Among Paine's most interesting articles were some on scientific matters, including a treatise on yellow fever, a scourge known well in the New World. There had been a serious epidemic in Philadelphia in 1793, and on Paine's return it also occurred almost annually in New York. Paine's pamphlet, *Of the Cause of the Yellow Fever; And the Means of Preventing it in Places not yet effected with it*, was published in London by Rickman in 1807. Naturally he lacked modern knowledge (the virus was not discovered until 1887) but with his extraordinarily quick intelligence and scientific flair he came remarkably close to a true understanding of the most likely environment to breed the disease. He connected it to an extent with marsh gas (now known as methane or natural gas), describing an experiment long ago with Washington in 1783 in a creek under Rocky Hill, New Jersey, when he and the General held rolls of lighted cartridge paper over the surface of the water. The experiment, made because of the creek's 'fiery reputation', proved the presence of gas and led Paine to think that yellow fever begins in the lowest parts of populous marine towns and in particular among wharves, where the vapour from the submerged dead matter in the water combined with a 'miasm' from the low ground. He suggests new ways of building wharves to avoid this, and as R. G. Daniels has written:

'Thomas Paine's comments about the disease occurring only where the banks are broken out and flattened to form wharves are entirely in keeping with the facts as we know them, for it is just in these areas that the mosquito finds the type of stagnant water it needs to breed. It is interesting that he uses much the same phrase in describing the site of the occurrence of Yellow Fever as does Sir Patrick Manson in his famous textbook on tropical diseases (6th edition, 1919)—"The ideal haunt of Yellow Fever is the low-lying, hot, squalid, insanitary district in the neighbourhood of the wharves and docks of large seaport towns . . ." '[1]

Paine's object was not a cure (in fact, although a vaccine is now

[1] 'Thomas Paine on Yellow Fever', *Thomas Paine Society Bulletin* (No. 2, Vol. 4, October 1971).

effective, there is still no treatment except good nursing). 'In taking up and treating this subject,' he wrote, 'I have considered it as belonging to Natural Philosophy, rather than medicinal art; and therefore say nothing about treatment of the disease, after it takes place.' But the pamphlet once again demonstrates the remarkable variety of his interests and talents, and his uncanny instinct for scientific truth. This applied, too, to his observations on mineral wealth in the United States and he had what R. W. Morrell, a geologist, has described as 'a grasp of geological time well in advance of his age'.

One extraordinary and dangerous incident in these last years almost cost Paine his life, and was quoted in the English papers. It has a curious resemblance to Shelley's famous and sometimes questioned story of the attempt to assassinate him, some years later, by a bullet fired through the window of his cottage at Tanyrallt. Paine's story, however, held no possibilities of mirage. During his residence in New York he had left the New Rochelle farm in charge of a Christopher Derrick. On his return he had discharged Derrick, but continued to employ him as an occasional farm labourer, to enable Derrick to pay off a debt of $48. On Christmas Eve 1805, Derrick drowned his difficulties in the most accepted way, the bottle, borrowed a gun and, according to the usual story, fired at Paine, who was sitting in his living room, through the window. The ball missed Paine by inches.

It is curious that in the circumstantial account of an English paper, the case even more resembles Shelley's, in that it is stated that the first shot on Christmas Eve occurred while Paine was absent, and a 'Mulatio woman (the only servant in Paine's employ) was alone in the house'.

'The servant related the transaction to Paine, who received it without emotion, and even neglected to make any further enquiries. On the third night after the first shot had been fired, while Paine was sitting with a young man of the neighbourhood, a gun was discharged under or near the window, two balls from which passed between Paine and the young man, and lodged in the partition of the apartment on the opposite side. Two months after, a man who had lived with Paine during the summer was apprehended on the oath of Paine, as the person suspected of the attempt, and is held to bail to answer the charge.'

Shelley also maintained that two attempts were made on his life in Tanyrallt, the first being an intrusion with shots within the room, when he struggled with his unknown assailant, the second some hours later when a shot was fired at him through the window. Shelley in 1806, when the accounts of Paine's experience appeared, was fourteen years old and highly impressionable, and it is interesting to speculate if some memory of Paine's experience lingered in his mind at the time of his Tanyrallt story, and helped to colour his account of it.[1]

It would seem the English account of Paine's escape was taken from American sources, for it quite closely follows the real event and shows no antagonism to Paine.

Periodically he was attacked by returns of ill-health, apparently stemming from his prison illness, which had undermined his constitution. In 1806 a fit of apoplexy deprived him of sense and motion and he was injured by a fall during the fit. But his tough frame and mentality recovered, and in spite of public and private bickerings he once again struck up a warm friendship with a much younger man, the thirty-year-old and rather inaptly named John Wesley Jarvis, an artist who was considered a great wit and who had much in common with Paine as a bohemian and perennial talker. 'I have had Tom Paine living with me for these five months; he is one of the most pleasant companions I have met with for an old man,' wrote Jarvis. His painting of Paine in old age was much admired, and he also produced a bust now owned by the New York Historical Society. Following more eminent scientific fore-runners such as Isaac Newton, Paine delved again into the Bible and wrote an *Essay on Dream*, published as a preface to Part III of *The Age of Reason* which dealt with the so-called prophecies in the Bible, in particular the prophecies concerning the coming of Christ. Although it is in no sense a psychiatric study, Paine's opening to the *Essay on Dream* is sufficiently striking.

'In order to understand the nature of dreams, or that which passes in ideal vision during a state of sleep, it is first necessary to understand the composition and decomposition of the human mind.

'The three great faculties of the mind are IMAGINATION, JUDGEMENT, and MEMORY. Every action of the mind comes under one or other of these faculties . . .'

In spite of the pleasant situation of New Rochelle, with its 'prospect always green and agreeable', as Paine wrote, and its quantity of 'grass and hay', his farm life did not go well and he spent the last three years of his life in New York, producing a great deal of journalism under pseudonyms, including much on the use of gunboats for defence and naval strategy generally (these were governed by fears of an attack by England on New York: and indeed, as we have seen, British armies were on American soil again within a few years of Paine's death). In March 1807, he reasserted his old passion for the writer's freedom in style, idea and expression by leaving a journal, the *American Citizen*, because the

[1] Shelley later wrote a 'Letter to Lord Ellenborough' on the punishment of Daniel Eaton for publishing *The Age of Reason*.

Editor, James Cheetham, altered his article before publication. 'I, Sir, never permit anyone to alter any thing that I write, you have spoiled the whole sense that it was meant to convey on the subject.'

Cheetham, whose enmity was thereafter to corrode with time and end in a particularly virulent biography in the year of Paine's death, perhaps had other sources for his hatred of Paine, which we do not know. They certainly included a journalistic battle with Paine over France, which Cheetham had attacked; and their politics were now wide apart. But psychologically the mainspring was probably the age-old and always despicable one of an inferior writer bitterly jealous and resentful of a greater and more celebrated one. His attempts to alter Paine's work suggest this; and Paine took it in the spirit one might have expected.

It was Cheetham's book that spread the story of Paine's drunkenness and of his immoral liaison with Madame de Bonneville. This story he obtained from an insinuation made by William Carver, the Englishman who claimed to have known Paine in Lewes and who had now emigrated to America. Carver took Paine into his house for a time but fell out with him over payments for his keep, claiming he had tended him after the fit that had ended in his falling downstairs. He added a good deal of unsavoury details about Paine's dirtiness and helplessness to look after himself, which in the circumstances were not surprising. Probably it is true he had tried to care for the sick old man; he certainly afterwards had qualms about Cheetham's use of his unguarded hint that the old man was actually Madame de Bonneville's lover and father of her sons, and he tried to retract. Just before Paine died he wrote a letter seeking reconciliation. But their attacks and counter-attacks (Paine claimed in his turn that Carver had neglected him and his nurse, Mrs Palmer, the widow of a deist friend) were not to be healed by time and Cheetham made the most of them, stating Carver's insinuation as fact. When Madame de Bonneville sued him, he lost the case, partly because Carver in court retracted his story; but it is a sign of the religious bigotry of the judicial view of Paine that in awarding damages of $250 (including costs), the Court highly commended the book which contained the libel, declaring that it 'served the cause of religion'!

In 1808, after the pleasant stay with Jarvis, Paine was ill again, and in July 1808, he was living with a family called Ryder in Greenwich Village. Here, in the house in Herring Street (now Bleecker Street), he was seen often in fine weather 'sitting at the south window of the first story room . . . the sash was raised, a small table or stand was placed before him, with an open book placed upon it, which he appeared to be reading. He had his spectacles on . . . and a decanter, containing liquor of the colour of rum or brandy, was standing next to his book and beyond it.' A charming print recalls this description, and shows the rural surroundings at that time of the now highly urban Greenwich Village centre of Bleecker Street, with its shops, cafés and night-spots.

By February 1809, Paine needed constant attendance and increased his payments from $10 to $20 a week (this, for those days, must have been quite a generous sum. In 1961 I was charged only $30 a week for a small hotel apartment in New York just off Times Square.) The paralytic illness he had had in France had returned, and the apoplexy of 1806 had further weakened him. But although in his last months he was confined to bed, his mind remained resilient and active and he welcomed all visitors, talking to them with his customary animation. A friend of Sir Francis Burdett, who had seen Paine off at Le Havre, went to see him and wrote: 'His conversation was calm and gentlemanlike, except when religion or party politics were mentioned. In this case he became irascible, and the deformity of his face rendered so by intemperance, was then disgusting.' No doubt Paine was drinking more heavily to dull the pain and discomforts of his illness: he was not a man who would accept helplessness easily. Nevertheless it was noted his intellect was unimpaired and his blue eyes were full and lucid. 'The penetration and intelligence of his eye bespeak the man of genius and the world,' wrote Alexander Wilson, a distinguished ornithologist with whom Paine had an animated discussion on his work, late in 1808.

Paine became lonely at Ryder's, and at his request Madame de Bonneville agreed to have him with her at 59 Grove Street, not many yards away in Greenwich Village. He was carried there very gently in an armchair early in May 1809. A strange nostalgia for his childhood seems to have returned to him in some degree. He made a request that he should be buried in the Quaker cemetery, and a kindly local Quaker, Willet Hicks, passed on the request; but the Quaker committee could not agree. Paine had offered Hicks to pay for the ground, and according to Madame de Bonneville was deeply moved at the refusal. She promised him he would be buried on his own farm, and he expressed a strangely prescient fear that it would be sold later and his bones disturbed and dug up. Madame de Bonneville protested, with tears, that this would not happen, and in fact she meant it and mourned Paine when he died with sincerity. Throughout May he had grown progressively weaker, and he died on 8 June 1809, at eight o'clock in the morning, after a peaceful night.

The funeral ceremony at New Rochelle took place in obscurity and was attended by only a few people. Madame de Bonneville, who had laid a rose on Paine's body when he died, wrote 'Death had not disfigured him. Though very thin, his bones were not protuberant. He was not wrinkled, and had lost very little hair.' Paine had lived and worked these last years mainly to leave her family a comfortable legacy; and he had, through the selling of some land on his farms, and by living abstemiously, managed to achieve this. According to his Will, his shares 'worth $1500', and movable effects were left in trust for Margaret de Bonneville; half of the proceeds from the sale of the north part of his farm to Clio Rickman and half to Nicolas de Bonneville of Paris; and the rents and profits of the south part of his farm, upwards of one hundred acres, in trust for the two Bonneville children, Thomas and Benjamin, for their education and maintenance. If the land were sold before they attained the age of twenty-one years they would inherit the stocks into which Paine directed the proceeds should be placed, to provide dividends to educate the children; otherwise they would inherit and share the land at the age of twenty-one.

It would seem from this Will that although not rich he had managed to husband his resources to leave a reasonable support for the Bonneville children whom he had made his responsibility, as well as something to express his gratitude to Clio Rickman for his friendship and loyalty. He also left $100 to Mrs Palmer, who had nursed him at Carver's house.

Madame de Bonneville left a full account of Paine as she had known him for many years in Paris and America. It was generous and often illuminating. And her picture of the scene at his grave is reticent and touching.

'On the ninth of June my son and I, and a few of Thomas Paine's friends, set off with the corpse to New Rochelle, a place 22 miles from New York. It was my intention to have him buried in the Orchard of his own farm; but the farmer who lived there at that time said, that Thomas Paine, walking with him one day, said, pointing to another part of the land, he was desirous of being buried there. "Then," said I, "that shall be the place of his burial." And, my instructions were accordingly put in execution. The head-stone was put up about a week afterwards with the following inscription: "Thomas Paine, Author of 'Common Sense,' died the eighth of June, 1809, aged 72 years."[1] According to his will, a wall twelve feet square was erected round his tomb. Four trees have been planted outside the wall, two weeping willows and two cypresses . . .

[1] Nevertheless, Madame de Bonneville later acknowledged she made a mistake in Paine's age and had the first stone engraved with the age of 74 years. This age clearly appears on a large broken fragment of the stone which was brought by Cobbett to England with Paine's bones in 1819. It remained with a Liverpool family and was photographed early this century. Another fragment remained in America; but souvenir hunters, as Madame de Bonneville says, early took away pieces of the tomb-stone and the trees.

'This interment was a scene to affect and to wound any sensible heart. Contemplating who it was, what man it was, that we were committing to an obscure grave on an open and disregarded bit of land, I could not help feeling most acutely. Before the earth was thrown down upon the coffin, I, placing myself at the east end of the grave, said to my son Benjamin, "stand you there, at the other end, as a witness for grateful America." Looking round me, and beholding the small group of spectators, I exclaimed, as the earth was tumbled into the grave, "Oh! Mr. Paine! My son stands here as testimony of the gratitude of America, and I, for France!" This was the funeral ceremony of this great politician and philosopher!'

XXII

AFTERMATH

No sooner was Paine dead, than religious and political enemies began to spread the story that he had recanted his opinions on his deathbed. The religious, as history shows, have not always been scrupulous, and the surest way to destroy any effects of *The Age of Reason* was to emphasize its author's own repudiation of it. There were, of course, no grounds whatsoever for this, but as the story continued to be published throughout the next century, a woman of 'impeccable respectability' called Mary Hinsdale was quoted as having heard the recantation personally, and the Religious Tract Society even circulated a publication repeating Paine's recantation, it is necessary to give the true evidence.

Paine was as consistent in his religious as his political views. He had stood at death's door before, in the Luxembourg prison, where he was visited by the English surgeon Dr Bond, who although not sharing Paine's opinions reported:

'Mr Paine, while hourly expecting to die, read to me parts of his *Age of Reason*; and every night when I left him to be separately locked up, and expected not to see him alive in the morning, he always expressed his firm belief in the principles of that book, and begged I would tell the world such were his dying opinions.'

The Age of Reason was completed, as Paine emphasized, under just such pressure.

On his deathbed at Grove Street he was persecuted by a number of people who gained entry simply in order to try and pressurize him into an admission that his religious views were wrong, in several cases out of a perhaps genuine wish to save his immortal soul. How much this eagerness was psychologically also due to an uneasy inner need for support in their own religious hopes perhaps a modern psychiatrist could conjecture. To the claim of one of these visitors, a Reverend Mr Hargrove, that his sect had found the key to a true interpretation of the Scriptures, which had been lost for four thousand years, Paine replied with a dying rally of his old wit that the key 'must have been very rusty'.

Paine was even tormented by his medical attendant, Dr Manley, on this question. In a letter to James Cheetham, Manley wrote the following (apparently without any conscience about his responsibilities as a *physician* to his dying patient):

'Mr. Paine, you have not answered my questions; will you answer them? Allow me to ask again, do you believe, or—let me qualify the question—do you wish to believe that Jesus Christ is the Son of God? After a pause of some minutes he answered, "I have no wish to believe on that subject." I then left him, and know not whether he afterwards spoke to any person on the subject.'

Cheetham did not scruple to make this a further basis for a vicious and sanctimonious attack on Paine's character. Paine's biographer Sherwin in 1819 confirmed the Manley story by printing a letter from a Mr Clark, who spoke to Dr Manley on the subject. 'I asked him plainly,' said Mr Clark, 'Did Mr Paine recant his religious sentiments? I would thank you for an explicit answer, sir.' He said, 'No, he did not.'

William Cobbett got to the bottom of the Mary Hinsdale story (which however continued to be repeated), by finding the girl and questioning her. It appeared she had been employed as a servant by the Quaker, Willet Hicks, who had been friendly with Paine and sent him many little delicacies in his last illness. These were carried to Paine by the girl and according to the story propagated by the 'recantation' theorists he had assured her personally that 'if ever the Devil had an agent on earth he who wrote *The Age of Reason* was undoubtedly that person'. Cobbett found her, some ten years later, to be an illiterate who shuffled, evaded, apparently did not understand him, and finally confessed she had 'no recollection of any person or thing she saw at Thomas Paine's house'. Hicks himself maintained that in conversation with Paine shortly before his death, 'he said his sentiments respecting the Christian religion were precisely the same as they were when he wrote *The Age of Reason*'.

As *Rights of Man* had to be equally discredited in the political field, the stories (unsubstantiated by precise details) of Paine's immorality and drunkenness continued equally to be maintained. Cheetham's biography clearly mentioned the 'habitual drunkenness' as a means of attacking the credibility of his political works, which was a main object of Cheetham's book as it had been of Oldys'. 'Wildness naturally followed this drunkenness,' wrote Cheetham, 'and begat a commotion of thoughts', thus producing 'his despicable work, *The Rights of Man*.' Paine was, of course, in addition 'a compound of all the vices'. 'Paine had no good qualities,' summed up Cheetham. It is an indication of the unscrupulousness of the propaganda of the time that a book so categorically emphasizing Paine's unmitigated villainy, in addition to his 'wretched' and 'uncouth' literary style, should have continued to have been accepted so long as the most reliable estimate of his character. Few could have read it: they were told its stories, and accepted them sometimes from sheer innocence and sometimes from wishful thinking. It is a curious fact that the English publisher of an edition of Cheetham's biography in 1817, while totally accepting Cheetham and expressing complete repugnance to Paine and his works, does in a Preface invalidate Oldys' earlier work, on which Cheetham to some extent rested. Even at this early date, the English publisher ascribes it 'to the agency of the ministry' and adds 'on a work so evidently of a party nature, one cannot implicitly draw'. Oldys, in fact, was already a known paid and tainted source, but Cheetham, who had known Paine only in old age, conveniently replaced him. Cheetham's attachment to the Federalists and anti-Jefferson bias would not, of course, have been realized by the English publisher.

It is significant that while Paine was within living memory of many who knew him well, this defamation of character failed to take hold. Until after the time of the Chartist movement he remained a hero of political reform and his works a rallying point of working class democracy: government propaganda had failed to register with Paine's fellow liberals because they, at least, *knew* it to be untrue. 'He Comes, the Great Reformer Comes', the song composed in his honour, became an anthem of the reformers, and the Reform Bill passed in 1832 was considered one culmination of the political campaign begun with *Rights of Man* (though in fact the Bill was a debilitated version of Chartist demands and repudiated by many of the radicals who had fought so hard, and suffered so much, for it). In 1842, the National Charter Association published a collection of Paine's writings to which they added a copy of the People's Charter. There were powerful unbroken links between the radical movement of Paine's time and the nineteenth century labour movement. W. J. Linton, a Chartist poet and engraver, wrote an anonymous *Life of Paine* in 1842, and an apprentice in Linton's workshop, Walter Crane, afterwards worked with William Morris in the socialist revival of the 1880s and 1890s. Charles Bradlaugh's journal, *The Investigator*, coupled Paine and Robert Burns with the words: 'priests have denounced them, but they are rising in the estimation of those who are best worthy of notice, men of literature and "the mob";' and Bradlaugh's daughter, Hypatia Bradlaugh Bonner, edited a composite edition of Paine's main works in 1912, thus extending the link into the twentieth century. But in the later part of the nineteenth century, and as Victorian morality spread, no one was left who could remember Paine himself or those who knew him best. Thus the legend of the uncouth profligate swelled again, assiduously fortified by religious bigotry and political fear; and as socialism, in industrial conditions, took on the colour of Marxism as a bulwark against landlordism and capitalism, Paine's importance began to be obscured by writers and reformers more directly tuned to the times. Robert Owen in his auto-biography (although he was twenty when *Rights of Man* was first published) did not even mention Paine. It was an oversight not to Owen's credit.

In 1892 the Fabian Society made some amends by affixing a com-memorative tablet to the Bull House at Lewes, but the general ignorance and apathy only began to lift in 1904 when *The Literary Guide* reported 'The First Paine Celebration in England' at the White Hart Hotel, Lewes, where a letter was read from Bertrand Russell deeply regretting his 'inability to participate in the homage to be paid to a great reformer and an illustrious heretical pioneer'. Even then, it was primarily a gathering of Rationalists, not of those associated with Paine's political ideals.

Paine, however, might have appreciated the fact that on 1 October 1929, the White Hart was the scene of talks between the British Foreign Secretary, Arthur Henderson, and the Russian envoy, M. Dougalovsky, which ended in the resumption of British diplomatic relations with the Union of Soviet Socialist Republics. (During the Parliamentary debate on this agreement Stanley Baldwin, perhaps not aware of the White Hart's early associations, complained of Henderson's 'surrender' to Soviet demands 'at a hotel where bitter beer is sold and where cricketers are wont to resort'.)

The fog really began to lift from the figure of Paine, the political writer and influence, at the time of the centenary of his death on 8 June 1909, when celebrations were held at Thetford and at St James's Hall in London, and reported at length in *The Times* of 3rd July. 'A hundred years ago nobody foresaw that Tom Paine's centenary would be the subject of a laudatory special article in *The Times*', wrote Shaw; 'and only a few understood that the persecution of his works and the trans-portation of men for the felony of reading them was a mischievous mistake.'[1] It is true *The Times* began with becoming caution: 'There is no need to believe in every word that Thomas Paine wrote, nor vouch support of his every action in a long and singularly adventurous life, to acclaim the most famous native of the little borough town of Thetford, on the borders of Norfolk and Suffolk . . .' The deputy mayor of Thetford, H. F. Millington, was however bolder and, as time has proved, over-optimistic when he stated: 'The myths and slanders which had gathered round the name of Paine had one by one died.' When Paine's bicentenary was reached in 1937 there was another outburst of political appreciation; but as late as 1963, when Thetford Town Council, at a stormy session, belatedly decided to make some permanent gesture of recognition by erecting a statue by Charles Wheeler, R.A., in Paine's

[1] 'The Case for Toleration': Preface, *The Shewing Up of Blanco Posnet* (1909).

honour, a Conservative Councillor promptly resigned ('A monument to Tom Paine on the Market Place would be an insult to the town'), and the Chairman of the Women's Section of the British Legion recoiled with equal horror: 'This is a shocking thing to happen. Tom Paine, the philanderer and an unmitigated scamp, is the last man Thetford should honour.'

The statue, unveiled in 1964, stands at the foot of King Street (diplomatically avoiding the Market Place and Guildhall): a graceful, gold-leaf figure with quill in one hand and a copy of *Rights of Man* (curiously held upside down) in the other, shining in the fitful Norfolk sun amid the flower-beds of a little garden. The most humanitarian of his sentiments are carved on the four sides of the pedestal base; but few read them. Paine's battles are not over and his spirit is not yet at peace. In 1970 the statue was sprayed with black and blue paint and in the Spring of 1971 Paine still gazed into the future, above the blowing tulips, with a darkened face, on which the gold leaf had not been restored. Perhaps he would accept the black face with pride, as a symbol of the coloured races he wished to free.

It might have amused and pleased him that since 1968 there has been an attractive new public-house named 'The Rights of Man' on the Thetford motorway, Brandon Road, with a 'Tom Paine Lounge' and posters of early editions of Paine's works on the walls. If reincarnated, he would undoubtedly be an enthusiastic client.

In America, although the revulsion of the ignorant and bigoted was violent, Paine always had champions among the great. He died in apparent neglect and ingratitude; but ingratitude is a human harvest reaped by the old, before Paine's time and long after it. Shakespeare's last bitter plays are full of the theme, and when, after *The Tempest*, he 'drowned his book' like Prospero and left the jealousies of theatre and Court for the rural placidity of Stratford-on-Avon, it may well have been for this reason above all others, a rejection of human betrayal. When the old, like Paine, have long since lost the success or prominence of their youth, and especially if they live alone, the rejection is nearly always total, even by those who owed them most.

There were always the few who would speak up. 'In my childhood,' Walt Whitman, who had known Paine's friend, Colonel John Fellows, told Conway, 'a great deal was said of Paine in our neighbourhood, in Long Island . . . Paine was double-damnably lied about. Colonel Fellows was a man of perfect truth and exactness; he assured me the stories disparaging to Paine personally were quite false. Paine was neither drunken nor filthy; he drank as other people did, and was a high-minded gentleman . . . Paine left a deep, clear-cut impression on the public mind. Colonel Fellows told me that while Paine was in New

York he had a much larger following than was generally supposed. After his death a reaction in his favour appeared among many who had opposed him . . .'

Gilbert Vale, Paine's first honest and conscientious American biographer (1841), also contacted a Mr Ward who remembered some of the local disapproval of Paine when he was a small boy living in New Rochelle. As a result, and with only a vague idea of the religious grounds for the disapproval, he and several other boys raided Paine's orchard, and were surprised when the kindly old man came out and helped them to collect the apples, 'patting one on the head and caressing another, and directing them where to get the best'.

Politicians like Abraham Lincoln and Woodrow Wilson were deeply read in Paine's works, and influenced by them to profound national and international effect. Nations do not always remember their benefactors at the time, only sometimes long afterwards. The tradition of Paine grew like a tree, and it was American airmen in Britain during the Second World War who unveiled a bronze plaque to Paine, to which they had subscribed, in Thetford and named one of their Flying Fortress bombers 'Tom Paine', painting on the side of it a paraphrase of Paine's words so applicable to Hitler: 'Tyranny, like Hell, is hard to conquer.' An American society devoted to Paine and his works long preceded the Thomas Paine Society in England, and on 29 January 1968, the anniversary of his birth, the United States issued a Thomas Paine commemorative stamp. In France a statue of Paine, shown pleading for the life of Louis XVI in the French National Assembly, was modelled by Gutzon Borglum in 1937, although its erection in the Parc Montsouris in Paris was delayed until after the War.

Among those who supported the Paine 'black legend', out of insufficient knowledge, and then admitted their error, were William Cobbett and Leslie Stephen, the scholar-father of Virginia Woolf, who wrote Paine's entry in the Dictionary of National Biography. Outside politics, he has had an unexpected range of posthumous devotees, from scholars, critics and philosophers to members of the stage and film world. Edward Gibbon, according to Rickman, sent repeatedly to France to try and get Paine's papers on the history of the French Revolution, 'upon a conviction that they would be impartial, profound, and philosophical documents'. William Hazlitt in *Table-Talk* preferred him as a writer to Cobbett; there were, he thought, 'no two writers who come more into juxtaposition from the nature of their subjects, from the internal resources on which they draw, and from the popular effect of their writings . . . But still if we turn to a volume of Paine's (his Common Sense or Rights of Man), we are struck (not to say somewhat refreshed) by the difference. Paine is a much more sententious writer than Cobbett. You cannot open a page in any of his best and earlier works without meeting with some maxim, some antithetical and memorable saying, which is a sort of starting-place for the argument, and the goal to which it returns. There is not a single *bon-mot*, a single sentence in Cobbett that has ever been quoted again.' Paine's writings, he sums up, 'are a sort of introduction to political arithmetic on a new plan'; he takes a bird's-eye view of things, while Cobbett sticks closer to them and inspects the component parts. Paine was to Hazlitt the 'metaphysical and poetical' writer, Cobbett 'more picturesque and dramatic'; but Paine was the one with the grip on first principles, about which Cobbett continually wavered.

Cobbett disturbed Paine's bones from a sudden excess of admiration, and probably not realizing the passionate depth of Paine's attachment to America. When he arrived with them on the *Hercules* at Liverpool in 1819, according to a newspaper report, 'An immense number of people met him on the beach, and cheered him to the inn, which is a considerable distance from the docks . . . *The bones of Paine* were deposited in a wooden box, and lodged in the Custom-house yard. When the box was opened, Cobbett observed—"There, gentlemen, are the mortal remains of the immortal Thomas Paine." The skull was shown and the coffin-plate accompanied it, but all that could be deciphered was, "— Pain, — 180 — aged 74 years." Cobbett was extremely attentive to the box, and looked rather serious during the exhibition . . .'

According to Hazlitt, the only time Cobbett ever grew romantic was in bringing over the relics of Paine, but he had scarcely landed 'when he left the bones of a great man to shift for themselves', travelled to London and disclaimed the political and theological sentiments of his late idol. Hazlitt was unfair to Cobbett in this; he was not a political apostate where Paine was concerned. As for the bones, they certainly either came with or followed Cobbett to London. It is interesting, though, to notice that Cobbett, when preparing his *Rural Rides* under two years later, stayed at the White Hart in Lewes but without, as far as one can tell from the book or his *Sussex Journal*, realizing the Paine connection. It was almost fifty years since Paine had left Lewes. Cobbett in *Rural Rides* recorded that the inns were good at Lewes, the people civil and not servile, and the town itself was a model of solidity and neatness. Perhaps Paine, the White Hart orator and fighter for the excisemen's rights, had helped to contribute to the character of a people conspicuously lacking in servility.

The lock of hair from Paine's skull acquired by Conway was not unique: Cobbett was reduced to selling these in the attempt to raise money for a memorial, from his London house at 11 Bolt Court, Fleet

Street. But the attempt was unsuccessful and, after Cobbett's death on 18 June 1835, at Normandy Farm, near Guildford, the auctioneer refused to include Paine's bones in the effects which Cobbett's son put up for auction. The main skeleton was rumoured to have been buried in 1849 in Ash churchyard, not far from Cobbett's Surrey home, although people for many years afterwards still claimed to have seen it; and the skull before disappearing is said to have been acquired by a Brighton phrenologist. According to Conway the skull and hand were examined by Professor John Marshall of the Royal College of Surgeons, who thought Paine's small and delicate hand 'the hand of a female . . . The head was also small for a man, and of the Celtic type, I should say, and somewhat conical in shape, and with more cerebellum than frontal development.' Later even these remnants of Paine disappeared.

The only thing that matters is Paine's soul, which like that of another freedom-loving American, John Brown, goes marching on. A man has a right to be judged, not on his declining years, but on his life and work in his prime, at the height of his powers. Paine's work lives and still has its warning message because it deals with recurring issues of human conscience and social needs, and forces which continue to oppose their solution, in subtly modernized but basically still dangerous form. Democracy is a word that changes emphasis according to the politics of the user, and even with Paine the attitudes can be retrogressive. In 1915 the Dent 'Everyman' edition of *Rights of Man* was published with an enlightened Introduction by George Jacob Holyoake. In 1959 the same series substituted for Holyoake's sympathetic estimate of Paine and his work a new Introduction which categorically stated that *Rights of Man* did not adequately reply to Burke, and deplored the fact that Paine's ideas on the social services had now been adopted by the British government, for the 'welfare state is, or in a free society should be, a passing phase'. It added a rider on the futility of much 'progressive' political theorizing, of which Paine's work, of course, is an important example.

So complete a *volte face* in the presentation of a famous political classic, within the space of hardly half a century, must give us pause when too inclined to think of society as always progressive. Human nature does not change, only the ideology which moulds or disciplines it at any given time: 'Tyranny, like Hell, is hard to conquer.' Within seven years of the publication of *Rights of Man*, Thomas Malthus was exploring the population problem and rejecting the idea of social welfare, for fear of the threat to wealth and trade. The poor man must stand on his own two feet, for 'if society does not want his labour, he has no claim of *right* to the smallest portion of food'.[1]

'Hunger is not among the postponable wants,' Paine had written of

[1] *Essay on the Principle of Population* (1798).

the poverty in so-called civilized countries in his own day; today his words are unconsciously echoed in organizations fighting starvation throughout large areas of the world, on a scale of which Paine never dreamed. In the 1960s and early 1970s, his work has taken on renewed topicality, and he is studied with increasing attention. His reputation is once again in the ascendant. Che Guevara, who takes his place with the young as the revolutionary hero of our own time, was very aware of Paine's works, and Fidel Castro, in his defence before the Court of Santiago de Cuba in 1953, remarked: 'Thomas Paine said that a just man deserves more respect than a crowned rogue.' The hostility is bound to revive in proportion, for the tug of social reform is always balanced by social reaction. To the end he never quite grasped this, and as has been said of Guevara in post-revolutionary Cuba, he was 'genuinely surprised that human nature remained unchanged when society had been changed so drastically'.

'Paine perused the face of civilization,' wrote Desmond McCarthy, 'with the astonished and indignant eye of a stranger from another planet.' But it was Paine's naïvety—'his inability to see that vested interests do not abdicate before logic', as Harold Laski put it—that constituted his strength and incorruptibility. 'In a great affair, where the good of man is at stake, I love to work for nothing,' he wrote; and he persisted in seeing the best in human nature, and therefore the ever-shining possibility of reform. In the end this almost visionary gaze into the future proved prophetic. 'History offers few examples of such confident and breathtaking foresight,' wrote Michael Foot, and when Cobbett declared, 'At his expiring flambeau I lighted my taper,' he was speaking, without knowing it, for generations who would keep that flame burning, passing the taper from hand to hand as in the Olympics of ancient Greece.

Today that taper-light is still assailable, but it throws a beam, like a nuclear-powered searchlight, that has penetrated throughout the world.

BIBLIOGRAPHY

(*including Articles and Collections*)

ALDRIDGE, ALFRED O.: *Man of Reason* (Cresset Press, 1960)

BAKSHIAN, ARAM: *Foreign Adventurers in the American Revolution* (*History Today*, Vol. XXI, No. 3, March 1971)

BARKER, AMBROSE: Paine Collection: at Branch Library of the Norfolk County Council County Library, Thetford, Norfolk

BARRAS: *Memoirs* (Paris, 1895)

BONNER, HYPATIA BRADLAUGH, and J. M. ROBERTSON: Ed. and Intro. *The Works of Thomas Paine* (Watts, 1912) (This includes English translations, which I have used, of Paine's Addresses and Manifestoes as Deputy to the French National Convention, 1792–3)

BONNEVILLE, MADAME DE: *Thomas Paine: a Sketch of his Life and Character* (Copied by Cobbett and printed in full, Appendix A, in Conway's *Life of Thomas Paine*, 1909, ed. Hypatia Bradlaugh Bonner)

BROPHY, BRIGID: *Mozart the Dramatist* (Faber, 1964: Harcourt, New York, 1964)

BROWN, P. A.: *The French Revolution in English History* (Allen & Unwin, 1918: Frank Cass, 1965)

BURKE, EDMUND: *Reflections on the Revolution in France* (1790: Ed. and Intro. Conor Cruise O'Brien, Pelican, 1968)

CARLILE, RICHARD: *Life of Thomas Paine* (London, 1820) (Carlile suffered a savage term of imprisonment for printing Paine's works)

CARLYLE, THOMAS: *The French Revolution* (1837)

CHEETHAM, JAMES: *The Life of Thomas Paine* (New York, 1809)

CLEMENCEAU-JACQMAIRE, MADELEINE: *The Life of Madame Roland* (Longmans Green, 1930)

COBBETT, WILLIAM: *Rural Rides* (1830)

COLE, G. D. H. and RAYMOND POSTGATE: *The Common People, 1746–1938* (1938)

COLLINS, HENRY: Introduction: *Rights of Man* (Pelican, 1969)

COLLINS, HERBERT F.: *Talma* (Faber, 1964)

CONNELL, J. M.: *The Story of an Old Meeting House* (Longmans, 1916)

CONNELL, J. M.: *Thomas Paine* (Longmans, 1939)

CONWAY, MONCURE D.: *The Life of Thomas Paine* (New York, 1892: Edition edited Hypatia Bradlaugh Bonner, Watts, 1909)

CONWAY, MONCURE D.: *Newly Discovered Writings of Thomas Paine* (*The Athenaeum*)

DANIELS, R. G.: *Thomas Paine on Yellow Fever* (*Thomas Paine Society Bulletin*, Vol. 4, No. 2, Oct. 1971)

DUMAS, ALEXANDRE: *The Flight to Varennes* (1856: Trans. and Intro: A. Craig Bell, Alston Books, 1962)

ERDMAN, DAVID V.: *Blake: Prophet Against Empire* (Princeton, 1954: Revised Ed. 1969)

FAY, C. R.: *Life and Labour in the Nineteenth Century*

FOOTE, G. W. and A. D. MCLAREN: *Infidel Death-Beds* (The Pioneer Press, 1887)

FOSTER, PAUL: *Tom Paine* (play) (Calder & Boyars, 1967)

FRANKLIN, BENJAMIN: *Autobiography* (Ed. Leonard W. Labaree, Ralph L. Ketcham, Helen C. Bratfield and Helena H. Fineman: Yale University Press, 1964)

GIMBEL, RICHARD: *The First Appearance of Thomas Paine's The Age of Reason* (*Yale*

University Library Gazette, Vol. 31, No. 2, Oct. 1956: reprinted *Thomas Paine Society Bulletin*, Vol. 4, No. 1, Jan. 1971)

GODFREY, WALTER H. and CONNELL, J. M.: *At the Sign of the Bull, Lewes* (1924)

GODWIN, WILLIAM: *Political Justice* (1793)

GODWIN, WILLIAM: *Sketches of History* (1784)

GOOCH, G. P.: *French Profiles* (Longmans, 1961)

GOTTSCHALK, LOUIS R.: *Jean Paul Marat: A Study in Radicalism* (University of Chicago Press, 1927. New edition, 1967)

GRAFTON, AUGUSTUS HENRY, 3rd DUKE OF: *Memoirs with Political Correspondence*, Ed. Sir William R. Anson (John Murray, 1898)

GRYLLS, ROSALIE GLYNN: *William Godwin and His World* (Odhams Press, 1953)

HARPER, CHARLES G.: *The Newmarket, Bury, Thetford and Cromer Road* (1904)

HART, ROGER: *English Life in the 18th Century* (Wayland, 1970)

HAZLITT, WILLIAM: *Table-Talk* (1821: Dent 'Everyman' edition, 1959)

HAZLITT, WILLIAM: *The Life of Thomas Holcroft*, including Holcroft's *Memoirs* of his early life (Ed. E. Colby, Constable, 1925)

JAMES, H. R.: *Mary Wollstonecraft: A Sketch* (Oxford University Press, 1932)

JUNIUS: *The Letters of* (2 vols. 1772)

KEGAN PAUL, C.: *William Godwin, His Friends and Contemporaries* (2 vols. 1876)

LAROUSSE *Encyclopaedia of Modern History from 1500 to the Present Day* (Hamlyn, 1964)

LENTIN, A.: *Catherine the Great and Enlightened Despotism* (*History Today*, Vol. XXI, No. 3, March, 1971)

MADAME DE LA TOUR DU PIN: *Memoirs* (Ed. and Trans. Felice Harcourt: Harvill Press, 1970)

MAO TSE-TUNG: *Quotations from* ('The Little Red Book') (Peking, 1966)

MARAT, JEAN PAUL: *The Chains of Slavery* (London, 1774)

MARAT, JEAN PAUL: *Plan de législation criminelle* (1780 and 1790)

MEE, ARTHUR: *Sussex* (Hodder & Stoughton, 1937)

NORTH, RENÉ: *The 'Marseillaise'* (*History Today*, Vol. XXI, No. 3, March, 1971)

NYE, R. B. and MORPURGO, J. E.: *The Birth of the U.S.A.* (Part I, *A History of the United States*) (Pelican, 1955)

OLDYS, FRANCIS: *The Life of Thomas Paine* (London, 1791)

OMAN, CHARLES: *A History of England* (Edward Arnold, 1895)

PAINE, THOMAS: *Theological Works* (Carlile, 1818)

PAKENHAM, THOMAS: *The Year of Liberty: The Story of the Great Irish Rebellion of 1798* (Hodder & Stoughton, 1970)

PENNELL, ELIZABETH ROBINS: *Mary Wollstonecraft Godwin* (W. H. Allen, 1893)

PERRY, SAMPSON.: *Argus*. Register of Occurrences, Miscellany, etc. for 1796. *Of Thomas Paine and his Imprisonment in the Luxembourg*

PIZZINELLI, LUIGI MARIO: *The Life and Times of Robespierre* (Hamlyn, 1968)

PLUMB, J. H.: *England in the Eighteenth Century* (1714–1815) (Pelican, 1950)

PRICE, DR RICHARD: *Observations on the Nature of Civil Liberty* (1776)

RICKMAN, THOMAS CLIO: *The Life of Thomas Paine* (London, 1819)

RIDGWAY, JAMES (Ed.): *The Speeches of the Hon. Thomas Erskine (now Lord Erskine) when at the Bar, on subjects connected with the Liberty of the Press*. Vol. II. *Preface to the Trial of Thomas Paine for a Libel* (1813)

ROUSSEAU, JEAN-JACQUES: *Social Contract* (1762: Dent 'Everyman' edition, including *Discourses*, Ed. and Intro. G. D. H. Cole, 1913)

RUSSELL, BERTRAND: *Why I am not a Christian* (Allen & Unwin, 1957)

SHAW, GEORGE BERNARD: *The Devil's Disciple* and Preface: from *Three Plays for Puritans* (1901)

SHAW, GEORGE BERNARD: Prefaces to *Man and Superman* (1901–3) and *The Shewing Up of Blanco Posnet* (1909)

SHERRARD, O. A.: *Lord Chatham and America* (Bodley Head, 1958)

SHERWIN, WILLIAM: *Memoirs of the Life of Thomas Paine* (London, 1819)

SUSSEX ARCHAEOLOGICAL COLLECTIONS, Vol. LVIII.

THOMPSON, J. M.: *Leaders of the French Revolution* (1929: Basil Blackwell, Oxford, 1968)

TREVELYAN, G. M.: *Illustrated English Social History of the 18th Century* (Longmans Green, 1942: Pelican, 1964)

WARDLE, R. M.: *Mary Wollstonecraft: a Critical Biography* (University of Kansas Press, 1951: Richards Press, 1952)

WILLARD, BARBARA: *Sussex* (Batsford, 1965)

WILLIAMSON, AUDREY: *Bernard Shaw: Man and Writer* (Crowell-Collier, New York, 1963: Collier-Macmillan, London, 1963)

WILLIAMSON, AUDREY: *Who Was Sarastro?* (*Opera*, Vol. 21, No. 4, April 1970: also pub. *High Fidelity*, U.S.A., Vol. 20, No. 2, Feb. 1970, under title *The Riddle of the Magic Flute*)

WOLLSTONECRAFT, MARY: *Vindication of the Rights of Men* (1790)

WOLLSTONECRAFT, MARY: *Vindication of the Rights of Women* (1792)

WOLLSTONECRAFT, MARY: *Historical and Moral View of the French Revolution* (1794)

WOODWARD, W. E.: *Tom Paine, America's Godfather* (Secker & Warburg, 1946)

YORKE, HENRY REDHEAD: *France in Eighteen Hundred and Two* (Ed. J. A. C. Sykes. Heinemann, 1906)

YOUNG, ARTHUR: *Travels in France* (1787, 1788 and 1789) (Ed. Constantia Maxwell, Cambridge University Press, 1950)

There are two comprehensive American collections of Paine's writings. *The Complete Writings of Thomas Paine* by Dr Philip S. Foner (New York, 1945) and *Thomas Paine: Representative Selections* by Prof. Harry Hayden Clark (New York, 1965). Prof. Clark's edition, although it professes to include *Rights of Man* 'complete', omits Paine's entire social security programme in Part II. Aldridge's biography also does not mention this.

Articles of interest on Paine include those by:
Harold Laski (*Manchester Guardian*, 29 Jan. 1937)
H. W. Nevinson (*News-Chronicle*, 29 Jan. 1937)
Desmond McCarthy (*Sunday Times*, 31 Jan. 1937)
Michael Foot (*The Observer*, 7 June, 1959)
Gwyn A. Williams (*New Society*, 6 Aug. 1970)

INDEX

Academy of Sciences Paris 101, 102, 104, 183
Acheson, Dean 268
Adam, Robert 108
Adams, Abigail 263
Adams, John 72, 85, 257-8, 260, 263, 268
Administration of the Finances of France (Necker) 140
Advice to the Privileged Orders (Barlow) 182
Aitken, Robert 66, 68
Alderson, Amelia 131-2
Aldridge, Prof. Alfred Owen 12, 48, 54, 58, 131n, 138, 213
Algerine Captive, The (Taylor) 126
Amar, André 208
America (Blake) 163, 164, 182
American Antislavery Society, The 66
American Citizen 272
American Society of Civil Engineers 106
American War of Independence 24, 69, 70, 76-97, 102
Ami du Peuple, L' 151, 173, 173n
Analytical Review 124, 150
Anchor, Thetford 23
Angoulême, Duchess of 248
Animal Farm (Orwell) 41
Anne, Queen 20
Annual Register 107, 184
Anson, Sir William 109
Appeal from the new to the old Whigs (Burke) 158
Argus, 1796 218n
Artois, Count of 142
Asgill, Captain 86, 97
Athenaeum 155, 214, 235
Audibert, Achilles 161, 162, 164, 165, 166, 171, 214, 215

Bache, Richard 63, 64
Bache, Sarah 92
Back to Methuselah (Shaw) 135
Bailly (astronomer) 113, 114
Baldwin, Stanley 279
Bancal, Jean Henri 148, 152, 194, 195, 248
Barbaroux 178
Barber, Alderman A. C. 38
Barber of Seville, The (Beaumarchais) 87, 149
Barère de Vieuxzac 180, 183, 195, 208, 209, 210-11, 216, 225, 235
Barlow, Joel 11, 156, 161, 182, 184, 200, 210, 213, 214, 215, 216, 235, 245, 255, 258
Barnaby Rudge (Dickens) 112
Barnave 147, 148

Barras, Paul, Vicomte de 196, 207, 244, 250
Basire 196
Beauharnais, Josephine de 258
Beaumarchais, Pierre Augustin Caron de 87-8, 89-90, 92, 102, 131, 149, 249
Beggar's Opera, The (Gay) 29
Belgrade Theatre, Coventry 149n
Bell, Thetford 21, 23
Benedict XIV, Pope 238
Bentham, Jeremy 111, 129, 130, 161
Bevis, Dr 28-9
Biddle, Charles 80
Biddle, Owen 93
Bien Informé 249, 250, 253
Birth of the U.S.A., The (Nye and Morpurgo) 65, 260
Bishop, Eliza 187, 257
Blackstone, Sir William 111
Blake, Catherine 162
Blake, William 30, 112, 124, 130, 142, 162-5, 166
Blake: Prophet Against Empire (Erdman) 162
Blanc, Louis 223
Blomefield, Rev. Francis 22
Bonner, Hypatia Bradlaugh 278
Bonneville, General Benjamin 205, 266, 267, 274, 275
Bonneville, Mme Marguerite de 53, 84, 183, 205, 255, 265-7, 272, 273, 274, 274n
Bonneville, Nicolas de 152n, 249, 250, 253, 265, 266, 274
Bonneville, Thomas Paine 266, 274
Borglum, Gutzon 281
Bosville, William 259
Boswell, James 29, 30
Bouillé, M. le Marquis de 146, 147
Bowling Green Club, Lewes 41
Bradford's Bookstore, Philadelphia 65
Bradlaugh, Charles 278
Brissot de Warville, Jacques Pierre 151, 152, 152n, 169, 173, 182, 183, 199, 201, 207
Bristol Old Vic 131
Brophy, Brigid 234
Brown, John 283
Brown, P. A. 165n
Brunswick, Duke of 170
Brutus (Voltaire) 150
Bull House, Lewes 41, 42, 46-7, 49, 51, 56, 279
Bunyan, John 73
Burdett, Sir Francis 259, 259n, 273
Burdett-Coutts, Angela 259n
Burgoyne, General John 61, 76, 79, 79n, 85